Visions of Progress

POLITICS AND CULTURE IN MODERN AMERICA

Series Editors: Glenda Gilmore, Michael Kazin, Thomas J. Sugrue

Volumes in the series narrate and analyze political and social change in the broadest dimensions from 1865 to the present, including ideas about the ways people have sought and wielded power in the public sphere and the language and institutions of politics at all levels—local, national, and transnational. The series is motivated by a desire to reverse the fragmentation of modern U.S. history and to encourage synthetic perspectives on social movements and the state, on gender, race, and labor, on consumption, and on intellectual history and popular culture.

Visions of Progress

The Left-Liberal Tradition in America

DOUG ROSSINOW

PENN

University of Pennsylvania Press

Philadelphia

Published by
University of Pennsylvania Press
Philadelphia, Pennsylvania 19104-4112

Printed in the United States of America on acid-free paper

10 9 8 7 6 5 4 3 2 1

A Cataloging-in-Publication record is available from the Library of Congress
ISBN-13: 978-0-8122-4049-8
ISBN-10: 0-8122-4049-9

". . . If I ever hear that 'can't make an omelet' phrase again, I'll start doing a little murder myself! It's used to justify every atrocity under every despotism, Fascist or Nazi or Communist or American labor war. Omelet! Eggs! By God, sir, men's souls and blood are not eggshells for tyrants to break!"

—Doremus Jessup, in It Can't Happen Here, *by Sinclair Lewis*

What was the "technique of liberal failure"? It was . . . the unwillingness of the liberal to continue with analysis once the process of analysis had become uncomfortable. LaFollette had been willing to continue with the analysis of the War; so had Bourne. But liberalism in general couldn't stand the gaff.

—John Chamberlain

A world in which all were happy, and every individual fully and freely realized his or her potentialities, in which freedom reigned and government that was coercion had disappeared, was the ultimate aim of both liberals and socialists. What distinguishes the various members of the ideological family descended from humanism and the Enlightenment, liberal, socialist, communist or anarchist, is not the gentle anarchy which is the utopia of all of them, but the methods of achieving it.

—Eric Hobsbawm

Contents

Abbreviations

ACLU	American Civil Liberties Union
ACPF	American Commonwealth Political Federation
ADA	Americans for Democratic Action
ADS	American Defense Society
AFL	American Federation of Labor
ALAWF	American League Against War and Fascism
ALP	American Labor party
ALPD	American League for Peace and Democracy
ANE	"America and the New Era"
ANES	American National Election Studies
APL	American Protective League
ARU	American Railway Union
ASU	American Student Union
AUAM	American Union Against Militarism
CAW	Congress of American Women
CCF	Committee for Cultural Freedom
CDC	California Democratic Council
CIA	Central Intelligence Agency
CIO	Congress of Industrial Organizations
CIO-PAC	CIO Political Action Committee
CIR	U.S. Commission on Industrial Relations
CLR	Californians for Liberal Representation
CNC	Committee for North Carolina
CORE	Congress of Racial Equality
CP	Communist party USA
CPPA	Conference for Progressive Political Action
CSO	Community Service Organization
DFL	Democratic-Farmer-Labor party
EPIC	End Poverty in California
ERA	Equal Rights Amendment
FBI	Federal Bureau of Investigation
FCC	Federal Council of Churches
FLP	Farmer-Labor party
FLPF	Farmer-Labor Political Federation
FOR	Fellowship of Reconciliation

GOP	Grand Old Party (i.e., the Republican party)
HUAC	House of Representatives Committee on Un-American Activities
IWA	Illinois Women's Alliance
IWW	Industrial Workers of the World
JCNR	Joint Committee on National Recovery
LIPA	League for Independent Political Action
LNPL	Labor's Non-Partisan League
MFDP	Mississippi Freedom Democratic party
NAACP	National Association for the Advancement of Colored People
NCL	National Consumers' League
NLG	National Lawyers' Guild
NNC	National Negro Congress
NNLC	National Negro Labor Council
NOW	National Organization of Women
NPA	National Progressives of America
NRA	National Recovery Administration
NSA	National Student Association
NWP	National Women's party
NWTUL	National Women's Trade Union League
OSHA	Occupational Safety and Health Administration
PCA	Progressive Citizens of America
PP	Progressive party
SANE	Committee for a Sane Nuclear Policy
SCEF	Southern Conference Educational Fund
SCHW	Southern Conference on Human Welfare
SCLC	Southern Christian Leadership Conference
SDS	Students for a Democratic Society
SNCC	Student Nonviolent Coordinating Committee
SP	Socialist party
SRC	Southern Regional Council
STFU	Southern Tenant Farmers' Union
SWOC	Steel Workers Organizing Committee
TUEL	Trade Union Educational League
UAW	United Automobile Workers
UE	United Electrical, Radio and Machine Workers of America
UMWA	United Mine Workers of America
USIC	U.S. Industrial Commission
WCTU	Women's Christian Temperance Union
WDU	Workers' Defense Union
WPP	Woman's Peace party
WSP	Women Strike for Peace
YWCA	Young Women's Christian Association

Introduction

Ours is an era of ideological illiteracy. Many Americans simply have no idea what terms such as "left" and "right" mean. The left half of the political spectrum is positively shrouded in a fog of conceptual confusion. Conservatives describe centrists, such as former president Bill Clinton, as "liberal" and liberals as "far left." When Ralph Nader ran for president in 2000 and 2004, he was treated by many liberals and conservatives alike as a wild-eyed radical, even though his views were little changed since the 1960s, when he was known as a liberal consumer-protection activist. Those, such as Nader, who stand to the left of the Democratic party denounce Democrats and many liberals as sell-outs to big business. Liberal Democrats themselves have felt like political outsiders for decades. Left, liberal, and progressive are terms whose meanings shift and float. Clintonite centrists, anti-imperialist peace agitators, and labor-union activists alike call themselves progressives, and no one can say definitely that any of them is wrong.[1]

Any Americans of the early twenty-first century who wish to revive something they call liberalism or progressivism, or who think substantial change, regardless of its name, is needed in our society—and such ambitions have been stated in some quarters for many years now—had better know something about the fate of similar hopes in the past.[2] Yet Americans' knowledge of political history often goes back no further than the 1950s and the 1960s—the childhood years of the baby-boom generation. The conflicts of these cold war decades formed images of liberalism and left-wing radicalism that remain powerful today. In contrast, the earlier era of the 1930s, featuring the triumph of New Deal liberalism and the vitality of a Communist movement, has become a dim and rapidly fading tableau, while the politics of the 1940s, the days of world war and post-war regrouping, have been blotted out by sentimental newsreel visions of sacrifice and social cohesion.

The images of liberalism and the left bequeathed to us by the cold war era are those of mutual antagonism. In the 1950s, the days of the "red scare" and Senator Joseph McCarthy—the most famous leader of the hunt for subversives in and out of government—many liberals joined in the anticommunist, anti-radical chorus. In the 1960s, a new generation of leftists (known as the "new left") believed that the crusading anticommunism of the 1950s had helped make America a repressive place, closed to new and critical perspectives on society; in their view, liberals shared responsibility for that setback. Radicals in the 1960s routinely denounced a "liberal establishment," led by men such as Presidents John Kennedy and Lyndon Johnson, as in fact far too conservative, too close to the "power elite," and insensitive to the plight of the socially excluded.[3] Liberals, who flocked to Kennedy's slogan of a "New Frontier" and Johnson's program of a "Great Society," returned the radicals' scorn, calling them irresponsible and unreasonable. In the late 1960s, the militancy of African Americans, on the heels of the civil rights movement's triumphs and frustrations, and the Vietnam War, escalated and prolonged by Kennedy and Johnson, drove liberals and the left ever further apart.

Against this backdrop of '60s antagonism, almost no one has written specifically on the subject of left-liberal relations in America. This makes sense, since people who came of age in the 1960s thought the American left and American liberalism had separate histories, linked mainly by animosity.[4] Historians at times gave the impression that rebellions in U.S. history—whether agrarian populist or urban and working-class, whether black or white—were authentic and inspiring only to the extent that they were free from any taint of liberal ideology. Some asserted the existence of an American "radical tradition" whose members fought for racial justice, economic fairness, and women's equality and who reflected an impressive integrity and independence.[5]

At the same time, scholars influenced by the radicalism of the 1960s surveyed American history and found liberals whose reform efforts aimed to quell discord and smooth the path of capitalist advances, not to achieve justice. They saw liberals who formed partnerships with business concerns and sought to control or repress radicals and the restive lower orders—in other words, liberals who committed the same sins that new left radicals charged to Great Society leaders. A leading concept of such scholarship was "cooptation," according to which liberals did the work of powerful interests, pacifying disruptive elements with empty promises of egalitarian change.[6]

Deep in American history, however, there lies a neglected middle ground of ambitious reform politics, forgotten amid the stark divisions of the cold war. This left-liberal tradition includes liberals who were deeply critical of American capitalism as well as leftists who saw great value in social reform, as opposed to revolutionary upheaval. During a roughly sixty-year period, between the 1880s and the 1940s, this vital political alliance constructed bridges of cooperation—not cooptation—between the worlds of liberal reform and radical rebellion. Reformers who adopted a deeply critical stance toward their society engaged in a series of extended, productive collaborations with radicals who saw in social reform a way toward a more acceptable society.[7]

Much of what was most creative and constructive in American politics in the twentieth century issued from this left-liberal tradition—from the work of radicals drawn to liberal principles and liberals who made deep criticisms of American society. Residents of the political zone where liberalism and radicalism overlapped championed, for example, the validation of free speech and free conscience and the imperative of racial equality in a diverse society whose origins lay in race slavery—causes that, by any reckoning, advanced dramatically in the course of the twentieth century. In the 1940s, this distinctive tradition of left-liberal politics fell apart. Leftists and liberals largely went their separate ways after that time, although they sometimes had more in common than was apparent.

This is not to say that the "real" history of left-liberal relations in America was simply an harmonious affair, the opposite of what it appeared to be when the baby boomers were young adults. There has been plenty of both conflict and cooperation between radicals and reformers, leftists and liberals, in the American past, and no single "natural" relationship exists between them. Neither periods of strategic collaboration nor those of mutual contempt have represented deviations from a norm. Almost two decades past the end of the cold war, a post–cold war history of left-liberal politics, one freed of the analytical blinders that we all have inherited from the 1950s and 1960s, is due.

Starting in the 1880s, middle-class reformers—most of them white, Protestant inhabitants of northern cities—rebelled against the doctrines of unregulated capitalism and sought to transcend class conflict by forming a political movement that would help forge a new society, a society newly harmonious and fair. Americans of the late nineteenth-century Gilded Age were aware that momentous economic and social change, characterized by heavy industrialization, rapid urbanization, the production of enormous wealth, and new extremes of wealth and poverty, was taking place all around them, and many believed that Americans could use political means to steer the ship of social change toward a desirable destination. Individuals such as the writer Henry Demarest Lloyd and the famous social reformer Jane Addams favored an activist government that would pursue humane and egalitarian policies, backed by a democratic mobilization—a mobilization based in Christian ethics and empowering both the industrial working class and middle-class reformers such as themselves. Such middle-class reformers wanted American workers to have a seat in the councils of power, but they definitely did not want to live under working-class rule.

These reformers pioneered the twentieth century's "new liberalism," which was associated with economic regulation and the rise of a welfare state, which represented a dramatic break from the doctrines of laissez-faire individualism that had been associated with political and intellectual liberalism in the nineteenth century. Political champions of new liberal proposals appeared not only among urban politicians—such as Tom Johnson and Hazen Pingree, the mayors of Cleveland and Detroit, respectively—but also in the southern countryside and the Great Plains, where white agrarian leaders such as Nebraska's William Jennings Bryan and Georgia's Tom Watson sought a farm-labor alliance to protect "the plain people" from capitalist abuses. African Americans were largely excluded from these alliances either through vicious demagoguery and violence or simply by means of reformers declining to discuss the issue of white supremacy. Women, predominantly but not exclusively white, organized in groups ranging from the Women's Christian Temperance Union (WCTU) to the National Consumers' League (NCL) and were pervasive in the political mobilizations of the new liberalism, even though they were excluded from public office and, for the most part, from voting before 1920. New liberals also included in their reform coterie relatively assimilated representatives of the enormous wave of immigrants, most of them Roman Catholic or Jewish, who furnished many of the workers for the mushrooming industrial centers. Yet even as such rising elements in the nation's populace shaped the agenda of twentieth-century liberalism, they joined a political framework of reform that had been shaped decisively by white Protestants in the late Gilded Age.

Many among these reformers embraced a transformative concept of social progress, a concept that opened a door between liberal reformers and left-wing radicals. From the 1880s to the 1940s, the efforts of many reformers and radicals were linked by a widespread conviction that American society was advancing from one stage of historical development to the next.[8] Most Americans, including most conservatives, believed that the country was becoming continually wealthier and more powerful. Various ideas of progress were commonplace in the United States.[9] For their part, grass-roots farm-belt agitators who advocated an enhanced government role in the economy to protect small landowners and workers saw society's transformation in a rather negative light and sometimes framed their proposals as a "counterrevolution" designed to stop or reverse that change.[10] In contrast, many urban new liberals believed that the country was in the midst of a fundamental transformation into a new society that held the potential to become more democratic, egalitarian, and united than the world of Gilded Age capitalism.

They embraced an especially robust concept of ongoing historical progress, one that asserted a tumultuous and—again, at least potentially—forward change that would be qualitative, not merely quantitative. In this perception, they agreed with many who called themselves socialists, whether or not they joined the Socialist party, formed in 1901.

This developmental, transformative vision of progress lent coherence during the period between the 1880s and the 1940s to a reform politics located where the new liberalism overlapped with the left. Those seized with this vision of change anticipated the eclipse of capitalism as they knew it in favor of a more united, fair, and democratic form of society. In 1888 the activist Florence Kelley derided efforts "to piece and cobble at the worn and rotten fabric of a perishing society" and called on her fellow Americans instead "to make an end of such a system."[11] She called for a political movement that could shape an ongoing social transformation; the existing society was "perishing," its fabric "rotten." It could not be maintained. In 1902, the philosopher John Dewey stated that he was "scientifically convinced of the transitional character of the existing capitalistic control of industrial affairs and its reflected influences upon political life." In the 1930s, the Communist Joseph Freeman wrote of his "belief that mankind is passing through a major transformation. The dissolution of capitalism compares in scope and significance with the origins of private property, the beginnings of Christianity, the ascendancy of the bourgeoisie." Views similar in some respects to Freeman's were not confined to the far left and they had been current for a long time when he wrote these words. Whether the anticipated new society, waiting on the far side of social and political transformation, would represent a new stage of capitalism or a society beyond capitalism was a question to which liberals and radicals gave a wide range of answers.[12]

From the 1880s to the 1940s, many liberals joined forces with leftists or debated the future with them amicably. The politics of transformation facilitated the construction of a broad political front whose politics often rendered moot distinctions commonly drawn between liberals and leftists, and even between evolution and revolution. Some liberals, including political leaders from President Woodrow Wilson to President Franklin Roosevelt and less famous strategists such as the journalist Walter Lippmann and the economist Adolf Berle, saw it as the liberal mission to stabilize the social structure of American capitalism and the political structure of the democratic republic. Others, mainly activists, ranging from Florence Kelley to the clergyman Harry Ward to the scholar W. E. B. DuBois to the writer Betty Friedan, at least during some phases of their careers, viewed American society as deeply flawed and saw it as their duty to express the perspective of the socially excluded. The latter type of liberals figures large in this book. Such liberals seemed to flirt with the idea of socialism, but generally they resisted it.[13] Some might classify them as leftists rather than liberals. In many individual cases, that distinction is of little use. Before the 1940s, liberal politics as such was not defined by a defense of America's political-economic system against those who made fundamental criticisms of "the American way." That came afterward.

After making considerable headway on their political and policy agenda during the Progressive Era, which stretched from 1900 to 1917, the broad front of left-liberal reformers experienced a traumatic disruption during World War I and the subsequent anti-radical red scare. As president, Woodrow Wilson backed regulatory and welfare-state measures associated with the broad and diverse ranks of "progressive" reformers. The early twentieth-century progressives, as that term was understood by contemporaries and later historians, included not only the social workers, labor activists, and religious reformers who are the focus of this study in its early chapters but also businessmen and others who desired a more efficient and highly organized society. The former congeries of activists—whom I call the new liberals—were relatively prolabor and embraced sharp criticisms of contemporary capitalism. Their sympathies with radical and militant labor organizations such as the Industrial Workers of the World (IWW), their tendency to oppose U.S. entry into the European war, and their support for the Bolshevik revolution in Russia brought them a world of trouble at the end of the 1910s, as they were sucked into the attack mounted by Wilson and conservatives alike against antiwar activists, labor agitators, and the left.

That attack, combined with the determination of some on the left to separate reformers from revolutionaries decisively, threatened to end forever the phenomenon of a broad liberal-left alliance. Women's gender-based political activism, as embodied in groups such as the National Consumers' League and the Women's Peace party, was linked closely to left-liberal politics during the Progressive Era, but the postwar feminist movement turned away from such damaging associations, taking on a more independent political profile in response to red-baiting in the late 1910s and early 1920s. Yet many women and men continued to believe in the left-liberal alliance, and they picked up its pieces and carried it forward. A politically disparate set of key activists who kept their faith in the broad front, including Harry Ward, the law professor Felix Frankfurter, and labor radical Elizabeth Gurley Flynn, worked together in the American Civil Liberties Union (ACLU), founded in 1920, which became the linchpin of left-liberal politics in the following years.

During the years between World War I and World War II, left-liberal activists mounted two significant strategic efforts to revitalize their broad front and to expand its agenda. The first such effort was the farmer-labor movement of the 1920s and 1930s, which involved third-party organizing activities and drew on the legacy of earlier agrarian movements. Its most important single champion was Senator Robert LaFollette, Sr. of Wisconsin, whose independent presidential campaign of 1924 gave hope to left-liberals that an updated version of farmer-laborism—William Jennings Bryan's old dream of a winning national coalition of "commoners"—might yet be realized, albeit outside the confines of Bryan's Democratic party. Into the mid-1930s, midwestern and western agitators roamed the Plains, the Rockies, and beyond, preaching the gospel of a third party. They found success in Minnesota, under the leadership of Governor Floyd Olson, and, to a lesser degree, in Wisconsin, with LaFollette's sons, Philip and Robert, Jr., at the helm, but they were unable to break out of this Upper Midwest ghetto, and in general their agenda was usurped by President Franklin Roosevelt in the 1930s. When Roosevelt revitalized the Democratic party as a reform vehicle and offered tangible benefits to farmers and workers, he cut the ground out from under interwar farmer-laborism.

The second effort, more innovative and more consequential for American politics, was the "Popular Front" of 1935–48. The Popular Front brought together Communists and liberals. It united old-stock reformers with African Americans and members of the newer industrial labor unions—which in 1935 formed the Congress of Industrial Organizations (CIO) under the leadership of John Lewis and others—in support of a pluralistic, social-democratic vision that embraced Roosevelt's New Deal program but sought to push the Democratic party beyond it. The industrial unions and the Popular Front spoke for a political-economic agenda intended to expand economic security and opportunity for American workers, but its success in advancing that agenda was partial at best. The frustration of social-democratic ambitions in the 1940s did much to dissipate hopes for social transformation in America and to channel the energies of those who had populated the broad front for transformation into new frontiers.

Faltering in their hopes to transform American capitalism, the activists of the Popular Front left their deepest mark in the pursuit of racial equality and the embrace of ethnic diversity. In the 1930s and 1940s, political liberals for the first time embraced at least a moderate form of racial egalitarianism, and they reached a consensus in favor of a mild version of cultural pluralism. Before about 1935, there was no such thing as racial liberalism, and political liberalism up to that time was a white political tendency. Occasionally an African American, most notably W. E. B. DuBois, had sought to involve himself in liberal politics in earlier times, but such efforts had met with frustration over the unwillingness of (white) liberals to extend their stated values to questions of race.

In the 1910s and 1920s, Catholics and Jews had begun to link their own agendas of empowerment and security to the programs then becoming associated with liberal reform, and in the process they altered the content of liberal politics. In the 1930s and 1940s African American activists, as well as Communists of all races, changed liberal politics perhaps more fatefully, insisting that the liberal movement could not be true to itself if it did not move to a position favoring civil rights and opportunity for black Americans and opposing Jim Crow segregation in the South, a particularly difficult task for liberals since their main vehicle by that time was the Democratic party, which was still committed to southern apartheid. Of the Popular Front's entire agenda, its racial egalitarianism was the element that, by far, was absorbed most fully and durably into the American political mainstream.

The left-liberal alliance was disrupted for a second time, and this time more definitely, during the 1940s, by the conflicts among American liberals over communism. The broad alliance did not survive this trauma, as it had survived the shocks it received during and just after World War I. American liberalism and radicalism both were redefined. Liberals in the 1940s shelved their longtime dreams of reshaping America's political economy through direct political action and began to strengthen their belief in the vitality and social promise of American capitalism.[14] By 1950, with the United States at an unprecedented peak of global power and the cold war between America and the Soviet Union having begun in earnest, anticommunist liberals vanquished their left-leaning rivals within liberal precincts and succeeded in redefining liberalism against the left, as an anti-revolutionary doctrine plain and simple. The left—or "radicalism," the term favored during the cold war—became a political identity defined in large measure by its differences with liberalism. In 1948, Henry Wallace, a former vice president, ran for president as a left-liberal who wished to preserve the Popular Front, taking a militant pro–civil rights stance and advocating peaceful coexistence with the Soviet Union. But he found himself excommunicated from the evolving politics of liberalism. The memory of liberalism's anti-capitalist heritage, of the fierce critique of American capitalism that long had animated one large wing of American liberalism, quickly faded, a memory that liberals had reason to wish gone during the era of McCarthyism. The earlier compatibility of liberalism with a supportive view of social transformation was erased from the nation's political rule book.

The years between the late 1940s and the late 1960s, the heart of the cold war, formed the classic era of estrangement between liberals and radicals. During this era, liberals generally supported the cold war abroad and some form of red-hunting at home. Self-proclaimed radicals often sympathized with third-world revolutionaries, expressed great suspicion of the U.S. government, and championed the rights of African Americans and other downtrodden minorities. Liberals gradually embraced the cause of civil rights and racial inclusion as well, but they did not welcome insurgencies against the American social and political system, either domestically or internationally, as cold war radicals did—and as some earlier liberals had. Liberals during the cold war maintained an attenuated belief in social progress, one that was basically quantitative. The question of capitalism's moral virtues and defects continuously faded from liberal politics, to the point where, in the post–Great Society years, political actors identified all around as liberals gave fulsome praise to the beneficence of America's economic genius and shrank from any fundamental criticism of the capitalist system. Programmatically, cold war liberals developed new initiatives, most dramatically during the 1960s, adding ardent civil rights advocacy, an opening of opportunities for women, environmental protection, and a celebration of diversity to their agenda. Yet, fundamentally, the cry of the cold war liberal was the same as that of the American labor movement, as the labor leader Samuel Gompers had expressed it long before: "More."

Leftists during the cold war era worked doggedly to extend the benefits of America's political and economic systems to social groups that had been excluded from these benefits. In other words, in the context of domestic politics, they did the work of liberalism. Leftists simply showed less hesitancy and more passion than most liberals showed and paid no heed to mass opinion. Breaking with liberals, leftists also opposed the cold war with the Soviets and defended a series of revolutionary socialist governments abroad, beginning with Fidel Castro's Cuban regime. But even leftists during the cold war advocated socialism in the United States only tentatively, sporadically, and far from unanimously. Leftists continued to malign American capitalism as immoral and exploitative, but they found it difficult to pose coherent alternatives to that system. They often consoled themselves in the role of prophets without honor, despairing of America's afflictions of the soul and disdaining strategies of power and change.

The thirty years after the Vietnam War ended, in 1975, were an era of scant optimism and ideological uncertainty for liberals and leftists. Ideas of transformative progress in an egalitarian direction faded rapidly from American political life, even as, ironically, the term "progressive" came into use as a euphemism, alternately, for liberal and left. Liberals swam, within the two-party system, against a resurgent tide of laissez-faire doctrine. Some liberals and leftists joined forces, either within the Democratic party or in issue-based activist mobilizations, to do battle against the political right, but with almost no explicit discussion of ideologies or long-range social and political goals. Many leftists found positions of substantial status and comfort in the cultural apparatus of post-1960s America, in some ways estranged from mass culture and in other ways absorbed in the culture of the professional class. They became awkward tribunes for downtrodden minorities and often appeared uninterested in championing the majority.[15] Perhaps most ironically, in light of the fervency with which earlier generations of leftists had embraced a doctrine of social progress in America, leftists in the post–World War II era developed grave doubts about any such doctrine, sometimes gravitating toward ideas of cultural renewal and spiritual enchantment and losing faith in the vision of knowledge-driven upward historical movement that had constituted the intellectual patrimony of the western left since the Enlightenment of the eighteenth century. Those who might have been, in the light of history, the most forceful advocates for a robust idea of progress in America became confused and ambivalent about it, their trumpets uncertain if not stilled.

Liberalism and the left, for all their differences, sprang from common Enlightenment sources, and this ensured that conflicts between liberal reformers and leftist radicals tended to take on a distinctively intimate quality. In fact, from the nineteenth century to the present, although American radicals and reformers criticized each other harshly, their disputes were often—although not always—bounded by bedrock liberal assumptions about the nature of a good society. Left-wing radicals were those who placed extremely high value on equality and who subjected capitalism to severe moral criticism over its allegedly exploitative and dehumanizing aspect. A leftist was not necessarily a socialist. Liberals' essential commitments were to individual freedom, natural rights, constitutional government, and the sovereignty of "the people"—concepts that, not only in the United States but also in world history, linked the anti-government liberalism of the eighteenth and nineteenth centuries to the welfare-state liberalism of the twentieth century and beyond.[16] As these definitions suggest, the line separating leftists from liberals often was smudged or downright invisible, no matter how often people to either side tried to mark it clearly and impassably.

As already noted, radicals frequently did the work of liberalism, fighting for a thorough application of liberal principles in society, and they often castigated self-identified liberals for failing to fulfill liberal principles. It is not hard to find exceptions to this rule: radicals who disdained liberal principle as well as practice. Nonetheless, it is striking how far the radical critics in our past were influenced by liberal ideology. American leftists generally championed individual liberties even as they pursued communal harmony. They sought new bases for individual freedom while extolling collective action. For their own reasons, leftists often shared with libertarians a distrust of the state, while nonetheless projecting visions of an expanded government that would tame capitalist power, express the will of "the people," and aid the oppressed. These multiple commitments may have entailed contradictions, but if so, these were contradictions shaped by the persistence of liberal themes in radical politics. Many of the dissenting forces in American politics were inhabitants of a deep liberal near-consensus—one also broad enough to include many conservative opponents of twentieth-century liberalism and the left.

If radicals very often were liberals in ideology and militant liberals in program, then is there no role for socialism in a history of left-liberal politics? In the context considered in this study, the idea of socialism functioned as a kind of enabling myth for radical egalitarians in America. To call socialism a myth is not to say it was merely a falsehood or a delusion. Instead, the idea of socialism served continually to push back the horizon of reform, to maintain a space for prophetic moral criticism of society, and to furnish a practically endless series of demands for the redefinition of liberal reform beyond what each receding generation had imagined. Socialism was the most striking formulation of the broader idea of transformative progress in America, describing the cleanest break between today and tomorrow. That clean break, that leap forward, never arrived and it likely never will. Radicals and liberals alike pushed for piecemeal improvements, but the idea of transformation, including the doctrinaire idea of socialism, prodded them onward in this path. In the absence of believers in a socialist alternative, one has to wonder if any similar spur to society's moral improvement will be felt. The term "progressive" returned to American politics as the twentieth century ended, but this was a euphemism for any among a wide range of political positions, not a signal that a coherent vision of progress had returned to American reform or radicalism. Leftists continue to claim a morally transcendent, prophetic vantage point from which they denounce the evils of contemporary society. Yet their vision of change is hazy. They are prophets without a promised land to which they might direct the people. Prophecy may be emotionally stirring, but prophecy without a coherent belief in progress may prove more disabling than inspiring.

In the early twenty-first century, liberalism—whether ambitious or cautious, whether establishmentarian or critical of American society's central tendencies—sometimes appears as the politics that dares not speak its name. Those who pine for a return of New Deal or Great Society designs for social equity often call themselves progressives because the political right has cast liberals into disrepute, defining liberals as cultural elitists and little more.[17] Others, who lean to the left, also call themselves progressives rather than liberals, but they mean that they side with society's outsiders and dissenters and liberals don't. Because of the success of cold war liberals in capturing the mantle of liberalism for themselves—in reading Popular Front liberalism out of what most Americans understood as "liberalism"—for a half-century or more, those who have adopted a militant pro–civil rights, pro-labor and anti-imperialist stance have tended to see themselves as "radicals"—or progressives—not as liberals.[18] Those who stand on the left flank of the reform tradition, whether they are particularly concerned with racial oppression, with the evils of capitalism, with the subordination of women, or with anything else, may think of liberals as timorous reformers who are hostile to protest and overly concerned with maintaining social order. Yet many protesters against such injustices themselves have laid claim to liberal politics, and American radicalism, as already noted, has been shot through with liberal values. Historians tend to assume that knowledge of the past will dissipate contemporary confusion. If that assumption is to find any validation here, the story has to begin rather far back, in the era that gave birth to both liberal and left politics as they were understood in twentieth-century America.

Chapter 1

The Emergence of the New Liberalism

During the Gilded Age, which stretched from 1865 to the 1890s, the anti-government doctrine of laissez-faire prevailed among the elites of American society. Some conservatives justified their dog-eat-dog economics with "social Darwinism," asserting that some individuals were "fitter" than others and that society would benefit if the "natural selection" of the powerful were allowed to proceed without interference. Others defended individualist, go-it-alone doctrine with the homely bootstrap precepts of Benjamin Franklin and Horatio Alger.[1] But many Americans held different views and mounted a succession of efforts to promote government intervention in the economy as just, necessary, and feasible. Such egalitarian movements were composed of farmers, industrial workers, and middle-class activists, of women and men, of old-stock Anglo Americans and new-stock immigrants, of white and black Americans, of urbanites and country people. The protest movements of the Gilded Age often presented themselves as a kind of secularized Protestant reform, justified with a millennial belief that Americans had a duty to create the Kingdom of God on earth. Many Americans found laissez-faire and social Darwinism offensive to Christianity or otherwise wrong.[2]

In the Progressive Era of 1900–1917, in the wake of unprecedented urbanization and business consolidation, social elements that previously had found laissez-faire thought attractive, particularly the "new middle class" of white-collar employees in large business concerns, as well as some business owners and members of the social and political elite, came over to the side of government regulation. Pro-reform "progressives" of that era concluded that large business concerns were interfering with the proper workings of republican government and that these incursions had to be repulsed. Often they also came to agree that some things—things as different as the labor of children and the national transportation system—should not be left to the vicissitudes of untrammeled market relations.[3] This widened and diverse constituency for reform brought success both to long-standing demands of farmers' and workers' movements and to new demands by middle- and upper-class groups for what was called "social control." Laissez-faire thinking would prove a resilient part of the political and intellectual fabric of American life, but it was put on the defensive during this period.[4]

By the end of the Progressive Era, many Americans had begun to call the reform outlook, which was justified with shifting proportions of concern for social justice and social stability, political "liberalism." Some historians have presented the protest movements of 1865–1917 as the "liberal" side in an eternal conflict between conservatives and liberals, but advocates of regulation or social control were not called liberals before the 1910s. Throughout the nineteenth century that name, in a political context, was reserved for the individualistic, laissez-faire perspective, and this libertarian stance remains known as "classical liberalism" today. Therefore the twentieth-century identification of *anti*–laissez-faire thinking as "liberal" is a problem in the history of political language worth pondering. The conceptual connections between twentieth-century reform politics and liberal ideas, which emphasized individual freedom, go back to the later Gilded Age. In the 1880s, reform thinkers who rebelled against laissez-faire thinking—people including academic thinkers such as the Christian economist Richard T. Ely, the labor leader Samuel Gompers, and the agitator Henry Demarest Lloyd—began laying the groundwork for a new kind of liberal politics and thought. Yet the practical politics and the ethics of their reform liberalism preceded the appropriation of the name "liberal" by those who shared their outlook. The naming of twentieth-century liberalism took so long to occur that as late as the 1930s, Herbert Hoover, a defender of classical liberalism, fumed with rage that his nemesis, Franklin D. Roosevelt, used the label that Hoover thought properly belonged to conservatives like him.[5]

The concept of early twentieth-century "progressivism" has saved historians of American liberalism some of the trouble of retracing the navigation between classical liberalism and the pro-regulation, pro-labor outlook that went by the name of "new liberalism" in Britain—a name that works well in analyzing the American scene, too. In many historical narratives, the procrustean individualism of nineteenth-century liberalism disappears during the Progressive Era, when all manner of Americans turned to reform efforts—whether authoritarian or egalitarian—and twentieth-century liberalism appears on the other side of the Progressive Era as a moderately democratic movement for fairness and security, its advocates proclaiming their solidarity with "the people." Somehow, liberalism was transformed from the laissez-faire dogma of President Grover Cleveland to the state interventionism of Franklin Roosevelt. Historians of British politics have compiled a substantial scholarly literature focusing specifically on the question of how classical liberalism got reworked on the road toward the welfare state.[6] Historians of America, in contrast, rarely have made the transformation of the "old liberalism" into the "new liberalism" an explicit problem.[7]

The new liberals of the later Gilded Age and Progressive Era, who favored state action as the key to preserving freedom and democracy in a new age of industrial behemoths, drove the process that shaped transformative politics in this new America. They played the greatest roles in crafting a reform politics visionary enough to draw in those radicals eager for concrete social improvement, while also appealing to farseeing members of society's ruling circles who wished to prevent class warfare. The new liberals included individuals such as social thinkers and activists Jane Addams and Henry D. Lloyd, lawyers such as the labor advocate Frank Walsh and future Supreme Court justice Louis Brandeis, and politicians such as Robert LaFollette, Sr. and William Jennings Bryan, among many others more obscure today. They were mainly people of the bourgeoisie, often from genteel or professional families if not usually from great wealth. But they were energized by and interacted with workers' and farmers' movements. The new liberals were those turn-of-the-century progressives who embraced a vision of qualitative historical change in America, of an egalitarian social transformation. Their ultimate ideological achievement was to forge a link between egalitarian, democratic reform and the American tradition of liberal thought. To understand the durable, influential politics of transformation in late nineteenth- and early twentieth-century America, we need to understand the thinking and activities of the new liberals and the social and ideological context that produced them.

Gilded Age America: An Era of Upheaval

The ideology of laissez-faire bulked large in the imagination of nineteenth-century Americans. Considering the wide belief in the self-made man as both a moral standard and a social reality during that century, the United States saw a rather high level of government intervention in the economy, including publicly funded roads and canals and, later, huge gifts of public land to railroad corporations. Political rhetoric proclaimed America the land of self-sufficiency, yet businessmen and civic leaders advocated publicly funded "improvements" as ways to develop national prosperity; "while the dish was spiced throughout with the rhetoric of democracy and sealed over with a thin pastry of orthodox textbook maxims, its meat and potatoes was economic nationalism."[8] In Great Britain, even those who called themselves laissez-faire liberals, in the early and middle years of the nineteenth century, in their own ways used the state vigorously to achieve their ends. But in the United States, even though Democrats were more strident than Republicans in proclaiming government irrelevant to prosperity, laissez-faire was the sustaining myth of a whole society, not that of one party.[9]

The broad mainstream of ideology throughout nineteenth-century America was liberal-republican, combining liberal beliefs in individual freedom and the progressive character of capitalism with the republican conviction that a good society, governed by politically free citizens, was sustainable only if built upon the foundation of widespread economic independence.[10] Political enemies almost always did battle from different positions within this shared terrain of liberal-republican ideology. But during the decades after the Civil War, which witnessed the epic rise of the U.S. industrial economy to giant status, massive social change challenged the basic precepts of liberal-republican ideology by raising grave doubts as to the future of economic and political freedom for vast numbers of Americans. The "Second American Revolution" of the Civil War had opened the field for the captains of northern commerce and finance by eliminating the rival ruling class of the slave South.[11] Cities now mushroomed across the North and West, fueled by capital, foreign and domestic, and mass migration, from abroad and from the American countryside.

The new industrial revolution of the Gilded Age generated unprecedented sums of wealth, but also inequality and privation on a scale never before seen in America. The working-class districts of the cities were squalid. Middle-class charity workers who came into such neighborhoods were disgusted by the conditions they saw. More than seven hundred people eventually occupied each acre of the Lower East Side of Manhattan, crammed into practically airless tenements. "Bubbly Creek," a waterway percolating with acid gas from packinghouse animal waste dumped in the Chicago River, ran close to the meat-workers' quarters in the Illinois metropolis. One eastern European immigrant worker said, "*My people do not live in America, they live underneath America.*"[12] The boom-and-bust cycles of American capitalism turned ever more extreme. The depression of the 1870s lasted longer than five years and brought the term "tramp" into the lexicon. The depression of the 1890s lasted about as long and was more severe; vagrancy laws, often created in the 1870s, were used twenty years later to imprison the jobless and homeless. Middle America was not insulated from industrial distress and feelings of dispossession. In the silk mill cities of Pennsylvania, girls with missing fingers could be seen around town, representatives of the under-age-sixteen females who sometimes made up half the mills' work force. And many of those in the economic middle found it harder to climb the ladder of wealth than they had expected. One historian, writing especially of the smaller towns, supposedly the beneficiaries of railroad penetration, observed of Gilded Age America, "A pall of thwarted opportunity, of frustrated dreams, hung over large parts of the nation."[13]

The industrial capitalist ascendancy brought forth fierce opposition. In the South, African Americans sought to wrest dignity and autonomy from the crises of Reconstruction. In the North, a nascent national trade-union movement became increasingly estranged from the nation's evolving economic regime and experimented with new political parties. So did the movements of small farmers that began with the Grange in the 1860s and led to the populist upheaval of 1885–95. The new working-class militancy was most alarming in the eyes of many Americans, partly because urban proletarians engaged in violent clashes with the minions of capital. Major strikes by workers, often sparked by wage cuts during the long depressions of the era, triggered violent state and capitalist responses, and whole communities sometimes formed along literal barricades. In 1877, the first national railway strike started in West Virginia, sparked a general strike in St. Louis and spread through to California; working-class men and women destroyed railroad equipment with abandon, and over one hundred were dead before the army fully suppressed it. The mid-1880s saw a massive movement for an eight-hour day; 340,000 workers struck for the cause on May Day, 1886.[14] The early 1890s gave no respite from conflict, as militias, army troops, and mercenaries rented from the Pinkerton agency squared off against steelworkers in Homestead, Pennsylvania, rail workers in Pullman, Illinois, and miners in Coeur d'Alene, Idaho. One can question whether or not the great egalitarian movements of Gilded Age America challenged the premises of the economic explosion, which destroyed as it created, in any basic way. Still, in the postbellum decades, prior to the emergence of a new liberalism, two major claimants to liberal-republican ideology emerged in the United States—one producerist, one elitist—and along this cleavage the ground shook.

Farmers and Workers Organize

The first generation of the new liberals grew up in the Gilded Age, and when they were young, the vital forces of rebellion against the injustices of the emerging economic order came from within the American producerist tradition. This was a variant of liberal-republican ideology that ignored the worker-capitalist divide and instead split society into wealth makers and parasites. The ranks of the dissenting small-producer army included both the farmers whose protest eventually inspired the People's party (and who became known as the populists) and the workers who formed the Knights of Labor, which was founded in 1869. The pop-

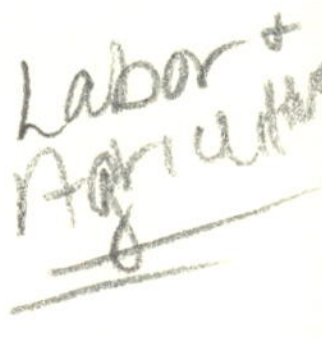

ulists and the Knights both spoke of creating a "cooperative commonwealth," a millennial ideal whose Christian utopianism has made these movements deeply attractive to historians searching for alternatives to acquisitive individualism in America's past. Indeed, the cooperative commonwealth was the most important idea on the American left before the 1930s, suitable to the writer Laurence Gronlund as the name of his socialist vision, but at the same time a respectable notion to many who inhabited the liberal-republican mainstream.[15] These fighting farmers and workers of the Gilded Age were creatures of traditional American ideology. They routinely paid homage to Jefferson and Jackson, and not idly.

Historians have raised the Knights, whose "Great Seal" announced to all that "profits are not a necessity," to heroic status in the annals of Gilded Age America. Such sympathetic chroniclers have exempted the Knights from the moral stains of narrow self-interest, elitism, and racism that have marked the reputation of the American Federation of Labor's craft unionists: the Knights opened their ranks to African Americans and women.[16] (The AFL was formed in 1886, the year the Knights peaked and then began their precipitous decline.) The moral distinction between the two labor groups is a sound one. Yet they were not as radically different as some have suggested. Many AFL activists listened sympathetically to populists, socialists, and advocates of every pro-labor nostrum under the sun during the Gilded Age and the Progressive Era, even while sticking to cautious strategies and a narrowly defined program.[17]

Ideologically, both the AFL and the Knights offered updated versions of labor republicanism, emphasizing the independence and competence of their members in economy and polity. Neither group had any basis for objecting to commercial expansion, much though they might protest some of the results of industrial capitalism. The AFL hardly could gainsay the capitalist system's interior logic, and the Knights of Labor's program never matched the radical suggestions of their Great Seal's rhetoric. The Knights denied the significance of class distinction, and they could decry the violation of lost privileges more easily than they could pose a coherent alternative to the emerging social order.[18] The question stands as to whether they really came to terms with the very evisceration of republican political economy that they decried.

In the 1880s, the Knights of Labor called for a cooperative spirit that would mitigate the harshest aspects of competition, at the same time that reform social scientists, who called themselves socialists, issued a similar plea.[19] "Cooperation" was a slogan of patent, and profound, ambiguity. It might signal a state-socialist agenda or a republican desire to maintain a wide dispersion of property or a cost-pooling arrangement by either producers or consumers or a call for the disgruntled to drop their complaints. Reform economists such as Richard T. Ely and Henry Carter Adams tilted their lances against laissez-faire thought as early as 1870, and in their hands "socialism" meant primarily a preference for cooperation over competition in society; the term for them was "a British borrowing, not a Marxian one."[20] But they were attacked anyway, and from the mid-1880s onward, social scientists increasingly resisted the "s-word." Their rhetorical retreat stemmed in part from the working-class militancy displayed by the Knights of Labor. Yet for both of these groups, the cooperative society was an alternative to class conflict, not its ultimate result. The tendency among the most vigorous dissenters of this era, regardless of their class, to identify competition as the main problem of industrial America reveals them as more acute cultural critics than economic analysts. They failed to understand that the titans of the Gilded Age economy viewed competition as almost as much a foe as they did organized labor, and perhaps as more wasteful. The folkways of economic individualism continued to justify economic developments that made Horatio Alger's tales of upward mobility increasingly implausible. Before the Progressive Era, liberal-republican social critics pressed at the limits of these individualistic mores but never fully took account of economic consolidation. In contrast, AFL union members, while determined to acquire as much in wages and shop-floor autonomy as they could force their employers to concede, harbored few illusions about becoming their own bosses.

It was the agrarian populists whose history has been the bloodiest scholarly battlefield in the annals of the Gilded Age. Squeezed by falling produce prices in the world market, exploitation by railroad shippers, and banks that saw no reason to show mercy when opportunities to foreclose appeared, the farmers of the South and the West organized and agitated after 1885 with an energy and a confidence in their collective righteousness that have made historians sympathetic to such insurgencies love them dearly. The southern populists were not crusaders against racism. Nonetheless, they made modest, temporary inroads against the caste system that has frustrated the strategic hopes of generations of southern leftists and liberals—as did the Knights. For no other predominantly white movement after Reconstruction and before the 1930s can one claim as much. There can be little doubt that the populist "movement culture" of mass meetings and economics lectures would have been as inspiring a thing to witness as it has been to imagine. Of all the thwarted attempts at fundamental political change that pass along in the historiographic pageant of American paths not taken, none is more heartbreaking than the populist alternative.[21]

But the substance of that alternative remains debatable. Edward Bellamy, author of the 1888 sensation, *Looking Backward*, which sought to resolve the class divisions of America by imagining a collectivist future of abundance for all, reflected on the populists with nice insight and subtle ambiguity: "It is not so much their specific propositions, however radical, as the tone and language of their papers, their campaign orators and their campaign songs, which give an adequate idea of the thoroughly revolutionary spirit of these men."[22] They forced onto the American political stage proposals for government intervention in the economy that seem more socialist than anything that ever occurred in the United States: public ownership of the railroad, telephone and telegraph systems, and democratic control over currency and banking. Private control of banking, transport, and communications gave big capitalists a stranglehold on the whole national economy; the populists wanted exceptions made to the rule of property, precisely so that productive smallholding, the "political economy of republicanism," could remain widespread. The right of the citizenry to make such demands was the essence of the concept of "commonwealth." The populists feared America might become a nation of vassals and lords if no such action were taken.[23] They also agitated for far-reaching reforms that achieved fruition in the twentieth century, such as a graduated income tax and extensive government assistance to farmers. For these reasons, the populists once were viewed as the harbingers of twentieth-century social democracy, American style. Beyond such specific proposals, on the level of their social vision, they projected into the American future a moral economy that would bind citizens together into a cooperative commonwealth rather than sundering them into exploited and exploiters. But the government activism they demanded was meant to make social change stop in its tracks, so that the Christian virtue of an agricultural, small-producer society could be maintained. The populists, paradoxically, were at once progressive, as their admirers in the 1930s claimed, reactionary, as critics of the 1950s charged, and humane, as sympathetic revisionists in the 1960s insisted.[24] They have been called both revolutionaries and counterrevolutionaries, yet they remained within the liberal-republican tradition. While the Knights of Labor harked back to Jacksonian labor republicanism, the populists breathed the last real life into Jeffersonian agrarianism. The Indians were virtually all exterminated or defeated, and now the continental republic was supposed to belong to the farmers, not to the railroads.

Populists were...

Unity between the producerist farmers' and workers' movements of the Gilded Age was prevented, in part, by discrepant economic interests. The high agricultural prices that the farmers wished the state to ensure were none too attractive to urban workers with families to feed. Factory employees favored the same high tariffs as did their bosses, while farmers, long enmeshed in global markets, urged freer international trade. Many on both sides of the farmer-labor divide tried to bridge these differences. The farmers tried harder, and their political delegates in Washington, largely Democrats and led foremost by Bryan, starting in the 1890s made consistent efforts to tailor their party platforms to meet organized labor's policy demands. But worker distrust of farm interests was too strong to overcome.[25]

Furthermore, by the 1890s ideological conflicts had driven a wedge within this would-be coalition. Traditional liberal-republicans stood ready to denounce those who strayed from familiar doctrine. In 1894 Henry George, author of *Progress and Poverty*, a critique of landed wealth published in 1879, which had a huge influence on egalitarian crusaders in America and elsewhere for decades, appeared in Chicago only to disrupt a regional attempt at a worker-farmer coalition. George chastised his audience for deviating from Jeffersonian solutions and for being tempted by theories of class conflict. In 1896 the Populists—that is, the People's party—who had been spokesmen for an indebted yeomanry, found fusion with the Democrats and the prospect of currency dilution through the remonetization of silver—expected to prove a boon to debtors—more attractive than continuing their insurgency against the two-party system.[26] Wage workers, by the 1890s, were trying to get the best price possible for their labor, while the radicals among them were becoming attracted to the Marxist hypothesis that this commodification of labor would lead to socialist revolution. Some of these radicals, such as Eugene Debs, were perhaps the labor activists most likely to have participated in the leadership of a rural-urban dissident bloc, so their motion toward socialism was damaging to such a prospect. Speaking more broadly, the potential coalition that might have counteracted the power of corporate capital at century's end was pulled toward two separate destinations in the social imagination: the liberal-republicanism of the nineteenth century and the self-concerned consumer liberalism of the twentieth. This was what Bryan discovered; or at least he should have discovered it.

The Old Liberals of the Gilded Age: Idealistic Elitists

The first expressly political use of the term "liberal" in the United States occurred in the 1870s, when a group of writers and activists criticized the major parties of the Gilded Age for their corruption and preached a bracing doctrine of individual independence that they called liberalism. The name was borrowed from "Manchester liberalism," so called for the English city whose name the activists Richard Cobden and John Bright had made synonymous with free trade and laissez-faire advocacy in the nineteenth century.[27] (Before the Gilded Age a "liberal" person in America meant a person who displayed personal and intellectual openness, tolerance, and flexibility, often a freethinker, in the tradition of Thomas Paine and Robert Ingersoll, hostile to religious orthodoxy—not an adherent of a political doctrine. Elsewhere the term had denoted specific political doctrines from the appearance of the "liberales" in Spain in the 1810s.[28]) In 1872 a renegade faction of Republicans, many of them former Democrats pining for a return to the small-government rhetoric of Andrew Jackson, broke with Ulysses S. Grant's administration and nominated the editor Horace Greeley for president on a Liberal Republican ticket. In 1884 some deserted the Republicans again, disdaining the party nominee, James G. Blaine, and preferring the Democrats' man, Grover Cleveland. On that occasion "stalwart" Republicans mocked the liberal aisle-crossers as "mugwumps," meaning turncoats who were aloof and self-important. I call both Liberal Republicans and mugwumps the "old liberals," since many of their leaders were the same people and they were united by a consistent doctrine. The old liberals saw the Gilded Age as a time of narrow, idiotic materialism, but they derided all movements from below that sought to change Gilded Age America. The old liberals hated the idea of social equality, and they expressed contempt for, as the *Chicago Tribune* sarcastically described it in 1873, "The spirit of Grangerism, Workingmanism, Communism, Grievanceism, or by whatever name the present fever among those who assume to themselves the title of 'the industrial and producing classes' may be termed."[29]

In order to appreciate just how far twentieth-century reformers wrenched the label of liberalism away from what it had meant in nineteenth-century America, it is necessary to grasp how elitist, how callous toward laborers, and how indifferent to the violent subjugation of black southerners the old liberals of the Gilded Age were. Yet these laissez-faire ideologues also hated imperialism and war, harshly criticized special government favors to business concerns, and believed in the existence of a public interest above the fray of special interests. Some of their values, for good and for ill, echoed through the reform movements of the Progressive Era and beyond, and in the 1910s, well-positioned commentators and activists, including President Woodrow Wilson, began to view liberalism as the most apt name for the widespread belief in political and social reform in an industrial age. The need to preserve and enhance the freedom of the individual amid a new society became a master rationale of twentieth-century liberals, and to privileged Anglophiles such as Wilson (quite an elitist and racist himself), the old liberals of the nineteenth century seemed the purest defenders of freedom in the recent American past.

In light of the old liberals' fervent embrace of libertarian economics, it would be a mistake to project today's distinction between liberals and conservatives into the Gilded Age. There were those in the Gilded Age whose whole ideology was order, property, and profit. Among their major ideologues were the Yale scholar William Graham Sumner and the steel magnate Andrew Carnegie. Some historians have called these iron-fisted gentlemen the conservatives of their day.[30] But both groups took a free-market view of labor relations, harkening back to Abraham Lincoln's belief that wage labor needn't be a permanent condition for any American man willing to work, save, and invest. The old liberals believed that their elitism and authoritarianism were unstained by, even opposed to, the corrupting influence of wealth; Samuel Clemens and Charles Dudley Warner, two liberals, coined the derisive term "Gilded Age" in their 1873 novel of that title. Yet the old liberals shared the social precepts of the nabobs of American business. Political corruption and personal shallowness, not wealth and inequality, were the targets of liberal satire in the Clemens-Warner vein. When Governor John P. Altgeld declined, in 1894, to intervene violently against the American Railway Union's (ARU) strike in Illinois, as when he spared the lives of some of the anarchists convicted without proof for the lethal explosion that occurred during a protest meeting in Chicago's Haymarket in 1886, business leaders and most old liberal opinion leaders alike were appalled.

Old liberal feelings toward labor unions ranged from toleration to disdain to outright loathing, and the foremost old liberals attacked labor organizations viciously. Both free-labor ideology and plain fear of the mob help to explain the vitriol of their anti-labor polemics. Edwin L. Godkin, the immigrant from Ulster who headed the *New York Evening Post* and *The Nation*, the country's leading old liberal organs, for much of the Gilded Age, led the old-liberal charge against economic regulation, whether of international trade or the market in labor. Godkin and the other old liberals loved Grover Cleveland above all other politicians most of all because Cleveland stood for free trade, regardless of political consequences.[31] To Godkin, Cleveland affirmed his worth when, over Altgeld's objection, he ordered the army into Illinois to break the ARU's strike. *The Nation* opined, "There is not even any just claim for the minimum wages necessary to keep a man and his family from starvation. . . . From an employer, a man is not entitled to an atom more than the employer is willing to give in a free market."[32] Godkin's barbed style and the prominent platforms from which he commented on events of his day made him the foremost spokesman for the Gilded Age liberals. While he attracted many admirers for both his style and his substance, Lincoln Steffens, who worked for Godkin at the *Post* in the early 1890s, found his editorials "shallow; clever, forceful, ripping, but personal and not very thoughtful."[33]

The situation of black southerners elicited many of Godkin's most obnoxious comments, the conventional racism of his day lending a cutting edge to his belief that calls for federal assistance to the former slaves spelled corruption and would prevent the emergence of a wholesome free-labor individualist society in the South. Most prominent old liberals had been aggressively antislavery before the Civil War, so this group's rejection of Reconstruction policies may seem surprising. The old liberals embraced the Democratic party's negative verdict on Reconstruction, but they did so less because of simple racism than because continued calls for federal involvement in social and economic affairs on behalf of the freedmen increasingly looked to the liberals like violations of their individualist dogma.[34] The liberals soured on U.S. military occupation of the former Confederacy as early as the first Grant administration. In 1869 Godkin, not content merely to invoke the standard republican emphasis on "self-reliance and self-deliverance" in this context—a message to which Frederick Douglass hardly could have objected—gratuitously added that the black American would do best if he heard fewer "gaseous lectures about his political rights."[35] While a republican such as Douglass continued, after the Civil War, to view all adult American citizens, regardless of gender or race, as fully deserving of the rights of citizenship, the white Gilded Age liberals took a narrower view. They resisted viewing women and blacks as worthy electors in their republic. At least they spared women the contradictory imprecation to self-sufficiency. In 1870–71, they opposed the proposed Force Bills, which were intended to curb the violence of the newly formed Ku Klux Klan, as "unconstitutional, unrepublican, un-American." Carl Schurz, a leader of the Republican party during the Civil War, equated the alleged abuses of the biracial Reconstruction state governments with the Klan's terrorism. *The Nation* deemed one senator's proposal for federal aid to public education in the South as an effort "to promote mendicancy."[36]

The old liberals were republicans, not democrats. They were equal opportunity elitists, viewing large numbers of white men as unfit for suffrage. In their support of suffrage contraction, they turned their backs on the tradition of the Manchester liberals. Godkin hardly wrote of democracy but to explain its defects. To him, "[t]he disregard of special fitness, combined with unwillingness to acknowledge that there can be anything special about any man, which is born of equality, constitutes the great defect of modern democracy." Since there were so many more of the poor than the rich, the rise of democracy in nineteenth-century America had allowed political power to slide from "the rich to the poor." This spelled disaster, especially in a society of increasing complexity.[37] The old-liberal complaint was a simple but deep one: the form of democracy itself posed a danger. Godkin's fear of the rising lower-class tide seems, today, a mistaken one.[38] *The Nation* might proclaim that "property-owners, taxpayers, and people of considerable intelligence and business experience" were those fit to rule, but Godkin made clear that "intelligence" was the most important criterion, and that this quality ought to be demonstrated in "the battle of life."

The old liberals' preoccupation with political corruption was closely linked to their elitism, even though their anticorruption fulminations would help to inspire later good-government campaigns that were far more democratic in spirit. The Gilded Age liberals discerned parallel forms of political corruption in the northern machines of "Boss" Tweed and others and in the biracial Reconstruction state governments of the South. In both the North and the South, they concluded, the wicked plied the ignorant with a few favors, and in return they received democratic license for their depredations. Such corruption might be avoided, they asserted, if "the best men" held office and if a nonpartisan civil service staffed the state. The old liberals saw in democracy a machine fueled by, and run largely to maintain, patronage. Offices were to be had, not performed. However, the old-liberal obsession with government favoritism and patronage echoed not only Manchester laissez-faire doctrine but also the antimonopoly thought of Jacksonian America, a tradition that found new life in the agrarian protest movements that the Gilded Age liberals derided. The old liberals criticized the riches showered upon the railroads by the federal government, and this was the preeminent example of government corruption decried by the late nineteenth-century farmers' movements. *Chapters of Erie*, the 1871 exposé of business and political corruption by Charles Francis Adams, Jr. and Henry Adams, a book much admired by the old liberals, paved the way for the muckraking works of the Progressive Era. Yet the old liberals tended reflexively to draw pinched, laissez-faire conclusions from evidence of such corruption. Godkin took from the Grant administration scandals this lesson: "The Government must get out of the 'protective' business and the 'subsidy' business. . . . It must let trade, and commerce, and manufactures, and steamboats, and railroads, and telegraphs alone."[39]

With the old liberals unable to pry themselves free of the laissez-faire rhetoric with which the plutocracy defended its own political economy, the liberals and the elite party regulars whom they disdained sought to explain their differences by questioning one another's manhood. Samuel Clemens called "manhood" more valuable than "mere life and property." In 1884, when the mugwumps bolted the Republican party, he proclaimed "that this idea of *consistency*—unchanging allegiance to *party*—has lowered the manhood of the whole nation—pulled it down and dragged it in the mud."[40] To him, manhood meant independence. But to many contemporaries, the liberals hardly seemed like good examples of strapping manhood themselves. Their aloofness from industry and finance and the writing with which many of them occupied themselves spelled effeminacy to some. An observer at the 1884 Republican convention wrote that the liberals "applauded with the tips of their fingers, held immediately in front of their noses," and, more pointedly yet, one reporter claimed that the "gentlemen from the East" were the only delegates in attendance who "pouted and sulked like whipped school boys" when the convention nominated Blaine. The mugwumps were called "eunuchs," "man-milliners," even "political hermaphrodites."[41] Since the middle of the century Democrats had swaggered their way through campaign seasons and ridiculed Republicans in similar terms, because the GOP called itself "the party of the home" and associated itself with the civilizing influence of wives and mothers, while Democrats emphasized the need for (white) men to rule, inside and outside the home. For example, in 1876 the Democrats claimed that Rutherford Hayes in childhood had been as "timid and nervous as a girl."[42] The mugwumps gave Republicans a chance to dish out what they were used to receiving.

Another reason why the mugwumps fell prey to charges of effeminacy was their distaste for war. Their idea of manliness stressed political and moral independence and personal self-control, not a capacity for bloodshed. They were not averse to state violence; plenty of the old liberals had wanted the Haymarket defendants hanged. But war seemed only a massive waste to them. Like the Manchester liberals, the American Gilded Age liberals saw war as the product of the same mischievous state power that granted economic monopolies. They believed that free trade, which would lead to economic interdependence, was the solvent of international enmities. Godkin had seen first-hand the Crimean War and it had horrified him just as it had Cobden and Bright, who had became scourges of British wars and empire. Godkin "once even [wrote] in his ardor that eventually the place of the soldier in the social scale would be next to that of the hangman."[43] The truest believers among nineteenth-century liberals tended to see themselves as citizens of the world. They followed in the path of Jeremy Bentham, intellectual forebear of the Manchester liberals, who had said, "I should reject with horror . . . the name of patriot, if in order to be a friend to my own country I must be an enemy of the human race."[44]

But in America, peace activism during the Gilded Age became closely associated with women, as groups such as the Women's Christian Temperance Union and the General Federation of Women's Clubs devoted themselves to the cause of arbitration of international conflicts. For much of this period Republican candidates embraced this world of female moral reform, but in the 1890s they turned to a more belligerent mode of male leadership as a way of competing with resurgent Democrats and bridging social divisions among male voters. They derided William Jennings Bryan as "the Emotional Candidate," implicitly questioning his manhood as well as his mental faculties. Then American jingoism reached a climax during the Spanish-American War in 1898, and Theodore Roosevelt led successful politicians in declaiming a martial ideal of manliness. He warned that "when men fear work or righteous war . . . they tremble on the brink of doom." Bryan, who aspired to lead the country, denounced the colonialism that followed the war in terms that few leaders of such stature would echo in twentieth-century America. He queried, "Is our National character so weak that we cannot withstand the temptation to appropriate the first piece of land that comes within our reach?" Most Democrats, like Bryan, wanted the United States to be a republic, not an empire—and they desired no additional nonwhite persons brought into the American realm.[45]

The remaining old liberals led the organized opposition to U.S. empire in 1898 on a republican basis, while also, at least in some cases and in muted form, sharing the racism expressed by many Democrats who resisted overseas colonialism. But the old liberals could not stand to make common cause with a demagogue such as Bryan and his rabble (as the mugwumps would have viewed things).[46] The old-liberal anti-imperialists positioned themselves as virtuous, disinterested moralists, replaying the arguments that the old liberals had made in 1870 against the Grant administration's effort at that time to annex the Dominican Republic.[47] In addition to their other concerns, they expressed genuine humanitarian outrage at the violence that marked the war and at the brutal subjugation of the Filipino independence movement that followed. Oswald Garrison Villard, a student at Harvard at the time, was deeply impressed by the outspoken opposition to the adventure that the famous Harvard professor Charles Eliot Norton and other Boston Brahmins organized.[48] Many twentieth-century liberals maintained the old-liberal tradition of opposition to war and empire. That opposition would provide the basis for friendly discussions between liberals and leftists throughout the twentieth century. Ever fewer would understand the complex lineage of American anti-imperialism.

Strange though it would have seemed to most of the old liberals had they lived long enough to see it, some of their number actually made the transition to the new, more egalitarian liberalism of the twentieth century. Perhaps strangest of all in light of the old-liberal abandonment of southern Reconstruction, Villard, who became the publisher of the *Evening Post* and *The Nation,* along with Moorfield Storey, another old liberal, helped found the National Association for the Advancement of Colored People (NAACP) in 1909, retrieving the antislavery heritage of old-liberal politics from beneath the weight of its postbellum mugwump betrayal. Villard's grandfather had been the abolitionist firebrand William Lloyd Garrison and his father the railroad executive Henry Villard, and Oswald Villard insisted that both were "complete liberals . . . ardent internationalists . . . they abhorred war, were devoted free traders, and believed in the brotherhood of man. Both were steeped in the doctrines of the Manchester school. . . ." While never repudiating the spirit of nineteenth-century liberalism, Villard abandoned some of its principles while clinging to others. He would become an obstreperous opponent of World War I, a sympathizer with the left, and eventually a supporter of the New Deal in the 1930s, while maintaining his belief in free trade and his disgust for machine politics.[49] He turned select elements of his old-liberal heritage leftward, demonstrating the complexity and critical potential that lay dormant within this elitist tradition, one so hostile to the contemporary forces of social protest in its Gilded Age heyday.

The New Liberals: Laborites and Fabians

When Villard, a legatee of the old liberalism, signed up, at an advanced stage in his career, with twentieth-century liberalism, he symbolically acknowledged that the ideological work of crawling out of laissez-faire individualism toward an industrial-era vision of freedom had been done, starting in the Gilded Age, not by the old liberals but by others—others who had sympathized with rather than scorned the producerist protest movements of the time and who had proved willing to break with ideological tradition. In the twentieth century's first two decades, Presidents Theodore Roosevelt and Woodrow Wilson and their camp followers, such as the Progressive Era writers Herbert Croly and Walter Lippmann, emerged as spokespersons for a new doctrine of regulatory government. Yet even they were responding, atop the political system, to conflicts and initiatives that rumbled below. The original new liberals emerged in America beginning in the 1880s and were closer in touch with those conflicts and initiatives. That decade was the time when reform scholars such as Richard T. Ely flirted with socialism, when Edward Bellamy's *Looking Backward* was published and sparked the formation of "Nationalist Clubs" around the country to promote his vision of an "industrial army," and when Henry George—who declared, despite his aversion to class analysis, "One millionaire involves the existence of just so many proletarians"—ran an insurgent campaign for the mayoralty of New

York City, almost winning.[50] The architects of the new liberalism were middle-class thinkers and activists searching for a way out of impending social disaster, and by the end of the nineteenth century they embraced statist and pro-labor views that would have made Godkin shudder. Both the old liberals and the new liberals uttered the traditional American shibboleths of "freedom" and "liberty," but they thought very different means were required to reach those ends.

By the 1890s, influential religious and social thinkers routinely denounced individualism as unsuitable for the new industrial society and called "*association*" the "next great principle," and at the local and state levels of the political system, politicians, thinkers, and activists who were linked to grassroots social movements started to win elections.[51] They understood the conflict between the dominant liberal-republican ideology of nineteenth-century America and the interests of workers and farmers in an industrial age. In the 1880s and 1890s, they sought to speak on behalf of these interests and to organize these groups into a political bloc that could challenge the prevailing order. This happened most dramatically in cities of the Great Lakes region, such as Detroit, Toledo, and Cleveland, where voters elected the troika of reform mayors Hazen Pingree, Samuel "Golden Rule" Jones, and Tom Johnson, respectively, between 1890 and 1901, and in Illinois, where Altgeld was elected governor in 1892.[52] While the national election results of 1892 and 1896 gave scant promise of meaningful reform, as the nation moved toward a new century discontent was turning to a new spirit of change among many Americans of different classes. In the first twenty years of the twentieth century, progressive reform—featuring good-government and direct democracy measures that promised change through procedural reform, but also bringing private industries and utility monopolies to heel and often strengthening labor rights—would overtake many of the country's statehouses, from Albany, where revelations of insurance-industry scandal broke the dam of political conservatism, to Sacramento, where the old specter of railroad influence finally found its exorcist in Governor Hiram Johnson.[53]

But the city most important in the origins of the new liberalism was Chicago, where beginning in the 1880s a critical mass of reform-oriented liberal intellectuals and activists worked to promote a new vision of social cohesion and social justice and broke through to lasting national influence. There Henry Demarest Lloyd worked to build a farmer-worker political alliance, Jane Addams established a center of social reform at the Hull House "settlement," where she welcomed immigrants and worked to improve living conditions for the urban poor, and Florence Kelley pioneered the regulatory state. All of them, moreover, forged a political identity that many new liberals would embrace in the coming century: that of the highly educated, upper- or middle-class advocate of the working class. These activists, whom I call "laborites" because of the centrality of their commitment to working-class welfare and empowerment to their political identity, initiated a reform tradition of cross-class alliances. As they helped forge the new liberalism, they also established the characteristic dilemmas of twentieth-century liberals, setting themselves amid the crosswinds of conflicting class loyalties.

Those crosswinds were created by the competition, within the hearts of the new liberals, between their laborite partisanship and their simultaneous desire to exert their own independent authority over a fractious society. The latter impulse can be thought of as an American version of Fabianism. The Fabians were a British group of genteel reformers, led by Sidney and Beatrice Webb, who in their long careers, which stretched from the 1880s to the 1930s, hoped to bring about a gradual transition to socialism in Great Britain through top-down methods. The Fabians thought that highly educated people like themselves should develop plans for the regulation of society by a powerful state. The essential battle was not one for the minds of the general public, they believed, but for that of the leadership of a political party, which, if it attained power, would allow people such as the Fabians to implement their plans for government administration. The British new liberals of 1890–1920 were influenced by the Fabian perspective, even if they did not call themselves socialists. Similarly, the American new liberals believed in their own capacity to provide solutions to social conflict, in their ability to midwife the birth of a new, unified industrial society by playing an independent role, transcending class conflict. This was the Fabian side of their political identity, one that they freely affirmed. American reformers enjoyed frequent visits to and from their British counterparts; it was not for nothing that Mary McDowell, another longtime Chicago reform leader, in the 1920s kept a copy of Beatrice Webb's autobiography on her desk at the University Settlement at all times.[54] But, at the same time, their laborite loyalty gave them a sense of partisanship in the social struggle and assigned a vital role to mass movements in the American new-liberal vision of social progress. While some of the new liberals tended more to the Fabian side and some leaned more to the laborite side of their persuasion, there were not two distinct camps within the ranks of the new liberals. The two basic elements of their outlook were present in each individual, and each of them struggled with this uncertain mix. They established no recipe that would help them measure fixed proportions of laborism and Fabianism in their politics.

Henry Lloyd was perhaps the most important thinker who early on charted a course from the old liberalism to the new, having begun his career as a propagandist for the American Free Trade League in the

1870s. He maintained an old-liberal hostility to monopoly and government corruption even as he rethought his social outlook in the wake of the railway strike of 1877. In the early 1880s he continued to see high tariffs and government favoritism at the root of the trust problem, saying, "Scratch a monopoly and you will find the Government underneath," and he still doubted the wisdom of strikes by workers, even though he had come to view himself as a friend to labor unions. Most important, by 1887 he explicitly rejected the free-labor dogma of the old liberals and the social Darwinists, condemning laissez-faire economics as "pseudo science with its fiction of free contract and gospel of competition teaching the extermination of the weak by the strong." He thought he risked no violation of natural law in asserting that "[t]he law of love" ought to be "part of the true political economy."[55]

As his invocation of "love" as an economic principle indicated, Lloyd advanced a secularized version of Christian ethics, and he trod a path closely tied to that of the social gospel, the surge of Protestant thought and activism that opened from its beginnings as a simple protest against social division in the 1870s onto a broader ideological spectrum, including a radical socialist wing, by the 1890s. In 1888, at Chicago's Ethical Culture Society, Lloyd delivered a landmark speech, "The New Conscience, or the Religion of Labor," in which he issued a creed of social solidarity, to be based in the labor movement. But in Lloyd's imagining, this movement—precisely because it would be a movement, as distinct from a mere set of labor unions—would include both workers and middle-class reformers. Lloyd called for a cross-class laborite reform movement that would point to a new social unity. In that same year, middle-class and proletarian women came together in a new organization, the Illinois Women's Alliance (IWA), which seemed to embody this "New Conscience." The IWA pressed for the enactment and enforcement of legislation protecting workers who were women and children from the worst effects of wage labor. Lloyd evinced a materialist outlook on political affairs, envisioning a new reform bloc as a marriage of major occupational groups. Yet he struck a strongly idealist note when explaining how a cross-class alliance was possible, arguing that an ethics of love could motivate those in the middle to embrace the cause of laboring folk. The working-class labor movement itself, while driven by crying economic need, was "the most religious movement of the day," said Lloyd, because it was trying to press "the Golden Rule into the market."[56]

All social gospel thinkers hoped to heal society's divisions in the new millennium that they believed was upon them, but there was no consensus among them about just how evil the present world was and how far from the harmonious Kingdom of God. In the hands of moderate religious thinkers such as Charles Sheldon, whose 1896 novel *In His Steps* popularized the phrase "What would Jesus do?," the new unity would rest on a social structure altered modestly if at all, and on a new spirit of understanding between members of the different classes. That didn't keep Lloyd from recognizing Sheldon as an ally. Early social gospel thinkers such as Washington Gladden likewise took up a position between capital and labor, seeking reconciliation, hoping never to take sides. But thinkers of the late Gilded Age, Christians such as Walter Rauschenbusch and Jane Addams, who were more alienated from social trends, insisted that only deep institutional change could bring about a new harmony. However, even social gospel thinkers deeply critical of their society often were inclined simply "to mediate between the competing classes" rather than to take the side of the working poor.[57] The middle-class laborites only rarely gave voice to their religious backgrounds and values, typically Protestant, but these were always at work close beneath the surface of political agitation, and the fundamentally ambiguous class loyalties of the social gospel foreshadowed those of the new liberalism.

Lloyd sought to make himself the hub of the whirling political-intellectual movement that he described in 1888, and he did not do badly. At his home in the peaceful Chicago suburb of Winnetka, from the middle 1880s onward, he hosted an astounding variety of activists and thinkers who sympathized with the working people of the country, including Addams, Kelley, and Ely, as well as the scholar of labor John R. Commons, Debs, the populist Ignatius Donnelly, and the feminist economist Charlotte Perkins Gilman. Of course, neither these people nor those of similar views ever exerted predominant authority in American life. However, it is significant in the history of reform activity that this brilliant and diverse group of thinkers ever came together, as they did under the temporary guidance of Lloyd in Winnetka and Addams at Hull House. This indicates the fluidity during the closing years of the nineteenth century and the opening years of the twentieth between socialist sympathies and social reform, between liberal reformism and left-wing radicalism. On the other side, the line between the new liberals and business-based conservatives sometimes seemed blurry. For instance, Addams served, as Lloyd would not, as a founding member of the Civic Federation of Chicago, largely a businessmen's attempt to quell labor-capital conflict by promoting mediation.[58]

Despite such flirtations with the forces of order, the sense of solidarity that accreted gradually between avowed socialists and many reform intellectuals during the quarter-century before progressivism captured the national political scene in 1912 is significant. Among the national political elite, socialism was anathema, and its growth during the Progressive Era occurred outside the two-party system. However, in the formative years of the later Gilded Age, many "respectable" middle- and working-class activists and thinkers, and even local political elites, treated socialism as a normal part of the political and intellectual system. Samuel Jones, Toledo's mayor, in 1899 stated that he was "willing to be called a collectivist, a mutualist, or Brotherhood of man," and sometimes called himself a socialist.[59] When a united Socialist party (SP) was formed in 1901 its leaders invited Lloyd to join but he declined; yet in 1891 he had framed socialism to mean merely "sympathy, a community of interest . . . a better share of civilization and of life, a broader Christianity," a definition designed to erase any clear barriers between radicals and moderate reformers. "Some intellectuals had no difficulty in alternately calling themselves collectivists, Nationalists, Fabians, socialists, or, simply, reformers."[60] This fluidity was present in European "social politics" in the 1880s and 1890s as well. French reformers "styled themselves radicals, *solidaristes*, economic *interventionistes*, or simply proponents of *la réform sociale*. . . . In Germany, a dozen rival socio-political parties and pressure groups constructed themselves around permutations of the core term, *sozial*."[61] In Britain, where the connections to America were strongest, the Liberal party theoreticians L. T. Hobhouse and John Hobson announced what they called a statist "new liberal" creed. Even though British new liberals generally were clear in their own minds that they were not socialists, they saw themselves and socialists as allied in a larger cause. Both the new liberals and leaders of the Independent Labour party in Britain had personal contact with Lloyd, and his writings as well as those of George were widely published there; influence ran strong in both directions across the Atlantic.[62]

Socialists, settlement house workers, social scientists, and trade union organizers seemed to be working in a single cause, forming a broad front for the extension of democratic and Christian principles into social life, yet the ambivalence of the middle-class new liberals about the issue of class loyalty never dissipated. Just as they projected an image of social transformation, they drew back from it in hopes of ameliorating the discord all around them. Some, such as Lloyd and Florence Kelley, seemed torn between the emotional loyalty to the underdogs of society that Lloyd expressed to his father and the Fabianism that they often betrayed. Lloyd, writing to his father about the Haymarket anarchists, said that he wanted always to side with the downtrodden. "The agitators on that side make mistakes, commit crimes, no doubt, but for all that theirs is the right side. I will try to avoid the mistakes and the crimes, but I will stay by the cause."[63] Lloyd sided with the left wing of producerist activism in the 1890s, seeking to forge an independent farmer-labor coalition in Illinois, advocating government ownership of at least some monopolies and lamenting, "The Cause is lost," when the Populists voted to unite with Bryan's Democrats in 1896. But, as already noted, he resisted the Socialist party in the short time he lived after its formation in 1901, partly because the concept of socialism had taken on newly strong Marxist associations in America, and Lloyd saw Marxism as a creed of exclusive proletarian loyalty that he could not embrace. In the course of his political activism he was "revolted . . . by the hard tone of the German socialists, who are about all we have," he said, "and by the practical falsity of the doctrine they constantly reiterate, that this crisis must be met by a class struggle, and that the working people alone are to be trusted."[64] "I cannot, for the life of me, see how the present social contest can be described as one between capitalists and the working class," he wrote near his life's end. "To me it appears to be a contest between the people and all those who commit depredations upon them."[65]

Moreover, Lloyd's political thought was bounded not only by class ambivalence but also by traditional liberal ideas about the importance of individual liberties. Of all the leading dissident political thinkers of the Gilded Age, Lloyd was the one who most emphatically sought a middle ground between individualism and collectivism and did so in the most plainspoken, politically aware way. He insisted to the end that the test of the good society was whether it made life "worth living for the individual," and that it was essential "never to surrender to [the] collectivity . . . the right of opinion and expression, right to home, wife, etc."—here sounding a patriarchal note—and the "right to vote."[66] Reform social scientists were saying much the same thing in more general terms when they justified an aggrandized state, as when E. Benjamin Andrews wrote that economic regulation by the state could "increase . . . average net freedom" or when Commons averred that "government," if it enacted a vigorous antimonopoly program, "is not socialistic but rather is supplementing the highest individualism."[67] As noted earlier, such scholars had distanced themselves from socialism by the early 1890s, some of them, such as Ely and Edward Ross, taking fire over their perceived inclinations. Regulatory action by the state might have become known as moderate socialism in America, but innovations in political culture instead took on other names.[68]

Lloyd, for his part, published his masterwork, *Wealth against Commonwealth,* in 1894, not as a socialist but as a liberal-republican in the Jefferson-Jackson tradition, outraged at the frustration of individual initiative by the new power of corporate behemoths. He might have agreed with Hobhouse's declaration that "[t]rue Socialism . . . serves to complete rather than to destroy the leading Liberal ideals," but if so, at the new century's dawn, the Socialist party could no longer be understood, in Lloyd's view, as a vehicle for "true Socialism."[69] A comparison of Lloyd to other thinkers with whom he is often grouped is instructive. George, the pure Jeffersonian ideologue, was sharply hostile to socialism and was somewhat puzzled by the British Fabians' enthusiasm for his ideas.[70] When a destructive row erupted within the ranks of his New York mayoral campaign between socialist and more conservative working-class factions, George kicked out the socialists and expressed his approval for the conviction of the Haymarket defendants. In contrast, Bellamy, who invested all in state and nation, had no use for traditional liberal ideology.

Florence Kelley, a veteran of leftist faction fights from years spent in Europe, was more willing than Lloyd to identify as a socialist, yet still she enacted a political identity fractured along class lines. There is no more memorable denunciation of middle-class charity work than her speech to the New York Association of Collegiate Alumnae in 1887. Kelley excoriated those who believed "giving doles to street beggars" was a serious solution to class exploitation, and she scorned those who wished to reform the morality of the poor. Rather, she said, one who felt sympathy with the oppressed needed to ask herself, "In the great strife of classes, in the life and death struggle that is rending society to its foundations, where do I belong?" Kelley associated different class loyalties with different programs for the alleviation of suffering, contrasting a systemic program with mere "palliatives." "Shall I cast my lot with the oppressors, content to patch and darn, to piece and cobble at the worn and rotten fabric of a perishing society?" she thundered at her audience. Her own choice was clear, and she threw down the gauntlet at her fellow middle-class women, challenging them to side with the workers of the world. "Shall I not rather make common cause with these, my brothers and my sisters," she asked, "to make an end of such a system?"[71] Kelley was nothing if not sincere. However, her major contributions to American life turned out to be more Fabian than laborite, and reformist not revolutionary. Indeed, Kelley called herself, as early as 1892, a convert to "English" socialism, meaning Fabianism.[72] Her groundbreaking work as a factory inspector for the state of Illinois epitomized American Fabianism, using the state as a balance wheel to achieve class fairness, with middle-class intellectuals overseeing the operation of the private economy. A trade union official, appointed to the same position, might have done the job exactly as Kelley did. Yet Kelley treasured her independence and performed her duties as labor's advocate, not as its instrument. If this made no difference, then perhaps Kelley exaggerated the importance of declaring, "Where do I belong?" Her activity as executive secretary of the National Consumers' League (NCL), starting in 1899, is a better example of cross-class solidarity than her factory inspection work. Despite Kelley's fiery rhetoric, the NCL's mission clearly was reform not revolution, aiming to reduce exploitation by raising the consciousness of middle-class consumers. Her brand of socialism was definitely reform socialism.

Jane Addams, besides Lloyd the other leading individual in marking the outlines of new-liberal ideas, was quite sure of her role in the process of social change. While Lloyd overhauled Democratic antimonopoly doctrine for the cause of a new liberalism, Addams imported into the new-liberal orbit the Republican tradition of moral reform and government activism, rendering it democratic in spirit yet somehow still calmly elitist.[73] Addams was a crucial figure because of her manifold authority. Through her writings and her celebrity she became a heroine to two generations of American middle-class women and men, a paradigm of social conscience. She was an advocate of the working poor and the immigrant, and she lived and worked among the toiling masses, even as she maintained a sense of her class difference from them and affirmed that she benefited from her relations with the poor. She had a deep and sophisticated influence upon reform intellectuals. Hull House, which she and Ellen Gates Starr established on Chicago's West Side in 1889, became the crucial experiment station for social scientists and social workers alike during the Progressive Era; it was the foremost national center for a synthesis of activism and detached inquiry into urban life.[74] Not simply a social service agency, Hull House was a venue created to let members of the urban working class get the kinds of assistance they desired and to enhance mutual understanding across lines of class and ethnicity; it quickly became a space for cross-class political organizing.[75]

Addams at first disdained labor unions as disruptive of social harmony, but she rapidly changed her mind when faced with actual working-class women and their conditions of work and life. She embraced an idealistic, liberal, and pacifist Christian ethics—while carefully avoiding identification with the social gospel or any conventional religion—but realized that the morals of Leo Tolstoy or George Eliot could not simply be pronounced from on high with any serious consequence. Grace Dodge, a wealthy founder of "Working Girls' Societies" in the 1880s who wished to bring "culture" to wage-earning women, said that women of different classes had to "combine forces" to realize "the great sisterhood of women."[76] But Dodge would not become a partisan of labor's cause. Addams turned out to be a different kettle of fish. When she invited Mary Kenney, a bookbinder trying to organize women workers in Chicago, to Hull House, Kenney feared that Addams was another do-gooder who desired interclass understanding but who would not address issues of social equity or embrace working-class organizations. However, Addams realized there was no hope of forging social unity if women like her did not prove that they were friends and comrades to proletarians, and especially to working-class women. Addams asked Kenney if she could help her in some way, and Kenney challenged Hull House's master by asking for a meeting room and money to produce fliers. Addams agreed. Privately she told a friend that "we hope to help them [the unions] on a conservative basis," but despite any hope she may have maintained of exerting a calming influence, Addams's support for union organizing crossed the essential political line. Eventually she served as vice president of the National Women's Trade Union League (NWTUL), which William English Walling and Mary (Kenney) O'Sullivan formed in 1903 in imitation of the British Women's Trade Union League.[77]

At the same time, Addams's Fabianism was pronounced, and therein lay the fundamental ambiguity of her class loyalties, an ambiguity essential to the whole project of the new liberalism. While she genuinely was on the side of women wage earners and the urban poor, she did not think this loyalty excluded others; she could be on everyone's side. Addams saw herself as someone who observed and spoke as if perched above the fray of class conflict. Soon after she founded Hull House, she expressed a strong belief in social democracy, pointedly contrasting this concept with the more limited one of political democracy that prevailed in the United States.[78] She was willing to countenance a radical alteration in the control of the country's economic and institutional machinery, but she saw no one class as the exclusive agent of change. Addams did not find it objectionable to identify the working class as a distinct group with its own entirely legitimate interests; yet she saw nothing wrong with the fact that women from middle-class backgrounds, like her and her New York counterpart, Lillian D. Wald, ran the NWTUL.[79] Addams adhered to no myth of a classless America. However, she cautioned against any analysis that simply split society into two classes, "capitalists and proletarians."[80] That, for her, was going too far. Economic class was a social role and location, and it represented a social truth that had to addressed realistically, but it did not have to—and if Addams had her way it would not—trump all other identities, such as that of citizen.[81] Moreover, Addams had no desire to see the have-nots take control of society. She saw herself as their champion, but not their instrument. She endorsed conflict as an inevitable step on the path to social reconciliation, but her ultimate vision of unity required her to limit the conflict she could tolerate. In her mind this was no contradiction. With her serene temperament, Addams was comfortable in her Fabianism.[82]

Despite the complexity and ambiguity of their class loyalties, there is good reason to see the women among the new liberals as the vanguard of this burgeoning movement in the late Gilded Age, more inclusive and adventuresome in their politics than were organizations run by men. In the 1890s the Chicago Women's Club advanced an agenda including advocacy for the rights of prisoners, for adequate and fair funding of public education, and for the interests of women employed in the schools—including the right of female teachers to organize a union. Many such activists also were ardent supporters of women's voting rights, and Emmeline Pankhurst, the famous English suffragist, went so far as to declare to her American counterparts in 1909, with characteristic exaggeration, "We have broken down class distinctions."[83] Although this goal would never be fully achieved, the aspiration was sincere among middle-class suffragists in the new century's early years. In New York, Elizabeth Cady Stanton's daughter, Harriot Stanton Blatch, organized the Equality League of Self-Supporting Women in 1907 as a suffrage group that might bridge the class gap. In California, Maud Younger, a daughter of privilege who had de-classed herself and gone to work as a waitress, started a union and also organized the Wage Earners' Equal Suffrage League. Such activists walked picket lines with women strikers and pressed for labor's legislative goals.[84]

White women's clubs, as well as settlement house women and other women's organizations absorbed in issues of class, were more open to working with African American women than were similar reform groups led by white men. However, black women were usually confined to separate black clubs, maintaining de facto segregation. In some cases, labor unions populated by women, for example those of waitresses and women working in stockyards, actually included black women in integrated locals. But even if the color line was honored within an organization or a movement, the notion of viewing African Americans as anything remotely resembling peers in the work of political reform was inconceivable in almost any reform environment dominated by white males throughout the late Gilded Age and the Progressive Era.[85] Black and white women, together and separately, joined forces in the Women's Christian Temperance Union (WCTU), the single most important women's organization of Gilded Age America. The WCTU, far from a mere temperance organization, strove for a broad reform of society that would make America a wholesome place for women and families. Frances Willard, the maximum leader of the WCTU and an enthusiast of Bellamyite Nationalism, asserted in her presidential address to the group in 1893 that "in every Christian there exists a socialist; and in every Socialist a Christian."[86] Her "socialism" was not doctrinaire, and she spoke for herself, not for the entire WCTU membership. Yet women's reform activism was clearly a channel through which the turbulent ideological waters of the late Gilded Age flowed into the Progressive Era.

Addams, Kelley, and uncounted other women played crucial roles in the reconstruction of liberalism from below. Women who worked in settlement houses and in groups such as the IWA formed "a crucial swing generation" offering a path between old-liberal reform activity and laborite progressivism.[87] Middle- and upper-class women reformers spearheaded cross-class activities, reform efforts that sought to train working-class women to help themselves get by, that demanded improvements in city life from government, and that placed public needs before free-market dogma. Once upon a time, historians tended to view settlement house workers as key players in the drama of American liberalism, depicting them as admirably altruistic, as some of the first members of the middle classes to call for a new social contract with the working poor of an urban, industrial society.[88] Scholars of the 1970s criticized such middle-class reformers for, despite their benevolent image, wishing to control a restive and newly diverse working class.[89] More recently, historians have turned anew to a positive evaluation of the settlement house workers, celebrating individual reformers as great American women and insisting that gender, and not class, is the salient factor in understanding their careers.[90] These reformers, like other social reformers of their background, showed an urgent interest in matters of class as well as those of gender, and their political impact was not confined to a women's sphere of any sort; they played an important, often overlooked role in the development of American liberalism as a whole. Individuals including Addams, Kelley, Wald, their colleague Julia Lathrop, the public-health pioneer Alice Hamilton, and many others are key figures in American women's history. But they also form a pivotal piece of the answer to the question of how the old liberalism became the new liberalism.

These reformers typically came from the same genteel milieux that had produced the old liberals, even if the settlement house workers less commonly possessed great individual wealth. Indeed, although the old liberals are almost always thought of as men, there is good reason to include many women in their ranks as well. Some Gilded Age women reformers, such as Josephine Shaw Lowell, who founded the Women's Municipal League as an anti-Tammany group in New York in 1894, shared all the characteristic classical liberal views on social issues early in her career.[91] Others, like Kelley and Lathrop, acquired through hard experience a disgust for machine politics and patronage that would have filled Godkin with pride. But the anti-machine sentiment that radiated from Hull House was based in a sense of solidarity with the poor, not in disdain of them. These middle-class do-gooders agreed with Oswald Villard that urban machine politicians merely exploited the poor for their own benefit and colluded with "monopolists and oppressors."[92] The settlement houses were founded and staffed by women who, having brought to the burgeoning cities of the nation their sense of mission and their confidence in their own moral leadership, both as bourgeoises and as women, could not ignore the exploitation they met there. Noblesse oblige was, perhaps, thought by their class best discharged by women, but once it began, it sometimes did not stop there. As Addams argued early in her career, the limits of political democracy as well as the obsolescence of the nineteenth-century concept of individual autonomy increasingly became clear in the thick of struggle.

However, the laborite loyalties of the new, insurgent liberals were continually tested, in one controversy after another. Liberalism began in Europe as the ideology of the business class, a class searching for its liberation from the structures of the past and seeking to justify its move toward power. The middle-class laborites of the Gilded Age and the Progressive Era came from backgrounds of genteel reform, a bit removed from family histories of successful business entrepreneurship. Moved by distress at human indignity and by hunger for a new social unity, they altered the liberal ideology they inherited. It tells a big part of the truth about early twentieth-century progressivism to state, as one influential historian did, that it announced "the ambition of the new middle class to fulfill its destiny through bureaucratic means."[93] The middle-class laborites stamped the other side of progressivism's coin with their own politics. They sought to accommodate their inherited ideology to their newly complicated class loyalties.

New Liberals and Progressives: Pluralism, Laborism, and Individualism

Around 1910, Americans began to see and hear the term "progressive" used to describe efforts at curbing business excesses and public-private corruption; historians later used this term to refer to activities that started at least as early as 1900.[94] As scholars have defined the progressivism of 1900–1917—and they have defined it in many different ways—it is a far broader category than the new liberalism that I discuss here. The new liberals were part of progressivism; only a minority of progressives were new liberals. Progressivism's center of gravity was more authoritarian than that of the new liberalism. Many progressives, following in Bellamy's footsteps, stressed nationalism above all as a solution to class division, and some even suggested discarding the concept of individual freedom completely.[95] Just as important, progressives, virtually always white, typically middle class, and mostly of north European Protestant extraction, often championed a forceful program of assimilation and segregation, one intended to discipline what they perceived as unruly working-class immigrants for service in a united nation and to confine African Americans in a ghetto for the supposedly unassimilable.

Those I count as new liberals sometimes shared in these attitudes and intentions, but their center of gravity was more egalitarian. At a conceptual level, the new liberals built upon the Gilded Age thought of Lloyd, Addams, Ely, and others in stressing the need to expand the idea of individual freedom beyond the limits imposed by laissez-faire dogma; they sought to make individualism newly plausible in an industrial, urban age by qualifying it with an emphasis on groups, nations, and classes, rather than abandoning it. They emphasized the salutary effects of working-class empowerment far more strongly than did other progressives. Finally, the new liberals reached no consensus on questions of race and ethnicity. Some, such as Addams, the philosopher John Dewey, and the scholar and peace activist Emily Greene Balch cautiously embraced cultural diversity as a positive force in American life, while many others ignored such questions. Some, for example Oswald Villard, embraced the pro-black heritage of his abolitionist forebears—despite the patronizing attitude he took toward W. E. B. DuBois, one of his few black comrades in the NAACP—while others countenanced the establishment of Jim Crow segregation.[96]

The example of DuBois offers a good measure of how far the egalitarian content of the new liberalism extended. In the early years of the twentieth century he echoed to perfection the new liberalism's compound of Fabianism and laborism. Yet the fact that he was almost alone in occupying the political niche of the black new liberal and the fact that his relations with white new liberals were strained show how limited the reach of this political formation was, even though its embrace of diversity went further than did that of the progressives in general. In 1909 the NAACP's founding board embodied the emerging reality of a broad front stretching from old liberals turned new, such as Villard and Moorfield Storey, to Socialist party members Mary White Ovington and DuBois. DuBois's political thought fit easily into the general framework of such a left-liberal front, making this group a logical place for him to work for reasons beyond his prominence in civil rights advocacy. DuBois's ideas neatly matched the Fabian environment of Anglo-American statist thought throughout his career.[97] He also, starting in the early years of the twentieth century, placed hope in a cross-racial workers' movement as an indispensable instrument of the social progress he sought. In 1907 he wrote, "It is only a question of time when white working men and black working men will see their common cause against the aggressions of exploiting capitalists."[98]

Such laborism was common currency among the new liberals, but it was unusual among African American leaders. When DuBois claimed in 1918, "I am among the few colored men who have tried conscientiously to bring about understanding and co-operation between American

Negroes and the Labor Unions," he did not really exaggerate.[99] During the Gilded Age, African Americans had participated in the Knights of Labor, and in the 1880s some black activists, such as T. Thomas Fortune, had denounced the exploitation of black labor and called for an interracial working-class movement in the South. But in the 1890s this laborite voice had all but disappeared within African American politics, swamped by Booker T. Washington's pro-capitalist, anti-union conservatism.[100] Most unions excluded black workers, and most African American leaders saw little reason not to side with employers in labor disputes. Not until the late 1910s were laborite and left-wing voices heard in substantial numbers in African American politics. Before then, DuBois moved with aplomb in several worlds—including that of an African-diaspora intelligentsia, that of African American political agitation, and that of a new-liberal movement that was a white movement. He was a singular individual, not an example of a broader trend within black politics or within the racial politics of the new liberalism.

More significant than interracialism in the development of the new liberal movement during the Progressive Era was the growing strength of an urban statist tendency, based among immigrant workers and led by labor and social work activists, pressing for reform at the state and national levels but comfortable with urban political machines and allied pragmatically with whichever parties and activists were in the offing. This tendency eventually became known as urban liberalism, but it did not go by that or any other one name in the twentieth century's early years. Safeguards for workers and a rudimentary social safety net were its goals. By the 1910s this urban laborism found new champions, such as Robert F. Wagner and Louis D. Brandeis, who, if they came from middle-class backgrounds and were rather easily accepted by established reform worthies as nicely assimilated, still expanded the circle of nationally known new-liberal activists beyond its pre-1900 predominantly white "Anglo-Saxon" Protestant definition.[101] Brandeis was particularly important in forging links between the previously existing new-liberal activist network and the new forces associated with the category of progressivism.

As early as 1904 Brandeis declared that "[i]ndustrial liberty must attend . . . political liberty," pithily adumbrating the abstract rationale for the new liberalism. "[T]he end for which we must strive is the attainment of rule by the people, and that involves industrial democracy as well as political democracy," he affirmed in 1915.[102] Brandeis was brought into the orbit of social work leaders and labor advocates, to a large degree, by his wife's sister, the consumer activist Josephine Goldmark, and he put his legal skills to work arguing in favor of legislation limiting the working hours and conditions of women—a goal scorned by declared feminists but one supported by most labor activists of that time, women as well as men. He became a close friend of Robert LaFollette, but he was fated to be tied politically to Woodrow Wilson, who, according to legend, swallowed whole Brandeis's antitrust doctrines in 1912 and dubbed them "the New Freedom." By that time Brandeis's Jewishness did not keep Wilson and LaFollette from consorting with his likes, but this was the case in part because his Jewishness seemed unimportant to his identity and his public persona. Like DuBois, Brandeis moved in more than one world, talking easily with senators, corporate magnates, and union officers (as well as, eventually, Zionist leaders). In contrast to DuBois, socialism formed no part of Brandeis's perspective; Brandeis found the cooperative experiments that the Webbs publicized highly attractive, but he rejected the Fabians' statism (though not their top-down vision of reform through administrative appointment). The significance of "socialism" is, however, questionable in this context, since theoretical differences over it did not bar individuals from inclusion in the broader project of the new liberalism.

The reformulation of American liberalism was an uneven process, not a matter of the first importance in the public mind, and one far from central to the partisan contests that dominated national politics during the Progressive Era. The situation was different in Britain, where one of the two major parties was called the Liberal party, whose leading thinkers by the 1890s, as mentioned earlier, argued outright for a redefinition of liberalism to fit a profoundly changed society. The "negative" liberty of freedom from government was to be replaced by a "positive" concept of freedom as the capacity for personally directed self-development, a capacity severely limited for most individuals without the support of a powerful democratic state and other agencies that could counteract the constricting forces of industry and urban life. In the United States, Dewey and his colleague George Herbert Mead declared that no person is an island, affirming the social character of the self and pointing to a positive concept of freedom. The salience of these conceptual developments for American political liberalism was not widely recognized at the time.[103] Neither of the two major political parties was quick to acknowledge the ideological change that was occurring all around. Wilson, Anglophile that he was, may well have thought he was following in the British Liberal party's path when, in 1912, he provided an American version of the new-liberal formula—the New Freedom—for the Democratic party. But at this national party level, American developments lagged behind those in Britain by twenty years.[104]

New liberals and other sorts of progressives mingled in the fluid reform currents of the Progressive Era, and the differences among them sometimes went unnoted. The publicists most closely identified with progressivism as such, such as Herbert Croly and Walter Lippmann, were not evangelists among the heathen, seeking to persuade Americans to give up laissez-faire. Instead, they constructed a rationale, often one that paid little heed to the plight of the individual or to that of working people as such, for a multifaceted political movement that was off and running. Croly argued, in *The Promise of American Life* (1909), for "Hamiltonian" means to "Jeffersonian" ends, but he was not a Jeffersonian reconsidering his premises; he was a nationalist, a disciple of the French thinker August Comte, seeking to justify a collectivist outlook to his fellow Americans. He did not even call his new creed "liberalism," instead emphasizing, as Bellamy had, the link between democracy and nationalism. Lippmann promoted the cause of "social control" no less than did Edward A. Ross, the sociologist who coined this phrase.[105]

It may be tempting to call the new liberals the "democratic" progressives, distinguishing them from more elitist and authoritarian progressives who emphasized "social control."[106] However, framing these differences among different Progressive Era thinkers and activists in terms of democracy may confuse as much as it illuminates. The most egalitarian of progressives believed they were striving for social control, which for them meant that "the people," not unaccountable elites or impersonal social forces, should be sovereign. And the most authoritarian progressive might believe that he fought for democracy, simply thinking that the nation embodied "the people" and that the achievement of important social purpose required national unity (and that unity required discipline and hierarchy). Liberal democrats, for their part, tend to call anything liberal "democratic," and this is often a mistake.[107] The new liberals were more likely than other progressives to endow the empowerment of labor with special historic meaning, to embrace ethnic pluralism, and to uphold the value of a transfigured individualism in a transformed society. While the first of these three differences did make the new liberals more democratic, the other two simply made them more liberal.

The House that Woodrow Built: Class Politics and the New Liberals in the 1910s

Theodore Roosevelt was the first national leader of the nationalist progressivism that, in the era of the New Deal and afterward, would be placed at the heart of liberal politics. Out of his commitment to both his personal popularity and the cause of social order, he was willing to forsake ideological rigidity and to consider the interests and desires of both capital and labor, casting the federal government in the role of honest broker between the classes. Roosevelt's presidential agenda was the first to match the aspiration of the "new middle class" of business functionaries and professionals to transcend class conflict. He decried Woodrow Wilson's "toryism" during the famous presidential campaign of 1912 in an effort to associate the Anglophile Wilson with British conservatism and to position himself to Wilson's left. Ironically, Roosevelt himself was at heart a Tory reformer, an American Disraeli, rather than a tribune of the nation's toiling masses such as Bryan, the "Great Commoner." Roosevelt sought to make the Republicans into "a party of *progressive* conservatism, or conservative radicalism," as he noted in 1908.[108] He eventually attracted the support of many progressives, such as Jane Addams, who were more partial than he to the lower orders. But for him the nation, its wholeness and its stability, was the only ideological framework he required or recognized. Roosevelt and the forces he represented played a key role in the refashioning of liberalism toward statism, but not in a highly self-aware way, and not by working from the principle of individual liberty toward that of government intervention. They were concerned to broker a truce in the class war, not to update liberal ideology.

Wilson, closely familiar with the laissez-faire teachings of Manchester liberalism as well as with British conservative thought, was better prepared to think through the ideology, but he actually did it much less definitely than many of his followers seemed to think.[109] Wilson derided Roosevelt's "New Nationalism" in 1912 as the dangerous doctrine of an authoritarian state, and might have approved the distinction drawn by the British statesman Joseph Chamberlain when he said, "[I]ntervention for the Tories is an act of 'patronage,' while the Liberal principle is that 'all people shall be assisted to govern themselves.'"[110] Wilson essentially repackaged his conservative views with his 1912 economic-policy slogan of "the New Freedom" as a flashy way of satisfying the demands of the day for boldness on the issue of business trusts. He came to power on a traditional Democratic party platform, emphasizing the need for a lower tariff regime. Political forces outside Wilson's control impelled him to suggest, carefully avoiding specific recommendations, a more intrusive state role than he truly envisioned, and it was left to others to apply his rhetoric to a broader agenda.

Most fundamentally, to the new liberals who were drawn to Roosevelt and Wilson in turn, the key area for this application of expedient campaign rhetoric, and the crucial test of progressive leadership, were the enduring questions of labor's rights and labor's welfare. As the 1890s gave way to the new century, continual conflicts between labor and capital and the formation of a nationally organized political left presented sharp challenges to the new liberals, and the new liberals sought to vindicate their laborite values while preserving their independence. Often the new liberals managed to work with socialists and radicals in the labor movement, while maintaining their attachment to the idea of a distinct middle-class voice in the great social questions of the day. They held to their ambiguous political stance. Despite their theoretical laborite commitments, they gradually developed, in the matrix of institutional growth, a political identity more distinct than before from the labor movement.

In the first two decades of the twentieth century both the moderate and radical wings of the American labor movement grew in strength. The AFL's membership total climbed from about 270,000 in 1897 to almost 1,700,000 in 1904, during the years when the captains of industry were consolidating their holdings in the greatest merger movement in American history.[111] The AFL flexed its political muscle in the early years of the twentieth century, trying to get an anti-injunction bill passed into federal law. The partisan maneuvering that followed, with the National Association of Manufacturing, the leader of the anti-union drive, supporting Republican candidates, helped lead the mainstream of the union movement toward an alliance with the national Democratic party starting in 1906. This alliance became solidified during Wilson's administration, and it became a central element in the new definition of liberal politics in the twentieth century.[112] While moderate unionists built the mainstream of the labor movement and pushed their agenda upon prominent politicians, labor radicals agitated in the lower orders of the American economy and pressed themselves ever more insistently upon the consciousness of the new American liberals. The Industrial Workers of the World (IWW) was founded in 1905, building upon the earlier work of the Western Federation of Miners. The new organization's cadres toiled in the West, and then in the East, preparing for the day when the proletariat would seize economic power. In practice, the Wobblies, despite their official position that contracts with capitalists were worthless, pressed for improvements in the lot of workers. The Socialists elected candidates to office in cities around the country, as they advanced the cause of a peaceful, gradual revolution through publications such as the *Appeal to Reason*, based in Girard, Kansas. The Socialist party kept alive the hope that a worker-farmer alliance could usher in the cooperative commonwealth (and not merely a Bryan administration). Yet miners in Montana, like workers elsewhere who looked to the IWW or the SP for leadership, wanted concrete gains, and they hailed as great advances not only victories won "at the point of production" but also those gotten in statehouses, such as laws establishing eight-hour work days and workmen's compensation requirements.[113]

A host of discussion clubs in New York City between 1900 and 1910 brought together Socialist and liberal activists and intellectuals, who clearly felt they had much in common. That common property was the

Fabian side of American reform. The flamboyantly named X Club, for example, begun by William James Ghent in 1903, had Algernon Lee, William English Walling, and Edmond Kelly among its members, and visitors to its meetings included John Dewey, Charles Beard, Franklin H. Giddings, Walter Weyl, Norman Hapgood, H. G. Wells, and Emile Vandervelde.[114] There were others whose reach extended even further, including broad-minded businessmen. These discussion clubs built upon the earlier cooperation among reformers of varying, but at that time vaguely defined, stripes within the Good Government efforts of the 1890s. New York's City Club had involved figures such as Washington Gladden, Giddings, Jacob Riis, Edward Devine (an important figure in social work), and Felix Adler (head of the Ethical Culture Society), as well as worthies such as Nicholas Murray Butler, John Jay Chapman, and Elihu Root. Here was a bridge between the old liberalism and progressivism. The Social Reform Club, going somewhat further, had included Adler, Gompers, William Dean Howells, Robert Hunter, Kelly, Ghent, and J. G. Phelps Stokes in its activities. Many of the same names appear with an almost numbing regularity. While the organizers of these clubs sometimes expressed the hope of involving trade union activists, the upper-class complexion of their participants could hardly have been stronger.[115] The Socialist intellectuals who traveled in these circles scarcely could have looked more different from the humble grass-roots base of the Socialist party, which was concentrated in places such as Milwaukee, Oklahoma, and the Lower East Side of New York. Many liberals had more contact with the former than the latter.

The first generation of new liberals, those who had come of age in the late Gilded Age, tended to look with hope to mainstream progressive leaders such as Roosevelt, Wilson, or LaFollette. While some, such as Kelley, joined the Socialist party, most did not. Without tying themselves too strongly to individual politicians or parties, they worked to make headway on a host of important social issues, including child labor, juvenile justice, and—for a small number—racial inequality. The cause of peace and international arbitration compelled their attention as well. The settlement house movement, the emerging social work profession, and the Protestant social gospel anchored the evolving political identity of this cohort, as ever more Americans became concerned, during the Progressive Era, with phenomena that long had impassioned them. Reform leaders such as Addams, Kelley, Wald, the minister John Haynes Holmes, Oswald Garrison Villard, and the social work leader Paul Kellogg, as well as somewhat lesser-known activists such as Amos Pinchot and John Lovejoy Elliott, worked together continually in countless single-issue organizations. They developed a base of operations in a host of institutional settings that ranged from the National Child Labor League and the Children's Bureau of the U.S. Department of Labor to the NAACP and the University of Chicago's School of Social Service Administration to the Henry Street Settlement and the *Survey* magazine (edited by Kellogg). Their numbers grew as social work channeled missionary tendencies among the college-educated young into constructive activities. The senior members of this new-liberal constituency grew into mature middle age, and as their contemporaries moved up in the world, the liberals' network of friends and acquaintances became an increasingly well-placed one. They could gain a hearing both in the corridors of power and in the public square through the many outlets for publication that they operated.

This group took on a collective identity separate from the trade-union movement, launching a tradition of genteel statist liberalism. But still they remained tied to the laborite vision of a new social unity that had emerged from the late Gilded Age. When Roosevelt advanced his New Nationalism and returned to the arena in the early 1910s, these older new liberals, generally speaking, found him irresistible. His toryism accommodated their new liberalism quite well. They played a key role at the Bull Moose convention, after the Republican regulars denied Roosevelt their nomination in 1912. The new liberals saw the Progressive party as a vehicle for the "Industrial Minimums," a set of standards for the conditions and terms of wage labor that the meeting in 1912 of the National Conference of Charities and Corrections, a leading venue for the settlement house liberals, had adopted.

The new-liberal reformers did much to prod President William Taft's administration (1909–13) to plan the U.S. Commission on Industrial Relations (CIR), whose investigations of conflict between labor and capital lasted until 1915, and which facilitated the forceful projection by new-liberal activists of a statist conception of class justice into public debate.[116] Previously, a U.S. Industrial Commission (USIC) had met and published its findings between 1900 and 1902. The USIC's conclusions had seemed heavily influenced by the conservative approach to industrial relations taken by the business-oriented National Civic Federation and the AFL. It had prescribed a private-sector collective bargaining model as the cure for the ailment of workplace conflict. But by the second decade of the twentieth century, laborites were well positioned to promote a different vision of how to achieve material equity and social stability, and such activists, including the commission's chairman, Frank Walsh, a lawyer and a Wilson appointee, and John Commons, dominated the CIR.[117] The lead investigator W. Jett Lauck stated blandly, "Industry, as regards its control, its methods, and its treatment of workers, has too long been considered heretofore as essentially a private and individual matter." The CIR framed government intervention in class relations as "extensions of sovereignty."[118] The official CIR report advocated a strong government role in setting wages at a level that would sustain a decent living (and recommended that female employees receive a minimum wage), as well as guarantees of workers' right to organize and to bargain collectively, using any nonviolent means, and unemployment insurance. Beyond such specifically labor-related issues, the commission advanced the view that the state might act as the caretaker of the national interest in all social and public policy matters. On this basis, the CIR championed greater public control over land and minerals, a graduated inheritance tax that would fund education and public works, improved rural credit for farmers, and immigration restriction (understood by most Americans of that time as a pro-labor progressive reform).

However, a split occurred among the laborites on the CIR, and Commons issued a minority report widely seen as less ambitious and less statist than Walsh's official recommendations. Some historians have taken this as evidence of a deep division between labor-oriented statist liberals such as Walsh and more conservative reformers, less sympathetic to working-class empowerment and perhaps naïve about class conflict in America, including Commons and social work progressives such as Paul Kellogg and Lillian Wald.[119] However, while there is some reason to see here a difference between liberals who embraced labor unions relatively tightly and loosely, the disagreement within the commission also reflected a strong measure of ideological murkiness in the new liberalism. The split over the CIR's recommendations revealed the ambivalent class loyalties that were essential to the new liberalism as such. That ambivalence sprang from the shifting and long-standing mix of Fabianism and laborism at the heart of this new persuasion. It is true that settlement house leaders, liberal university professors, and those deeply influenced by the Protestant social gospel did not always see fit to defend organized labor. They intermittently criticized corruption or "bossism" within unions. They did not view labor *exclusively* as the agent of promise in American society's development. While Walsh and the CIR took a dim view of corporate-sponsored philanthropies such as the Rockefeller Foundation, seeing them as rivals to government investigation that were designed to treat corporate malefactors with relative leniency, social work liberals often supported such private funds. (The Rockefeller Foundation was indeed begun as a public relations initiative by the oil tycoon after his Colorado Fuel and Iron Company's violent tactics led to the massacre of striking miners and family members by National Guardsmen in the town of Ludlow in 1914.) Kellogg, at the *Survey*, took the latter view most publicly, leading to a rather nasty dispute with Walsh and the crusading Colorado journalist George Creel, who charged that Kellogg and others in the new nonprofit sector were compromised by the philanthropic subvention of their work.[120] Addams had worked with Civic Federations, and many who followed in her footsteps were not beyond working with private philanthropies. But they labored under no illusion that such funds would eliminate class conflict. Mary van Kleeck, who in the 1930s became the most visible representative of the social work profession's militant left wing, made the Russell Sage Foundation her base of operations.

The social work liberals tended to speak, in good progressive language, of a public interest that was not necessarily identical with labor's interests. Sometimes they identified "the public" with consumers and envisioned this group as the third leg of the stool that would support just and balanced economic decision making, along with capital and labor. At other times the definition of "the public" was entirely vague, although the concept seemed designed to open a door through which the new middle class could enter debates about public policy. At yet other moments, the working class seemed to overlap greatly with the new-liberal category of the public. The slippage in this concept reflected the unstable and mixed loyalties of many new liberals. As they developed an independent base of operations, they might indeed see the labor movement as less central than before to their own hopes of renovating society. Their Fabian tendency found opportunities and outlets in both the nongovernmental sector of public life and the progressive vision of an aggrandized state. Although this evolving political identity did represent some movement away from Henry Lloyd's vision of a new religion of labor, the new liberals by no means discounted the importance of economic class, either socially or politically. They remained highly supportive of a proletarian political mobilization, and they retained their laborite loyalty as one aspect of their complicated political outlook. They still were susceptible to the appeal of laborite visions of social reconstruction. Walsh and those like him also had dual political loyalties: both groups were drawn to the labor movement and, increasingly, to the state as the sites of progressive political action. Neither liberal grouping viewed labor as the only embodiment of forward movement. The new liberals who enjoyed an independent institutional base saw that apparatus as a third possibility, because for them it was a possibility; for Walsh, the unions and the state were the only two choices. All of the new liberals were laborites, and none of them sought to build anything like a proletarian state.

The new liberals overall pinned much of their hope for social regeneration on the labor movement. Whether or not the new-liberal alliance would take a partisan form and, if so, which party would become its vehicle were not clearly answered questions in the era of Bryan and Theodore Roosevelt. Yet, by the 1930s, the liberal-labor constituency clearly saw the Democratic party as its home. To answer the question of how this came to pass, we must look to the very consequential presidency of Thomas Woodrow Wilson.

Wilson had been only a mildly pro-labor politician before entering the White House, and his momentous role in the embrace of the Democratic party by labor and laborites would have been impossible to predict in 1912. In the first decade of the twentieth century, the Democratic party was rent by conflict between its left and right wings, and the outcome was by no means certain. Wilson himself first came to national prominence as a spokesman for the conservative, anti-Bryan sector of the party. Bryan, nominated for president in 1900 and 1908 (in 1904 he was thrown over for a conservative judge, Alton B. Parker), still sought to weld farmers and workers together into a winning combination, but the workers continued to play hard-to-get. The Republicans' claim that their own program, emphasizing a high tariff to protect northern industry, would bring prosperity to all classes continued to compel many wage earners. Among the Democratic leadership, the leveling legacy of populism competed with the party's traditional embrace of states' rights and laissez-faire economics. Bryan railed against the "centralization" that he claimed marked Roosevelt's program in office, but this bit of rhetoric was at odds with Bryan's progressive agenda, which gave new life to old populist demands for regulation of transportation, finance, and utilities, for a graduated income tax, and for workers' organizing rights. In 1910, when Roosevelt, plotting his return to the White House, announced his "New Nationalist" program, which sounded more statist (and more laborite) than anything he had done as president, the Democrats had a good year. They attacked Roosevelt from the right, with the New York State Democratic convention criticizing Roosevelt's proposed "exaltation of Federal centralization power" and declaring that "whatever advance its adoption would bring is advance toward socialism."[121]

In 1912, while Roosevelt attracted the support of most of the new-liberal intellectuals and activists, many conservatives viewed Wilson as a reasonably safe compromise candidate. One prominent Republican told a conservative U.S. senator, "We can't elect Taft and we must do anything to elect Wilson so as to defeat Roosevelt."[122] Once elected, Wilson's agenda focused on reducing tariffs (the agricultural interests in the United States, which tended to support the Democrats, would benefit from freer trade),[123] the symbolically important progressive goal of securing new antitrust legislation (the Clayton Act of 1914 and the establishment of the Federal Trade Commission), and the urgent capitalist need for a reorganization of the country's banking system (accomplished, through a compromise that satisfied demands from moderate farm spokesmen in Congress, in the Federal Reserve Act, the most important legislation of Wilson's presidency). With these tasks addressed, late in his first term as president Wilson felt that his "New Freedom" program had been consummated. He seemed to be a moderate progressive who wished to look after the interests of urban and rural businessmen no less than those of labor, and especially the interests, as he memorably said, of "the men who are on the make, and not the men who are already made."[124] Although calibrated perfectly to appeal to the new middle class, this rhetoric was uninspiring to leaders of opinion. The *New Republic*, which in only a few years would become a kind of party organ of the White House, sneered that Wilson's Democrats had "the vitality of a low organism" that could "temporarily assume almost any form, any color and any structure without ceasing to recognize itself and without any apparent sacrifice of collective identity."[125]

When the Republicans chose Charles Evans Hughes as their presidential nominee in 1916, Wilson's camp knew it had a real fight on its hands. Hughes was a highly respected progressive in the mugwump tradition, a Supreme Court justice who had overseen an extremely well-publicized prosecution of insurance industry and utilities corruption in New York State. Although acceptable to the conservative forces in his party who had frustrated Roosevelt's desire for another nomination in 1912, Hughes could not be easily characterized as a reactionary. With the AFL having shown itself willing to mobilize a labor vote for friendly candidates (or, perhaps more compellingly, against unfriendly ones), Wilson competed openly for these ballots. His main bid for the labor vote was his support for the Adamson Act, which mandated the long-sought eight-hour day for railway workers. But this was not all. Wilson masterfully engineered the passage of national laws restricting child labor and ensuring workmen's compensation for the federal government's employees, as well as other legislation that, all told, enacted quite a bit of the Progressive party's 1912 agenda. By election time he also had changed his long-standing opposition to woman suffrage, gaining support among supporters of the vote for women. Wilson's successful nomination of Brandeis to the Supreme Court so antagonized conservatives in Congress as to do wonders for the president's reputation as a genuine progressive. With his accomplishments in the election year, and with his credentials as a peace candidate who had kept America from getting sucked into the European war, Wilson was reelected in a close contest.

A great many of the new liberals who had been Bull Moosers in 1912 turned to Wilson's banner. One of them, Lippmann, in explaining his defection admitted that there seemed to be more than one Wilson. He intended to back "the Wilson who is temporarily at least creating, out of the reactionary, parochial fragments of the Democracy, the only party which at this moment is national in scope, liberal in purpose, and effective in action."[126] Wilson himself had anticipated Lippmann in the equation of progressivism with liberalism by a good half-decade. After winning election to the office of governor in 1910, Wilson stated—privately—that the Democrats needed to wrest the mantle of progressivism away from Roosevelt's Republicans if they hoped not to lose "the chance of a generation . . . to constitute the ruling party of the country." The supporters of reform whose loyalty he wished to capture he called "the liberal elements of the country."[127] This was a new way to put it.

Essentially, Wilson succeeded in his aim. This partisan accomplishment was associated with organized labor's gravitation toward the Democrats. It was remarkable that Wilson cemented the alliance with the unions while also capturing the loyalty of a large chunk of the new middle class. When Wilson ran the peace ship aground and mobilized the country for war, he shrewdly brought Samuel Gompers into the center of economic decision making, offering organized labor a lucrative partnership in the war economy, which it was delighted to accept.[128] By 1919, under the shadow of the Russian Revolution, Wilson had declared to Congress, "The question which stands at the front of all others amidst the present great awakening is the question of labor." Workers built and sustained the world, he said, and deserved an improvement in their standard of life. Perhaps the state would have to take possession of the railroads, utilities, and even some basic commodities, he informed his brother-in-law. "Some people would call me a socialist for saying this," he acknowledged, yet he insisted that this was mere liberalism. "We can meet Bolshevism only with bold liberalism," he stated, forecasting the strategy of social democrats around the world throughout the long cold war against communism.[129] Indeed, although Wilson distinguished sharply between liberalism and socialism, his shifting position would have placed him, in any European country, safely within the confines of evolutionary socialism. Meanwhile, just as important, the Republican progressives saw their power within their party steadily diminish from 1912 until the 1920s, when the GOP developed the overwhelmingly pro-business, anti-labor profile that it retained ever afterward. By that time, there was little partisan competition for an organized labor vote. Out of these political circumstances, the Democrats and the AFL gradually tightened an alliance that became a linchpin of American politics for the next half century. In all, it is no great exaggeration to say that, for better and for worse, all American liberals since World War I have lived in the house that Wilson built. Roosevelt, if we take him at his word, was, like some of his contemporaries in Europe, laying the groundwork for national socialism.

The Youth Movement of the 1910s: Liberal and Radical

By the 1910s, a new generation of liberals who had been educated in the nation's elite universities and by the political movements of the Progressive Era had become politically prominent in America. This was the generation that included publicists such as Lippmann, who was taken under the wing at various times by Steffens, Croly, Wilson, and George Lunn, the Socialist mayor of Schenectady; artists such as Amy Lowell, evangelist of the "new" poetry and sister of Harvard's president; and little-known activists such as Lucille Milner, who was captivated by Lillian Wald at the Henry Street Settlement and who went on to a long career in social work, political lobbying, and civil liberties. Most of this younger crowd had been born between 1875 and 1890, the years when the first generation of the new liberals had been learning what the world was really like. The two generations had close and warm relations. The younger liberals also were so friendly and worked so regularly with radicals in the SP, and even the IWW, that it is difficult to draw a clear line between liberals and radicals when considering the "innocent rebellion" of the 1910s. The "young liberals" and the "young radicals" were often the same people.

Frederic Howe, an advocate of Henry George's "single tax" on land, a student of Wilson at the Johns Hopkins University, and a protégé of Mayor Tom Johnson in Cleveland, was one of the generation of the 1890s who kept up with the times. In his 1925 memoir, *The Confessions of a Reformer,* Howe wrote of the early 1910s, "It was good form to be a liberal. Conservative lawyers, bankers, and men of affairs stepped out from their offices and lent their names to radical movements. They presided at meetings and contributed to causes. Branches of the Intercollegiate Socialist League were being organized in the colleges, woman suffrage was enlisting the most prominent women of the country. . . ." Howe was part of a "liberal movement," he said, but it was also a "youth movement," despite the involvement of a middle-aged element. It "stood for variety, for individuality, for freedom." In 1925, his definition of the liberalism of the 1910s as more a cultural movement than a conventional political movement was novel, but that characterization would be echoed often in later years.[130]

In the 1910s, "Feminism was born ideologically on the left of the political spectrum, first espoused by women who. . . . considered themselves socialists or progressives leaning toward socialism. . . ."[131] The appearance of this new tendency was inextricably tied both to the prevailing sense of generational insurgency and to a revolt against the culture of capitalism, a revolt whose cadres did not shy from leftist associations. In 1915 Miriam Allen de Ford, a suffrage activist, bequeathed to us a priceless statement of how the pursuit of personal freedom mingled with feelings of opposition to society (and concomitant feelings of self-importance) for young rebels. "I have taken it and embraced it all—the Social Revolution, the life of rebellion, the certainty of misunderstanding," she wrote. Rejecting what she called "the horrible, sugar-coated world of reform and philanthropy," she declared dramatically, "The world's honor is my degradation; the world's condemnation must be my pride and victory."[132] She was talking about sex, but clearly she felt that was not all she was talking about.

The young liberals were, in their own way, evolutionary socialists. Some of them streamed into Socialist party meetings, rejuvenating the party with talk of Nietzsche and Sorel, sex and feminism, while others had little use for political parties.[133] It made little difference. Whether they are called liberals or the "lyrical left," as historians have dubbed them, they wanted a big change, and they thought it would happen soon and, by and large, peacefully. Many of them took an understanding view of occasional proletarian violence (which typically had nothing to do with socialism), such as the McNamara brothers' confessed bombing of the Los Angeles *Times* building in 1910. The young liberals envisioned a future society more rational, fairer, and more expressive; they celebrated the modernist avant-garde and embraced Freud (as they understood him).[134] As Howe noted, their rebellion reflected disgust for the culture of capitalism as they knew it. "To me," he wrote, the youth movement "was a renaissance of America rising from the orgy of commercialism."[135]

Some activists continued earnestly to try to make distinctions, but these often crumbled at the touch. Croly wrote in 1914 that his new journal, the *New Republic,* would be "radical without being socialistic."[136] Croly and Lippmann welcomed working-class empowerment while fearing proletarian revolution and dictatorship, but that stance hardly lay outside the ambit of social democracy, notwithstanding their protestations that they were not "socialistic." Years later, the American writer John Chamberlain recalled the tenor of the times, of an era when "the extreme intellectual Left . . . hobnobbed with liberal thought. Between a Lippmann and an Eastman the hopeful bourgeois convert to reformed democracy made little distinction. Weren't both men calling for Utopia? Freedom was the watchword, not the harsher slogans of the class struggle."[137] Max Eastman, the editor of *The Masses,* who throughout his journey from far left to far right consistently championed what he called "enjoyment of living," made no bones in the 1910s about his commitment to class struggle.[138] But for many observers, the lyrical left's commitment to a cultural renovation that was not framed as a class project dulled the edge of revolutionary commitments like those Eastman proclaimed. Besides, liberal progressives expressed support for working-class mobilization. Eastman might wish for a revolution, but the larger movement of which he was part seemed to advance a cause—"freedom"—more multifaceted, more ambiguous, more resonant with the tradition of liberalism and less threatening to middle-class minds.

The young liberal/radicals of the 1910s combined bohemian lives with Enlightenment values, mixed artistic and political rebellion as if this made sense to everyone, and grounded the romance of revolution in the pragmatic philosophy of the Progressive Era. They made Manhattan's Greenwich Village their headquarters. The movement's beginning is commonly located with the move of the Liberal Club downtown from Gramercy Park. The club began as a meeting ground of progressives and Socialists, much like the X Club. A disagreement over the case of the feminist Henrietta Rodman, head of the Teachers' Association, the precursor to unionization, who had been fired from her job as a schoolteacher for getting married, led to a secession of the more conservative faction. Those who remained moved their meetings to the Village in 1913, next door to Charles and Albert Boni's Washington Square Bookshop. The Liberal Club, founded in 1907, was probably so named in connection with the earlier tradition of "liberal" clubs that had celebrated unrestricted intellectual inquiry. As noted earlier, the few lonely free speech activists of the Gilded Age and the Progressive Era, generally freethinkers who revered Robert Ingersoll and anarchists in the Garrisonian tradition, also tended to call their local associations "liberal."[139] But now a connection was made between that identity and the lyrical left, whose neon glow and buzz emitted from the Liberal Club's salon. Only some of its members called themselves socialists, but it might have been hard to guess which ones.

To some, spirit and attitude made the difference between liberals and radicals. *The Masses* ran a famous statement of intent on its masthead starting in late 1912, after Eastman took the helm. It would be "a revolutionary and not a reform magazine: a magazine with a sense of humor and no respect for the respectable: frank, arrogant, impertinent, searching for the true causes: a magazine directed against rigidity and dogma wherever it is found."[140] Radicals were for throwing over the system, not patching it up. No matter for the moment who would run the show after the revolution and to what end. The desire to erase the present order stood alone as a kind of politics. *The Masses* did indeed propagandize against capital's crimes and for the militant working class. But it is more remembered today, and in truth it was more noticed by some in its own day, for being "frank, arrogant, impertinent." To some this simply meant free love, birth control, and feminism. It drew on the same Enlightenment inspiration as had the Manchester liberals, back when they were considered "radicals" even if only in their philosophy. The habit of irreverence—toward the past, toward the present—that descended from the French *philosophes* was taken over wholly from the most iconoclastic of the old liberals, such as Samuel Clemens, by twentieth-century radicals. That the Liberal Club maintained its old name was a small salute to this tangled lineage.

But if liberalism and radicalism were hard to unknot, the difference between statism and anarchism was, at certain moments anyway, a clearer dividing line. The great intellectual struggle of the first generation of the new liberals had been to justify collective public action, particularly state action. For the young radicals of the 1910s, legitimizing the state was one of the least urgent of tasks. (Small wonder that the generation of the 1960s chose the lyrical left as their special historical rediscovery.[141]) Sympathy for anarchism ran high among those who gravitated to the lyrical left. In a 1916 number of the *Little Review*, whose name stands in for a host of Greenwich Village publications of the 1910s, Margaret Anderson counseled fellow liberals not to despair of defining anarchism's notoriously vague social aims, any more than they would hope to define art. "Because," she said, "anarchism and art are in the world for exactly the same kind of reason."[142] The reason was liberation from the dead wood of the past.

This convergence of art and politics was what John Reed sensed in his love affair with the IWW. While Socialist ideas made inroads among the first generation of new liberals, it was the IWW that really captured the imagination of the middle-class liberal of the 1910s. Big Bill Haywood and Elizabeth Gurley Flynn became culture heroes of the youth set in the pre–World War I days of "Young America." The Wobblies crisscrossed the country, attracting crowds and inspiring the strongest of feelings in Nevada and Montana, on the Mesabi Iron Range of northern Minnesota, in New York and San Diego. Gravitating to the bloodiest, most primitive scenes of class conflict in the country, they embraced the bottom dogs of American society—itinerant lumberjacks, rough-hewn miners, migrant produce-pickers, even bindlestiffs without work. In the process they created a romantic myth that endured to invigorate American radicals for decades after the U.S. government effectively killed the organization. The IWW slogan of "One Big Union" suggested a monumental response to the capitalist behemoth, the crude but compelling power of a united working class. It also renovated the familiar ideal of a new social unity, which might, in this version, be founded upon the proletariat. At the group's founding convention, Haywood declared, with as much a sense of theater as of history, "This is the Continental Congress of the working class."[143]

Wobbly organizers' reputation for fearlessness, which they came by honestly, made them heroes to middle-class idealists as well as rebellious workers. When the IWW energetically involved itself in strikes among textile workers in Lawrence, Massachusetts, and among silk workers in Paterson, New Jersey, in 1912 and 1913, eastern liberals, many of them new to street activism, found an opportunity to work with the Wobblies. The Paterson Pageant, directed by John Reed, in which strikers reenacted recent events in Madison Square Garden, marked the dramatic culmination of this alliance. When the IWW sparked a series of protests on behalf of the unemployed in New York City in 1914, Steffens and Lippmann were unafraid to join Haywood and Emma Goldman as speakers at an outdoor meeting, black flag or no black flag.[144] Such gestures of solidarity among reformers and radicals, even declared revolutionaries, were common. They were encouraged, though unintentionally, by Wilson's and Roosevelt's repeated embrace of the label "radical." Of course, Wilson and Roosevelt meant something different from what Reed or even Lippmann meant. Roosevelt's Tory reform program was clear enough, and to Wilson, radicalism also referred to progressivism but was defined more vaguely as a spirit of change and renewal rather than a specific set of proposals. The "so-called radicalism of our time," he said almost mystically in 1911, "is nothing else than an effort to release the energies of our time."[145] His meaning was the same as when he spoke of liberalism. The continued rhetorical fluidity of the political scene was in itself consequential, preventing dissident or far-reaching social ideas from being forbidden from public discussion. A fresh generation of laborite hopes for a new society had come on the scene. But this generation mixed the call for revolution with the dream of the cooperative commonwealth. Eventually, much of the liberal constituency would settle on the ideal of "reconstruction" as a middle ground, one that might, theoretically, accommodate both a Wilson and a Reed.

Perhaps it made little sense that the young liberals should have viewed anarchists as comrades-in-arms even as they thrived within the intrinsically statist atmosphere of progressivism. But the meaning of anarchism was perhaps less than literal. Whether or not the Wobblies truly were anarchists is an open question. For those young liberals more interested in cultural revolt than in taking power, anarchy meant bohemia for all, and utopia was only a figure of speech, since it was real for them. In the aftermath of the Great War, dreams of organization were sifted out from the atmosphere of permanent opposition. But while it lasted, the era of "the innocent rebellion" was innocent because the desire for power and the resistance to power somehow seemed to go together. And the linkage of cultural liberation to political revolt helped to cement liberals and leftists in their youthful alliance. From the desperately sober vantage point of the early 1930s, the writer John Chamberlain looked back with wonder and sadness, writing, "It looked like a good bet, in 1913, for a fairly intelligent, fairly good-natured and fairly easy transition, via the ballot, via a liberalism called to terms by radicalism, to the millennium." It remained a reliable source of poignancy to consider "how something that started so gaily ended so seriously."[146]

Chapter 2

War and Revolution

> *The massive influence of the [American Civil Liberties] Union was [Roger Baldwin's] unique and heroic work. In the beginning this work was dangerous, as it was regarded, almost by common consent, as subversive in character, and thus edging on the border line of treason. For years it seemed impossible to make plain that our defense of radicals in our courts of law was not because of any sympathy with their ideas. . . .*
>
> *—John Haynes Holmes, 1959*

In the early and mid-1910s, many liberals and radicals alike were content to work within the tradition of the broad front that descended from the 1880s for the goal of progress into a new, more just social unity. The question of evolutionary versus revolutionary change troubled some, who insisted on making a sharp distinction between movements for reform and for total transformation. But such either/or stances did not dominate progressive politics at that time. Then came World War I. The war broke out in Europe in 1914 and the United States entered the war three years later. The atmosphere of political repression generated by the Wilson administration and other supporters of U.S. entry into the war, and the thunderbolt of the Communist revolution in Russia in 1917, together created crises of political faith for many. The events of the late 1910s and early 1920s inflicted the first major trauma on the broad front of reformers and radicals.

The fraying that the broad front experienced during these years constituted the first step in the long process of redefining liberalism and the left, in the minds of many Americans, into mutually incompatible political faiths. The issues of war and peace provoked this phase of ideological reconstruction and estrangement. Yet the emerging, not always coherent differences between "leftists" and "liberals" did not turn fundamentally on questions of military action. Instead, the bitter disputes among erstwhile members of the broad progressive front over World War I, combined with the appearance of actual socialist revolutions around the world, brought activists to consider anew whether they wished to reform or to upend the American political and social system. To both reformers and radicals, this meant evaluating the depth of American capitalism's moral depravity and judging whether democratic politics could create a cooperative commonwealth by working within that economic system. The broad front for progress toward a more equal and unified society survived the crisis of the late 1910s and early 1920s, though not without strain and the loss of some participants. Moreover, the moral indictment of American capitalism that was longstanding and basic within the broad front also survived this crisis. Newly sharpened differences over the U.S. political system emerged within the broad front, but the front was held together by the shared imperative to transform American society.

The Early ACLU: Liberals and Radicals

One morning in 1920, Lucille Milner reported for work in her ground-floor office at the American Civil Liberties Union (ACLU). The organization, founded in that year, would come to exemplify a major strand of American liberalism, aggressively advocating for the rights of individuals against the state and for dissenters against majority opinion. In principle, this type of liberalism resonated deeply with classical liberalism and might have found itself allied with conservative opponents of statism in the twentieth century. Yet when Milner, the executive secretary of the group, appeared this particular morning at the three-story brick structure on West Thirteenth Street in lower Manhattan, she discovered Big Bill Haywood seated behind her desk. By this time Haywood, the leader of the Industrial Workers of the World (IWW)—also known as the Wobblies—was an enemy of the state as well as of the capitalist class. Milner, the daughter of a well-established southern family, was surprised but not scandalized to find Haywood in her workplace. She listened sympathetically as he recounted for her the latest installment in his tale of woe.[1] Federal agents had spent the war years hunting down hundreds of Wobblies and the courts had sent them to federal prison, often for many years, essentially for the crime of their radicalism. Haywood was on the run from the law, and Milner seemed not to fault him for his subsequent action: as his comrades were tried, he fled to the Soviet Union, where he lived out the rest of his days.

In 1920, the conversation between Milner and Haywood would have taken very few by surprise. If Haywood had left Milner's back-room office and ascended the stairway to the second or third floor, he might have paid a visit to Max Eastman, a leading spokesperson for the lyrical left of the 1910s. Eastman was editing *The Liberator*, the successor magazine to *The Masses*, on the top two stories of this same house. *The Masses* had been the venue for the most hard-hitting protests against the war, and in response the postmaster general of the United States, the Texan Albert S. Burleson, had banned the magazine, along with other publications he deemed seditious, from the mails. In 1917, Judge Learned Hand had found this to be a violation of the First Amendment to the U.S. Constitution, but his superiors in the federal judiciary disagreed. Bohemianism continued to find space in the magazine until the publication's distribution was suppressed, but the hard hand of persecution affected the mix of radical elements in the journal. *The Liberator* heralded the worldwide proletarian revolution to which Eastman felt freshly committed but, paradoxically, it did not call for an overthrow of the U.S. government. At the insurrectionary water's edge, the lyrical left still stopped, despite its sympathy for the new government in Russia.

If political protest now held pride of place over cultural experimentation, liberals and leftists continued to mingle without care in these quarters, and it remained hard to tell who was which. Milner had embarked upon a career in social work just before the outbreak of the war in Europe. After she finished her course of study at the New York School of Philanthropy, Roger Baldwin, the leading figure in social work in the city of St. Louis, got Milner a job working to reform child labor laws in Missouri. Baldwin would lead the ACLU for decades, and Milner worked with him there for almost as long. Each recognized a kindred soul in the other right away, according to her account. Both Milner and Baldwin "wanted to see the old social order replaced by a new one, though neither of us had decided upon the formula," she recollected. "Roger called himself a 'philosophical anarchist,' a follower of Thoreau, Kropotkin and Emma Goldman. I hoped for a socialist state to bring about the brotherhood of man and universal peace, but I did not join the Socialist Party."[2] Despite his ease among blue-blood do-gooders, the young Baldwin held the IWW in high esteem. He was also a bohemian, known to lead a footloose bachelor life; for an "anarchist" admirer of Goldman like Baldwin, the political and the personal went together.[3] Perhaps it was, as she put it, their common uncertainty as to "the formula" for social revolution that kept them both out of the Socialist camp or some other revolutionary party. But these leading liberals were in fact non-doctrinaire socialists who expressed no great concern for an incremental pace of change.[4]

The civil libertarians of the ACLU were both radicals and liberals. Indeed, their ideological position provides the best evidence of all of the continuing involvement of liberalism with socialism, since we might expect activist civil libertarians to be the *least* likely of all liberals at this time to have maintained such an involvement. The theoretical conflict between legal individualism and social reconstruction that a later generation of political liberals would assert simply did not obtain in the minds of most political activists on the left half of the political spectrum in these years. Liberals in the 1920s became more persistently concerned with preserving individual rights because of the state repression that Americans experienced during and right after World War I.[5] But, in the minds of many self-identified liberals of the World War I era, individual freedom was no barrier to social democracy. It would be a mistake to project a rigid antagonism between individualism and socialism, one characteristic of more recent politics, backward into the 1910s and 1920s.[6]

Progress and War

When Milner first ate dinner at the Henry Street Settlement, it was 1914 and the talk was of war. The "idealists and social workers" gathered at the long table under Lillian Wald's supervision thought the prospect of a world war "seemed insane," Milner wrote. "If war should come to America or if the advocates of militarism had their way, I heard them say, all the social movements would be dead for a generation if not for a century."[7] Many liberals and radicals of that time were enveloped by this sense of dread at the approaching juggernaut. Yet many other liberals welcomed the war as a cause that would focus national purpose, welding state and society together to produce long-lasting benefits.

Liberals who opposed U.S. entry into the war harked back to the classical liberal belief that international peace was a necessary condition for human progress. Wald and Jane Addams, leading the effort to organize liberals against U.S. entry as early as September 1914, only a month after the war had begun, reflected that the spirit of war was "inevitably disastrous to the humane instincts which had been asserting themselves in the social order" during recent decades.[8] Wald emphasized how "much is at stake in both war and reconstruction."[9] Her incantation of the liberal mantra of "reconstruction" conveyed a double meaning. When the war ended, a necessary process of rebuilding would occur, and the outcome of that rebuilding process would be of interest to the whole world. But she also referred to an existing liberal agenda for social change, an agenda that had developed during the Progressive Era and that she feared the war jeopardized. Those who had labored to establish a more extensive role for the state in pursuing the general welfare worried that war would drain money and attention away from the cause of social progress at home.

The antiwar liberals' sharp suspicion of warmongering paved the way for links to the radical left. Liberals since the heyday of Manchester had believed that wars tended to occur as a result of the vile machinations of "interests" in league with governments over which these interests gained untoward influence. This explanation for war would continue to have a large purchase among both liberals and leftists in the years after World War I, and it would be endorsed by an investigating committee of the U.S. Senate under the leadership of Joseph P. Nye in the 1930s. "Every day it became clearer, and yet more clear," wrote John Haynes Holmes, the pastor of the Unitarian Church of the Messiah in New York, "that the war across the sea was just one more armed clash between contending empires for the mastery of mankind."[10] The common view among socialists and other radicals—that wars, like imperialist expeditions, were instigated by and for capitalists—was merely a sharper-edged version of the same idea. Leftists emphasized that members of the working class did most of the dying for the benefit of the bourgeoisie, and antiwar liberals had no trouble agreeing. By 1914 the American left had been swelled by the huddled masses from southern and eastern Europe—as well as Ireland—among whom it was a common enough family tradition to flee from service in the king's army, or the kaiser's or the czar's. Perhaps only in the United States were the poor truly expected to line up alongside their betters for service in the trenches. The Socialist party vote increased greatly in cities around the country after the United States entered the war.[11] There were not enough social workers in the land to account for this result.

Protestant liberals of the era before the Great Depression, such as Addams and Villard, have been called sentimental and unrealistic in their assumption that social progress, as they defined it, was natural and inevitable. Reinhold Niebuhr made this criticism most memorably, in his 1932 book, *Moral Man and Immoral Society.* Support for this view might seem to be offered by Emily Greene Balch's comment, in her draft suggestion for an antiwar statement to be signed by the group of activists whom Addams and Wald were organizing, that "[t]he world is too highly developed for war to be endurable any longer—too complex, too interrelated, too artificially organized, above all too sensitive." Obviously this was wrong: the wars of the twentieth century turned out to be more murderous and destructive than those of any previous age. However, statements like Balch's were more prescriptive than descriptive. She was urging that citizens of the United States and the world act, not presuming that war could no longer happen. In this same draft, Balch, a professor at Wellesley College and a leading pacifist and suffragist, wrote of the European conflict, "Not only in the theatre of war but in the world at large there is felt an unspeakable shock to the fabric of our civilization. It has lowered our *painfully acquired* sense of the value of life as life." Mornay Williams, the chairman of the New York Child Labor Committee, likewise saw the war as a threat to the "corporate consciousness" of the "sins" of "injustice and preventable poverty," a consciousness that he felt was "very slowly" being accreted in America. (By "corporate," he referred not to views within the business sector but more broadly to the public mind of American society.) He saw the war as "retrogression into barbarism," just as racism and economic conflict appeared to Balch "like a legacy from a baser age." But these antiwar liberals had no confidence that the forces of barbarism would fail. They did not hold to a complacent or automatic concept of progress.[12]

Balch and Williams gathered with others, heeding Wald's and Addams's call, at the Henry Street Settlement at the end of September 1914. The small but prominent group of twenty came primarily from the world of social work, particularly the settlement house movement. The gathering formed the nucleus of the Anti-Preparedness Committee, which in turn changed its name to the American Union Against Militarism (AUAM). The group's eventual statement was published in *The Survey* in March 1915 under the title "Towards the Peace That Shall Last." It repeatedly stated, with a long series of punishing metaphors, the thesis that an American war would be "disastrous" for the causes the *Survey*'s readers held dear. War, they said, had "tortured," "rent," "blasted," and "bent" the society of the living in myriad ways. The war, they said, "has sucked into its blood and mire our most recent conquests over the elements—over electricity, and air and the depths of ocean; and has prostituted our prowess in engineering, chemistry and technology, to the service of terror and injury." The triumphs of the civilized world were being perverted and ruined.[13]

Instead of focusing on the need for the United States to stay out of the war—perhaps they thought their view on that question was clear enough—the statement's authors looked to longer-range objectives that foreshadowed Wilson's eventual proposals for a settlement of the war (his famous "Fourteen Points"), specifically the need for open and democratically informed diplomacy. Where they went beyond anything Wilson would propose was in implying a call for the nationalization of the arms industry. A government takeover of arms manufacturing was a consistent demand of the militant antiwar groups of World War I, endorsed for example by the Woman's Peace party (WPP) at its opening meeting in January 1915.[14] Despite the excitement this idea generated internationally among political activists, it died at the door of government. The committee members were so defensive that they felt constrained to include in their statement several paragraphs on "our right to protest." It was no wonder, given the atmosphere of the moment, when Theodore Roosevelt could publicly hope for the time when America would enter the war and Senator Robert LaFollette, a war opponent, could be hanged.

Some associates of the signers of "Towards the Peace" were loath to add their names to the document. Florence Kelley signed only after first refusing, for obscure reasons, Paul Kellogg's request that she do so. She rather lamely told Kellogg, "I cannot tell you how I hate *not* to be one of the signers." After changes were made to accommodate those who, like Kelley, were wavering, she came on board.[15] Julia Lathrop, who was employed in the federal government's Department of Labor, consulted the secretary of labor, who unsurprisingly "questions advisability" of her involvement, she reported, and she stayed away. Louis Brandeis apparently attended the initial Henry Street meeting and not only declined to attach his name to the committee's eventual product but also told Kellogg, "I think it wiser that my name should be omitted from the list of those who were present at the conference." Doubtless Brandeis was concerned that signing such a statement might negatively affect his well-justified hope of nomination to the Supreme Court.[16] His understanding that a militant antiwar statement would not sit well with the Wilson administration might have sobered the Henry Street group's optimism about the president's pacifist bent.

Prior to U.S. entry into the war in April 1917, despite the continual schedule of large antiwar gatherings in which the AUAM's members played a vital role, some in the antiwar camp became radicalized, while others trimmed their sails. Lillian Wald did not like the sound of the Anti-Preparedness Committee, preferring that the group officially name itself the "Rational Defense Committee," which would have implied a large rhetorical concession to the concept of "preparedness," Wilson's term for war mobilization.[17] As their cause increasingly appeared lost, the antiwar leaders stripped the varnish off their analysis of the war's origins. The idea that the global bloodletting was simply the product of capitalist greed, a view offered early in the going by Balch and Holmes, gained ground among the antiwar liberals. At the initial meeting on Henry Street, Balch and Holmes proposed an alliance with the labor movement, which they thought would be against the war (despite the stunning collapse of Socialist-labor opposition to the war in almost all the combatant countries).[18] The increasingly extensive and close contacts with the antiwar wing of organized labor, with the Socialist party, and with the international women's movement sealed the radicalization of many antiwar liberals during World War I. These liberals would see many of their newfound allies in the United States subjected to shocking political persecution.

The Woman's Peace party, organized in the months following the start of the war, might not have taken a left turn had it not been for its internationalism. It brought together socially conservative suffragists such as Carrie Chapman Catt, eminent activists for social justice such as Jane Addams, and younger women inclined to the lyrical left such as Crystal

Eastman (aged thirty in 1917). Quickly the WPP decided to send a delegation to an international meeting of women calling for peace, planned for April 1915 in The Hague, long a site of worldwide peace meetings. The American delegation included four social workers, five labor activists, and three Socialists. In the Netherlands the Americans mingled with the likes of Rosika Schwimmer of Hungary and Emmeline Pethick-Lawrence of England. American activists including Eastman previously had met Schwimmer when they were representatives to the Congress of the International Woman Suffrage Alliance, held in Budapest in 1913. Schwimmer, like some in the WPP, had long worked in the causes of the working class and of women and only came to the crusade for peace under the pressure of circumstances. The meeting at The Hague called not only for the nationalization of armaments industries but also demanded that "the people" take part in the peace conference that would eventually settle the war. Who would represent the people was not clear, but the attendees insisted that women be involved in this process of democratization.

Some remained attached to the Victorian notion that women were naturally pacific and nurturing, and therefore were well suited to making peace. Others, however, simply thought that women were in a position to broker an armistice because they were excluded from political power in the combatant countries. Their position as bystanders was analogous to that of neutral nations, which the conference hoped to enlist in an effort to mediate an end to the war. After the meeting, a chosen group of delegates fanned out across the continent and the globe to make their case for "continuous mediation," an enterprise that would keep on producing armistice proposals until it devised one that all the warring parties could accept. Of course, the war was not ended through mediation. But the extensive contact that American women in the WPP, especially Addams and Balch, had with European women peace advocates and with sympathetic governments, many of which drew heavily on the European tradition of social democracy, encouraged the Americans' radical tendencies.[19]

American women appalled at the outbreak of war in Europe quickly organized a solemn protest march of fifteen hundred women down Fifth Avenue in New York at the end of August 1914, seeking to assert a special moral authority for women. Fanny Garrison Villard, daughter of William Lloyd Garrison and mother of Oswald Garrison Villard, led the parade. Almost a year later, when Addams spoke at New York's Carnegie Hall, reporting on her European activities, Oswald Villard introduced her with his own fiery oratory, claiming abolitionism as a precursor to the peace movement and calling the movement "revolutionary." Summing up all the available liberal outrage at what war wrought, he intoned,

1914? NO US involvement?

"Why, it is a revolution in itself that women have dared to assert in an international council that they were concerned in this matter of war. For centuries they have been told that they had no further interest in it than to breed like cattle the progeny that was to be the food for the cannon at a King's whim, and then, when war came, to bind up the wounds of the injured and to be the prostitutes for the armies."[20] While to call Villard's comments feminist would be anachronistic, he displayed a sympathy with women closer to modern feminism than to stereotypical Victorian pedestal-building; he styled women more as an oppressed class in revolt than as the vessels of a redemptive moral power. Women (and men) who advocated woman suffrage and equality between the sexes, including Harriot Stanton Blatch, Crystal Eastman, Ruth Pickering, Rose Schneiderman, and many others, would be in the thick of virtually every American antiwar effort during the war and every radical-liberal formation that took shape immediately after the war.[21]

While Addams and Balch mixed with what remained of the independent European left, young opponents of the war such as Louis Lochner and Crystal Eastman gravitated toward the American left of the 1910s. The younger members of the AUAM and similar groups drawn from the privileged classes sought the alliance with labor that some at the Henry Street meeting had anticipated. Eastman, leader of the New York branch of the Woman's Peace party, was interested in bringing speakers such as John Reed to the group's gatherings. As early as 1915 some in the WPP expressed alarm at the prominence of New York women such as Eastman who supposedly harbored dangerous sympathies with the Wobblies. One critic called Eastman "such an extreme socialist that she cannot greatly help the movement. . . ." The secretary at the New York branch commented with pride that, in her view, the party's mission was "not simply an emotional anti-war cause but . . . part of the fight for freedom for the great masses of people."[22] The younger, more militant AUAM members transformed the group, through their energetic mobilization efforts, from a small discussion clique into a network of local chapters in twenty-two cities comprising six thousand members.[23]

Shifting from indignation at the fate of women to prophetic denunciation, Villard declared at Carnegie Hall, "Surely some one must arise to drive from the very temple of our humanity the money-changers who are coining their millions out of the manufacture of arms—arms that deny our Christianity and stamp us indelibly as those who profess Jesus, and abide by him not at all."[24] Clergymen who maintained a stalwart opposition to the war, like Holmes, reached yet greater heights of jeremiad. "War is an open and utter violation of Christianity," he declared. "If war is right, then Christianity is wrong, false, a lie. If Christianity is right, then war is wrong, false, a lie." Most of the American clergy, like most liberals, thought different. The Hun was denounced from pulpits across the country as the beast at civilized society's door, and opponents of the war found themselves only slightly less the target of pious scorn as the Hun's minions.[25]

Holmes found himself on the losing end of debate within the Federal Council of the Churches of Christ in America, which had been founded in 1908 as part of the national and global movement for ecumenical Protestant conciliation. In the tense days before the outbreak of the war in Europe, it seemed that organized international Christianity might really try to stop the war. In the United States in late 1914 and 1915, some leaders of the Federal Council allied themselves with anti-preparedness advocates. But, predictably enough, the tide turned against the peace advocates among the clergy. Americans flocked to churches as the war fever heated up, eager to have the fires of their indignation stoked. In 1919 Holmes denounced his colleagues on the Federal Council for having climbed on the war bandwagon. Looking back on this period, the prominent liberal pastor Harry Emerson Fosdick remarked, with the condescension that is one of the few consolations available to the politically defeated, "What a temptation war is to a minister."[26]

The War Divides the Liberals

The People's Council of America for Democracy and Peace of 1917, in its short, controversial life, hung over a precipice that had opened among political liberals over the question of war. The People's Council remains one of the important but little-known stories of twentieth-century American dissent. It was a broad cooperative effort that brought together trade unionists, Socialists, and genteel liberals from the AUAM in a militant antiwar coalition.[27] The People's Council began at the Conference on Democracy and Terms of Peace, which was convened in New York City at the end of May 1917.

By that time the country was at war and the atmosphere for dissenters was nearly murderous. As early as the second of April, when Wilson delivered his war address to Congress, a protester who exchanged insults with Senator Henry Cabot Lodge was dragged off and thrashed by patriotic bystanders, after the senator threw the first punch. George Norris's antiwar speech in the Senate, in which he echoed left-wing views of the war, saying, "We are going into war upon the command of gold," provoked cries of "Treason!" A Senate colleague denounced LaFollette's views as "anti-American President and anti-American Congress, and anti-American people," setting the tone for all future red-baiting in Washington.[28] Wilson promised "repression" for anyone who manifested disloyalty, and by early June the Espionage Act was law, empowering the postmaster general to ban from the mails anything he saw fit and allowing the attorney general to indict anyone who, in his judgment, obstructed the war effort in any way. The law was interpreted broadly. Postmaster General Albert Burleson started to crack down on Socialist publications before the Espionage Act was actually in force. Speakers against the war found themselves harassed in halls by thugs and chased around the nation's streets by mobs. In no Old World capital was opposition to war treated more harshly. Oswald Villard, who was horrified at what transpired on these shores during the war, later recalled how different things had been in Great Britain. "Mrs. Philip Snowden," a Labour party activist, "told me that, in 1918 alone, she had spoken at fifty peace meetings, only two or three being interrupted," he wrote. "I told Mrs. Snowden that in the United States she would have been assaulted at her first peace meeting and jailed on attempting a second. No one in London could understand the bitterness in America or the severity of the sentences given to conscientious objectors, to Debs, or those accused of pro-Germanism."[29]

The Socialist party became the spearhead of opposition to the war after it adopted a militant antiwar resolution at its emergency convention in St. Louis in April 1917. The "majority report" of the SP at St. Louis reiterated the view that the war was a capitalist-imperialist "crime" and went so far as to encourage active resistance to the military draft by workers around the world. Opposition, the report stated, should be "continuous, active and public," using "all . . . means within our power."[30] Startlingly, virtually all the best-known Socialist publicists—most of them native-born and from middle-class backgrounds—found themselves on the losing side of the debate and quickly made public their support for the war. These individuals included Charles Edward Russell, Robert Hunter, Rose Pastor Stokes, and Upton Sinclair. Their effective desertion from the party was a significant blow to the organization.

Responding to the challenge from St. Louis, moderate Socialists such as Morris Hillquit, the SP's national chairman, trade unionists, and middle-class antiwar activists such as Louis Lochner, a young protégé of Addams, shaped the subsequent Conference on Democracy and Terms of Peace to broaden the support for antiwar politics. The conference's specific proposals do not seem very far to the left, featuring demands for fair labor standards in time of war, the preservation of the right of workers to strike, taxes on war profits, an end to the draft (which many Americans, regardless of their political differences, disliked), and the protection of civil liberties.[31] The conference called for a quick end to the war that would confound the imperial and undemocratic agendas of the combatants. There should be no annexations and no indemnities, and all peoples should enjoy self-determination. Despite the U.S. government's claims that it was fighting to gain exactly nothing, the demand for generous and idealistic peace terms would prove politically hazardous. The conference laid plans for the People's Council, which would meet in Minneapolis in September. In the interval, peace advocates generated support for the People's Council in localities and organizations around the country, holding meetings, giving speeches, and organizing chapters.

The People's Council's only potential mass constituency lay in the labor movement. Council activists hoped that the long talked-of but only intermittent alliance of labor with middle-class liberal leadership might emerge in a lasting way out of the conflict over the war. Ironically, this was yet another progressive vision of the good the war could do. The largely Jewish clothing trades provided the single biggest contingent of union support for the idea of the People's Council; Jewish workers generally had had difficulty swallowing the claim, often made by supporters of the war, that the alliance of the British Empire with the czar had been a condominium for democracy. The support of the new republican government in Russia for continuing the war apparently did not alter their view of the matter, despite the hopes of war supporters that this development would eliminate all liberal squeamishness about joining in the fight. Members of the Iron Moulders, Machinists, Teamsters, and Mine Workers unions, among others, were also prominent in planning the meeting in Minneapolis. This labor involvement far outstripped that of any earlier peace effort. From the other side of the class divide came not only Lochner and both Eastmans (Crystal and Max), but also Emily Balch and Norman Thomas (at this time a Christian pacifist). Amos Pinchot, Roger Baldwin, and Lillian Wald kept a safe distance from the People's Council's planning activities while still indicating their friendliness to the enterprise. The eminent rabbi Judah L. Magnes became very involved in the People's Council, lending a distinguished air to the undertaking. Finally, left-leaning intellectuals and bohemians, running the gamut from Charles Beard to Fola LaFollette to Randolph Bourne, made their presence felt. The People's Council became a virtual directory of those in America who, because of their radicalism, their fears for the fate of reform, their feeling that they bore a special responsibility to those whose blood would pay for the European crusade, or just their plain orneriness, could not be brought along on Wilson's crusade.

The peace terms that formed the salient demand of the People's Council were controversial in part because they were closely associated with the Russian radical left, specifically with the Bolsheviks. They were habitually referred to by their advocates as the Russian peace terms. Some leaders of the People's Council were explicit about taking the

Soviet, or Council, of Soldiers' and Workmen's Delegates in Petrograd as their model. The Petrograd Soviet was the hothouse of the Bolshevik Revolution, which overthrew the provisional government in Russia in the fall of 1917, based largely on the Bolshevik promise to withdraw from the war. The People's Council's financial secretary, Rebecca Shelly, achieved brief notoriety for her speech in New York calling for a "lay congress" that could shadow the government in Washington, D.C., which, she said, "does not represent the American People," just as the Petrograd delegates shadowed the Kerensky government. Like many progressives, she envisioned a regime in which functional economic groups, not just geographic areas, would enjoy formal representation. Like liberal progressives, she thought that labor and farmer groups should predominate in such an assembly. Many schemes that had gone by the name "industrial democracy" seemed similar to Shelly's proposal. Indeed, Scott Nearing, who had been fired from his post as an economics professor at the University of Pennsylvania's Wharton School of Finance for his left-wing and antiwar writings and other activities, became the chairman of the People's Council in advance of its September 1917 assembly in order to work for industrial democracy (which, he told the council's executive committee, did not equal socialism).[32]

Immediately the People's Council was denounced from many quarters as the vanguard of bolshevism in America. Samuel Gompers, safely on board the war wagon, set out to undermine the People's Council by establishing a rival group, the American Alliance for Labor and Democracy. AFL unions were expected to back this pro-war labor group if they wanted their sliver of Gompers's slice of the war-profits pie. The pro-war Socialists lent their talents to the group, and the federal government footed the bill through the Committee on Public Information (CPI), the wartime propaganda outfit run by George Creel, formerly a crusading progressive journalist. In all these ways the alliance perfectly foreshadowed the anticommunist propaganda vehicles of the cold war in the United States and elsewhere. Throwing down the gauntlet to the People's Council, Gompers scheduled the alliance's first big meeting for Minneapolis, at the same time that the council was to meet there. It was not much of a contest in the end, since the governor of Minnesota, J. A. A. Burnquist, forbade the People's Council from convening within his state. It is not clear how big or successful the council's assembly would have been in any case, but its organizers had been holding meetings around the country in preparation for the gathering in Minneapolis, and local chapters had been formed from coast to coast. The need to scramble for a new venue turned the People's Council into a fugitive group. "Big Bill" Thompson, Chicago's anti-British mayor, welcomed the council to his city, yet the city's police disrupted the first day's events, throwing the council's leaders out of the West Side Auditorium. The next day, state militia troops arrived to disperse the delegates, but found that the assembly had come and gone.[33]

The People's Council fizzled after this. The pain of official obloquy was too much for many, and the labor unions clambered off the peace train and onto the war wagon one after the other. The British government's wartime promise to establish a Jewish state in Palestine helped sway the heavily Jewish unions. Before long the unions that initially had joined the council were selling war bonds. The left-liberal dream of a broad revolutionary laborite front quickly died in 1917, to be resurrected in 1919 on the far left with the outbreak of huge strikes in the steel industry and others, and then in the imagination of the right during the red scare that followed. The few remaining staffers of the council spent the group's last days propagandizing in favor of the Bolshevik regime, as Nearing, ironically in light of his earlier effort to distinguish his own politics from socialism, moved sharply to the left.

Some historians have downplayed the radicalism of the People's Council, emphasizing instead its civil libertarianism and its pacifism.[34] Shelly's call for a reprise of the Bolshevik Revolution in Washington did not represent sentiment within the People's Council as a whole. Such feelings received expression in the heat of the moment, not to survive long after. Still, there is no reason to dismiss such views as insignificant. Shelly announced the U.S. government's illegitimacy, and this assertion was the basis for all calls for radical measures heard from the council. Many in the council doubtless thought that the government's decision to go to war in Europe did not reflect majority opinion. More fundamental, the requisite belief of any participant in the council was that this decision did not truly represent the interests of "the people," but rather advanced the cause of certain powerful special interests in the country. Furthermore, the allure of the Russian Revolution, at least in its early days, for both socialists and many liberals in the United States, ought not be dismissed.

The People's Council, abortive though it was, presaged the "Popular Front" coalitions of the 1930s. It renewed the idea that liberals and radicals, reformers and revolutionaries could act together along a broad front of action for political change. That desired change, which was amenable to the liberals who played leading roles in organizing the People's Council, was bold and drastic, leaving open the possibility of an unpredictable and convulsive process of revolution even if liberals carefully refrained from endorsing such an outcome. In 1919 the leftist Anna Louise Strong would urge on a general strike by workers in Seattle, declaring dramatically, "[W]e are starting on a road that leads—NO ONE KNOWS WHERE."[35] She perhaps had an idea of where she hoped it would lead, while others were excited by the notion of their society entering a truly plastic moment. With all its ambiguity, this aggressively formulated vision of impending change, galvanized by the actual occurrence of socialist revolution on the margins of Europe, appeared all over the United States in 1917–19.

To say this may seem to confirm the most feverish accusations that contemporary American rightists hurled at the political left during and after the war. Leading the way in this red-baiting campaign was the New York State Joint Legislative Committee Investigating Seditious Activities, under the leadership of Representative Clayton R. Lusk. The Lusk Committee compiled a massive two-volume report on such activities, real and imagined, and published it in 1920 with the title *Revolutionary Radicalism.* Primarily written by Archibald E. Stevenson, who had first achieved public attention as a witness testifying in support of a proposed federal peacetime sedition act in 1919, which did not become law, this report was in truth a compendium of almost any and all political activities and organizations in America to the left of the U.S. Chamber of Commerce. The authors lamented, "In the radical dictionary . . . the word 'autocracy' refers as often as not to a genuine democracy, such as our own; the words 'democracy,' 'democratic' and 'democrats' are used to connote Socialism, Socialistic and Socialists; and the very word 'Americanism' has been prostituted to mean things as wholly un-American as, let us say, the Socialist Party."[36] Once the committee's report established that American revolutionaries spoke with forked tongue, it was a simple matter to assert that political actors who spoke out for democracy really aimed for something very different. It was up to the committee's experts to discern the malign intent and the deception that stood behind this false use of language. This became the characteristic logic of professional red-baiters in both of the century's red scares.

In the short term, the Lusk Committee set the pattern for the "exposures" of vast left-wing conspiracies that materialized and circulated widely in America in the 1920s. The best known of these are the "spider-web" charts that first appeared in 1923, offering a frighteningly dense vision of a liberal establishment's entanglement with the revolutionary left. The charts, like *Revolutionary Radicalism,* spotlighted those involved in antiwar efforts and, more generally, the prominent liberal reformers of the prior two decades. Jane Addams topped the charts, followed by most of her well-known colleagues in political and social work, including Kelley, Lathrop, Baldwin, the Catholic priest John A. Ryan, who had been the leading light behind the influential bishops' document of 1919, which propounded a plan for the "social reconstruction" of American society, and virtually all other activists mentioned in this chapter. These liberals were mixed in with leftists from Debs to A. J. Muste to

Sinclair.[37] Those sounding the alarm about the red danger seemed most urgently concerned to identify the liberal front groups, since the openly radical groups were just that, open. Of all the liberal entities called on the carpet in these publications, the American Union Against Militarism and the American Civil Liberties Union seemed to come in for the hardest scrutiny. The Lusk Committee's staff went to great pains to assert that Lochner and Judah Magnes, in organizing the American Conference for Democracy and Terms of Peace, kowtowed to the desires of the AUAM contingent, depicting the latter organization as a kind of shadowy executive committee of the larger peace effort.[38] The ACLU, according to *Revolutionary Radicalism,* was the culmination of a years-long effort to bring revolution to America in the guise of reform, and was the worst of all liberal front groups.

In fact, there were several grains of truth in the Lusk Committee's accusations against the ACLU and similar liberal groups. Liberals involved in efforts such as those of the AUAM, the People's Council, and the ACLU certainly did not endorse violent revolution in the United States. Yet throughout the long era of the broad front, new liberals consistently carved out some ambiguity for their ultimate social and political objectives, at the terminus of their political vision. In the 1910s, the entanglement of numerous liberals with distinctly left-wing groups, including some ostensibly revolutionary ones, was real and extensive. It was rooted in the longstanding laborite commitment that had been pervasive among the new liberals since the 1880s, and it was made rhetorically adventurous by the war and the Bolsheviks' seizure of power. On the other side of the left-liberal fence, the revolutionary commitments made so explicit by the IWW and the SP are open to question. Liberal reformers, especially those who opposed the war, had one ideological foot in the same boat as did the American left during these years.

But this view benefits from almost a hundred years' hindsight. In 1917–19, not only conservatives and other enemies of radicalism viewed the People's Council as a dangerously left-wing group, but so did some liberals, and conflict over the council helped split the AUAM and thus helped create the ACLU. The ACLU came from the left wing of the AUAM, and not merely from among those who wished to defend strenuously the right of conscientious objection. However, the issue of conscientious objectors also helped drive a wedge into the ranks of antiwar activists. Once the United States entered the war, some in the AUAM preferred the role of loyal, rather private opposition to the Wilson administration's policy. Others, such as the Eastmans, Baldwin (who had moved east from St. Louis to become associate director of the organization), Nearing, and Norman Thomas, favored continued and even escalated militancy against the war.

Some believed that patriotism demanded that the AUAM close up shop once the government had made the decision to enter the war. Although only a small number of the AUAM's members took this position, their viewpoint reflected the larger environment of political pressure for conformity that opponents of the war confronted. The prominent rabbi Stephen Wise was the earliest such defector, changing his course when Wilson cut off relations with Germany. The AUAM meeting in which Wise announced his intention to desert the opposition was by all accounts memorable. According to Oswald Villard, "He asked us to state our frank opinion one after the other and he got what he asked for. Crystal Eastman, Walter Fuller, Lillian D. Wald, Amos Pinchot, Agnes Leach, L. Hollingsworth Wood, Mary W. Ovington, Norman Thomas, I and others told him exactly what we thought. Never have I heard such plain, straightforward language; never have I seen a man so flayed to his face."[39] Apparently the prospect of harsh disapproval by his peers weighed less heavily with Wise than the factors on the other side of the scale. After this meeting, he and his son very publicly took jobs in war-production factories.

Once the United States entered the war, the fissure within the AUAM widened, with the issues of conscription and involvement in the People's Council bringing a definite break in the ranks. Baldwin, who went to prison for refusing to cooperate with the draft system in 1918, led the militants in forming a suborganization to support conscientious objectors, and this prompted Wald and Kellogg to threaten to resign. Crystal Eastman kept them in by proposing that the new branch of the AUAM be called the Civil Liberties Bureau, which seemed more decent to these worthies than a Conscientious Objectors Bureau. This was a temporary solution. In August 1917 the AUAM decided, by a vote of eighteen to four, to send representatives to the People's Council gathering in Minneapolis in September. Wald was absent from this vote, and when she learned of it she wrote a stern letter to Eastman, saying, "I feel very strongly that it would be a blunder for representatives of the American Union Against Militarism to participate in the Conference." She explained, "There is a cleavage and we must recognize before we send representatives to the Council that its place in the opinion of the public is of impulsive radicalism. . . . The American Union has stood before the public as a group of reflective liberals. . . ." (She wanted the vote taken again, and if it went the same way a second time, then she wanted the AUAM to set policies from which its representatives at the People's Council would not deviate.) She finished her letter predicting that either she or Eastman might have to resign from the group.[40] Wald and Kellogg did leave the group that they had taken the lead in founding

(Addams stayed), leaving those remaining to participate in the inconsequential council. After this the Civil Liberties Bureau, the forerunner to the ACLU, formally struck off from the AUAM, which quickly atrophied.

Wald had had difficulty defining the "cleavage" within the AUAM in terms of political ideals or goals and could only describe the difference between liberals and radicals as a matter of tactics and temperament. She reflected that those who held out until the end against the war effort were the "free lances," activists who were not enmeshed deeply in institutions of social welfare, either inside or outside the state. There was something in this. Social work leaders such as Wald, Lathrop, Kelley, and Edward Devine eventually took positions on various government boards during the war, enjoying reasonable success in helping to ensure that workers and soldiers got what they could out of the conflict.[41] Even Jane Addams came around sufficiently to lecture for Herbert Hoover's Department of Food Administration, although she maintained her pacifist stance and as a result found herself shunned by colleagues, experiencing "a bald sense of social opprobrium" and put under surveillance by the Department of Justice.[42] The social-welfare liberals who joined the war effort could point to concrete improvements in social welfare stemming from the war effort, just as labor had been able to get more work, better wages, and more power.[43] But, of course, labor's new deal didn't last. The Wilson administration had to purchase labor's loyalty only for the war's duration.

Most of all, opposition to the war simply became politically hazardous, threatening to bring an odor of disloyalty and disreputable radicalism upon any person or cause associated with it. Eastman and other feminists discovered in 1921 that their comrades in the National Women's party (NWP), run with an iron hand by Alice Paul, wanted no part of a peace and disarmament agenda. The NWP also refused to pursue complaints by civil rights supporters that African American women in the South were being denied the voting rights that the suffrage movement supposedly had won for them with the inclusion of the Nineteenth Amendment in the U.S. Constitution in 1920. The party convention in that year also refused to embrace a broad feminist program, aimed at retaining the support of younger women, that included support of birth control. Involvement in one or more of these causes had been de rigueur for the party's members previously; the chilling effect of wartime repression and the postwar red scare was evident. The NWP now would focus narrowly on an elitist, legalistic equal rights agenda. It would lose a great many of its members but it would remain "respectable," and the early entanglement of feminism with the left would be quickly forgotten by many.[44]

Start of Bad Rep?

The War at Home

The war was a time of pervasive intimidation and violence.[45] The CPI, newspaper publishers, and Hollywood motion picture studios joined forces to convince Americans that the war was a righteous crusade to stop the sacking of the civilized world by the Hun, who was epitomized for most U.S. citizens by Erich von Stroheim's movie portrayals of rapists in uniform. Symphonies around the country consigned themselves and their audiences to the unhappy prospect of hearing only music not "Germanic" in origin. Less amusingly, the Department of Justice deputized large numbers of private citizens and allowed them to run rampant, to break down doors, to make large numbers of arrests, and to flash makeshift badges. Ultra-patriot groups such as the American Protective League (APL) and the American Defense Society (ADS) claimed to represent the national government. Attorney General Thomas W. Gregory enlisted the services of the APL in a series of "slacker raids" around the country in 1918. The APL's personnel, generally right-wing members of the respectable business class enjoying their lark as storm troopers, swept into public and private locations; union halls were favored targets.

APL members and their counterparts in government used the war abroad as an opportunity to make war at home on their class enemies. Only about one-twentieth of those hauled away in the raids could be called real draft dodgers. The IWW had not taken an official stand on the war and was not as an organization involved in antiwar efforts (although most of its active members no doubt were against the war). Yet it was a major object of government prosecution and persecution during the war, its offices raided and wrecked, its files either seized or destroyed (this happened to the Civil Liberties Bureau, too), its leaders indicted. Prisoners who belonged to the IWW faced terrible jail conditions around the country; in some cases they were held awaiting trial for up to two years, circumstances associated more often with military dictatorships than with democracies at war.[46]

Jane Addams's reputation among her countrymen never recovered from the episode early in the war in which she relayed the stories, which she said she had heard in countries all over Europe, that soldiers needed to be given stiff doses of liquor before they would embark on bayonet charges.[47] She was lucky to be so famous and to have made her comments before America entered the war, or she might have lost more than her reputation. Obscure Americans, and sometimes well-known ones, who said such things after mid-1917 found themselves either beaten or imprisoned. Tales abound of war critics or guiltless German Americans forced by mobs to kneel and kiss the American flag in the streets. This kind of humiliation often sated the mob's appetite for its proverbial pound of flesh; sometimes it wanted more. The old custom of tarring and feathering witnessed a revival. So did horsewhipping, the best-known instance of which was the literal flaying of Herbert Bigelow. A leading Cincinnati reformer and minister, Bigelow was kidnapped and taken into the Kentucky woods to receive his punishment, which his attackers told him they administered "in the name of the poor women and children of Belgium." This assault was consistent with the pattern of targeting crusading liberals and radicals broadly, rather than opponents of the war specifically; Bigelow actually supported the war. Walter Nelles, a Civil Liberties Bureau attorney, noted simply, "It seemed likely that his subjection to outrage was due mainly to the fact that he had led successful political campaigns inimical to public utilities interests."[48] Roger Baldwin tried to organize a public meeting of liberals to protest Bigelow's torture, but few luminaries were willing to participate. The Methodist clergyman Harry F. Ward, Lincoln Steffens, and Norman Thomas showed up, as did James H. Maurer, the president of the Pennsylvania Federation of Labor and a Socialist, but the list of those refusing to appear was longer, including not only pro-war Socialists but also Charles Beard and Theodore Schroeder, the best-known advocate of free speech on libertarian grounds in the early years of the century. Liberals and independent radicals both for and against the war, including Dewey, Thorstein Veblen, and Helen Keller, proved more willing to defend labor radicals than others against repression, signing an appeal for funds to defray the legal costs of the IWW defendants. Many who were abused by vigilantes had no one even to try to convene protest meetings on their behalf. The most grotesque of all such incidents was perhaps the torture and lynching of Frank Little in Butte; not surprisingly, he was an IWW organizer. This American tradition was directed not just against white labor radicals like Little, but also against more customary targets. Any graph charting the incidence of lynchings of black Americans throughout time shows a sharp spike during World War I. The influx of African Americans to northern cities looking for war-production work brought rioting by whites anxious to defend their prerogatives. Spontaneous popular hatreds and the will of the organized political right flowed together like two streams forming a powerful river.

The government perpetrated its violence behind prison walls. While the ADS freely printed pamphlets denouncing antiwar dissent, an Iowa man received a twenty-year prison sentence for circulating his own literature urging the defeat of a congressman who had voted in favor of conscription. Another man in Minnesota who expressed doubt that socks, supposedly knitted by women for soldiers, ever reached the doughboys was taken to jail; the Minnesota Espionage Act, like similar laws in many

woah!

other states that were modeled on the federal statute, was intended to forbid damaging actions like this one. More notorious was the case of *The Sprit of '76*, a movie about the American Revolution that contained scenes depicting the redcoats as suspiciously Hun-like thugs. The film was repressed and its producers were tried, convicted, and sentenced to ten years in prison for seeking to undermine the morale of the U.S. armed forces.[49] Genuine leftists, of course, were ripe for arrest and prosecution, and found little mercy from the courts. Eugene Debs, a serious candidate in the fragmented presidential election of 1912, which first put Wilson in the White House, gave an antiwar speech in Ohio outside the jail in which three other Socialists were serving one-year sentences for themselves having made peace speeches. His oration netted him ten years in federal prison under the Espionage Act, supposedly for having sought to undermine the military draft. His speech said nothing specific about conscription, but it praised the IWW and lauded the Bolshevik government for its antiwar stance. "Our hearts are with the Bolsheviki of Russia" was a more incriminating sentence than any Debs made about the war, in the view of the criminal justice system, which featured, in this case, a jury of twelve men all above the age of fifty and enjoying average incomes over fifty thousand dollars, making them very affluent. Supreme Court Justice Oliver Wendell Holmes, Jr. upheld the conviction. In prison, Debs got almost a million votes for the presidency in 1920. Kate Richards O'Hare, an old Populist who was famous for telling farmers to "raise less corn and more hell," and by World War I a leading Socialist, received a sentence of five years in Fargo for her utterances. Rose Pastor Stokes turned against the war and got ten years (though she never served any time) for a letter she wrote to the Kansas City *Star*.[50] A. J. Muste, then the general secretary for the Amalgamated Textile Workers of America, reached deep into the store of traditional American political rhetoric when he wrote to Eugene Lyons, "Orientals have been accustomed to these things from their despots; Russians endured them under the Czar; but the traditional American attitude toward social and political heresy is not that of repression but of liberty."[51]

In late 1918, the prominent progressive journalist Norman Hapgood made a personal plea to the president on behalf of political prisoners. Wilson replied, "I do not think the men you refer to are in any proper sense political prisoners. They have in fact violated criminal statutes of the United States."[52] A dictator could not have put it any better. Wilson's position on the matter of amnesty only hardened with time if it changed at all. After the huge steel and coal strikes of 1919 and a rash of mail bombs sent to prominent government officials, including the new attorney general, A. Mitchell Palmer, what historians call the red scare was on. But it really was a continuation of what the government had done during the war; vigilante action simply played a lesser role now. States around the country enacted "criminal syndicalism" laws that effectively outlawed leftist political organizing, and a raft of similar legislation was introduced in Congress. Such attempts to extend the federal regime of political repression and surveillance by law were scuttled but, law or no law, war or no war, Burleson, Palmer, and others continued their wartime practices until the conservative Harding administration took office in the spring of 1921. The armistice did not bring freedom of speech and of the mails. The "Palmer raids" of 1920, involving the arrest of hundreds of political radicals in the union movement, merely echoed the "slacker raids" and other actions during wartime.

Foreign-born radicals, especially those from Russia, were arrested and slated for deportation in large numbers by the mail-fisted Department of Justice, but then they were turned over to the immigration service, which was housed in the Department of Labor, where Louis Post, assistant secretary of labor under Wilson, and Frederic Howe, commissioner of immigration, took action on their own to stem the still onrushing tide of repression. Again, political radicalism, not antiwar agitation, seemed to be at issue. Defenders of such prisoners often asserted, as a Chicago lawyer, Caroline A. Lowe, did of twenty-one members of the IWW awaiting exile, "The records show that they do *not* advocate violence; do *not* advocate destruction of property; do *not* advocate a bloody revolution nor the overthrow of the Government by force; that they *do* advocate the organization of the working class into industrial unions, to the end that industrial democracy may be achieved without bloodshed or chaos."[53] The champions of repression really had no response to the charge that such individuals were targeted for their radical activities and not for any specifically antiwar actions; neither those in power nor the general public, the available evidence indicates, felt this distinction was important. To them, in either scenario, those accused were displaying un-American attitudes. Post, able to act only because his superior, William B. Wilson, was ill, so that Post was acting secretary, canceled over 70 percent of the approximately sixteen hundred pending deportation orders the government had issued.[54] Aliens held for deportation were housed on Ellis Island, which was overseen by Howe. He took steps to reform the conditions there, allowing prisoners better access to legal counsel. Perhaps his actions had something to do with appeals like the one that the Workers' Defense Union (WDU) sent him in July 1919. The appeal stated, "The forward looking elements in our community have . . . learned to expect from you outspoken and unafraid opposition to high-handed, blatant iniquity," and expressed disappointment at his "persistent silence in the face of rank inhumanity" within the immigration bureau. Howe replied blandly that the conditions on Ellis Island of which critics complained, such as vermin, poor food, and untimely deaths among inmates, were imagined rather than real, or were at worst "isolated instances."[55] He made no direct response to the appeal to his conscience. Yet in his memoir of 1925 he acknowledged, "Always there was some just cause for complaint" by the detainees, and he sought to improve conditions on the island.[56] Despite these rearguard efforts to ameliorate the government's treatment of the targeted immigrants, Palmer boasted later that he had managed to deport 505 of them, including 249 to Russia—among them Emma Goldman and Alexander Berkman—aboard the so-called Soviet ark, the *Buford*.

The president himself continued to profess his liberal attitudes regarding political freedom to his tender-hearted friends, expressing doubt that any abuses of political liberty were occurring and offering assurances that he would inquire into any such matters personally. Wilson showed his aide, Joseph Tumulty, his real face. Speaking of Debs, the president told Tumulty, with the war well over and the Socialist leader a sick man, his movement split and mangled, "I will never consent to the pardon of this man. This man was a traitor to his country and he will never be pardoned during my administration."[57] In early 1921, Roger Baldwin "doubted . . . if the President was capable of 'anything human.'"[58]

The bitterness felt by antiwar liberals and leftists against Wilson by war's end is difficult to overestimate. Oswald Villard went as far as he could when he reflected on the red scare in the late 1930s, "Much has occurred under Adolf Hitler in Germany which could be paralleled by official misconduct in this country during this period."[59] If this seems a bit purple, consider that in 1920 a very sober—and pro-war—group of liberal lawyers, including Felix Frankfurter, Frank Walsh, Roscoe Pound, Ernst Freund and Zechariah Chaffee, published the "Report upon the Illegal Practices of the United States Department of Justice," which played a large role in encouraging criticism of the Palmer raids. In only a very few other instances in American history—perhaps only during the later years of the Vietnam War and the Watergate crisis—can one imagine such a plain-spoken indictment of government treatment of political dissent from such distinguished legal figures.

Conservatives such as Lodge were not the only ones to oppose the Versailles Treaty and the proposed League of Nations; so did liberal voices such as Villard and *The Nation*, from the left. Liberals saw in the league a scheme by the great powers to consolidate global dominance and thwart the ideal of self-determination. Villard's radicalization showed in his enthusiasm for the Second International, which reconvened in Bern, Switzerland after the war. He wrote, "Though no Socialist myself, if I had the power to decide on which conference to rest the future of the world I should unhesitatingly, and with real joy, decide for this simple conference with its plain membership."[60] No piece of writing better reflects the disillusion of the liberals than a scene painted in words by John Dos Passos in his novel, *1919.* With the war newly ended, one of Dos Passos's heroines, Eveline Hutchins, something of a naïve liberal, meets some acquaintances in a café while traveling in France.

> Robbins was there with a redheaded newspaper woman from San Francisco. They sat at a wicker table together and drank Alexanders. The bar was crowded. "What's the use of a league of nations if it's to be dominated by Great Britain and her colonies?" said Mr. Rasmussen sourly. "But don't you think any kind of a league's better than nothing?" said Eveline. "It's not the name you give things, it's who's getting theirs underneath that counts," said Robbins.
>
> "That's a very cynical remark," said the California woman. "This isn't any time to be cynical."
>
> "This is a time," said Robbins, "when if we weren't cynical we'd shoot ourselves."[61]

In 1920 *The Nation* endorsed Debs.

In this bitter atmosphere, the ACLU began to make its mark. Baldwin, jailed for a year for draft resistance, emerged to freedom in 1919 newly radicalized. He declared, "I am going to do what a so-called intellectual can do in the labor movement and aid in the struggle of the workers to control society in the interests of the masses."[62] In contrast, Albert DeSilver, a patrician colleague of Baldwin's at the ACLU, offered a different, more strictly civil-libertarian view in explanation of his work rallying support for the IWW defendants during the war: "I just want to see those fellows have a chance."[63] In fact, it is not easy to line up the civil libertarians of this era on one or the other side of this tension between laborism and the disinterested commitment to political fair play. The two tendencies existed together, perhaps uneasily, within any number of individuals.

A good many liberals, when justifying their own political dissent, struck a transcendent pose, above the fray of class conflict. Mornay Williams, explaining why idealistic social work crusaders like himself ought to oppose U.S. entry into the war, had hailed the dawning "recognition," during the Progressive Era, "that *the man* in the mass was of more consequence than *the class.*"[64] Such humane and individualist sentiments ought to militate against nationalism as well as class enmity, he thought. DeSilver addressed the contemporary political situation in the United States in slightly less abstract terms during Wilson's first term as president. "Most people instinctively align themselves, either because of their economic position or because of their sympathies, with one or the other of the two great classes," he told his wife, Margaret. "My ambition is to belong to neither class, but to try to form part of the intellectual pivot upon which the balance of our civilization must be gained."[65] Such sentiments had been present for a long time among members of the middle classes who felt themselves particularly enlightened, part of a tradition that included the mainstream of the social gospel and the American Fabians. The ambition to mediate the conflict between "the two great classes" that had shaken American society since the 1880s found a global analogue in the progressive hope that the United States could mediate the European war in 1914 and 1915, before it spread further. "By that good fortune which has placed us outside the conflict": This might have introduced a proposal by progressives such as DeSilver or Jane Addams to bring an end to a local labor conflict. In fact, it prefaced a suggestion by the authors of "Towards the Peace That Shall Last" that the United States was particularly well positioned to assist in the resolution of the war.[66]

The Civil Liberties Bureau first sounded the call for a defense of labor radicals based in a sense of fair play and a desire to broker peace between warring classes when it organized legal and political support for the IWW defendants during the war. The bureau published a pamphlet in 1918 that defended the Wobblies, and it organized the appeal by prominent liberals, mentioned above, for money to pay for the IWW's legal defense. This group ran an advertisement in the *New Republic*, beginning, "Never mind what you think about the IWW. They are at least entitled to a fair trial and an open-minded public hearing. That is a primary American right."[67] The academic Carleton Parker, author of the bureau's pamphlet, took a different tack in soliciting liberal sympathy for the Wobblies, arguing at length, based on his own research, that the IWW's talk of sabotage and seizing power was mere rhetoric, and that the organization was basically a union like any other. Its fiery words and occasional violence resulted from the extraordinary exploitation and repression its members faced. This analysis both placed the moral blame for class conflict on American capitalists and deflated the anxious fears of the middle class that the IWW was bent on insurrection. Baldwin echoed the first of these points when, during the trial, he instructed the bureau's publicist to "put the burden of guilt where it belongs, on the shoulders of private capital exploiting the workers." He wanted to "put the whole industrial system on trial."[68]

When the bureau reorganized itself as the ACLU at the end of 1919, it planned to begin a "dramatic campaign of service to labor."[69] The ACLU did not undertake the defense of political prisoners from a substantively neutral political position. Baldwin and his colleagues saw themselves fully as part of the movement that included the People's Council and the radical unions. While the council itself enjoyed only a short life, and while the IWW, it turned out, was effectively destroyed as a social force by the repression of the war era, the ACLU and other affiliated groups carried on the council's work. In the aftermath of the war, the most urgent task at hand for this movement was to get its cadres out of jail, "to free the class-war prisoners," as Fred Biedenkapp of the Workers' Defense Union put it, "who people the prisons of this glorious country by thousands."[70]

The ACLU announced forthrightly, "Today the organized movements of labor and of the farmers are fighting the big fight for civil liberty throughout the United States as part of their campaign for increased control in industry. . . . The union of organized labor, the farmers, radical and liberal movements is the most effective means to this. That union is everywhere spontaneously taking place." The statement continued, "It is that union of forces which the American Civil Liberties Union serves. The practical work of free speech demonstrations, publicity and legal defense is done primarily in the struggles of the organized labor and farmers' movements." The dominant view in the ACLU saw left-wing unions, radical farmers' groups, and assorted liberals and leftists comprising a broad front, a "union of forces" standing clearly on one side of the struggle between "the two great classes."[71] There was no neutrality here; perhaps that was reserved for private moments, such as those between Albert and Margaret DeSilver.

The composition of the ACLU essentially reconvened the People's Council's dramatis personae; it also reconstituted the broad front of laborite liberalism that had marked the Progressive Era. It was as if the Henry Demarest Lloyd–Jane Addams circle of the 1890s had been reborn, now more firmly than ever joined by a new generation of activists. The national committee was headed (following alphabetical order) by Addams herself; it also featured Sophonisba Breckenridge, John Fitch, and George Nasmyth, all representing the older social work leaders. Lucille Milner carried on this tradition, too, taking up duties as the organization's field secretary. Other turn-of-the-century new liberals on the national committee included Oswald Garrison Villard, John Haynes Holmes, William S. U'Ren, Lincoln Colcord, and Frederic Howe. But the war had brought others into the fold: Frankfurter and Freund, appalled by the political repression of the era; young radicals such as Crystal Eastman, Nearing, Arthur LeSueur, and Norman Thomas; prominent individuals whose leftist sympathies were (and remain) less well known, such as Judah Magnes, Helen Keller, and James Weldon Johnson; and a host of labor radicals. This last group was perhaps, in light of the stated desire of the ACLU to serve the cause of labor and of the long-standing liberal hope to forge a cross-class alliance, the most important addition. It included James Maurer, Rose Schneiderman, Elizabeth Gurley Flynn, A. J. Muste, and, perhaps most eyebrow-raising in light of his later history, William Z. Foster. Flynn, in 1940, would find herself expelled from the organization because of her Communist party (CP) membership. She took some satisfaction in later recalling, "My name on their early listing was followed by William Z. Foster of Pittsburgh and his name was followed by Felix Frankfurter of Cambridge, Massachusetts."[72] At that time, Foster had been a revolutionary syndicalist and was certainly identified with the left. But he was best known for leading the 1919 steel strike, having received Samuel Gompers's somewhat reluctant blessing in that role. Only later, after he became the top leader of the CP, did his cheek-by-jowl association with Frankfurter and other ACLU liberals become something for the organization to regret and obscure.

Black and Red: Fears and Realities

One aspect of American life that the broad front of leftists and liberals, throughout the period from the late Gilded Age through World War I, largely failed to address in a meaningful way was racism and white supremacy. A handful of liberals, white and black, formed the NAACP in 1909, and many liberals and radicals alike viewed manifestations of racism with distaste or outrage. But the broader ranks of reformers in the Progressive Era included many who advocated Jim Crow segregation and apartheid, and who turned a blind eye to violence and exploitation directed at African Americans. Liberalism was basically irrelevant to black Americans, and the left, while more willing to make an issue of white supremacy, addressed this dimension of American society only in limited ways.

African Americans in the Gilded Age and the Progressive Era did not inhabit an ideology-free zone. But the ideological map was drastically different for them than it was for whites. The defining issues were accommodation versus militancy, the relation between economic development and political rights, and elite versus plebian strategies for group empowerment. The abstract question of liberal versus radical orientations, or even of revolution versus evolution in society, was less pressing than pragmatic questions of resources, allies, and enemies in the battle to survive and to become secure. In the late nineteenth century many black Americans were drawn, by hopes of both incremental political improvement and visionary social change, to populist agrarian organizations and the Knights of Labor. Starting with the "Great Migration" in the 1910s black leftists, many of them from the Caribbean, appeared prominently in print and on street corners in Harlem and other urban neighborhoods.[73] The southern history of political struggle, experience with industrial wage work, the heady cosmopolitanism of large northern cities in the 1910s and 1920s, and excitement over a world in upheaval combined to encourage an openness to radical perspectives among the generation of African Americans who would become known as "the New Negro."

The events of World War I and its immediate aftermath, when African Americans participated widely in the huge strike wave of 1919, brought hopes for racial change to a new high point. After the Bolshevik Revolution, word of the dramatic support the new Russian regime offered to the colonized peoples of the world spread rapidly among African Americans and generated respect for the Communist movement. In the wake of awful race riots in the "red summer" of 1919, *The Liberator*, a bridge between the lyrical left of the 1910s and the Communists of the 1920s, consistently ran scorching indictments of white racist violence and stirring calls for militant interracial resistance to both racism and capitalism. Attorney General A. Mitchell Palmer feared that "the Negro is 'seeing red,'" and fretted that both Russian and American Communists would find fertile ground among a group with little stake in American society as it existed. Kelly Miller, a conservative African American academic at Howard University, likewise feared that the Bolsheviks would inspire a revolt among his brethren. "Revolutions always lessen the domain of oppression and increase the area of liberty," he conceded, as if this were a commonplace. Most who welcomed such a prospect, both black and white, saw it the same way.[74]

Yet the reluctance of white reformers and dissidents to champion the interests of African Americans and welcome them as comrades in the cause of social progress severely restricted the plausibility of such hopes and fears for change in America's racial regime in the World War I era. Only a handful of liberals took an interest in racial justice. In contrast, leftists in the early twentieth century often denounced white supremacy, but just as often they carefully circumscribed their antiracism within strategic limits. The Socialists specifically and the American left generally took the position that racism was wrong, stupid, backward, and destructive to the project of building a social-democratic coalition; that black and white should unite in a single movement and in labor unions without prejudice; but that there was no reason for the left to make a distinctive or particularly fervent appeal to black Americans, instead addressing them as working-class Americans or simply as citizens and human beings. The SP has taken much criticism by latter-day historians for this "color-blind" politics. Some party members expressed a different view through their actions. Highly visible among these were the New York Socialists, for whom the need to break through to the swelling local African American population during the Great Migration, and the presence of black leftists such as Hubert Harrison, outweighed the force of color-blind party doctrine. The New York SP newspaper *The Call* excoriated

Madam Walker

not only southern lynchings but southern Socialist capitulation to white supremacy as well.[75] However, such active opposition to white supremacy at that time represented only the seeds of what would later become a vital interracial push for racial equality. Such a forceful interracial effort would materialize only after the Communist movement made the issue of white supremacy impossible for other radicals and many reformers to ignore.

Reconstruction or Revolution?

Although the broad laborite front was revived and continued in the war's aftermath, the ambiguities of this broad front became matters of deeper tension after the Bolshevik Revolution. In 1921, Max Eastman and others from *The Liberator* met with H. G. Wells, a figure of considerable influence among leftists for many years. "Wells was about as remote from our political attitude as anyone who called himself a socialist could be. 'A bourgeois, boys, a bourgeois, by the sacred whiskers of Karl Marx!' Mike Gold remarked after he had gone." But writing years later, Eastman recalled to his readers what had bound Wells to people like him and even to Gold, a literary commentator who was to labor in the Communist cause for many years. Wells, he said, "knew as well as we did the gulf that divided the revolutionary from the Fabian socialist. But there is—or was up to Lenin's time—a fraternity among all those who like to disturb the established inanities. To this fraternity of disturbance, at least, we all belonged."[76] The abrupt triumph of the Bolsheviks put this "fraternity" in question even more than had the issue of opposing an ongoing war.

The new rift within the broad front for social change resulted first and foremost from the appearance of insurrectionary politics on the American left, for the first time since the "anarchists of the deed" in the late nineteenth century, in the form of the Communist movement. Following the dictates of the government in Moscow, to whose leadership the American movement early on pledged fealty, an underground Communist network was formed, alongside an aboveground party structure. This overseas loyalty is worth pondering. Discussions of the "Russian question" have been tortured into exhaustion by the polemics of axe-wielding avengers and defensive apologists. After clearing away the detritus of debates that have produced as much heat as light, one still needs to ask, Why did leftists in the United States adopt developments in a remote and radically different country as their lodestar, and why did they not deviate from this guide for decades?

The immigrant character of the American left in the first half of the twentieth century is one answer. The political base of the Communist movement in this country came directly from the foreign-language federations that broke with the Socialist party. With these emigrants from central and eastern Europe, the presumption that American society was profoundly different in ways that made individualism in politics and social thought natural had little purchase. Immigrant and first-generation Italian Americans followed Italian politics closely, and within the precincts of this ethnic group prominent anarchist and fascist tendencies would shape political life up until World War II. Similarly, Slavic and Jewish immigrants who came from a political world dominated by the czarist empire and the struggles against it continued to orient themselves to that world once in America. The internationalist character of socialist ideology facilitated a feeling that a drastic shift of perspective was unnecessary. In the time of the Bolsheviks, the American left, dominated numerically by immigrants, pushed hope into expectation that the red tide would sweep across the ocean. Many American radicals anticipated some reorganization of the worldwide revolutionary forces in the epoch of victory. The prestige and authority of the first victorious socialist revolution in a major country made it so. The Bolsheviks were quick to declare this authority, and all relearned the lesson that Lenin long had taught: the assertion of will amid turbulence commanded assent.

It remains harder to understand why so many prominent native-born leftists saw things this same way, and why American radicals stayed with this Soviet-oriented perspective for so long. Political events account for much of this durable attachment. This was an affective link, not merely a matter of organizational ties. It was annealed in the heat of the revolutionary era of the Great War. In later years, the antifascism of the 1930s and 1940s reinforced these chains of loyalty. If not for those developments, perhaps the initial gravitation of American leftists, and many liberals, to the Soviet beacon might have weakened earlier than it did. Max Eastman explained the original basis for the outpouring of American leftist emotion for the Soviet Union. He recalled the vitriol that members of the American social and political elites, particularly in the daily newspapers, directed at the Russian Revolution. The Bolsheviks were "so fabulously lied about in the American press, pulpit, barroom, and drawing room, in Congress and on the lecture platform, that truth itself seemed to be crying for help. I think over half the country actually believed that 'Lenin and Trotsky' had decreed the 'nationalization of women'—whatever that might mean." The social democratic forces in Russia and the United States long had been allied. The October Revolution in the first of these countries was a major event for the world and even more for socialists everywhere. Sympathetic Americans wished to correct the outlandish charges flying about and to call attention to the good points of the Leninist regime.[77] Their feeling of loyalty to comrades requires no special explanation. What is odd is that this developed into a loyalty of follower to leader, of vassal to liege. This change occurred, it seems, with some not fully understanding what was happening. It stemmed from the combination of Russian assertiveness, immigrant enthusiasm, and the reaction of the left to harsh repression in the United States. American leftists started by defending beleaguered comrades across the sea and soon found themselves feeling like failures, looking to the tutelage of successful peers.[78]

However, Communist loyalty to Moscow should not overshadow the diversity of responses to the Bolshevik regime among American leftists and liberals. Socialist enthusiasm for the Russian developments did not imply support for revolution in America. Flynn called for "monster May Day demonstrations" around the United States in the spring of 1919, hoping that these protest gatherings could rally support for a general amnesty of political prisoners jailed during the war. But she also wished to rouse "conscious[ness] of class interests" in America and declared that the demonstrations would "be a celebration of the rising tide of proletarian dictatorship in Europe." She did not call for such a dictatorship in America.[79] Eastman later recalled the position *The Masses* had taken up before the war: "I left the concept of revolution abstractly defined: the conquest of power by a new class. I did not envisage the overthrow of the United States Government. . . . [W]e had not a notion of that armed assault of the proletariat on the state and the pillars of society which extreme-left Marxists in Continental Europe projected."[80] This was also a fair description of *The Liberator*'s outlook. But the accusation that revolution, not reconstruction, was what Eastman or Flynn really wanted in America would always stick, at least a little, to Americans who condoned the overthrow of Kerensky and defended the ensuing Soviet government.

Despite leftist assertions that the Russian and American situations were very different, the Bolshevik insurrection of October-November 1917 did appear to many laborites, both radical and liberal, in a highly general sense like the victory of the cause they themselves had worked for. The method seemed reasonable under the circumstances of war and within a political system that offered little chance for real progress through parliamentary means. Moreover, the soviets in Russia seemed from afar to resemble so closely the schemes of industrial democracy that progressives had long traced on paper that once the soviets' rivalry with the reformed Duma emerged clearly, many elsewhere took the side of the workers' councils. Many American progressives agreed with the British philosopher Bertrand Russell that proponents of class or occupational representation "ought to pay great attention to bolshevist methods of organization . . . because of their partial adoption of an industrial instead of a geographical basis for the Soviets."[81]

In the 1910s, the concept of reconstruction, endlessly intoned in liberal journals, both captured and accommodated the liberals' ambivalence over the scope and depth of the changes they sought in American society. The ambiguity remained after the revolutions in Russia. Liberals generally implied that support for bolshevism in reactionary countries, such as Russia and Hungary, where Béla Kun's Communist regime briefly reigned in the turbulent postwar period—and where Crystal Eastman and others turned up to look at the thing firsthand—did not require advocacy of bloody revolution in the United States, or in Britain or France.[82] Of course, this represented a reversal of Marxist theory, which held that proletarian revolutions ought to occur in the most economically and politically advanced countries first.[83] American liberals' feeling that democratic political institutions, if vigorous, were a preferable alternative to revolution spared them the specter of smoke and guns. The blatantly illegal removal of elected Socialists from the New York legislature during the war seemed to suggest a different lesson, but faith in the American political system died hard, especially among native-born reformers.

The metaphor of reconstruction took off in the United States during the war and stayed popular right afterward, partly because after any major war there is talk of physical and economic rebuilding in the war zones, and this offered an opening into which liberals hoped they could insert their long-standing social-justice agenda. "Between November 1918 and mid-1919, the American Federation of Labor, the U.S. Chamber of Commerce, the Federal Council of Churches, the National Catholic War Council, the Women's Trade Union League, social workers, farmers, and state federations of labor all cobbled together reconstruction programs. Six states established official Reconstruction Commissions."[84] "Reconstruction" projected a feeling of bold and fundamental social change even as it suggested an orderly process different from revolution. In the early postwar years left-liberals sounded a note of caution as they painted the outlines of reconstruction. They began to make clear that they did not seek to import the Bolshevik program or method to the United States. Even a group so radical as the Fellowship of Reconciliation (FOR) suggested as much. The FOR, founded in 1915, was a pacifist group that would become a pioneer in the techniques of nonviolent protest, so it would have made little sense for it to promote insurrection. Yet conservatives like those on the Lusk Committee's staff nonetheless painted the FOR as "pseudo-pacifists."[85] Certainly it was a left-wing group, deeply sympathetic to the cause of organized labor as well as that of Christian peace. Its annual conference in 1917 offered a program featuring Harry Ward, Joseph Cannon, and Elizabeth Gurley Flynn.[86] Of these, only Ward came from the world of the churches, while all of them were identified strongly with the labor left.

In the midst of political repression, pacifist radicals clung to the idea of peaceful change. The masthead of the *World Tomorrow,* the FOR's journal, whose editorial board included Ward, Holmes, and Villard, announced that it was committed to "the reconstruction of society on the enduring foundation of freedom and fellowship." In 1920, in protest against the red scare, Norman Thomas, writing for the *World Tomorrow,* observed, "No nation is really democratic which is so afraid of a relatively small group of Reds" as Palmer and Wilson seemed to be. Rhetorically, this put some distance between the future Socialist party leader and the "Reds." It also may have suggested to some that, since the United States was not really democratic, a revolutionary course might be justified. Yet Thomas discouraged such an inference by lamenting that the state's harsh treatment of dissent "makes for violent revolution. Those radicals who say that there is no such thing as civil liberty are strengthened in their argument by the attitude of the government."[87] He seemed to warn those left-liberals who wished to continue working within the existing political institutions of the United States that things were approaching a point of crisis. Henry Neumann, leader of the Brooklyn Society for Ethical Culture—a local branch of a movement long part of the broad laborite liberal front—was more explicit in stating his philosophy of social change. "Believing as I do in peaceful political methods," he wrote, "in the slower but more fruitful process of educating public opinion, I deplore the resort to direct action." He lamented that political repression was "likely to drive the discontent underground, to breed the resentments which flare up in violence and to postpone the only step which will halt discontent, namely the reconstruction of our present society."[88] If the red scare did not encourage revolutionary violence in America, it did encourage the Communist movement (united in a single party in 1921) to go underground. The red scare eased the way for the parallels that a minority within the left drew between America in the 1920s and Russia in the 1910s.

Liberals, even those who leaned to the left and supported the Bolshevik regime, thought it foolish to consider imitating Lenin and his followers in America. American and British liberals insisted that their countries shared a special heritage of political democracy and flexibility that especially resisted the appeal of Bolshevism. Bertrand Russell, in a powerful statement of support for international socialism in 1920, qualified that support in stating that "England, ever since 1688, has had a love of moderation. Methods such as those of the Bolsheviki would alienate ordinary people. Nor is the opposition of the reactionaries sufficiently ruthless to justify such methods."[89] American reactionaries had behaved more ruthlessly during the war and immediately afterward than had their opposite numbers in Britain. Nonetheless, this was the sort of exceptionalist comment that would echo through America as well as Great Britain so long as the Bolsheviks inspired admiration.

Russell, like many other socialists and liberals, quickly became disillusioned with the Bolsheviks as they traveled to Russia and found the ruling party more violent and dictatorial than they had expected. Anarchists such as Emma Goldman and Robert Minor were the first to tread what would become this well-paved road, after a Soviet crackdown on Russian anarchists, who once had played an important role in that country's left. Minor quickly changed his mind in the unconventional direction: after writing a widely read "J'Accuse" in which he lamented the political evils of the Soviet rulers, he abruptly became a dedicated and leading Communist, which he remained for decades. Goldman had trouble finding a publisher for *My Disillusionment in Russia*; she went on an anti-Soviet speaking tour where she was treated unsympathetically by her longtime comrades.[90] After one speech the only audience member who applauded was Bertrand Russell. All this helped the Soviet government's reputation in the United States. As early as 1918, Bolshevik repression of anarchists convinced some conservative Americans that this might, after all, be a responsible government they could deal with.[91]

Socialists such as Debs had more trouble renouncing their initial support for bolshevism. In 1918 Debs proclaimed the October Revolution "the soul of the new-born world," and he wrote, "We stand or fall by Russia and the revolution—the whole program clear-cut from start to finish."[92] Morris Hillquit, like many Socialists a refugee from the tyranny of the czar, also welcomed Kerensky's fall. Hillquit was a leader of the "right-wing" forces in the SP. Yet in 1921 he averred that a new socialist government like that in Russia would need to use "repressive force" against "the forces of surviving capitalism aiming at its overthrow." Such a regime would be "frankly a limited form of democracy," he wrote, but "a higher form than the democracy of the bourgeoisie, because it means the actual rule of the majority over the minority, while the latter represents the rule of a minority over the majority." This was strong brew from a man commonly derided by the militants of his own party as a champion of "sewer socialism." But, after the initial flush of joy at Marxism's triumph in a large country had passed, many SP members entered a crisis.[93]

Debs's radicalism owed as much to Jesus and Lincoln as to Marx and Lenin, and it was not long before Debs wired Lenin to protest "with all civilized people in the name of humanity" the planned executions of Social Revolutionaries (a peasant-affiliated group, formerly allied with the Bolsheviks, but now targeted for violence after besting Lenin's party in elections to the soviets).[94] But he could not turn his back on what was supposed to be the first successful proletarian revolution. It seemed difficult as well for him to say simply that bolshevism was fine for the Russians, but that socialism in North America would take a very different path. He eventually implied such a view when he chastised William Z. Foster that he, Debs, had "no Vatican in Moscow to guide me."[95] He was castigated in Communist-oriented journals. Still, Debs's imprisonment, his stature among American leftists, and eventually his early death saved him from a good deal of the public left-wing agony over the Russian question. Harding released him at the end of 1921, and Debs, ill and frail, died in 1926. In his last years he was a picture of obsolescence, a man from another time.

A commitment to a broad and vaguely defined "reconstruction," led by workers and visionaries of all classes, became harder to maintain in the early 1920s. According to Max Eastman, "Both Debs and Hillquit receded" from their initial stance of solidarity with the Bolsheviks, "as the purpose of Lenin to split the world's socialists into hard and soft began to grow clear. . . . The hards were those not only sympathetic to the October revolution in Russia, but ready to agitate and conspire toward a similar seizure of power in their own countries. The softs were those who, while glad of what happened in Russia, were unwilling to take the role of idealistic traitors to their own governments."[96] As the October Revolution and its legacy combined with the punitive atmosphere in which American radicals struggled to advance their cause, both leftists and liberals felt new pressures to choose sides. Reform versus revolution was not the only critical choice that haunted them. Starting at this time, they began to hear, and sometimes to express, more talk of national loyalties than ever before. As far back as the days of the French Revolution, conservative forces in the United States had declared revolution a foreign import.[97] The bearded anarchist of the Gilded Age was virtually always pictured as an immigrant. The members of the Lusk Committee reached into the counterrevolutionary quiver for this straight shaft, sharp-tipped as ever, seemingly without having to think hard.

In this atmosphere, radicals and liberals themselves often sped to deploy the language of "Americanism." This was not a new theme for dissenters in the United States, but it now acquired fresh saliency. Typically, those who talked this way were native-born, mainly from the WASP genteel reform tradition. In 1917, Roger Baldwin wrote to Lochner with advice on the September meeting of the People's Council: "We want . . . to look like patriots in everything we do. We want to get a lot of good flags, talk a good deal about the Constitution and what our forefathers wanted to make of this country, and to show that we are the folks that really stand for the spirit of our institutions." To the Lusk Committee, this statement was evidence of deception.[98] To those on the right, real patriots would not need to think about how to "look like patriots." The committee, of course, thought anyone against the war must be unpatriotic, as Baldwin and Lochner understood.

But the interest in asserting one's patriotism was more than merely tactical. Many on the American left truly felt that a libertarian spirit marked the tradition of democratic dissent in the United States. Muste's 1920 comment, mentioned above, that political repression was "fundamentally un-American," revealed that immigrants (Muste was from the Netherlands) were fully capable of adopting this point of view. However, the strongest statements of this kind came from those proud of their Anglo-Saxon heritage and their families' deep roots in North America. A revealing exchange of letters comes down to us from Harry Weinberger and William Nye Doty. Weinberger was one of the most prominent civil liberties lawyers in the United States. A friend of Elizabeth Gurley Flynn and many other left-wing activists, he handled many cases, high profile and not, that the Workers' Defense Union brought to him. Doty, a railroad brakeman in Iowa in 1917, found himself taken off his train at Waterloo by a U.S. marshal because he had refused to register for what he called "Prussian conscription." Apparently someone had reported him. He twice declined to sign a registration card and was tried, convicted, and sentenced to sixty days in the Blackhawk County jail. He told the draft board "that it was against my convictions," he wrote Weinberger, "to sign away my Birthright for a morsel of liberty."

After serving his time, in the spring of 1918 Doty received a card from the adjutant general of Iowa informing him that he was registered in accordance with the Selective Service Act and instructing him to report for military service. Doty ignored this summons because he had never registered and insisted that the adjutant general's orders "misrepresented the facts." On 9 August, working as a switchman in Mandan, North Dakota, he was arrested for desertion. The local War Board again sought his consent to enter the army, and again Doty stood firm. The authorities brought him to an army base, where, according to Doty, "[They] ordered me to be a soldier and I refused." He was court-martialed, convicted of desertion, and sentenced to thirty years' hard labor in military prison at Fort Leavenworth, Kansas. Six months later his sentence was cut down to five years, set to end in late 1923. Doty contended that he had been tried, convicted, and jailed twice for what was, in essence, a single offense: resisting the draft. This seemed to him to violate his constitutional protection against "double jeopardy."

Weinberger, learning of Doty's case, was keen to emphasize the prisoner's patrimony. "Certainly I think," Weinberger wrote to Flynn, "when he submits the fact that he is a descendant of those who came over on the 'Mayflower', it would be good for publicity. Certainly pro-Germanism cannot be thrown at him." When Doty learned that Weinberger wished to put this lineage to good tactical use, his response was prickly. In November of 1920 he expounded at some length on his interpretation of the American legacy of liberty. "Since you are interested in my Mayflower Lineage, I wish to inform you that the Mayflower Folks held all their [property] in common with a desire of conforming to the simplicity of the early Christians," he wrote. "I hold these very same convictions and the military *cannot* change them by calling me a 'Socialist and an Agitator' for the Devil called Jesus Christ all of the nasty names that his wicked heart could think of, and I care not what they call me and my Class."[99] Doty combined a quasi-religious reverence for the U.S. Constitution with a Christian primitive communism that he traced back to the Puritans. To him, this was his heritage, and it was to lay claim to it that he mentioned his family background. He was not interested in making himself seem less radical by trumpeting his Mayflower pedigree. From this time forward, many left-wing Americans, fending off newly potent charges that they were not true Americans, would cite a specially American radical tradition. Harry Weinberger might not have taken it too seriously, but others, such as William Doty, meant it with excruciating earnestness.

Weinberger had a hard time of it with his clients on more than one occasion. The small crusade to free political prisoners jailed during and right after the war continued for several years, solidifying the new civil liberties constituency. One debate within that community concerned the two strategies of pressing for a blanket amnesty and pursuing the cases of individual prisoners. In 1922 a group of left-wing activists in the Workers Prison Relief Committee, based in Paterson, New Jersey, put the case for a comprehensive approach in a way designed to cut a civil liberties activist such as Weinberger to the quick. These prisoners had refused Weinberger's request that they support the application by a single prisoner, Manuel Rey, for his freedom. The committee took the view, which it claimed to share with "the large majority of the I.W.W. prisoners," that "the individual clemency men are not made of the stuff out of which a sound labor movement can be built." If a few individual prisoners with especially strong cases applied for and perhaps got amnesty, what would be the fate of those remaining in jail? But Ulrich Frueh, Peter Talsma, Bernard Hagedoorn, and Peter Braak insisted that this was not just a question of tactics. "This committee is a class-conscious proletarian group, interested primarily in strengthening the labor movement. We are not sentimentalists seeking to alleviate individual distress." They did not see much common ground with liberals who cared primarily for abstract individual rights and who sought, like Albert DeSilver, to function as the "pivot" on which class relations turned. As in the late Gilded Age and the Progressive Era, class loyalty seemed the most pressing concern. But now the basis of that loyalty was formulated more sharply than before, in stark Marxist terms. In the grim and angry aftermath of the war, a broad labor-liberal front was, as far as one could tell from this rhetoric, not in the offing. The members of the Workers Prison Relief Committee, as they told Weinberger, "do not expect you to accept or even to understand our point of view. It is not that of the lawyer or the bourgeois, no matter how liberal, but of the class-conscious proletarian. . . ."[100]

In response, Weinberger struck the pose of a put-upon ally, trying to help those who would scarcely help themselves. "I suppose you feel," he replied, "that with your committee is all wisdom and with you it will die. I am sure benighted Paterson needs your illuminating intelligence." He took the view that the choice between the goals of individual and general amnesties was not a matter of principle. While some, harking back to the IWW and now attracted to the Communist movement, took a hard line, separating proletarian revolutionaries from bourgeois liberals, many continued to believe in and seek to reconstitute the broad left-liberal front. The Workers' Defense Union, its Communist links notwithstanding, functioned as an affiliate of the ACLU. Radical groups like the People's Freedom Union, a successor of sorts to the People's Council, and its publishing arm, People's Print, were housed "under the same roof" with the ACLU at the house on West Thirteenth Street.[101] People such as Lucille Milner and Harry Weinberger, as well as Elizabeth Flynn and William Foster, continued to believe in left-liberal unity. The American left, broadly understood, was poised in the 1920s between these two alternatives of the broad front and the class war, which tended, rhetorically, to coincide with the choice between reform and revolution.

"They Couldn't Stand the Gaff": The Left Critique of Liberalism

The searing experience of World War I set the tone and the substance of left-wing criticism of liberalism for many years afterward, criticism that soon extended well beyond the obscure ranks of New Jersey revolutionaries. Harold Stearns and Lincoln Steffens were among the prominent writers who embraced what became the standard left critique of liberalism. In 1919, Stearns defined liberalism as "a temper and an attitude towards life as a whole rather than an explication of a program."[102] Steffens, in his *Autobiography*, which was not published until 1932, depicted liberalism as a political and social creed. Stearns and Steffens represented the radicalization, respectively, of liberals of cultural and political stripes. To radical critics of liberalism, the problems seemed essentially similar in 1919 and 1932, even if the salient form of the problem appeared to shift with the passage of time. To critics such as Albert J. Nock, it came to seem obvious that a yawning gulf lay between "radicalism" and "liberalism." When, in 1920, he began a new journal, *The Freeman,* he rejected the congratulations that *The Nation* proffered to his supposedly liberal venture. Nock, whose libertarianism later took him far to the political right, explained to Oswald Villard that he was appealing to "Radicals" not "Liberals." He wrote, "I hate to seem ungrateful, but we *haint* liberal. We loathes liberalism and loathes it hard."[103]

The anti-liberal analysis was simple. Liberals always had prided themselves on being quintessentially modern, yet they could not cope with the momentous changes of the twentieth century. John Chamberlain, too, expressed the charge concisely, in terms of economic doctrine, when he derided "'reform' in America—the reform that has talked, endlessly, about going back to the primitive capitalism of our fathers while an economic revolution has been beating about our ears."[104] Frederic Howe, chastened by the Great War and the ensuing red scare, returned to the scheme of class-based historical development that the original new liberals had held dear, and from which many contemporary American liberals now shrank. In the conclusion to his 1925 memoir, *The Confessions of a Reformer,* he wrote, "My political enthusiasm was now for a party of primary producers. . . . Such a party was the last step in political evolution. . . ."[105] Howe called on liberals who believed in progress to support a worker-farmer party, yet he feared that many liberals were stuck, mentally, in a bygone stage of history.

Critics charged that liberals thought they could manage the transition to a new society but could not. There were irreconcilable choices that would not be managed. Liberals in the highest positions of power and influence came, first in the 1910s and with increasing stridency after 1917, to define themselves by their opposition to both reaction and revolution. They favored orderly and balanced progress. There were extreme dangers to avoid on either side. Left critics condemned liberalism precisely as a politics of avoidance. In dissecting what he considered "the technique of liberal failure," Chamberlain homed in on "the unwillingness of the liberal to continue with analysis once the process of analysis had become uncomfortable. LaFollette had been willing to continue with the analysis of the War; so had Bourne. But liberalism in general couldn't stand the gaff." Here Chamberlain helped cement the reputation of Randolph Bourne, the lyrical left writer who denounced John Dewey for supporting the war, as a fearless truth-teller. Chamberlain directed most of his fire at what he termed the "economic fundamentalism" of American reformers. The economic thinking of the progressives "suggested many problems, but shied away generally from a rigorous portrayal of the conditions necessarily attendant upon solution."[106] Yet his most biting, and rather personal, comments frequently returned to the issue of the war. For many of his generation, Wilson betrayed the liberal cause in taking the United States into the European conflict. What joined the indictments of foreign and economic policy was Chamberlain's criticism of the liberal's habit of mind. He was not far from Stearns in seeing liberalism as an attitude. To Chamberlain, it was a pathetic attitude, in love with moderation for its own sake, defined by intellectual cowardice. Liberals "couldn't stand the gaff," meaning they couldn't stand the flak, the intense criticism, the attacks, that any radical political analysis was certain to call forth. Chamberlain, like Stearns and Steffens, helped to forge an enduring leftist image of liberals as humanitarians whose cowardice in the face of criticism from the right literally defined them.

Steffens focused on Wilson, "perhaps, the greatest liberal we had." To Steffens, Wilson's motion toward intervention in World War I after it began in 1914, protesting all the way that he wanted to keep out of it, had been idiotic and, in retrospect, easy to predict. "England sent man after man over here to get Wilson, till finally they found in Arthur Balfour a man, a liberal who could, as the president said, 'talk his language,' the liberal language, principles—bunk."[107] The sources of Wilson's woes were specifically the war and its settlement; he proved as tragically ignorant of international affairs as he was expert in domestic matters. Therefore it can be questioned how deep his "failure" cut into the soft belly of liberal ideology. However, in order to understand the atmosphere of bitterness that enveloped so many who hovered between liberalism and the left in the era of war and revolution, one has to recapture the thorough entanglement of the war issue with the perceptions of a class conflict that the war itself merely interrupted. Will Durant's acerbic portrait of "the liberals," penned after the war's end, can be read as a caricature of Wilson. "The very word is in bad odor . . . it has come to betoken a mild and bespectacled indecision, as of a man who dispenses radical rhetoric but cannot forget that he has some shares in Bethlehem Steel."[108] His point of reference was the class war, but the Great War had called up the image.

Steffens was more concerned with the mental qualities of political leaders than with the specific question of class loyalty, and when he compared Wilson unfavorably to Vladimir Lenin, it was in the former regard. To Steffens, Wilson's liberalism seemed a weird combination of lofty principles and situational vacillation. The gap in between ought to have been filled by strategic goals and plans, but there were none. "That is the advantage of a plan," he wrote with satisfaction after recounting

Lenin's lesson. "You can go wrong, you can tack, as you must, but if you know you are wrong, you can steer back on your course. Wilson, the American liberal, having justified his tackings, forgot his course. To keep himself right, he had changed his mind to follow his actions till he could call the peace of Versailles right. Lenin was a navigator, the other a mere sailor."[109]

Yet Steffens's critique of liberalism was double-edged and perhaps contradictory. He saw liberals as not only strategically crippled by their inability to see that social reality did not conform to their models of human behavior, but also as dismally lacking in a real moral vision. Their principle was rather hollow, or perhaps just overly rational. He had experimented with applying the golden rule to American society when he came to grasp the galvanizing, radical potential of Christianity. This was, to him, perhaps the only available alternative to socialism as a creed of true principle that could fire men's souls and move them to rise above corruption. Here he implied a stark difference between radicals and liberals. In his experience, "Socialists were not particularly honest. . . ." Yet "their vision, their imminent hope, of a better world . . . made them unpurchasable. They were as honest as any fanatics are; they were believers in some hopeful vision. . . . If it was vision that made such a difference in men, vision is what we need in the world."[110]

In fact, Steffens himself immediately undermined his own contention that the Socialists alone were possessed of a "vision." He saw the moral core of Christianity—the part he never saw in the churches—at work not only among Socialists but also among the best of the progressives and the liberals. Tom Johnson and Bob LaFollette were Christ-like figures to him, believing that we all should do unto our neighbors as we would have them do unto us, and finally betrayed not only by politicians and judges, but also by "the mob, led by the best people." The Sadducees were afoot in the land. "I have never heard Christianity, as Jesus taught it in the New Testament, preached to the Christians. But I did see it practiced, in politics. It was an element in every reform movement that won the support of the people." The "neo-democratic" progressives, as Chamberlain called them, were, in their hearts, cut from the same cloth as Debs and Altgeld, doctrine aside.[111]

When Steffens considered his heroes among American politicians, it became clear that his broadsides against liberalism were less than perfectly targeted. His summary indictment could not hold fast. In fact, the whole critique that Stearns, Steffens, and Chamberlain directed against the liberalism of the Progressive Era represented, in the end, a distortion. The new liberalism of the twentieth century was not simply a politics of blind and impracticable principle. It featured a set of concrete social goals and political strategies. The liberals, for their part, viewed themselves as brave in their willingness to forge compromises and to choose the lesser of whatever evils were at hand. They were wont to feel that they, and not those who launched jibes from their left flank, understood how the world worked. It was the left-wing radicals, in this view, who sought to force the world into an ill-fitting framework of principle. And, certainly in the 1910s, liberal thinkers, activists, and leaders continued to grapple with the question of class relations, weighing their sympathy for labor against their belief in order and in the historic role of a class occupying the space between capital and labor.

The war ripped away much of the liberals' claim to such a sober and self-respecting politics in the eyes of the most idealistic in their own ranks. Complaints by critics of the war and of those who followed Wilson blindly into it were all too telling. However, it was unfortunate that the war, and the role played in it by Wilson and his most visible liberal supporters, came to dominate the postwar image of American liberalism for the critics. Although a majority of liberals, from all indications, came to support the war, many others rightly feared the domestic political consequences of "militarism," a word implanted firmly in the American lexicon in the course of the war. If the numbers of liberals who steadfastly opposed the war were small, their legacy was large—for American liberals and leftists both.

But a more grievous error in the portrait of liberalism painted by Steffens or Chamberlain was the less than fully accurate depiction of liberals' role in the class war. The Great War and the repression of the left that it brought in the United States distorted the earlier record of liberals on the question of class relations. In the first two decades of the century, the new liberals had become somewhat less sure than they had been originally that they must simply be partisans of labor. Some found firmer footing in nongovernmental organizations separate from the trade union apparatus; some increasingly looked to the state as a neutral arbiter of class conflict. Still, as Chamberlain himself noted, "even those Progressives who presumed to speak for the Jeffersonian state" were "inevitably conditioned, to a small extent at least," by the spectacle of class conflict and the rise of a vigorous political left based in the union movement. Walter Weyl and Lippmann, two editors of the *New Republic*, liberals perhaps more attracted to the ambience of the White House than to that of union halls, "had to reckon with industrial unionism and the ineluctable encroachments on that shibboleth of an earlier liberalism, 'freedom of contract.' "[112] Self-described socialists of all kinds called for the empowerment of the organized working class at war's end. But most liberals favored this as well. Socialists and radicals tended to want labor to have more leverage in economic matters, aspiring to make labor equal with capital, but only a small number sought a proletarian dictatorship. The differences between liberals and most leftists on this matter were differences of degree, not of kind.

As it happened, the events, domestic and international, that the war brought in its train strengthened the backbone of American liberals precisely in the ways that many of their left-wing critics ought to have appreciated. The forceful, often violent suppression of political dissent during the war, the ensuing red scare, and finally the Russian Revolution, sparked in liberals a stronger appreciation of civil liberties and also reinvigorated their laborite tendency. In the era of Theodore Roosevelt and Woodrow Wilson, the loyalties of liberals gravitated toward the state, toward the middle class, and, for some, toward youth. The war was a slap in the face to many of them. Like Howe, they hoped anew after the war that the labor movement could be the repository of their hopes for historic progress.

Chastising himself for his earlier naïveté, Howe wrote, "We liberals had the truth. If we talked it enough and wrote it enough, it would undoubtedly prevail. . . . The one thing I had clung to all these years was a belief in my class convinced by facts." But after his wartime experience, he wrote, "[I] now began to see that men were not concerned over the truth. It did not interest them when economic interests were at stake. . . . Aside from a few young men, I could not remember a person of prominence . . . who had been converted from his class by intellectual appeals. It had been a war of classes."[113] Perhaps he caricatured his own former innocence. Regardless, in his telling, as we have seen, the war jolted him back into the long-dormant awareness of the evolutionary, class-based vision of historical progress with which so many American liberals seemed to have lost touch. Many liberals took his call to arms quite seriously, setting the stage for further efforts at left-liberal collaboration.

Chapter 3

Third-Party Organizing and the New Deal

During the Progressive Era, many American radicals and liberals were bound together in a broad front for change to a new, more unified, and fairer society. That broad front sustained some damage in the era of World War I. But, despite these internal strains, the idea and the political reality of a broad progressive front continued to exist and to be politically vital in the 1920s, 1930s, and 1940s. Activists in the broad front alternately were called "progressives," "liberals," and "radicals" in these years. One prominent feature of the period stretching from the mid-1920s to the late 1940s was the increased explicitness with which adherents of the broad front asserted their belief in a transformative, sequential vision of social change, a vision descended from the eighteenth-century Enlightenment. They were called progressives in part because they talked all the time about "progress" with this transformative meaning. Because of the pervasiveness and importance of this theme of historical progress, I call the years 1924–48 the "Second Progressive Era."

In the Second Progressive Era, activists who believed in progress to a new stage of American history continued their efforts to forge practical political instruments that could help to achieve that goal. In the 1920s this meant forming political vehicles that were independent of and more radical than the two major political parties, both of which had become quite conservative. In the 1930s it meant responding adequately to the social crisis of the Great Depression and figuring out how the politics of the broad front ought to relate to the vigorous but inconsistent reform policies of President Franklin D. Roosevelt's government. In the 1920s, activists bent on breaking out of the two-party system formed a "farmer-labor" movement that updated the antimonopoly tendency that had enlivened American politics throughout the Gilded Age and the Progressive Era. In the 1930s, a largely different set of political actors, including Communists and various liberal reform elements, forged the "Popular Front" and worked within the Democratic party. Both of these initiatives amounted to efforts to push American politics to the left and to bring incrementalist reformers along on the movement for social transformation. Both efforts reflected a stubborn belief that such a movement for change could transcend the difference between reform and radicalism. Both efforts embodied a continuing conviction that capitalism in America was morally bankrupt and that it should be superseded by a new, more just society. Each effort in turn became known as "progressivism." Each effort fell well short of facilitating social transformation and instead ended up invigorating and changing political liberalism.

Third-party farmer-laborism, rooted in the American Midwest and the mountain West, embraced a vision of historical change stemming from the Protestant ideal of the cooperative commonwealth that had animated rural and urban reformers since the Gilded Age. Farmer-laborism, in the Second Progressive Era, was not a promising road-not-taken, an unrealized alternative to New Deal liberalism. Instead, it was a road that was taken, and whose limits were revealed during these years.[1] Despite these limits, farmer-laborites succeeded in revitalizing preexisting traditions of protest and they meaningfully addressed and contributed to the strengthened creed of statist liberalism. Third-party organizing, for all its generally weak twentieth-century record—in terms of insurgents' own stated aim to displace one of the existing major parties—continues to compel some activists and thinkers in the early twenty-first century.[2] In order to understand the genuine potential of the third-party approach in modern, industrial American society, one needs to grasp the true history of the most successful such efforts. Those efforts, which took the form of farmer-laborism, found their leaders among midwestern insurgents who claimed the mantle of "progressivism" in the 1920s and 1930s.

From the Old Progressivism to the New

In the early New Deal years, "liberalism" primarily described adherence to Franklin Roosevelt's program of economic recovery and moderate social equity, and "progressivism," which was sometimes used as a synonym for New Deal liberalism and sometimes to hark back to the programs of Woodrow Wilson and Theodore Roosevelt, most often referred to farmer-laborism, a non-Communist left-liberal set of political forces with an ambivalent relationship to the New Deal. Farmer-labor progressivism traced its ideological lineage to late nineteenth-century agrarian populism. Yet beginning in the 1920s—as small farmers entered a terrible crisis of dropping commodity prices and as labor unions reeled under a successful employer anti-union drive—farmer-laborites expressed a newly radical conviction that American capitalism was mired in a deep crisis and that so were the major political parties, which these activists believed were fundamentally corrupted by their involvement with that system. The onset of the Great Depression in 1929 merely reinforced these perceptions. It was not surprising that the farmer-labor progressives came early to this ambience of crisis, since the depression began in rural America about a decade before the great stock-market crash.

In elite political and intellectual circles, the newer meaning of progressivism vied with the seemingly less radical, older meanings of this term throughout the 1920s and in some quarters into the 1930s. In 1928 the *New Republic,* although it had begun to embrace the idea of centralized economic planning, inserted the contested idea of progressivism into its argument against the Socialist party (SP). The editors spoke for a politics that was "piecemeal, realistic, and experimental." They said, "This sort of thing is what we understand by progressivism—not a magnificently loyal adherence to some ready-made set of comprehensive principles."[3] While on one level they simply objected to doctrinaire programs in favor of more tentative steps, their resistance to the radical anti-capitalism of Norman Thomas, the SP leader, makes their idea of progressivism look like New Deal liberalism *avant le lettre.* In 1931 the writer Edmund Wilson attended a Progressive Conference in Washington, which was peopled by senators such as George Norris of Nebraska and Bronson Cutting of New Mexico—men sympathetic to farmer-laborism and known as progressives in pursuit of piecemeal reform. Apparently, President Herbert Hoover himself attended this conference, clinging to the shreds of his own long-standing reputation as a businessman's progressive—technocratic and elitist, yet humane.[4] That same year Wilson registered the shifting sands of political terminology when he issued a call for "Progressives" to "take Communism away from the Communists." Progressives as he defined them stood close enough to the far left to capture the standard of radical anti-capitalism.[5] To Hoover, this may have seemed baffling. It was not to Senator Burton K. Wheeler of Montana, who had said in 1926, "A radical is a progressive who knows what he wants." He made the left associations he imputed to the idea of progressivism yet clearer with a rhetorical question and answer: "Has the movement become a class struggle? It has always been a class struggle."[6] Wheeler was an extreme example among the crowd of western progressive senators who alternately would support and disdain the New Deal in the 1930s. The tribune of Butte miners hardened by long years of brutal class conflict in their remote state, Wheeler would support Franklin Roosevelt early on but would harbor suspicions of such an eastern dude with a moneyed background.[7]

The most important way station on the passage to farmer-labor progressivism came in 1924, when the Conference for Progressive Political

Action (CPPA) nominated Senator Robert M. LaFollette, Sr. for the presidency on a new Progressive ticket. LaFollette, with Wheeler as his running mate, did not come close to beating Calvin Coolidge but still threatened to upend the political system by getting 17 percent of the vote, to the dismal 29 percent of Democrat John W. Davis. Although the Progressives of 1924 boasted no institutional continuity with the Progressive party that Roosevelt had started in 1912, the use of the old name roused the spirits of those Bull Moosers who worked for LaFollette.[8] However, Fighting Bob's campaign was supported by Samuel Gompers, by the railway workers and other unions—who were particularly angry at corporate America at that moment—and by assorted socialists.[9] These were not the standard progressive dramatis personae of the years 1900–1917. As a public servant, LaFollette's characteristic triumph followed from the close inspection of tariff bills to see who had the fix in. His platform of 1924 was standard antimonopoly fare, with plenty of promises for farmers and workers; its radical flourish, actually conventional enough in midwestern politics, was its expressed hope for the eventual public takeover of the railroads.

That did not keep the powers that were from denouncing his platform in terms of flaming crimson. There is some merit in the view that LaFollette was a spokesman for "nineteenth-century competitive capitalism" who, frustratingly, "suffered from an inability to convince businessmen that he was in fact a conservative."[10] But the businessmen saw that, even if LaFollette looked to equality of opportunity for the petite bourgeoisie and not to a social transformation, he led a promising coalition of the near left. Who knew what might come if they took power? Moreover, the concept of the cooperative commonwealth, still so resonant with the rural and midwestern bases of LaFollette's appeal, kept alive a millennial desire for a new heaven and a new earth—even if the Kingdom was to be achieved through postmillennialist reform—that beckoned to those far more radical than the senator from Wisconsin. A candidate whose monumental integrity, accrued through a lifetime of political work, lent him great credibility, LaFollette in 1924 stands out starkly against the dismal third-party presidential exercises of the left throughout the succeeding decades, as this summary indicates:

> The 5,000,000 votes he actually received in the election—despite his stand against prohibition, his anti-war record, his opposition to the Klan, his history of serious illness, his inability to handle an extensive speaking itinerary, the poorly financed Progressive organization which received almost no money from the unions . . . the lack of press coverage and distorted reporting . . . were all a personal tribute to the senator and a sizable endorsement of his reform and isolationist views.[11]

In the 1920s, the progressive cause drew on the leftover appeal of the antimonopoly tradition but was flecked with the spirit of new insurgencies. Now, progressives were most likely genteel WASP reformers, rural populists, or labor radicals. Progressive, radical, reformer: the terms were used promiscuously. In 1926 *The Survey*, the central organ of social-work politics, asked a roundtable of eminences, "Where Are the Pre-War Radicals?"[12] The ones they were talking about—the freelancing, pro-labor reformers on liberalism's left flank—were still around; their side just wasn't winning. Their attraction to socialists and libertarians alike, borne of the wartime experience, lingered. No longer so confident as before that nongovernmental organizations provided them with a promising base of power, they yearned for partners.

A worker-farmer-reformer alliance seemed the obvious formula throughout the late 1910s and the 1920s to those upset with bipartisan conservatism—those who thought, "There is nothing between the parties, save the desire of the Republicans, who are in power, to stay in power, and the desire of the Democrats, who are not in power, to get back in power."[13] From 1915 through 1917, A. C. Townley got the Nonpartisan League of North Dakota and the Farmer-Labor party of Minnesota off the ground, providing the upper midwestern model that came close to dominating strategic thinking in the United States about insurgent politics for the next twenty years. That model's application was limited by the distinctive social and cultural situation in that region, but there weren't many models that could boast any success in winning political power. In 1920, Farmer-Laborites convened in Chicago; the Committee of Forty-Eight, a group of reformist worthies heavy on ACLU types, came and then left. The convention offered its nomination to LaFollette, who spurned it as too far left. The railway brotherhoods called together the first CPPA in 1922 as a more pragmatic affair. Forty-Eighters and Farmer-Laborites both threw in, as did radical social gospel groups such the Methodist Federation for Social Service and the Church League for Industrial Democracy (an Episcopalian group), and the Socialists too, who were down on their luck and not so keen as before on going it alone. This seemed to be the best effort possible for a progressive third party, and the CPPA tried its hand at endorsing candidates in the off-year elections. The candidates they supported did well, mainly in the Midwest, giving LaFollette a solid base for his leadership in Washington. This led inevitably to his CPPA-backed candidacy of 1924, a pivot on which the meaning of progressivism swung. That meaning was changing less because it referred to an evolving agenda than because of its shift to a clear worker-farmer appeal, the urban businessmen who supported Theodore Roosevelt and Wilson having abandoned the standard.

The Communists thought about joining the CPPA in 1923–24 but were turned aside. The Communist party (at that time called the Workers party) spent the 1920s with at least one foot in "underground" mode. It devoted much of its public effort to "boring from within" labor unions, through its Trade Union Educational League (TUEL), but it also dipped its toes into third-party politics. The CP managed to take over the Federated Farmer-Labor party and thought to maneuver the CPPA into a partnership by nominating LaFollette for president itself. But his public rebuke rid them of that notion. He wrote, "To pretend that the Communists can work with the Progressives who believe in democracy is deliberately to deceive the public. The Communists are antagonistic to the Progressive cause and their only purpose in joining such a movement is to disrupt it." (Striking a softer note, he also called Communists "persons who may be well meaning but who can be very troublesome.")[14] His analysis of the Communist party's strategy—that it sought to divide and conquer the left, rather than work sincerely in a coalition for progress—became the standard one for all anticommunist leftists and liberals. There were some non-Communists willing to take a "no enemies to the left" approach. But even in those circles, the question of who would be top dog always got in the way of unity. Communist authorities favored a united front with them in charge. John Fitzpatrick, the left-leaning president of the Chicago Federation of Labor, wanted it the other way around, saying, "[L]et's get this straight. . . . [W]e think you Communists should occupy the back seat." By 1923 the tension between these versions of a labor-left movement had erupted into conflict. Government officials unleashed a new offensive against the CP, reviving the red scare. Organized labor, led by Gompers, with Fitzpatrick and Philip Murray playing supporting roles, turned ferociously on the Communists in their midst.[15]

While the problems on LaFollette progressivism's left side were complicated by factionalism, those to its right were simple and overwhelming. During the 1920s, career reformers within the Democratic and Republican parties scored some legislative victories in Congress, but they also trimmed their sails, more fearful than before of associating with insurgent forces. They lacked sufficient electoral backing to put one of their own in the White House and to continue the sense of inexorable forward momentum that had marked reform politics in the 1910s. The decline of Roosevelt-Wilson progressivism, a decline rooted in the loss of middle- and business-class support for the concept, opened the way for the term's new meaning to coalesce. It can be argued that the 1920s were not a time of conceptual lassitude on the American left broadly defined. The Sheppard-Towner Act provided federal funding for maternal and child health services around the country until it was repealed at the end of the decade; it was a big (if temporary) progressive

achievement.[16] The hardiest of the old social justice progressives, such as Paul Kellogg and Mary van Kleeck, doggedly continued to develop plans for social insurance on a national basis, even when they found few takers among officeholders; when the New Deal came, they were ready with detailed policy blueprints (much as the right-wing Heritage Foundation was when Ronald Reagan took up residence in the White House in 1981).[17] Still, there is no denying that the 1920s were a disheartening time for most old and new progressives.

What efforts at a united front there were in the 1920s focused on the defense, which the ACLU spearheaded, of political prisoners. The most famous and consequential such case was that of Nicola Sacco and Bartolomeo Vanzetti, whose long ordeal, ending in their execution in 1927, stirred in many who tried to save the immigrant anarchists that rare anger that never passes away. Sacco and Vanzetti, as much as anyone or anything else, make sense of Wilson's 1931 "Communist" urgings to "Progressives." When John Dos Passos said "all right we are two nations," he spoke for a good many socialists and embittered liberals.[18] But they were all shouting in the wilderness while the masses were busy buying radios, a wondrous invention of the 1920s, on the installment plan. (By 1929, 30 percent of working-class families in the country owned an automobile; the portion of U.S. homes with electricity basically doubled in the 1920s, to 68 percent).[19] Dos Passos's vision of a big-money police state oppressing the common people prepared him and many others for any insurgent opportunities that might arise, but his lament for the traduced "Lincoln republic" was shared by relatively few Americans in the years before the Great Crash.[20] For these dishonored prophets, and as well for many trade unionists of varying political stripes, the lack of promise on the domestic front made for a continued investment of hope in "the Soviet experiment." It was widely known how anarchists fared under Lenin and Stalin. But foreign sympathizers with the Soviet regime viewed the complaints of such individualists differently in the context of socialism than under liberal capitalism. There, history was at least still moving forward, if bloodily.

To the Eighteenth Century

A sequential view of American society's development, the belief that the United States was passing through a fundamental transformation, had been widespread since the 1880s among radicals and reformers, and this belief emerged as the sine qua non of the second progressivism, becoming more explicit than ever amid the apparent breakdown of the capitalist system during the 1930s.[21] During that decade, the belief in the obsolescence of capitalism as it actually existed in the United States was sharpened into the belief that a "revolution" in social relations was ongoing and that a similar upheaval in politics lay in store. Depression-era expressions of this belief in social transformation showed the influence of Marxism.

But just as striking were the common references to the eighteenth century by Americans of the 1930s. The writer Matthew Josephson took strength from the examples of eighteenth-century defenders of the French Revolution. He cited Karl Marx's "vision of the continuity of man's revolutions" as "a most appealing hypothesis in the 1930's." "Marx . . . was a true heir of Humanism and the eighteenth-century Enlightenment as well as an intellectual son of the great French Revolution." The Reverend Harry F. Ward, as prominent a left-liberal activist as any in 1930s America, challenged those who celebrated earlier "transitions" to assist in the one that lay ahead. "The intellectual liberals," he wrote, "played a creative part in helping rising capitalism to smash feudalism," and Ward urged the "liberals" of his day to help usher in the rise of a new social system for the further fulfillment of their ideals. Edmund Wilson put it bluntly in 1932: "When the middle class upset the feudal landlords and the serfs and the slaves got free, we had the modern bourgeois-governed world; now there is only one more step to go." This sounded like plain Marxism. But Wilson's vision of modern history had deeper Enlightenment roots; he wrote, "I believe in progress as the eighteenth-century people did." In 1936, Joseph Freeman opened his memoir of his journey to Communist loyalties, *An American Testament*, thus: "This narrative is rooted in the belief that mankind is passing through a major transformation. The dissolution of capitalism compares in scope and significance with the origins of private property, the beginnings of Christianity, the ascendancy of the bourgeoisie." He closed his book on a similar note, recalling that by 1927 "it was becoming clear to me that there was a deep continuity between the great aspirations of the Renaissance, the French Revolution, the American Revolution, and the modern aspirations of socialism." In this way Freeman implicitly justified violent revolution as simply the price to be paid for upward progress toward increased democracy and freedom, for the fulfillment of liberal values; and he yoked past and future revolutions in a golden chain of progress. The economist George H. Soule painted a stark picture in 1934: "Just as feudalism was compelled in the end to give way to the rise of the middle classes and capitalism, so capitalism must in the end give way to the rise of the working classes and socialism."[22]

However, the politics Soule advocated in his book, *The Coming American Revolution*, did not square with this momentary projection of proletarian rule. The American tradition in which his vision of change followed was not one of working toward domination by a single class; instead it was the ambivalent tradition of Fabianism and laborism combined. This led to ambiguity and slippage in sketching the future political system when that tradition was reinvigorated by Marxism in the 1930s. Many reformers had shared in earlier decades this dynamic view of historical change, but gradually in the interwar years it became the exclusive property of liberal reformism's radical critics and radical supporters. The progressives thought the story of progress, of transformative social change, was not over yet. This brand of progressivism was not simply synonymous with the left, as opposed to liberal reformism. Only gradually, between 1924 and 1948, did "progressivism" come to be equated with the left, and even more specifically with the Popular Front—conceived as something clearly separate from liberal reform.

Those who thought competitive capitalism was finished consigned the individualist ethics associated with it to the same dustbin. All the doctrines of the classical liberals were becoming obsolete. Believers in a cooperative commonwealth always had an easier time evoking the values that would underlie the coming order than laying plans for future institutions. Even in the realm of values, however, potentially disruptive ambiguities lurked beneath the millennial chorus.

Chief among the disagreements, and one not often noted by historians, was one between true devotees of collectivism and those who sought a new social framework for the realization of liberal values. The latter group faced a challenge in distinguishing what was good in the liberal tradition—as they understood that tradition—from bad old individualism. Among activists, Frederic C. Howe spoke for this camp in 1925, but in the conclusion of *The Confessions of a Reformer*, he had a hard time explaining exactly which liberal values would carry over into the post-bourgeois world.[23] John Dewey took the lead in clarifying this matter at a theoretical level. Building upon the concept of the social self that T. H. Green, George Herbert Mead, and Dewey himself had elaborated starting in the 1880s, Dewey drew political inferences from the idea that, in a new world of industrial consolidation and big organizations in general, the individual could find freedom only through social action and through the support of a community (meaning a society and a government, as well as a more immediate community).[24] While the political implications of the idea of the social self no doubt had occurred to a good many of the new liberals for a number of years before the 1930s, having been discussed openly by British new liberals going back to Hobhouse, only now did Dewey fully develop them for a broad American audience, in *Individualism Old and New* (1930) and *Liberalism and Social Action* (1935). Ever afterward this retooled individualism served as the careful social democrat's root justification for his or her politics.[25]

In fact, Dewey went further than stating that liberal ideology needed an overhaul for new conditions. He sought to incorporate the capacity for this kind of adjustment itself into liberalism as a principle. "The fundamental defect" of nineteenth-century liberalism, he contended, was not its hedonistic epistemology or its cheery view of unregulated capitalism—though he lamented these—but rather its "lack of perception of historical relativity." He proclaimed that the new liberalism was "committed to the idea of historical relativity. It knows that the content of the individual and freedom change with time." So he tethered his historically specific new individualism to a timeless value of flexibility, although he preferred to call it "experimentalism." Dewey castigated what he saw as the "doctrinal absolutism" of those, like Herbert Hoover and other political conservatives, who were still, in the 1930s, wedded to classical liberalism. Since he could logically argue that experimentalism was the opposite of dogma, he allowed himself to conclude, happily, "The connection between historical relativity and experimental method is intrinsic."[26]

During the 1930s, the political center witnessed a battle between advocates of the new liberalism and conservatives who continued to assert that their doctrine of small government as essential to individual freedom remained the true liberalism. Unlike many on the left, Dewey continued to engage that argument occurring to his right. He called economic libertarianism a "pseudo-liberalism." He sounded most radical when, in tracing a history of liberal ideology from the eighteenth century to the twentieth, he spoke the language of class and group. "Even when words remain the same," he wrote, "they mean something very different when they are uttered by a minority struggling against repressive measures and when expressed by a group that, having attained power, then uses ideas that were once weapons of emancipation as instruments for keeping the power and wealth it has obtained." Although he was careful to shear away the specific references that might have left him open to charges of Marxist influence (charges that would have been false), he clearly was talking about the upward journey of the western bourgeoisie, from its battles against the aristocracy and the mercantilist state to its more recent position of dominance in America. For his part, the Communist leader Earl Browder pinned Dewey's philosophy to the historical epoch the professor sought to escape, calling pragmatism the outlook of "the bourgeoisie in ascendancy." This charge was a bit obscure, although Dewey himself made it clear that he sought less to escape the perspective of the business class than, like his protégé Sidney Hook, to revise and universalize it. That class threatened to make the ideal of individualism an empty shibboleth, but Dewey had no intention of letting them decide its fate. Even when analyzing the power of social classes and discerning the meaning of political ideologies in that context, he remained in the end a champion of the individual. A search for conditions of individual freedom, in the context of a community and society, was the basis for his leftward shift in the 1920s and 1930s, and he argued sincerely with conservatives over the true contemporary meaning of individual liberty.[27]

In truth it is not easy to identify new progressives who based their politics in anything but the yearning for individual freedom. What would an entirely new ethical basis for society look like? Few could, or would, say. For many it was difficult even to imagine transcending the individualistic values long identified with liberalism and the modern era of capitalism. Yet if one truly thought that a transformation in human history was underway, comparable to the transition from medieval society to modernity, then it made sense to think that a shift in society's ethical basis would accompany that change in social structure, producing something as new as individualism had been in the early modern era. The readiest candidate for this new ethics was cooperation; it was hardly a new ethos, but one that had been far from dominant in the bourgeois era. American apostles of cooperative thought in the early decades of the twentieth century emphasized consumer cooperatives almost exclusively, seeing in them "an anti-capitalist, revolutionary movement," as Albert Sonnichsen, a leading thinker in the cooperative movement, put it in 1919. The blossoming of worker-run producer and consumer cooperatives, for example in Seattle in the aftermath of the famed general strike there in 1919, for a time seemed to promise a new, alternative society. But this alleged revolutionary potential never materialized.[28] In practice, most cooperatives worked to advance the interests of individuals, mainly small economic producers, within the capitalist system. Even the most visionary farm radicals righteously demanded debt relief and price supports *for the individual farmer.* Farm "cooperatives" were purchasing and marketing cooperatives. One searches in vain for American advocates of collective farming (or at least for advocates of American collective farming). Save for a few completely apolitical, religious intentional communities, the Upper Midwest was not sprinkled with kibbutzim. The new progressivism almost always came back, often only by sheepish implication, to the individualistic justifications that Dewey forthrightly embraced. Here was the precipice at which new liberal thought stopped.

A few thinkers among the new progressives were willing to take the leap. They broke with liberalism in all its forms, rejecting individual freedom as the basis for the new society they heralded. So few even among their political comrades could go where they went that readers have passed over these farewells to individual freedom with little comment, finding it hard to understand them and recoiling from them if they did understand. Edmund Wilson hinted in this direction in his angry expression of hope, early in the Depression, for the liquidation of the dominant capitalist class:

I should be glad . . . to see a society where this class was abolished. It seems to me plain from my reading of history that the tendency of society is progressively leveling. And with this tendency I am in complete sympathy. I take no stock in the alleged precious "values" cultivated by aristocratic societies and destroyed in democratic ones. Poverty and degradation below and unearned wealth and idleness on top have been implied in all these values.[29]

His sense of what these stupid values had been was vague, and he admitted he didn't know what would replace them. He just hoped it would be something entirely new. Moreover, in Wilson's rendering of his hatred's object, he seemed to tangle together the society of the joint-stock corporation with that of the manor and the demesne. But the bitterness of his indictment made a deep impression, as did his willingness to speak of class abolition—indeed, of the "liquidation" that, as he noted wryly, was then usually the exclusive rhetorical province of American Communists.

Others who, like Wilson, sought to follow through fully on their belief in a continuing sequence of historical change, directed their fire specifically at the values of modern capitalism, at times even drawing upon the allegedly more communal values of medieval society for some of the makings of the new collective ethics. That neo-medievalism was most prominent among Roman Catholic thinkers in the interwar period, but it appeared among Protestants as well, particularly among those steeped in the social gospel. (Actually, Wilson himself, around this same time, offered an appreciative account of the Tennessee Agrarians, the most aggressive of all American anti-modernists. His reputation was not built upon the consistent or systematic character of his thought.) No Protestant activists were more important in the interwar world of the new progressives than Sherwood Eddy and Harry F. Ward, and they both sang the praises of a new collectivism that echoed the communal ways of medieval Europe. They located the pioneers of this collective life in the Soviet Union. Indeed, whether or not communism featured this particular anti-modernist flourish, the true collectivists among American new progressives were united by their genuine sympathy for communism. Theirs was not merely a belief in peaceful coexistence between American capitalism and Soviet communism, but a conviction that the Russians were leading the way down a path that, at least in some ways, Americans would and must follow.

In the fall of 1939, in the turbulent aftermath of the pact that made a temporary peace between the Soviet Union and Nazi Germany, Max Eastman rather shrewdly anatomized the appeal of socialism to American radicals, finding three different constituencies for such sympathies. One of these was comprised of those who "saw in the principles of socialism a modern version of Christian brotherhood." This Christian socialist impulse to end the "loneliness and isolation" of the modern condition aimed to replace it "with a sense of communal solidarity." It was among this Christian collectivist faction of the new progressives, which included Ward and Eddy, that anti-modernist sentiments were most likely to appear.[30]

Ward, generally explicit in his evolutionary social thought, nonetheless occasionally sounded a reactionary note that embraced the totalism of life in the Soviet Union (as he understood it). Accompanying the theme of sacrifice was that of "unity," which Ward asserted had been lost in the modern world; this premodern unity might be recaptured under socialism.

> The essential characteristic of that manner of living which in the past has in common usage been called civilization, whether it was in China, Greece or Medieval Europe, is unity. Life was within the compass of a scheme; it had unity. Its relationships were ordered; there was a universal sense of status and obligation. But this is exactly what it lacking in the Western world, and most of all in these United States. And over its absence we even exult.[31]

Manchester liberals and twentieth-century civil libertarians alike viewed the Middle Ages as "the dark ages," the emancipation from which they viewed as the watershed of freedom in human history. Therefore Ward's sarcasm is shocking: "The transition from the obligation of status to freedom of contract is hailed as a great step forward. Is not the road to the top always open for the most able? Let every one look out for himself and the common weal will automatically be taken care of! . . . The actual outcome of course is mostly chaos and conflict." Many social critics would have agreed with this observation, but few would have added, as he did, that "in the high days of Medieval Europe feudalism gave everybody his place and duty in the common life for which they all lived."[32] What liberal could actually suggest a wish that the shift "from status to contract" be reversed? Some may have suspected as much of Eddy, the editor of the Protestant-pacifist journal the *World Tomorrow*, who escorted many groups of American liberals and intellectuals to the Soviet Union to show them the future. He lamented the "philosophic decadence and disintegration" of the West, in contrast to the unity that had existed under feudalism, and he hailed in Soviet Russia "the experience of almost a whole people living under a unified philosophy of life."[33]

Since the Enlightenment tradition of deriding medieval and "oriental" darkness drew strongly on anti-Catholic sentiment and found a home in America mainly among Protestants, it was doubly unusual for these religious Protestants to invoke this anti-modernist radicalism. As had William Morris, Ward and Eddy projected a vision of a holistic life, marked by certain "duty" and shared vision, both backward into premodern society and forward into the socialism of the future—and, indeed, they directed the same vision across the sea, into Russia. Karl Marx had predicted that communism would integrate the holism of precapitalist societies with the freedoms made possible by modern political and economic revolutions. Those in this tradition saw in socialism movement both forward and backward, the achievement of things as yet unknown and at the same time the end of the anomie that so many theorists of modern life bemoaned. Such thinkers sketched an ideal society that would synthesize the different phases of human history (the medieval thesis of community, the modern antithesis of individualism) into a higher and more spiritually satisfying form.

Needless to say, the audience for neo-medievalism in the twentieth-century United States was small, Depression or no Depression. American admirers of the Soviet Five-Year Plan often expressed a longing for a common vision that might marshal the efforts of a demoralized society, and many of them envied Soviet citizens in this limited respect. But, typically, progressive attraction to the Soviet Union took the form simply of a prosaic call for planning. Indeed, the stronger note in Harry Ward's own advocacy at home was the "necessity to complete the democratic revolution" in America, not an inclination to look backward.[34] This is not to say that there was no constituency for true collectivism at all in the United States. There had been one at least since Edward Bellamy's *Looking Backward* (1888) inspired middle-class Americans around the country to set up Nationalist Clubs to plump for an "industrial army." But in the interwar period, outside of religious circles, that was a constituency that the Communists had largely to themselves.

FDR and the Senate Progressives

Franklin Roosevelt, for all the conservatism of the balanced-budget platform on which he first ran for the presidency, was strongly associated with Wilsonian progressivism and with New York State's regulatory program, and his run for the White House gave hope to many reformers that the major parties might discover new courage in making policy. The second incarnation of progressivism had been germinating among farmer-laborites; now it competed with the last breaths of the term's older meaning. In the months before the general election in 1932, George Norris and Frederic Howe organized the National Progressive League to voice the support of old progressives for Roosevelt. Norris, as an old Bull Moose and a Republican progressive, was especially important. The next time around, in 1936, he and Robert LaFollette, Jr. (who had replaced his father as a U.S. senator) formed the Progressive National Committee (at Roosevelt's request) to serve the same function. This group had old progressives such as Paul Kellogg, the editor of the leading social-work and reform journal *The Survey*, on its letterhead and involved other familiar names such as Frank Walsh. But it was funded by the United Mine Workers of America (UMWA), which was "a good indication that the word 'progressive' now denoted reformers of a different type" than previously.[35] In addition to labor leaders such as John L. Lewis of the UMWA and Sidney Hillman of the textile workers, "Young Turks" of the 1930s such as Maury Maverick of Texas, Thomas Amlie of Wisconsin, and Fiorello LaGuardia of New York were prominent in the group. These politicos represented a coalition loyal to Roosevelt that drew its strength from organized labor, urban workers, and anguished rural folk nourished by decades of militancy.

However, on Capitol Hill the terms "progressive" and "independent" attached most strongly to a group of midwestern and western senators, mentioned above, that included Norris, the LaFollettes, and Wheeler. Intellectuals and activists, including some of the members of the U.S. House of Representatives mentioned above, looked to these senators as prospective leaders of a farmer-labor political movement that would be based primarily in the Upper Midwest and that harked back to LaFollette, Sr.'s campaign of 1924. These activists, who sought a non-Marxist political movement to the New Deal's left, and such Senate progressives were preoccupied with demonstrating their "independence," meaning independence from the Democratic party, which they tended to view as a corrupt party unsuited as a vehicle for their hopes. (As explained below, in Wisconsin, which was, along with Minnesota, one of the two main hotbeds of this activity, it meant independence from the Republicans, the party in which the LaFollettes and their followers had made their home.) The Senate progressives often gave Roosevelt only grudging support since they thought he never went far enough. To take one example, Roosevelt's emergency banking bill, which was passed in the beginning of his term of office, had sailed through Congress with only seven senators voting against it: five of these were LaFollette, Jr., Edward Costigan of Colorado, Henrik Shipstead of Minnesota, Gerald P. Nye of North Dakota, and William Borah of Idaho. They favored more radical action, either a nationalization of the country's financial system or at least the establishment of a national bank.[36] They would never see such things come to pass.

The Senate "insurgents," as they sometimes are known, may have pushed Roosevelt to more aggressive stances on particular policy issues. The western progressive senators supported Roosevelt on key roll-call votes less than half the time in the years 1933–38, which was more than very conservative Democrats did, but often, as with the banking bill, they criticized Roosevelt from the left. Their support for liberal measures was always possible, but they were willing to go their own way, so it was always worth the time for the administration to seek their support. The most notable instance when these senators sought to influence Roosevelt came on 15 May 1935, when the most prominent of them (LaFollette, Norris, Wheeler, Costigan, and Hiram Johnson of California) joined their allies in the cabinet—Harold Ickes and Henry Wallace, the two former Republican progressives in high administration positions—and Felix Frankfurter to confront the president together to ventilate their frustration over his weakness in pressing their reform agenda on Capitol Hill. The U.S. Chamber of Commerce recently had gone on the attack against Roosevelt's program, and the progressives urged the president to stop trying to woo business leaders. This meeting may have fortified in Roosevelt a new determination to press a liberal agenda, propelling him into the historic initiatives—Social Security, the Wagner Act, the Public Utilities Holding Act, and the Wealth Tax—that followed and became known as the "Second New Deal." This was very much the influence of a group of insiders, depending on the same outstanding characteristics of personal leadership that had marked the Senate progressives for many years before this. It did not reflect the democratic pressure of new and large political forces, which was what the architects of a left-right realignment envisioned. Officials in the administration continued to view congressional progressives as brilliant but somewhat unreliable freelancers, not as delegates of such broader forces. Even Rexford Tugwell, generally seen as a left-leaning member of the administration, expressed frustration with them, saying, "I think it can fairly be said that they cannot lead, they will not follow, and they refuse to cooperate."[37]

The Senate independents lost their independent footing in the late 1930s, some of them becoming loyal New Dealers and some drifting to the right and finding new comfort in the Republican party whence most of them had come. Roosevelt's so-called court-packing scheme of 1938 caused an enormous controversy in Washington and aroused concerns about enlarged presidential power among these lions of the Senate. Just as important in the advancing process of alienation were Roosevelt's moves toward involvement in the European war, a prospect that appalled many in this group. Wheeler, for one, moved sharply right, flirting with the less savory elements in the movement against intervention and, as an isolationist and a severe anticommunist in the years after World War II, becoming a fan of Joseph McCarthy. Others, likewise recalling how Woodrow Wilson had helped kill the first progressive movement by stirring the nation's martial spirits, saw themselves opposing Roosevelt on the war from his left. Those who stayed most loyal to Roosevelt and lived to see the 1940s, Norris and LaFollette, found the ground cut out from under them, losing their seats as they kept the Democrats at arm's length while campaigning as New Dealers.[38] The political extinction of their species makes it seem odd that anyone once saw the Senate progressives as potential leaders for a national ascendancy of the left. Yet farmer-labor activists in the 1930s saw other potential sources of leadership; these lay in the states of the Midwest, not in Washington.

The Farmer-Labor Option

Paul Douglas took the lead in forming the League for Independent Political Action (LIPA) in 1928 and 1929, and brought Dewey on board as chairman. Echoing many previous American reformers with large ambitions, the LIPA stated early on that it hoped it would become a kind of "American Fabian Society." Its roster of officers replicated the LaFollette coalition of five years earlier: in addition to Dewey and Douglas, the list included Howard Y. Williams, a Minnesota farmer-laborite and a Methodist minister who preached the social gospel; James Maurer, a labor Socialist; Zona Gale, a novelist involved with the American Union Against Militarism, by then a moribund group; and W. E. B. DuBois. DuBois was exceptional in this context; black activists were not a regular presence in any "progressive" formations in the 1910s and 1920s, and this would not change until the second half of the 1930s. Other left-liberal worthies such as the redoubtable Oswald Villard and assorted Socialists including Reinhold Niebuhr and Norman Thomas were involved, too. The Christian left was well represented by, in addition to Williams, Sherwood Eddy, Harry Ward, and Kirby Page. The LIPA had no luck in building bridges to the old progressives still ensconced in the U.S. Senate, but House members such as Amlie and LaGuardia were readier to bolt the two-party system. Beginning in 1933, their resident publicists were Alfred Bingham and Selden Rodman, the champions of economic planning and political democracy at the journal *Common Sense*. That magazine's statist tendencies were echoed in the elevation of Edward Bellamy and Thorstein Veblen, apostles of planning by the state and by a soviet of engineers respectively, to the status of "patron saints" within the LIPA.[39]

Theoretically, the LIPA made one essential point: the American capitalist system was a failure and had to be replaced. Since both major political parties refused to recognize this essential fact, the logical corollary was that a new political formation had to lead the way to a new, workable economic system. Howard Williams averred in 1930 that the Democracy was merely the "false face of Republicanism," and the advent of the Roosevelt candidacy two years later did not change his mind. Considering Roosevelt as against Al Smith, Williams judged, "Neither of these men are [*sic*] real progressives," and while his midwestern roots lent an ambiguity to his use of this tortured term, he meant to indicate their continuing faith in politics as usual.[40] Those involved with the LIPA, understandably, eschewed labels, both for their politics and for the system they hoped would replace the collapsed house they and all other Americans inhabited.

The only label they even sometimes embraced, given its suitably "American" past and its nice ambiguity, was the cooperative commonwealth. "Production for use" was a warmly embraced slogan. Their vision was one of collective empowerment and rational administration, in place of individualist ethics and economic dysfunction. "We the masses of the people, must rise up and win economic and political control. We must organize to establish a new social order, a scientifically planned system" whose design would aim at satisfying "human needs," not at making profits. This was how the statement of goals read at the conclusion of the conference that the LIPA convened in Chicago in 1933 and that ended with the formation of the Farmer-Labor Political Federation (FLPF), which was intended to be a national force.[41] Who would do the planning and whether "control" by "the people" would be confined to election day were questions answered only in the fine print, if at all. Following in the well-trod path of agrarian agitation, some of those who went under the farmer-labor standard in the 1930s would promote the activities of producers' cooperatives quite seriously, especially in Minnesota. But virtually no one seriously proposed this as the model for the entire U.S. economy. The "independent" vision was clearly that of a "mixed economy." Whether this would have qualified as the end of American capitalism as it was known in 1933 is a question with no definite answer. It certainly would not have spelled the liquidation of the profit motive as a force in society.

Alfred Bingham and others associated with the LIPA believed that a truly promising radicalism in the United States of the 1930s would aim at a middle-class audience, perhaps at a consumer constituency. They often used "consumer" and "middle class" as synonyms.[42] They believed a proletarian movement would hold little appeal even to proletarians. It was a commonplace among production-for-use advocates, from Bingham to Upton Sinclair, that American workers identified themselves as "middle class." This was part of what they meant when they spoke of an "American" or "native American" radicalism. Sinclair, a longtime Socialist and founder of the End Poverty in California (EPIC) movement that captured control of the Democratic party in that state in 1934, wrote, "Ours is not a working-class country. Our workers act and speak and dress middle-class." Thus radicals needed to speak a special "American language."[43] Clearly what this meant was that Marxism was unwelcome; Bingham and Sinclair felt certain that this tradition, with its language of proletariat and bourgeoisie, would seem alien to Americans of all classes and meet with firm rejection.

This fear of seeming alien indicated the second meaning of the call for an "American" radicalism. This imperative linked Marxism to immigrants from eastern and southern Europe. The predominantly white Anglo-Saxon Protestant activists of the LIPA might have recoiled from a suggestion that they were nativists or that they bowed to nativist prejudices abroad in the land. But in fact they embraced the nativist thesis that political traditions imported from Great Britain and from other lands populated with "Nordic" and "Alpine" stock were acceptably American, but that those associated with other nations were not eligible for naturalization. When Bingham commented that the movement the LIPA was helping to build represented a "cross section of the native American radical movement without the benefit of the European ideas," he clearly indicated his primary concern with keeping Marxism, in which he didn't believe and which he considered a political nonstarter in the United States, out of the movement. At the same time, when he spoke of "native Americans" he wasn't talking about American Indians. This was both a reference to ideological content and a piece of ethnic commentary. In his widely noted book *Insurgent America: The Revolt of the Middle Classes* (1935), Bingham, using a phrase to chill the blood of cultural pluralists, called for a "one-hundred-percent American" radicalism. Giving full vent to his traditionalist gambit, he wrote that this politics would be one of "defending the home, the family, the church and the nation," one built on "patriotism" and "puritanism," abjuring violence and revolution and looking to a peaceful democratic transfer of power to a new regime. This went considerably further than most of Bingham's comrades, but it reflects the importance—fifteen years after the post–World War I red scare and ten years after U.S. borders had been all but sealed to immigrants from southern and eastern Europe—attached in many precincts of the American left to the project of developing a nativist radicalism. It was a project that would live on.[44]

The last element in the "independent" movement's call for an "American" radicalism was a desire to keep the Communists out, which was a practical matter, separate from the question of Marxism. No one better illustrates this concern than Tom Amlie. A person of universally recognized intelligence, learning (largely self-educated), and leadership qualities, he was usually seen as the most important elected official among those actively committed to national third-party organizing. It was Amlie, with his tall bearing and fiery speech, who would galvanize the meeting in 1935 that launched the actual attempt to create such a party, discussed below. First elected to Congress as a Republican from Wisconsin, he thereafter ran as a Progressive. He followed in the path of the Norwegian American political tradition that accounted for much of the strength of the new progressive movement in the Upper Midwest during the interwar period. Contrasting himself with Alfred Bingham's rather elitist perspective and solicitation of middle-class support, Amlie said, "Emotionally, I still continue to live in the miserable frame building where I was born on a North Dakota farm." Politically, some changes lay ahead for him. But his distrust of the CP is a striking and consistent feature of his career. Not a red-baiter, he abstained from the anticommunism that sought to stigmatize or punish Communists. Yet he saw no possibility of working with Communists in a true coalition. He thought Communists were sectarians bent on control of anything they touched. They, he said in 1936, "are out of sympathy with our program and philosophy, and . . . seek admittance to our councils not to work with us toward the ends which we seek, but to gain control of our organization for their own purposes." At that time the CP had moved to its Popular Front stance, but Amlie wasn't buying it. While some figures in this third-party movement, especially Howard Williams, at that time became willing to work with Communists, Amlie and most of the other LIPA figures did not. This dominant faction succeeded in pushing the question of the CP's involvement into the background of the third-party movement's strategic work for some time, but not permanently; in the late 1930s it became a point of fierce conflict, especially in Minnesota.[45]

The use of the farmer-labor label made clear that the organizers thought that their best option, certainly given these requirements of their ideological position, was to play the midwestern gambit. In the early 1930s it quickly became obvious that the LIPA brain trust could locate no other vehicle for its third-party hopes than a radicalized version of LaFollette progressivism. As Amlie said bluntly, "There is nothing else available." The broad, national middle-class constituency they had dreamed of, reminiscent of progressivism's support, was not to be found. The platform of the conference in 1933 championed aid to workers, farmers, and consumers; advocated a state takeover of the nation's financial system as well as utilities; sought civil rights for all; and spoke for international peace and against imperialism (including U.S. power in Asia and Latin America). On the one hand, Norman Thomas complained that they were merely "rewriting the Socialist platform of 1932"; on the other hand, A. J. Muste, an independent labor radical with a growing following, left the LIPA in 1931 because he was dissatisfied with

its grab-bag appeal to "diverse economic interests." Indeed, the LIPA endorsed Thomas for president in 1932 and subsequently sought to move beyond his party's appeal by dropping the s-word while retaining his agenda.[46] Still, it wasn't only his agenda. The similarities to LaFollette's 1924 platform are striking and indicate the stability of the left-liberal agenda throughout the passage to the new progressivism in interwar America, bridging both sides of the cataclysm of 1929.

At bottom, the LIPA and the FLPF were part of a movement for political "realignment." That became the watchword of left-liberal politics in the United States into the 1960s. It meant that the progressives or liberals would concentrate their forces in one party and induce the conservatives and reactionaries to congregate in another. Instead of each faction fighting a two-stage war for victory in any political season, first contending with its ideological foes in a party primary or convention and then, if successful, moving to the general election campaign, each ideological tendency would have its partisan vehicle, presenting the general public with a simple and clear choice. As Ickes put it, "I'd like to see all the progressives together and all the conservatives together. Then you'd always be facing your enemy and not wondering what was happening behind your back."[47] Students of the U.S. political system long have considered 1936 to be a year of political realignment. But only some of the new progressives of the 1930s considered it the realignment they had worked for. There are two different meanings to the concept of realignment. The "realigning election" of 1936, like that of 1896 when McKinley defeated Bryan, redistributed regional voting patterns into a stable and new balance of power between the two major parties. Such realignments do not necessarily sort out left and right so that this ideological conflict coincides with a partisan divide, and the results of 1936 certainly did not. The resulting "New Deal coalition" continued to house a legion of extremely conservative white southerners, and in fact it brought them to a level of power within the national government not matched by that constituency since the days before the Civil War. Urban bosses including Frank Hague of Jersey City, a bane to the ACLU's liberals, also figured large in the Roosevelt coalition.

What did the new progressives of the 1930s really want from their ideological realignment? Drawing upon the store of demands that insurgents had built up from the days of the Grange through to the Coolidge era, they embraced long-standing radical farm demands for the nationalization of national transport and banking as well as less ambitious reform proposals to benefit farmers and wage earners. The ambiguities of their vision of economic change were as real as their commitment to the vision of historical dynamism. By this time, it was not unusual in the global history of social-democratic movements to mask the this-worldliness of a militant interest-group agenda with revolutionary rhetoric that was destined to go unfulfilled. European socialists had addressed this discrepancy head-on some time before, as a result of agitation by Eduard Bernstein and his "revisionist" followers. The farmer-labor economic agenda was typically so specific—focused on raising commodity prices and bringing debt relief to the farmer, and secondarily calling for collective bargaining rights for labor—as to render it susceptible to cooptation by a state willing to spend some money and to curb some of the traditional prerogatives of employers.[48] Moreover, the rhetorical insistence on the primacy of economics masked the real strategic priority of politics.

The elections of 1934 marked big gains for Democrats in Congress (breaking with the historic tendency of the victorious party in the prior presidential election to lose legislative seats in the off-year elections), and for the small left-leaning bloc on Capitol Hill. In March of 1935, a group of left-liberal representatives and senators met in Washington to decide on a legislative agenda they would share and to talk about caucusing in order to push it forward. They also wanted to work for a political realignment. Many of them were in the thick of the farmer-labor movement, and the FLPF had encouraged the meeting. Maury Maverick and Gerald Boileau of Wisconsin were the ringleaders at this time. At that point there were seven Independent Progressive representatives from Wisconsin and three Farmer-Labor representatives from Minnesota. Some fifteen to twenty Democrats and half that number of Republicans from the House also were considered likely members of such a caucus, along with eight to ten senators, almost all of them, such as Lynn Frazier and Henrik Shipstead, from the Upper Midwest. Reports of this group's cohesiveness vary. Still, what became known as the "liberal bloc" in the House emerged from this effort and included others such as Amlie, Ernest Lundeen of Minnesota, Usher Burdick of North Dakota, and Vito Marcantonio of New York.

At the most, the officeholders involved were advertising their availability as a congressional leadership group that might support any political formation that would lead the way to realignment. At the least, they championed Roosevelt's liberal initiatives and reminded him that he had a left flank to keep happy. Some, like Robert LaFollette, Jr., routinely played Roosevelt off against the independent progressive forces to gain as much in the way of patronage and power as they could. Those who attended the caucus's meetings agreed on the need for the federal regulation of the credit and currency systems and for higher taxes on inheritances, gifts, stocks, and bonds. They also wanted a guarantee of cost-plus returns to farmers for their produce and other benefits for hard-hit farmers and agreed on the need for a living wage, a shorter work week, and collective bargaining rights for workers. They called for social insurance against unemployment, illness, and old age. Like virtually all liberal and leftist groups at this time, the caucus favored a neutralist foreign policy, one it thought could be assured by a pledge by the government to tax away war profits in the unfortunate event of a conflict. And, most radical and echoing long-standing demands of agrarian radicals, the caucus demanded a government takeover of monopolies and natural resources.[49] While some of these public servants were cool to the idea of third-party organizing that had propelled the leaders of this caucus to Washington, few (if any) of them were closed to the prospect of following Roosevelt's leadership, if he would absorb more of their agenda. Others who remained out of office and out of Washington remained more certain that no matter how good Roosevelt's intentions might be, he could not bring his party along to the left. Dewey spoke for the stand-fast activists, arguing that the "only way to preserve as well as extend whatever is good in Rooseveltian measures is the formation of a strong, united, radical third party."[50] At this point, with the success of the independents in getting some of their people into office, these two strategic tendencies began to compete among the new progressives: one was open for business, highly pragmatic, and amenable to an (almost) "no enemies to the left" policy; the other was firm in its conclusion that the American political system needed a true upheaval if realignment were to occur. These two tendencies would ebb and flow among progressives as the dramatic election campaign of 1936 wore on. To a large degree, this became a debate between a midwestern tendency steeped in the agrarian revolt and a northeastern movement anchored in industrial labor unions.

At mid-decade, progressive advocates of a third-party realignment thought they saw materials around the country ready to be formed into the nucleus of a new party. A few of these independent political organizations were far more substantial than the rest, and not all were equally as enthusiastic about breaking with Roosevelt.[51] There were numerous potential adherents of similar organizations in other states, including Montana, where Wheeler and Representative Jerry O'Connell were aligned with the new progressive forces, and in Idaho, where Senator William Borah sometimes was. These forces were concentrated in the Upper Midwest and in the West and the Northwest, often in old hotbeds of the populist movement and Bryanism. The FLPF engineered a call for a conference in July 1935 to organize the national party. It was signed by Amlie and current U.S. Representatives Marcantonio, who ran on the American Labor party (ALP) ticket in New York, Lundeen, and Byron Scott of California. Sounding the now familiar themes of realignment activists, they said the "old order" was collapsing and the crying need was to "substitute planning for chaos." They invited everyone who wished for realignment to come—except for the Communists, who were changing their tune about coalition building with moderate socialists and progressives. The CP's old image as mischief-makers held fast.[52]

The meeting, again in Chicago, drew over three hundred activists from over thirty states; while the first total was not very impressive, the latter number gave heart to farmer-laborites because it suggested that their effort might draw on a geographically broad network of organizers. The attendees chose the name American Commonwealth Political Federation (ACPF) for their organization of state-level organizations, pointedly eschewing the farmer-labor label in a clear effort to transcend the movement's current rural and midwestern constituencies. But the choice of leadership, which necessarily reflected the organization's areas of strength, reinforced the regional accent of the effort. Amlie became the chairman of the ACPF, and John H. Bosch, the head of the Minnesota Farm Holiday Association, became the vice chairman. Howard Williams became the national organizer, and Lundeen and Congressman George Schneider of Wisconsin went on the executive committee. It was here that Alfred Bingham commented that the ACPF was a "cross section of the native American radical movement." No doubt Bingham knew that the "new immigrants" and their children, who filled the cities and factories of the country, had to be approached with some success if the ACPF were to achieve its goals. But the federation's roots in midwestern agrarianism—and the success of independent progressivism in Depression-era California bore no small debt to the large influx of midwesterners that state witnessed at the time—and the preoccupation among the new movement's thinkers with maintaining its "American" quality reinforced one another and foreshadowed its difficulties in breaking through to the third-party status it coveted. Bingham himself was selected as the ACPF's executive secretary, but this did little to include the East. Frank Rosenblum, the vice president of the Amalgamated Clothing Workers of America, a politically ambitious union, also joined the executive committee. He was the only prominent liaison to the labor movement.

The Vanguard: Minnesota and Wisconsin

The ACPF's disappointment, as 1936 wore on, had been foreshadowed by the flexible and opportunistic behavior of Farmer-Labor party (FLP) leaders in Minnesota since its breakthrough in 1930, when it elected a governor, Floyd B. Olson, for the first time. This party supposedly provided the chief model for the national movement. Olson gained a reputation as the most radical governor in the country, and his early death from cancer in 1936 is still looked on by some as a major blow to the hopes for social democracy in the Depression era. While Olson's ambitions may have matched those of his most ardent admirers, his radicalism was somewhat elusive. He proclaimed it in 1934 in a memorable speech in which he accepted his party's endorsement for reelection. Presaging what would become a rhetorical commonplace, he contrasted radicalism with liberalism, saying, "Now, I am frank to say that I am not a liberal. . . . I am a radical in the sense that I want a definite change in the system. I am not satisfied with tinkering. I am not satisfied with patching." From the other side of this rhetorical divide, Rexford G. Tugwell had defined it differently the year before. He had written,

> The essential contrast between the liberal and the radical view of the tasks which lie before us is that liberalism requires . . . experimenting and that radicalism rejects it for immediate entry on the revolutionary tactic. Liberals would like to rebuild the station while the trains are running; radicals prefer to blow up the station and forgo service until the new structure is built. Their ultimate objectives may not be so very different. . . . But there is all the difference in the world in the ways of achieving what is hoped for.

Olson rejected such definitions. No bomb thrower, the governor immediately followed his declaration of radicalism with his assurance that the change he desired would be "orderly . . . sane," "constructive" and "gradual." But this evolutionary perspective was not necessarily a retreat either from radical goals or from the third-party approach. Olson's avowed gradualism left unanswered questions about his actual aims and his strategic thought.[53]

As to his goals, the governor implied that he favored some comprehensive, systematic change, but he never offered such a vision, even while he signed into law important reform measures, one of which initiated the beginnings of an old-age insurance system and several of which strengthened the rights of organized labor. Olson stuck to the concept of a cooperative commonwealth but tested the winds regularly to detect how much the electorate desired, or indeed would tolerate, talk of public ownership. The FLP's platform of 1934 became famous for its call for the government of Minnesota to take over all manner of major economic enterprises, going far beyond the familiar discussion of utilities and railroads, and its endorsement of production-for-use cooperatives along the lines Upton Sinclair laid out in his EPIC campaign in California that same year. Olson's close advisers were badly scared, and the governor quickly embarked on a damage-control effort during which he repeatedly disavowed the goal of a government-directed economy. Olson said that the FLP desired "a cooperative commonwealth in which enterprises will be carried out cooperatively by organizations of producers and consumers. . . . essentially . . . private business, but . . . business carried on for mutual aid and not avaricious profit," no doubt seeming to many Minnesotans merely to describe long-standing practices by dairy farmers and others in their state.[54]

This backtracking made Olson's repudiation of liberalism seem like a rhetorical sop to the left-wingers who had gathered to hear his convention speech. Then again, he tacked sharply to the left in 1935, with an article in *Common Sense* affirming what he termed farmer-laborism's "challenge to the basic claims and principles of capitalism," specifically its badly unequal distribution of wealth and the underlying principle of "*production for private profit.*" Olson wrote of "*the necessity of production for use,*" instead. The ideal of a cooperative commonwealth might be called "vague and nebulous," he conceded, but he insisted that "it is nevertheless an attack on the fundamental concepts of the present system." Going yet further, seeming to embrace what he had rejected in the heat of an election campaign the previous year, Olson declared, "*A third party must arise and preach the gospel of government and collective ownership of the means of production and distribution.*" This struck a different note from the one he had sounded in a debate in 1934 with the British Marxist John Strachey, when the Minnesotan embraced the title of "opportunist," defining this happily as "one who will use any agency he finds at hand—whether he believes in the entire program—to translate into action such part of his own program as is possible."[55] Now, a year later, those wishing to bid adieu to the Democracy took heart. The article in *Common Sense* was everything they could hope for, and it was committed to print in the public domain. But this rhetorical salient was as far as the Minnesota governor would venture. Such radical statements, coincidentally or not, most commonly issued from his pen in odd-numbered years. In retrospect they are most persuasively interpreted as an effort to push the New Deal in a more courageously reformist direction, partly by stoking the fires, during nonelection years, of the third-party forces whose strength would do the most to achieve that goal.

It was no wonder Olson so admired Franklin Roosevelt: both were masters at placating supporters on all sides. In 1932, Howard Williams, the leftist Minnesotan who had long been active in third-party organizing, sought to become chairman of the Minnesota party's statewide election campaigns, but Olson vetoed the pending hire. During the famous Teamsters' strike in Minneapolis in 1934, which led to repeated violence and several deaths as workers and their supporters squared off in the city's streets against a business-organized militia and police, Olson had to tread a fine line between supporting labor—a major part of his coalition—and "maintaining law and order," meaning protecting the safety and convenience of the general public. (While he incurred the anger of some of the Trotskyist leadership of the strikers, overall Olson pulled off the tightrope walk successfully.) In 1936, Olson personally disrupted Williams's efforts on behalf of the ACPF to build toward a national third-party campaign, entering a planning meeting unannounced to state flatly that he opposed this course. As was widely understood by the fall of that year, Olson and Roosevelt had worked out a deal whereby the Minnesota Democrats either would stand down or would receive no support from the White House in statewide races. This left the FLP to reap the New Deal's benefits as the sole viable alternative to Republican conservatism in the state; in return the Farmer-Labor leadership would support Roosevelt in the presidential race. "In Minnesota *hands off*," Roosevelt wrote in a note to James Farley, his national patronage supervisor. The Minnesota party's left wing, based in the major cities of Minneapolis, St. Paul, and Duluth, was substantial, but it could not alter matters; the course of events in the 1930s demonstrated that its links to power came not through its own popularity with the public, but through that of pragmatic spokesmen such as Olson and Shipstead.[56]

Even so, Olson's victories in 1930, 1932, and 1934 plotted a descending line of popularity, and he won the last of these elections with a plurality. The rural component of third-party insurgency was on the wane, as the hand of the conservative American Farm Bureau Federation and its affiliates grew very much stronger under the pacifying effects of New Deal payments and loans. In March 1933, six counties in Iowa were under martial law; a year later, they were refinancing mortgages at lowered interest rates through the new Farm Credit Administration and trading worthless crops for "loans" (whose repayment they could forgo so long as they let the federal government keep the produce) from the Commodity Credit Corporation.[57] By election time in 1934, many of those who had held onto their farms were ready to move back to their accustomed standard of conservative Republicanism. In Olson's last election in that year he actually lost the rural vote, maintaining only the old populist stronghold in northwestern Minnesota's Red River Valley. Elmer Benson was elected governor of Minnesota in 1936 in a victory bigger than any of Olson's, and Benson's Popular Front politics (featuring a clear welcome to Communists) gave heart to many leftists in his state. But he benefited from the Olson-Roosevelt deal and Roosevelt's landslide, and the next election cycle would show his popularity to be a questionable one.[58]

As 1936 progressed the base of support for a national third-party effort proved thin even in Minnesota, which had been envisioned as the base for such a national drive by enthusiasts such as Howard Williams. He could muster only eighty-one attendees at the meeting that formally invited the Minnesota Farmer-Labor party to issue a call for an ACPF-based presidential bid. That the FLP was not moving on its own to issue such a call and needed to be called upon to issue this call by an ad hoc assembly of activists, said a lot in itself, and the idea died on the vine after that. Bingham and Nathan Fine, a scholarly expert on third-party efforts who was also involved in the ACPF, had warned Williams that he should cancel these plans, but Williams had moved ahead. Now, leaders of the ACPF realized that they would have to console themselves with working for independent congressional candidates. Amlie charged that Williams's undeterred efforts were "apparently to be under the domination of the Communists," who now, under the banner of the Popular Front, were working as Farmer-Laborites in the North Star State. Embittered, Williams concluded that Olson was "out for himself to build his own personal machine and win elections regardless of movements or principles."[59] While there is an element of wisdom in this harsh judgment, the larger truth is that Olson and others, despite their disavowals of patchwork liberalism, saw much in common between their state-level efforts and the New Deal.

Many of the "third-party" advocates in these states really were trying to build true second parties. They, along with the Non-Partisan League in North Dakota and the LaFollette Progressive party in Wisconsin, formed an unusually strong "independent" movement because they emerged in the Upper Midwest, long a one-party fiefdom for the Republicans (a legacy of the U.S. Civil War). Prior to the New Deal, the Democratic party did not appear to farmer-laborites as a viable framework for a new progressive politics. There were plenty of genuine leftists among them who took the cooperative commonwealth seriously and were really socialists (some had been SP activists), and their parties' programs and legislative achievements were far-reaching in some respects. They effected on their part of the map a political situation that approximated that which advocates of left-right realignment hoped for on a nationwide basis. So it was logical for ACPF activists to look here for the spark that would spread a prairie fire across the country. But overall—if one considers what voting constituencies and elected officials seemed to desire, and not just the goals of the most articulate and ideologically self-aware spokespersons of a political movement—farmer-laborism was a kind of New Deal progressivism unbound, as if the most liberal and democratic of the national administration's impulses did not have to contend with powerful conservative forces within their own party. In these states farmer-laborism was a movement with a broad constituency and not simply, as was the case with the ACPF, one of devoted thinkers and activists. Ironically, because of the movement's successes in the Upper Midwest, it became less likely than activists such as Williams and Amlie had thought to lead a national challenge to Roosevelt's "tinkering" and "patching." Some thought that this was sheer opportunism among officeholders such as Olson and the LaFollette brothers, who could use the unrealized threat of a national third party to their personal career advantage. But a more powerful inhibiting consequence of state-level success was the realization among such leaders that if they took their "independent" politics national, they ran a dire risk of leaving their voters behind. This was just what happened to Governor Philip LaFollette of Wisconsin when he finally made up his mind to initiate a national third party in 1938.[60]

By this time the moment had passed. The LaFollette brothers and their associates had formed an independent Progressive party in Wisconsin in 1934, and in that year and 1936 they too had enjoyed great success in the general election. Even more than the Minnesota Farmer-Laborites, the Wisconsin Progressives relied on a rural constituency that was up in arms in the early 1930s, its anger cresting by mid-decade. The LaFollettes added to their column the strength of urban wards in Milwaukee and other cities along Lake Michigan at that time, working with Socialists who had learned the arts of plain-and-simple politics in the state's largest city. When Philip LaFollette was turned out of the governor's office—for the second time—in 1938, it was most of all because his ticket had bled votes in the farm areas and smaller towns that had given him and his father before him their political base.[61]

The LaFollettes' commitment to an independent farmer-labor movement was highly questionable, in Senator Robert LaFollette's case because of personal bonds of affection with Franklin Roosevelt and a desire to be part of the New Deal coalition in Washington, and in Philip LaFollette's case because of his ideological uncertainty and stark opportunism. Robert was a reluctant partner in the formation of the Wisconsin Progressive party, and he led the way in organizing the Progressive National Committee to support Roosevelt in 1936. (Of the 150 attendees at the committee's main meeting, perhaps 20 were from Wisconsin, including Amlie and Schneider.) Philip, meanwhile, continually dallied with national third-party organizers at home while privately offering expressions of fealty to Roosevelt. On one occasion he opined that "a real leftist party" was what was needed on a national basis; at another moment he averred, in fine exceptionalist fashion, that class politics was irrelevant in America, because of the absence of a feudal past. When the organizing meeting of the ACPF occurred in July 1935 the LaFollettes shunned it—as Olson sent cordial greetings but stayed away—and Robert LaFollette derided it as "largely a group of crackpots who cannot possibly get anywhere in the formation of an important and new party movement." Later that year, Socialists, Farmers' Holiday Association members, and Wisconsin Federation of Labor activists further complicated the Wisconsin political scene by forming the Wisconsin Farmer-Labor Progressive Federation as a kind of state-level affiliate of the ACPF. Tom Duncan, a Socialist and Philip LaFollette's top aide at the state legislature, was involved in the effort, but the governor remained aloof, declined to join, and disdained the production-for-use language in the new group's platform. Behind the scenes he told Progressive party activists to build up that party, not the new federation, in Wisconsin. He wanted to confine the new group to the eastern, urban parts of the state and preserve the rural West as the Progressive stronghold. Urban-rural tensions mounted within the Progressive coalition in the state in the ensuing years as unionization rates rose sharply among workers, giving rise to opposition among farmers and small-town inhabitants, especially when employees at rural cooperatives tried to organize.[62]

Matters of ideology were inextricably attached to the conflicts attendant on industrial unionism's rise in the second half of the 1930s, dragging the farmer-labor camp past dysfunction and into irrelevance. In Minnesota, Trotskyists and the leadership of the state Federation of Labor formed a tag team with resurgent Republicans led by the "boy wonder" Harold Stassen to do battle with their antagonists in the Congress of Industrial Organization's (CIO) affiliates, which included numerous Communists. Popular Front activists in the FLP's left wing made Elmer Benson their man, and he went down to defeat in 1938 at Stassen's hands after a vicious Farmer-Labor primary battle. Benson's primary opponent, Hjalmar Peterson, unhesitatingly red-baited Benson and his supporters and at the very least tolerated an anti-Semitic campaign directed against top Benson advisers; Stassen followed suit in the general election campaign.[63]

Wisconsin's third-party tumult was less openly ideological and, for the last time, driven by LaFollette family decision making. Philip LaFollette plotted his own final defeat in 1938 by initiating a quixotic effort at national third-party organizing that would (in his mind) be held together by nothing so much as his own irresistible leadership qualities. Having dithered when third-party activists were on the march a few years earlier, he now seized the bull by what he mistakenly thought were the horns. In his first stint as governor between 1931 and 1933, he had touted the underconsumptionist explanation for the economic disaster and advocated redistribution of income as the solution. Those days were gone. The second time around in the executive offices, LaFollette argued against what he considered Roosevelt's destructive method of limiting production in order to raise prices and artificially engineer an anemic equilibrium. Now he said that increasing production was in fact the problem that government should tackle. This made him seem to lean to the conservative (supply) side, as he dropped redistribution in favor of "multiplication," meaning increased productivity, which supposedly would absorb the unemployed in something other than government-paid make-work, in turn creating the needed new consumption.

In fact, this critique of New Deal economic policy was a familiar one and had both strong and weak points. Typically its exponents targeted agricultural policy, which of course was aimed precisely at decreasing production and raising farm prices. Here the usual quip was that Roosevelt sought to eliminate the paradox of want amid plenty by erasing the plenty. Many agreed with that assessment, based on the well-publicized slaughter of surplus pigs and plowing up of cotton under Agricultural Adjustment Administration authority early in the New Deal era. Later in the 1930s, however, the government altered the mix of policies used to raise farm revenues, and in 1938 Henry Wallace, the secretary of agriculture, called the standard criticism "the worst misrepresentation I ever heard." The same indictment of U.S. industrial policy could not be sustained, given that there was no U.S. industrial policy after the U.S. Supreme Court's decision in *Schechter* v. *United States* in 1935 and the resultant dismantling of the National Recovery Administration (NRA). Philip LaFollette's criticism of the New Deal's policy was in some respects out of date.[64]

The policy proposals that LaFollette offered as the platform of his new party, the National Progressives of America (NPA), excited far less interest than the symbols and trappings with which he announced them, and it was these that brought condemnation down on his head. His principles, while playing for conservative support by implying criticism of the New Deal's relief programs, conformed to the farmer-labor tradition, declaring that the nation's financial system should be "under public and not private control," and that everyone was entitled to a job that would provide a "decent annual income."[65] This platform was so lacking in distinction from other third-party manifestos that it drew little attention and hardly justified LaFollette's lone-wolf approach to the enterprise. What everyone noticed was his use of theatrics and symbols in announcing the NPA's formation. From his travels in Europe in the era of fascism he apparently had concluded that this was the kind of thing needed to rally fervent popular support of movements for political and economic revival. He unveiled a flag that was to serve as the NPA's banner: a simple blue "X" inside a red circle, on a white field. It was immediately attacked as a "circumscribed swastika," with one-time admirers genuinely shocked and many others cynically calling LaFollette a fascist and would-be dictator (a charge his opponents in Wisconsin had leveled at him before this, as had Roosevelt's at him). LaFollette explained that the symbol expressed his belief in the need for economic "multiplication"; years later in his memoir he pinned the idea on his wife. In any case his effort did not appear to be built upon the solid foundations of independent political organizing that had taken shape over the previous ten years. Eschewing such support, which would not be under LaFollette's personal control, the NPA made feeble efforts to field slates of candidates in a few states in 1938, efforts that came very close to absolutely nothing. It became a curious footnote to the Depression decade, notable in that it brought Philip LaFollette's career in politics to a finish, amazingly, at the age of forty-one.

Thunder on the Right?

The NPA's dismal showing was one of several indications in that election season that the movement for left-right realignment was going nowhere fast as the Depression entered its tenth year. It also revealed the trenchancy of antifascist politics in the America of the late 1930s. Liberal and left commentators had derided the NPA in the idiom of antifascism. This was partly because, as the feckless LaFollette failed to see, the deep political background of European fascism was not present in the United States. In Germany, Italy, and elsewhere, the political systems antedating fascism had lacked broad legitimacy; those systems were eagerly attacked by aggressive, powerful forces and found few formidable allies willing to rally to the cause of the existing order. The economic despair of the American people in the 1930s was not linked to a widespread hostility to the U.S. constitutional order. A political revitalization movement did not need a new flag in the United States; the only flag that would elicit a deep and broad response of loyalty was the Stars and Stripes, and another standard perceived as a replacement for it could only be met with incredulity and anger. This does not mean that the makings were not available for a North American variation on fascism. But any such movement, if successful, would have been couched in an affirmation of traditional political symbols and values, not in the assertions of novelty so characteristic of European fascism, with its claim to revolutionary status.

In 1936, even as some continued to work for a third-party challenge to Roosevelt, the percolating fear of fascism served to express the building terror of forces to the New Deal's right, a terror that helped undercut the remaining support for such a challenge. After less than one term in office—and only a few years since angry farmers had threatened to lynch mortgage agents in the fields and "independent" activists had talked pityingly of Roosevelt as a hapless, transitional figure like Hoover—Roosevelt seemed inoculated against challenges from his left. The brash planning for a new national party fizzled within a year of the ACPF's founding. Even some of the most promising leaders of the ACPF defected to Roosevelt at the moment when the hypothesis of an independent politics was to have its first true test. Of these, none was more important than Tom Amlie. Both in and out of Congress in the decade's first half, he had been the foremost spokesman among professional politicians for an independent party to Roosevelt's left. But when Roosevelt came up for reelection for the first time, Amlie and many others who were like him, if less talented and thoughtful, got cold feet. It is true that, when the president delivered a stemwinder in his annual address to Congress in January, condemning "autocrats" who sought to crush the people's liberties and rule over all, the main left-liberal journals remained cool to him. The *New Republic* and *The Nation* criticized the speech harshly as cheap talk that did not correspond to a populist program and as "a political diatribe," respectively.[66] But within months most on the near left walked or ran into the Democratic fold, either with heads down or smiling philosophically. The American Liberty League, established in 1934 to defend nineteenth-century liberalism against its twentieth-century offspring, began its attacks on the New Deal (with Al Smith fronting for conservative big business). Actually, by late in the campaign season, the national Republican party, hoping to put Alf Landon in the White House in part by making him seem reasonably progressive, distanced itself from the Liberty League, which in short order had made itself something of an embarrassment. It took the briefest of scares from the right to make many farmer-laborites and other new progressives abandon ship. A handful remained outside the tent—Villard, Niebuhr, Dewey, Hook, Freda Kirchwey—and pulled the lever for Norman Thomas, who was always ready to offer himself as a repository for the stricken social-democratic consciences of these generations. As it turned out, of course, Roosevelt's victory in 1936 was an historic, crushing one. The independent progressive votes hadn't really been needed to stave off a return to Hoover's policies, nor to block fascism, whose coming some had not hesitated to predict if Landon had won.[67]

Why did the apostles of "independent" left-liberal politics run back to the two-party system when they had their first chance to test their ideas on the field of election-day politics? It is tempting to answer that the threat from the right was real, and that people such as Amlie, who were knowledgeable about American politics, realized it in time to help save America from disaster. However, they merely saved themselves from political oblivion, although in Amlie's case even that can be questioned; the New Deal was safe without their help. The Liberty League's denunciations of the New Deal as a red plot to bolshevize America seem silly to us now and may have been shocking to contemporaries. But intelligent and experienced American social democrats could hardly have expected conservatives to surrender to Roosevelt in 1936 without a stiff fight.

Doubtless all those deeply involved in national politics expected harsh attacks from the right. Fears of the threat from the opposite side of the spectrum are always available as a reason for erstwhile dissenters to get on board with the lesser of evils. Some will be compelled to do so and others will not. One cannot say that one decision or the other was the truly rational one; this was a matter of inclination. The fact that so few in the "independent" camp were left off the New Deal Express in 1936 must be taken as an indication of the deep, underlying aspirations and desires that prevailed in that precinct of American politics. Murray Kempton's was one way of putting it. What was remarkable, he wrote of radicals in the 1930s in general, was not "how much they demanded, but . . . how little it took them to be satisfied."[68]

There was little taste for an apocalyptic showdown between clashing visions of the future. Communists—had they not received instructions to the contrary at mid-decade—would have cared little about whether Franklin Roosevelt or Alf Landon and Al Smith ruled the roost down Pennsylvania Avenue from Capitol Hill. In their early Depression mode, they had been certain that they should just keep plugging away at their revolutionary plans for total change and had thought disaster for the halfway measures of the New Deal might even be good for such a project—"the worse, the better." In a way this was what the author Sherwood Anderson meant when he replied, famously, to the question of what set Communists apart from Socialists and liberals, "I guess the Communists mean it."[69] By contrast, when push came to shove, people such as Amlie, Bingham, and Olson, in spite of their radical words about the insignificance of reform politics within "the System," seemed relieved to see any positive response to social and political distress emerge from that system. They were Roosevelt's almost for the asking.

The "coup de grace" to third-party hopes in 1936, as Bingham put it, came with the strong move by organized labor to Roosevelt.[70] This took the form of the organization of Labor's Non-Partisan Committee to Elect Roosevelt in 1936. This became known as Labor's Non-Partisan League (LNPL); no one took the "Non-Partisan" part seriously, but it did at least indicate that the LNPL operated outside party structures. The LNPL was formed by Sidney Hillman, the supreme leader of the Amalgamated Clothing Workers, with John Lewis of the Mine Workers and George Berry of the Printing Pressmen's union. The Amalgamated was as important a defection from the ACPF as was Amlie. Having broken with the AFL, the new industrial unions eventually gave hundreds of thousands of dollars to the Democrats that year; the total contributions from unions amounted to $800,000, which helped Roosevelt at least compete in 1936 with the far more massive Republican fundraising among America's wealthy.

Although some unionists, including Hillman, long had harbored a vision of an industrial democracy spearheaded by a labor vanguard in politics, the hope of realizing that dream through a long effort at building a new party paled beside the promise of continuing support from the administration for union organizing and collective bargaining of the most basic kind. The NRA's labor provisions and the Wagner Act of 1935 had spurred and protected the huge wave of strikes and organizing successes of the years 1934–35. Even though Roosevelt had switched from his opposition to the Wagner Act only late in the game, when it became clear that Congress would pass it strongly, he and his appointees were widely seen as pro-labor, and the mainstream of the labor movement, both the rank and file and the leadership, gave every indication that four more years of this was what they wanted.[71] The most committed leftist sector of the industrial union movement was pervaded with the energy of Communist organizers and administrators, and ironically they were antipathetic to new third-party efforts at a national level. The only alternative party they might support privately was the CP, but its national campaign, under the influence of the new Popular Front conception, aimed mainly at attacking the Republicans and effectively was a pro-Roosevelt lobby. Communists in the CIO unions were unlikely to do any electioneering for the CP. The Democrats took labor's money while keeping union leaders largely out of leading roles in the 1936 campaign. The connection between the CIO and Roosevelt in 1936 seemed to belie definitively the assertions, from LaFollette's presidential run in 1924 through the LIPA's manifestos and all the farmer-laborism of the 1930s, that organized labor would join hands with reform professionals and protesting farmers in a movement for a new America. In a more limited, less radical way, the unions did form just such an alliance in 1936, but it was the Democratic alliance, in bed with the Bourbons of the South and the bosses of the cities, under Roosevelt's smiling aegis.

Some of the former "independents" tried to pick up the pieces of the farmer-labor constituency and lead a left wing of the Roosevelt coalition. In the fall of 1936, some had said that *after* the elections—*then* we'll return to party building. Amlie was more honest and realized that he had joined the Democrats for good. His further political failures remain instructive. He had gotten back into the House, and he ran for the U.S. Senate from Wisconsin in 1938 but didn't make it out of the Progressive party primary. Herman Ekern defeated him and then went on to lose in the general election. Ekern was a name from Wisconsin's past: a former state attorney general, he had been the recipient of the letter LaFollette, Sr. had made public in 1924 spurning Communist support. He ran hard against Amlie, contending that the deceased LaFollette's antimonopoly views remained perfectly suitable, in need of no revision. Amlie had introduced an industrial expansion bill in the House in 1937, along with Maury Maverick, Jerry Voorhis of California, and Robert G. Allen of Pennsylvania; it provided for national economic planning and featured fixed prices and production quotas, all of which would be overseen by a national advisory board, in order to achieve full employment. Ekern compared the proposal to the Soviet Union's Five Year Plans. Perhaps this did not exactly qualify as red-baiting—American admiration for Soviet planning was widespread among the new progressives, and therefore arguably fair game—but it had a similar effect. In fact, the charge was misleading, since Amlie proposed something like a return to the NRA, not a centralized government planning scheme. The bill aimed at increasing production levels and featured participation by all major functional economic groups. Its main inspiration lay not in any foreign government's policies, but in the widely circulated ideas of Mordecai Ezekiel, an economist with the Department of Agriculture. Unfortunately for Amlie, the bill met with little enthusiasm two years after the Supreme Court's decision in *Schechter* and amid the "Roosevelt recession." It must have been difficult to say whether this exhaustion with economic planning proposals was more or less disappointing to left-liberals than the discovery that Ekern's economic fundamentalism appealed to Wisconsin's Progressive voters more than Amlie's up-to-the-minute faith.[72]

Roosevelt made his only significant effort at forging a left-right realignment in American politics in 1938. The result was a debacle for the forces of New Deal liberalism. He supported liberal candidates in Democratic congressional primary races and worked to oust five conservative southern Democratic senators. But the voters in many of these localities, particularly in the South and uniformly in the Senate primaries where Roosevelt challenged incumbents, rebuffed him and his proxies. In fact, unlike the results of 1934, those of 1938 returned American politics to its familiar pattern of off-year congressional losses for the party holding the White House, with a vengeance. The Republicans gained seventy-five seats in the House of Representatives, rebounding in one election cycle from the bottom along which they had bumped since losing control of the Congress in 1930; the House's "liberal bloc" was cut in half. In the new Congress Republicans would join with conservative Democrats to halt further efforts to expand the power of Roosevelt and the New Deal agenda.[73] All of this came in addition to the ouster of the independent governors Benson and LaFollette in Minnesota and Wisconsin, respectively, and the pro-labor governor Frank Murphy in Michigan. The death knell was sounding around the country for dreams of further progressive realignment. (This year did, however, see the first election of a Democrat, and a liberal one, Culbert Olson, to the California governor's office in the twentieth century.)

Roosevelt's breakthrough election of 1936, in which he had taken 46 of 48 states and 104 of 106 large cities, and solidified the partisan realignment of four years earlier, had been largely wasted on failed attempts to alter the Supreme Court's composition and to reorganize the executive branch, with a watered-down Fair Labor Standards Act (1938) practically the only important reform legislation passed in the ensuing session of Congress. Now the New Deal's legislative innovations were over. An effective Keynesian spending policy would completely end the Depression, but only because of World War II. During the war, conservative forces would gain increasing control in both the legislature and the executive branch and important New Deal programs would be shut down.

All of this began in 1938, when many voters had felt far enough from the precipice to place opponents of the New Deal in office. Paradoxically, both the "Roosevelt recession" of 1937–38 and the prior easing of the economic crisis—the government considered effective joblessness, when federal work relief was taken into account, to have fallen below the 10 percent mark in 1937—undermined the call to strengthen the president's hand. Furthermore, the split in the labor movement, while it benefited Roosevelt and the Democrats in 1936 through the CIO's political involvement, cut the other way two years later. The AFL went on the offensive against its jurisdictional rivals, whom the craft unionists thought (with some justice) got preferred treatment from the National Labor Relations Board, and joined Republicans in widely publicized attacks on Communist involvement in the industrial unions. William Green, the head of the AFL, went so far as to support Governor Frank Merriam of California and Senator James Davis of Pennsylvania, both conservative Republicans, and he claimed to have caused Maverick's defeat in Texas.[74] Nineteen thirty-seven and 1938 were the years of the sit-down strikes in Michigan and elsewhere, and these proved unpopular with middle-class voters. Roosevelt distanced himself from the tactic, but conservatives succeeded in sticking it to numerous Democratic candidates, on the one side, and to the allegedly decisive and destructive influence of Communist organizers, on the other. The House of Representatives in 1938 established its Committee on Un-American Activities (HUAC), charging it with ferreting out both Communist and fascist agents in the United States. This investigation was supported by many liberals and leftists out of either anticommunism or antifascism. In the late 1930s the committee enjoyed a brief spell of publicity regarding allegations relating to each. But its real fame, of course, was yet to come.

Relating to FDR

At the New Deal's high tide, its liberal cadres were animated by the twin drives of the new liberalism since the late Gilded Age: laborism and Fabianism. Reform professionals—lawyers, social workers, and others—finally were able to migrate out of the nongovernmental sector that they had built up, into an elaborate national government of agencies aimed at achieving many of the goals these professionals long had held dear. Although the American state was limited by traditional ideology and vigorous conservative hostility, American Fabianism seemed finally to have come of age. The passion of the attachment to the New Deal was uneven, as some of the reformers, such as Paul Kellogg—who served on an advisory board involved in devising the Social Security system—continued to criticize Roosevelt's program as a series of sell-outs that would not do the job. But enlistment rates were high, certainly among the younger and lower ranks of reformers.

More notable is how unequally returned their devotion was. Lucille Milner of the ACLU exaggerated in remarking that Roosevelt's "official family read like a roster of the Civil Liberties Union," but it was true that the group "found an open door" at virtually all executive branch departments. There was a touch of Wilson about Roosevelt's patronage of these reformers, but this second of their Democratic "friends" in the White House would never betray or attack them, even if he did only some of what they hoped. To Roosevelt and his right-hand men, the full-time reform bunch was one useful interest group among many, whose support they were happy to have. Paralleling other interest-group vote-getting outfits in the campaign of 1936 was the Good Neighbor League. White House officials procured names from Lillian Wald, George Foster Peabody, Frank Graham, and other genteel reformers whose enrollment in the league was solicited for the duration of the contest.[75] Aside from election time, Roosevelt valued professional reformers, whom executive agencies hired in large numbers, not as representatives of a Fabian bureaucracy-in-waiting, administrative plans in hand, but as individual retainers whose personal loyalty was expected. His politics combined a democratic defense of the average American's aspirations and an embrace of traditional political practices with a Tory organicism that sought to head off revolution through reform. He wasn't looking for a group of Sidney and Beatrice Webbs to help him run things.

Yet laborism, too, occupied an uneven status on the scale of liberal commitments, as labor itself joined the Roosevelt coalition in a big way. To the professional reformers, labor's importance tipped downward, as their own involvement with the state rendered them ever less troubled by their perennial failures in actually making connections with labor unions. From the Washington perspective, labor was not the vanguard of a new historical bloc. Rather, it was cast in the role of one highly important interest group, more important than the reformers, in a grand alliance. This harmonized with the long-standing liberal emphasis on a broad front for progressive change, while the ambiguous status of labor in the liberal vision was clarified as that of a junior partner whose constituents deserved protection and the right to protect themselves.[76] Beginning in the 1930s ardent liberals viewed the New Deal as the full flowering of a "broker state" under which workers, farmers, racial minorities, and consumers would engage in "counter-organization" to balance the power of big business and parley at the table of the national government over the rules of the economic game. Enthusiasts of such a scheme viewed labor as the most important of all such historically unrepresented groups who now would be brought into the councils of power as an essential player.[77] Yet Roosevelt's own commitment to a strategy of counter-organization in reality was rather "iffy," to use a favorite term of his, and he never saw labor as the kind of inside player that many imagined.

The "independent" efforts at a left-right realignment in the early 1930s, based on the hope of a farmer-labor movement, clearly failed. The realignment was a partisan one that allowed for substantial reform, both in the way the state did business and in the ensemble of political forces that held sway over the state; that liberal realignment was adjusted to the right only a few years after its initial appearance.[78] Roosevelt remarked on one occasion, "I am trying to get across the idea that if we have the right kind of people, the party label does not mean so very much." Naturally, among those close to him this most pleased the former progressive Republicans Ickes and Wallace, who hoped for "political parties divided on real issues," in Ickes's words. On many occasions Roosevelt supported progressives without regard to party loyalty. He assembled a coalition of all liberal forces, in the new meaning, reaching through party structures to do so. But this realignment was always momentary, coming together for elections or specific legislative pushes and never followed up with vigorous party-building activities designed to strengthen the hand of the liberal forces in a permanent, institutionalized way. As already noted, the only attempt to purge conservatives from the Democratic party ended unhappily for Roosevelt. Indeed, one could say that he took the pursuit of a broad governing coalition too far to put it to use for partisan ends; in 1936, Roosevelt "mentioned the Democratic party by name no more than three times in the whole campaign."[79]

Where politics and policy were concerned, Roosevelt was impressed with numbers, and the farmer-laborites were by this measure not that threatening. His administration felt most strongly compelled, during the heyday of farmer-laborism in the early 1930s, to appease farmers. Thus the allotment program, with all its conservative influence, as well as "loans" and mortgage refinancing, can be traced in part to the agrarian wing of this midwestern agitation. Labor never joined the farmer-labor movement in the 1930s, so Roosevelt's pro-labor moves were responses to stimuli from other directions. Eventually the work relief offered through the New Deal was quite significant, even if it did not erase mass unemployment and privation. Arguably this came in reply to agitation by the poor and jobless, such as those organized in the Unemployed Councils of the early years of the Depression.[80] This is significant for its contrast with the administration's stance toward property owners. For their rebellions, the poor got relief and workers got new organizing rights; farmers and aspiring homeowners got property. The Home Owners Loan Corporation and the Federal Housing Authority did for urban homesteaders what the rural aid programs did for yeomen and agribusiness. Roosevelt and his top administration officials were most responsive in a substantive and lasting way to middle-class protest, and that was the key to their understanding of the farmer half of farmer-labor protest; the government did not respond to the pitchforked masses as part of a political left, but as part of the threatened and threatening middle, in both ideological and class terms. As far as potential third-party challengers went, by all accounts Roosevelt was far more worried about the troika of "demagogues" afoot in the early 1930s—Huey Long, Francis Townsend, and Charles Coughlin—than about the "radicals," to use one scholar's categories, not only because the demagogues were less susceptible to horse-trading and personal charm but also, and more important, because they demonstrated their access to large constituencies.[81]

Once again, these were perceived to be constituencies of the middle, and perhaps most of all of the dread "lower-middle," which figured large in the direst scenarios of political upheaval sketched in liberal heads during the Depression. Indeed, the president seemed quite unworried by a traditional left, and he responded most positively to those on his left flank when they approached him professing loyalty. Farmer-labor progressivism marked out for future advocates of non-Marxist, left-liberal politics in the United States pathways that proved less promising than farmer-laborites had hoped. Nonetheless, this movement played an important role in shaping American political discussion. It helped shape new meanings of progressivism and liberalism. More controversial, however, and more formative for the ensuing political culture, was the second variation on the new progressivism of this era. That was the progressivism of the Popular Front, whose adherents joined with the independents in ringing the tocsin against the menace of fascism, whose specter increasingly shadowed the politics of the 1930s.

Chapter 4

The Popular Front and Racial Liberalism

The fact is that though communism uses dictatorship brutally, it does not exalt it as an end in itself. Nor does it worship either race or war. Its moral cynicism is only provisional, and it is never morally nihilistic as the Nazis are. It is, in fact, ultimately utopian in morals, just as is the liberal-democratic world. . . . We have, on the whole, more liberty and less equality than Russia has. Russia has less liberty and more equality. Whether democracy should be defined primarily in terms of liberty or of equality is a source of unending debate. But history proves fairly conclusively that if we subordinate one too much to the other, we shall end by losing both.

—Reinhold Niebuhr, 1943

Nobody thought I was a Communist. Even Jim Eastland didn't think I was a Communist. He thought I was a "fellow-traveler," which was even more dangerous.

—Virginia Foster Durr, 1985

The most successful left-liberal political effort of the Second Progressive Era was the Popular Front. This was a coalition of Communists and liberals that, from the mid-1930s until the late 1940s, promoted the interests of workers and people of color in the United States and fervently supported the Soviet Union politically. These domestic and foreign agendas were welded together by the idea and rhetoric of antifascism. The Popular Front developed an alternative form of political liberalism, one allied with Franklin Roosevelt's New Deal but one that pressed for a more expansive and aggressive agenda for egalitarian change. Liberals in the Popular Front welcomed the prospect of revolution in some parts of the world, and even their domestic reformism was joined, perhaps incoherently, to a continuing hope for a fundamental transformation of American society.

The Popular Front achieved some of its goals, even though it was vanquished by its political opponents in the late 1940s. It did much to include industrial workers and African Americans and other people of color in the American political system. It made ethnic and racial "diversity" a mantra of political liberals for the first time, injecting cultural pluralism into the mainstream of American politics in a way that no movement had done before. In these ways the Popular Front exerted an important influence on the political liberalism that succeeded it. Despite this influence, Popular Front liberals found themselves effectively demonized, in the 1940s, by early cold war liberals who called them untrustworthy agents of the Soviet government, either witting or unwitting. The "vital center" liberals who supported the cold war triumphed over the Popular Front and succeeded in redefining liberalism as an antirevolutionary doctrine. The long era of the broad front between reformers and radicals came to a close, and the lingering liberal hope for social transformation took the single biggest step toward its expiration.

The Popular Front: Semi-Independence

The Popular Front was the second of the major efforts in the interwar period to forge a new, distinctly left-liberal political movement that could push the United States toward social democracy. A loose constellation of forces loyal to Roosevelt but committed to creating a political world that would stand to the New Deal's left, the Popular Front was similar to what Max Lerner, in 1936, called a "liberalism of the progressive labor movements."[1] Unlike the farmer-labor movement in the 1920s, the first of the two big left-liberal initiatives of the Second Progressive Era, the Popular Front was not bent on "independence." Only in 1948, as the cold war set in, did adherents of the Popular Front move toward a third-party model, and that helped to put this most successful of left-liberal efforts in its coffin.

The Popular Front was more successful than farmer-laborism because of the superior vitality of its social and organizational base and because of the shrewder political strategy it pursued during its successful periods. Those periods coincided roughly with the years when the CP embraced the Popular Front (1935–39, 1941–46). The Communists did not dominate the Popular Front in the way that many anticommunist historians allege, but they were certainly the dominant organized group in the coalition in the normal meaning of the term; they led primarily by means of superior organization and discipline and through persuasion, not by deception and mind control. To Communists and other avowed leftists, a "People's Front" meant that they should make common cause with "rotten liberals," as Communists would have called reformers in the early 1930s, in order to keep fascism from coming to power in additional countries. Liberals joined the Popular Front for the same reason, and also because the Popular Front's efforts seemed to embody the multiracial, labor-based liberal politics to which, they hoped and trusted, the future belonged.

In practical terms, whether in France and Spain, where Popular Front coalitions actually came to power in 1936, or in the United States, where this coalition simply supported the reformist Roosevelt administration starting in 1935, the Popular Front became the vehicle for a broader agenda of far-reaching change at home. In the American Popular Front, the slogan was "democracy," not "socialism." The more radical members of the coalition saw this as a gradual path to socialism, and they openly advocated that goal, for example in Corliss Lamont's modest invitation of 1939, *You Might Like Socialism.*[2] Most of the Popular Front's foot soldiers considered themselves antifascists before anything else. The categories of left and liberal, socialist and democrat became blurred and lost some of their distinct relevance for them. The Popular Front's leaders expressed the view that liberals and leftists held both short- and long-term goals in common that ought to unite them into the foreseeable future. The Popular Front was based in the belief that there was another chapter to come in the story of America. Its political vision was based upon the old Enlightenment belief in a sequential developmental pattern in human history, and in the belief that the present dispensation was not the final one. Liberals and Communists could welcome one another as fellow "progressives," and that is exactly how Popular Fronters became known.

The strategic sense of the Popular Front came through in its recognition that supporting a reformist regime that lay within the two-party structure was a far better bet than seeking to remake that political structure. The Popular Front could come to power in France and Spain because those countries were governed on a parliamentary basis, through coalitions built in a multiparty legislature. The United States was dominated by two heterogeneous parties, and here the chief executive was chosen directly on a single ballot, separate from the national legislature. Popular Front leaders did not engage in discussions of these differences, but their behavior indicated an awareness of the specific institutional setting of U.S. politics. Encountering the fortuitous circumstance of a reformist president in the White House who seemed to welcome their support, they backed Roosevelt's program, particularly after his shift in 1935 away from "corporatist" formulas of industrial recovery and toward the construction of a national safety net and open support for labor's "counter-organization." Because they weren't a political party, but simply a set of organizations that encouraged support for prolabor politicians, Popular Fronters maintained enough independence of the Roosevelt administration to allow them to ventilate differences of opinion where these occurred. This created no issue of party loyalty. More important, they did not have to devote their resources to the near impossible task of building a viable third party that could challenge Democrats and Republicans nationally. This was the project that the farmer-laborites embarked upon, and they did not even have the kind of organizers that the Popular Front had in the Communists. Popular Front groups therefore could devote themselves to direct support of the causes and people they felt passionately about.

The Popular Front was not based socially in the farm belt or in the northern European ethnic extractions dominant in the farmer-labor movement. By the 1930s such constituencies had been declining for some time in proportionate size, economic power, and cultural significance. This was the larger reality for which Fighting Bob LaFollette's "economic fundamentalism," his outmoded nineteenth-century small-producer faith, was a metaphor. While the organizers of the Minnesota Farmer-Labor party and the American Commonwealth Political Federation went beyond such doctrines, they never matched their new economic analyses with a mass constituency that would be moved by them.

New themes and new appeals made for a mass following in the nation's large cities that Franklin Roosevelt swept in 1936: the comforts of "the American way of life," inclusion in a society stratified by ethnicity, and a fair bargain for workers. This was not the sort of control that small businessmen sought over their own fates; it was simply respect, an opportunity for material betterment, and a little security. This was the "New Deal." The Popular Front folded its rhetoric of a people's democracy and its left-leaning "Americanism" into that appeal, emphasizing, first, labor organization, and second, respect for racial minorities and ethnic latecomers as part of a proud mongrel America that gained strength from its diverse origins. The Popular Front swept through the country's urban centers when these locales were where the action was, politically, socially, and culturally. Of the two efforts at forming left-liberal political movements in the Second Progressive Era, it was the one appropriate to what some call the "Fordist" era of urban concentration, large-scale bureaucratic organization, mass production, and mass consumption. The Popular Front was comprised of several basic constituencies: organized industrial workers and "culture workers" who were largely children of the turn-of-the-century "new immigrants" from southern and eastern Europe; African Americans, to whom the Communist party and other leftists in this period made a special, targeted appeal (as well as some other low-caste racial minorities concentrated in the American West); and the professional reformers who had pioneered the "new liberalism" of the century's early years, most of them white Anglo-Saxon Protestants, who now were joined by a new cohort of Jewish and

Catholic reformers who staffed the middle reaches of the New Deal state and the top ranks of the CIO unions.

The CIO's Politics

Most historians of the constituent elements of the Popular Front, most of whom express left sympathies of one degree or another of intensity, have celebrated these constituencies, seeing in them a promise of socialism, or at least of the transcendence of America's traditional ideologies of classlessness and white supremacy. For any historian with such retrospective "hopes" for the America of the 1930s, the industrial unions of the CIO have carried much of the freight of historical possibility. Invariably this version of the past has assumed the form of "alternative" histories, of paths not taken, thwarted not only by conservative enemies of the left but also by liberals without vision. A brief accounting is needed. Union members in the 1930s could hardly be unaware of class differences. The question is whether that consciousness extended into the realm of politics—consciously understood.

The place of organized labor in the Roosevelt coalition was discussed in Chapter 3. It was that of one among several loyal interests. It was particularly important in terms of financial contributions and ground operations turning out the vote. The LNPL's successor, the CIO Political Action Committee (CIO-PAC), which was Sidney Hillman's brainchild, sought to entrench the industrial unions in the latter function during the election cycle of 1944. It had some success, helping Roosevelt and the Democrats in a handful of important states, although friends and enemies alike were wrong to claim it was the key to the entire outcome. That claim resulted from the extremely vicious, red-baiting, and anti-Semitic propaganda produced by Republicans and their backers that year, propaganda that claimed that Hillman was the all-powerful rabbi in Roosevelt's camp. The CIO-PAC's legacy was not a permanent role in the inner circle of a ruling Democratic majority, but rather its inspiration for countless other fundraising operations that took the name Political Action Committee for themselves in later decades. Roosevelt derived an enormous share of his support from wage-earning Americans—many of the CIO unions' members and their families were among the surge in first-time voters in 1936, who swelled the voter participation rate that year to an astounding 83 percent (among those registered)—but no one seriously disputes that this was his own doing. He reached through and around union structures to make a direct connection with working-class voters.[3] By 1938, "More than Harry Bridges, or even John L. Lewis, this Hudson Valley patrician and graduate of Groton and Harvard had become the symbolic leader of organized labor. Roosevelt defined labor's program; workers fought in the ditches to defend it."[4]

This sober assessment leaves cold those who look for inspiration to the "turbulent years" of the Depression. Is there no vision of a new society, no hope for transformation in all the heat of the sit-downs, the mass marches, the street confrontations of Minneapolis, Akron, and San Francisco? The evidence for it is rather slender. There are two different versions of the thesis of revolutionary, or otherwise very radical, potential within the turbulence of the CIO organizing drives. The first is the "rank and file" thesis, which sees the radical "self-activity" (as distinct from activity) of American proletarians as the source of working-class militancy in the Depression era, and which further sees this militancy smothered by the "bureaucratic" (implying elitist, routinized, boring, selfish) development of national union structures and collective bargaining machinery overseen by the state. Sometimes the self-interested mischief of sectarian political parties plays a stultifying role as well in this version of the story. Evidence indicates that, indeed, a great deal of the shop-floor militancy during the 1930s emerged rather spontaneously and was under no one's control outside small circles of employees; what labor historians call "quickie" strikes abounded, and even the massive strike waves of 1934, 1937, and 1945–46 were far from centrally coordinated, stemming in impressive measure from countless, decentralized, often impulsive decisions to "go out" or to sit down. It all seemed quite anarchic, or syndicalist, to many close observers. The difficulty in the "rank and file" interpretation is that it confuses militancy with radicalism. This is no surprise when one considers the political roots of that interpretation's purveyors in the new left of the 1960s, which made this specific confusion one of its hallmarks.

When the radical potential of 1930s unionism is the topic, the Communist unionists are the ghosts lurking in the machine. The second version of the 1930s labor radicalism thesis centers on them. As noted above, this argument too is hard to credit, since the function of the CP cadres within the unions of the CIO was to work as dogged, devoted union organizers and institution builders. The Communists were concentrated in the national ("international" in the parlance of organized labor) offices of these unions and within the paid staff. John Lewis met with Earl Browder and other leading Communists when the rift with the AFL occurred, and he hired Lee Pressman, who was known as at least a close fellow traveler, as the top lawyer for the CIO; horse-trading occurred within individual unions over which national officers would come from Communist-led factions and which from others, whether Socialist-led or conservative. All of this contributed to the charges, which gained traction within the CIO only in the late 1940s but which were made vociferously by AFL rivals and others starting with the schism in 1935 between the AFL and its Committee on Industrial Organization, that an innocent and distinctly nonradical rank and file was under the malign control of Communist bureaucrats. But the CIO Communists were local organizers, too, and John Lewis called upon their assistance in the organizing drives in steel, automobile manufacturing, and other heavy industries after the break with the AFL. William Z. Foster claimed that of the two hundred organizers hired by Lewis to staff the Steel Workers Organizing Committee (SWOC), sixty were CP members. Lewis had repressed radical dissidents within the UMWA viciously before this, and he would not remain a friend to the left forever. Here was a tactical alliance that both sides entered knowingly. Lewis responded to questions about that alliance pithily: "Who gets the bird, the hunter or the dog?"[5]

Why the Communists? Because they boasted a corps of devoted, battle-hardened organizers who in many cases had been through the worst that any labor organizers could face, weathering not just the "lean years" of the 1920s but also the implacable hostility of conservative craft unionists and government officials, as well as the problems posed by their own party's zigs and zags. They certainly were used to the AFL's hatred. Their history of "underground" work had accustomed them to the habits of hunted men, which remained useful in organizing workplaces where employers, throughout the 1930s, used espionage and violence without hesitation against unionists. When Wyndham Mortimer, the open leader of the CP's forces within the Auto Workers, sought to organize General Motors plants in Flint, Michigan in the 1930s, for safety's sake he began by relying on cells and clubs allied to the party. In this dangerous atmosphere, no one but the Communists possessed such an extensive, if small, network of trustworthy cadres. Moreover, in the early Depression years Communist labor organizers had been the most prominent advocates of industrial unionism. The Trade Union Education League had titled one of its publications *Amalgamation*, arguing in it for industry-wide labor unions. The Communists offered by far the largest available pool of experienced labor organizers who were familiar with the challenges facing industrial unionism. The bottom line for the Communist organizers' new allies was expressed by one union member, who said, "The Coms, they say, are fighters, they've got ideas on strategy and they keep their noses clean on money."[6] This last point was no small issue in itself.

Lewis gave the Communist organizers the kind of backing they had never dreamed of, and they gave him and the CIO quite a bit in return. Not least of what they gave was to leave their politics largely at the workplace door. They insisted on offering resolutions at union conventions supporting whatever the current Soviet line was in international affairs, and often they got these passed. That mattered little. It did indicate to anyone who had not noticed what loyalties were at work and where. Sometimes workers did not know who was a Communist and who was just a union stalwart. Among the top union leaders, there was little ignorance about who was, if not an actual CP member, then at least a close fellow traveler. Only a small number of the CIO Communists were open party members, mainly the older ones who had been through more than one generation of red-baiting, often having been Wobblies or Socialists in earlier days. The "secret" Communists, and their party superiors, feared attacks from forces outside the union movement, and also, it must be said, from the more conservative elements within the rank and file. In this single respect they were like many a drug addict: their secret was only a secret to those who did not know them.

When considering the relations between radicals and liberals in the labor movement of the 1930s and 1940s, it is hard to keep the discussion from devolving completely into a debate over the CP. But it is worth the effort to try. The story of left-liberal politics in the Second Progressive Era is more the story of the far larger numbers of Americans who worked in the space between the New Deal and the left-wing parties. A focus on the CP's role in the Popular Front can easily take the form of a strident, prosecution-and-defense debate over who knew whom and when, who took orders from whom, and who tricked whom. The less sensational matters of broadly shared goals and visions are more important for an accurate understanding of "progressive" politics in this era, and even specifically of Communist-liberal relations within the Popular Front. "During the Popular Front, broad agreement existed between Communists and others in the CIO on central policy goals and strategies, including aggressive organizing of the unorganized, establishing inclusive industrial unions regardless of workers' skills, race, or political beliefs, using mass strikes as a tactic of last resort, and mobilizing workers to elect New Deal Democrats."[7] Of course, fierce anticommunists always insisted on the overriding importance of the Communist issue narrowly defined, and between 1946 and 1950 their viewpoint achieved hegemony within the CIO. The numbers do, of course, matter, although their exact meaning is debatable. "Communists were partners, although not dominant ones, in the CIO's largest affiliate, the United Auto Workers. State and city CIO councils in New York City, Minnesota, Wisconsin, and Washington were effectively controlled by Communists." Different estimates place the overall share of CIO union members in unions with at least very significant Communist leadership, variously, at one-third and one-half at the end of World War II, before the uncertain political interval that ended with the expulsion of eleven of these unions from the CIO in 1949 and 1950. One can usually infer the interpretive position of historians of these events from the terms they employ when describing these unions: "Communist-controlled," "Communist-dominated," "Communist-influenced," or "left-led."[8]

The purges actually began as early as 1938, amid what some historians call the "little red scare," which lasted from that year, when the House of Representatives formed the Committee on Un-American Activities (HUAC), until 1940, when President Roosevelt signed into law the Smith Act, which criminalized not revolutionary activities themselves but the "advocacy" of revolutionary doctrine. After the sobering gains made by Republicans and conservatives in the elections of November 1938, Philip Murray, the head of the SWOC and the man who would succeed Lewis as chief of the CIO, started firing CP cadres from the SWOC. It was easy to see that more red-baiting was on the way, since it had worked well during the election campaign, and he was determined to shed people he considered political liabilities (especially now that they had helped achieve a good bit of their assigned mission). Communists in the CIO responded to this chilly atmosphere by resolving to move yet further into the background *as Communists*. Party caucuses within unions stopped meeting and putting out their own publications, and Communists showed a willingness to support anti-Communist candidates for union office and even anti-Communist resolutions at union conventions. While this willingness to take abuse seemed intended in part to show good faith to non-Communist union allies who were in the know, in the end it would be used against them, as evidence of duplicity.[9]

The red scare, when it came to the union movement in the half-decade after war's end, did not deradicalize the movement, although it did foreclose the possibility of sharp independence from the Democratic party. By the last years of Truman's presidency, whatever direction the leadership of that party took, the heavily politicized leadership of the AFL and the CIO would follow. Criticisms would serve only as mild qualifications of that loyalty; the game was an insider's game by then. This newly complaisant face of labor would remain in place throughout the cold war, long after objective observers saw how shamelessly the Democratic party's leaders took union support for granted. The impact of the purges of the early cold war imprinted the labor movement of this whole era so deeply as to make the national leadership of the union movement the last redoubt of hard-line international anticommunism within this party's orbit in the post-1965 era, when the Vietnam War triggered substantial rethinking about the value of that stance among both Democrats and Republicans. For George Meany and Lane Kirkland, where U.S. foreign policy was concerned, it would always be 1946.

Still, even if the move within labor to amputate its own left wing set the union movement's international stance in concrete, it cannot be said to have prevented the survival of a vital radical alternative in domestic American politics. That is because the industrial union movement, by 1945, did not constitute such a radical alternative, Communists or no Communists. This conclusion is inescapable if one admits of the Communists what their defenders traditionally have said of them: they were good trade unionists first and Communists a distant second. They were fierce and Jesuitical in their devotion, in their vocation for the workers' cause. But they accepted and worked within the prevailing consensus of aspirations among the American working class, a class that looked to the New Deal state for guarantees of its living standard. Hillman pioneered the formulation of New Deal labor liberalism that perhaps expressed best this consensus of president and workers. He said that workers wanted "security" above all. That was obviously a consumerist rendering of blue-collar hopes. The Roosevelt era witnessed the withering away of the "labor question" as a question of who would govern industrial America, material hopes displacing visions of class empowerment.[10]

Walter Reuther of the United Automobile Workers (UAW) tried to keep the old question alive during the strike wave of 1945–46, when he demanded that the automobile manufacturers open their financial books to outside scrutiny and bargain with the union over product pricing. He hoped to focus public attention on the question of corporate America's profits and to make the distribution of the economic surplus the basis for a social-democratic coalition of workers and consumers—groups that, for all that they overlapped, might be pitted against one another by a narrow focus on retail prices. But that demand had little chance of fulfillment and it went by the wayside.[11] During the 1940s Philip Murray, as the head of the CIO, fielded a plan for localized industrial councils with labor included in a functionally based power-sharing arrangement. That idea was rooted in Murray's study of Catholic social doctrine and theory and resonated with the whole tradition of "industrial democracy" that had sought to replace geographic with functional representation. But it was a deader letter than Reuther's product-pricing demand. Murray's scheme was truly utopian in the context of the post–World War II years. The culture of consumerism was well advanced, despite the deprivations of the Depression and the war. Time would show that these experiences had primed American workers to try to live as well as they could in the coming years, not to struggle for a refashioning of American capitalism.

The Black Left

Whether in Birmingham, Detroit, or Memphis, black Communists and leading black CIO union activists were frequently the same individuals.

Such people were often the driving forces within local struggles for rights and equality by African Americans. This represented a remarkable turnabout in the traditional hostility between black Americans and trade unions, which with a few exceptions (such as the UMWA) had been racially exclusive by design. It is not putting the matter too strongly to state that American labor unions on the whole, prior to the era of industrial unionism, were agents of white supremacy, viewing the prospect of black entry into white occupations and unions as degrading in the extreme. Almost the only exceptions to this rule were unions organized by left-wing radicals. In this situation, black workers were ripe for use by employers as strikebreakers; that role for black workers was widely embraced by African American leaders of all classes for decades, a view that went hand in hand with the Republican loyalties of black voters and activists (where blacks were permitted by whites to vote). This in turn exacerbated white unionists' preexisting anti-black animus.[12]

The CIO unions extended their hands to unorganized black workers, raising the prospect of a working class no longer riven by race. This historic change resulted from the understanding by leaders of the CIO, seasoned observers all, that racial division functioned at the end of the day to the advantage of anti-union employers. Racial solidarity was a more familiar tradition in America than proletarian solidarity, and the former tended to overwhelm the latter when they competed. In fact the CIO's leaders often found themselves backtracking on issues of racial equality, or at least soft-pedaling such concerns, in order to appease white union members who were far more clannish and bigoted than they. But the CIO's interracial gambit also stemmed from the determination of Communists and other leftists in the industrial unions to make antiracism, interracialism, and indeed a passionate pro-black stance some of their hallmarks. In particular, the aggressive antiracist militancy of the Communists—who made James Ford, an African American, their vice presidential candidate in 1932—was so extraordinary, virtually unique among predominantly white political organizations in the United States of that era, that it had an outsized effect on black and white Americans, rippling outward into the labor movement and other precincts. "White chauvinism" was a phrase introduced by Communists into the American lexicon (as was "male chauvinism," a matter of somewhat less ardent concern, if still a pioneering one).

Black activists, workers, and intellectuals alike joined the Popular Front in large numbers in the 1930s and 1940s, seeing in it a vehicle for progress toward a society of equal opportunity and acceptance. That enthusiasm for the antifascist coalition was based in large measure on the apparent sincerity of the antiracist appeals made by CIO union activists and Communist-led leftists. The CP's special emphasis on battling racism did not compromise the universal terms in which the Communists preached the socialist message. Richard Wright, long an adherent of the Communist cause, reflected, "I'm black. I'm a man of the West. . . . How can the spirit of the Enlightenment and the Reformation be extended now to all men? How can this boon be made global in effect?" Certainly to black intellectuals, the appeal of the CP in its heyday was less that it was race conscious (rather than colorblind) than that its direct confrontation with racism expressed a distinctively fervent commitment to universalist values.[13]

The special appeal that Communists made to African Americans during the interwar period had little precedent within either the American left or American liberalism. As discussed in Chapter 2, before the World War I era, the organized left had made no special bid for African American support and declined to view American racism as an issue worthy of attention in its own right—separate from class oppression. Starting in the late 1910s, some Socialists had begun to address white supremacy directly. In the 1930s, the interracial organizing cadres of the Southern Tenant Farmers' Union (STFU) in the Deep South of the 1930s, most of them Socialists, many of them ministers, provided the most spectacular example ever of the SP's antiracism. With the active support of Norman Thomas and other top Socialist leaders, they performed extremely brave and hazardous work, sparking a fast-growing movement that lasted for several years in the teeth of violent opposition. Franklin Roosevelt, who was unwilling to alienate the political-economic power structure of the South, turned a deaf ear to Thomas's pleas that he speak out against this violence, just as he opposed a federal anti-lynching law for fear of alienating powerful white southerners in Congress.[14]

Before the mid-1930s, liberalism always had meant white liberalism. It had been virtually an all-white political formation. The new liberals of the Gilded Age and the Progressive Era, but for exceptional figures such as Oswald Garrison Villard—who joined W. E. B. DuBois, the white Socialist Mary White Ovington, and others as a founder of the NAACP—simply had given little thought to race matters. In the pre-1935 period, even when white liberals did think or act in response to the predicament of African Americans, they enunciated no coherent and distinctive doctrine that should be termed "racial liberalism." White liberals were relatively likely to adopt a moderate stance regarding race relations, and even to be known as figures friendly to African Americans, yet they never defined their liberalism in terms of their characteristic aloofness from race hatred.

Liberalism was understood as fundamentally a creed of political economy, and this creed's indifference to white supremacy made it irrelevant to African Americans. Black Americans from the time of Booker Washington onward might be conservative; they might be radical; they rarely saw anything to draw them to liberalism. It is very hard to identify African American activists who called themselves liberals before the 1940s. The irrelevance of liberalism in black America began to change during the Second Progressive Era, as white liberals, with painful slowness, began to see the political wisdom of competing with the left for the mantle of Friend to the Negro. Reuther eventually sought to promote anticommunist liberal civil rights cadres within the UAW in an effort to overcome the suspicion of his camp among black automobile workers, who tended to support the union's CP-led caucus. He drew on an impressive group of Socialist African American activists; he could not draw on the interracial ranks of fighters for racial justice within the previous generation of political liberals because such ranks had not existed.[15] Franklin Roosevelt demonstrated the dividend to be reaped by white leaders from even the faintest reputation for benevolence toward African Americans. But until the 1940s, there were not many others who could claim this reputation for themselves. During the Depression, "a man like George Norris could oppose an antilynching bill and still be counted a liberal in good standing," since after all he was only doing (or not doing) the same as Roosevelt.[16]

The retrieval of "liberal" as the denotation of a political identity and program relevant to the situation of African Americans in a time of severe industrial distress occurred haltingly during the Second Progressive Era. DuBois, a case to himself, occasionally used the term to denote an enlightened white view of black rights, as he did in criticizing Alfred Smith in 1928 for a timorous stance on this matter: "Mr. Smith is posing as a liberal."[17] But this usage was definitely idiosyncratic at that time. In the late 1920s DuBois involved himself in the LIPA, but by 1930 he had grown frustrated at the group's inattention to racial issues. Paul Douglas wrote a pamphlet for the group, "Why a Political Realignment," that made no mention of the need to enforce the right to vote for all; a testy exchange between the two men followed, and DuBois exited the group. Farmer-laborism and the groups associated with it showed virtually no interest in questions of race. More typical among African American thinkers before the mid-1930s was the emphatically backward-looking meaning that Abram Harris, Jr. gave to the term "liberal." Harris, the Howard University economist who coauthored the classic study *The Black Worker* (1931), castigated the NAACP's emphasis on formal civil rights as the answer to African Americans' problems as "18th century liberalism." Like other left critics, he viewed liberalism as quintessentially the ideology of the bourgeoisie, plain and simple.[18] A vital liberal-left politics that showed an interest in questions of race awaited the integration of Communist antiracism into the broader antifascism of the Popular Front.

BTWs era

Here too, DuBois was prescient, as he criticized the U.S. news media for their positive coverage of Mussolini's regime in 1928, a time when antifascism remained a somewhat eccentric taste.[19] The potential "new" liberalism that DuBois implied appeared among students at Howard University in 1934, when they formed a campus Liberal Club. The club pursued an overt Popular Front path, complete with antiwar agitation, American Student Union (ASU) involvement, and expressions of hope that an interracial workers' movement might become "a front neither storm troops nor private armies can stop." This politics bore no resemblance to the liberalism that Harris criticized.[20]

In 1935 a specifically African American wing of the Popular Front appeared on the political scene in the form of the National Negro Congress (NNC), which was launched at a gathering at Howard University that year, a conference convened by the Joint Committee on National Recovery (JCNR). The JCNR, which was partly funded by the NAACP, was the work of John P. Davis, a young economist and activist close to the CP. The JCNR was intended to lobby for black economic interests during the crisis of the 1930s; its main legacy lay in the 1935 Howard conference, titled "The Position of the Negro in Our National Economic Crisis," which offered a setting for brainstorming by a dynamic assortment of younger African American political thinkers and doers. Davis and Ralph Bunche, the key figure in political science at Howard, did the heavy lifting in organizing the NNC. Numerous Communists participated in the conference at Howard, but so did many others who could hold their own, including Lester Granger of the Urban League, Charles Houston, the law professor who shaped the emerging legal strategy of the NAACP, and Alain Locke.[21] A consensus emerged on the need for a new overarching political action group such as the NNC's organizers hoped it would become. The NNC succeeded in becoming a highly visible umbrella organization for African American politics and protest in the late 1930s, collecting support and participation from a wide range of black leaders and groups—with the very notable exception of the NAACP. Walter White was wary of the Popular Front and could not have been pleased at the challenge the NNC presented to his organization's preeminence in national black politics. African American Socialists succeeded in getting some important white unions to withhold support, but many others made contributions. The NNC's position was that interracial trade unions were the proper route to economic and political empowerment for African Americans. A. Philip Randolph served as the chairman. The longtime Socialist hardly would have held this position for as long as he did if he had thought the Communists were acting as puppet masters. Up until 1939, the fateful year of the pact, Randolph kept his caustic views on the Soviet Union under wraps. In the late 1930s, the CP's "power" within the NNC "rested largely on consent."[22]

For five years the NNC maintained a position at the center of political debates and activism among African Americans. Yet its vitality and effectiveness as a black unity organization has been questioned. As early as 1937 it was developing close ties not only to the CP but also to John Lewis and the CIO. Arguably this represented a deviation from the NNC's initial aim of bringing together a comprehensive *African American* movement. The NAACP's abstention from the NNC was a serious blow. The NAACP was at that time receiving an infusion of fresh, more militant blood, certainly at the local chapter level, but the friendliness of some of that group's new cadres to a Popular Front orientation did not extend to a defiance of White's hostility to the NNC.[23] For all this, the NNC's accomplishment was not minor. It signaled the possibility of a nationwide black *activist* mobilization, as opposed to the legalistic and lobbying efforts of the NAACP and the Urban League. It made peace between, on the one hand, the black-nationalist sentiment that had bubbled through Harlem and other urban black neighborhoods since the heyday of the Marcus Garvey movement around 1920 and, on the other, a left-liberal politics that foresaw genuine progress for black Americans through inclusion in the programs of the New Deal and an unashamed interracial coalition. (As far as the CP and its fellow travelers were concerned, the earlier doctrine of self-determination for a southern "black belt" was gone, but the militancy associated with that doctrine remained.) The Young Turks of the NNC offered the hand of partnership to whites of whom they demanded the same. This offer met with more success than anyone had had a right to expect in 1935.

If the NNC's political limits had already come into view by 1939, the pact and its fallout damaged the organization beyond recovery. African American liberals and leftists proved just as exercised as their white counterparts over matters of European diplomacy. Granger, Wilkins, and Adam Clayton Powell all directed their fire at the NNC and the whole Popular Front, essentially saying that the Communists had removed their smiling masks and revealed the true and terrible nature that lay underneath. Surprisingly, Randolph, with a more substantial history on the anticommunist left than any of these others, did not bail out right away. But it was not long before he did. In 1940, at the third convention of the NNC, John Lewis and the CP succeeded in pressing for an anti-intervention stance. This tore it for Randolph, who had agreed to give the keynote address. He denounced the CP as the agent of a foreign power and called the Soviets and the Nazis so many peas in a pod. Not surprisingly, he left the NNC. When he organized the March on Washington Movement soon afterward to demand an end to the exclu-

sion of black workers on federal government contract jobs, he kept out not only Communists but their allies in the Popular Front as well.[24] His estrangement was complete. Their anticommunism given full rein, Randolph and the NAACP were well positioned for the second red scare when it came.

At the same time, the memory of the Popular Front's left-liberal interracial politics could not be erased from the minds of the young African American cadres who had populated the NNC. New Popular Front efforts, notably the Southern Negro Youth Congress and the continued activities of the Council on African Affairs, presented an interracialist alternative during the remainder of the 1940s, an alternative that, in the harsh atmosphere of the election campaign of 1948 and its aftermath, appeared alarmingly radical to many liberals, black and white. Although it has received far less attention from historians, a Popular Front initiative among Mexican Americans materialized in the late 1930s as well. The Spanish-Speaking Peoples Congress ("El Congreso"), organized in California and elsewhere in 1938 and 1939, pressed for the inclusion of Latinos in an empowered working class. El Congreso adopted the CP's line that Mexican Americans (and Mexican nationals in the United States) formed an "oppressed national minority," not a separate nation. Communists and others in left-wing CIO unions with many Latino members, such as the Cannery and Packinghouse Workers, supported this activism. Although it was short-lived, El Congreso offers further evidence that the Popular Front was a vital pathway inviting largely working-class racial minority groups into the mainstream of U.S. politics and specifically into the orbit of New Deal liberalism, even as the Popular Front reflected a marked enthusiasm for militant citizen action that might press U.S. politics beyond the New Deal. Thus the Popular Front would pave the way for the emergence of racial liberalism in mid-century America.[25]

The Reformers: The Last Phase in American Fabianism

The last of the three major elements in the Popular Front, the middle-class professionals and intellectuals, many of whom can be captured in the category of "the reformers," was the one that had ploughed the field of left-liberal politics by far the longest. The productive tension between Fabianism and laborism, pursued through the late Gilded Age and the Progressive Era, had been the invention of such reformers. Many of the Progressive Era generation, such as Roger Baldwin, Mary van Kleeck, Harry Ward, and Paul Kellogg, entered the prime of their professional careers during the Second Progressive Era and provided the senior leadership for the Popular Front reformers. They dominated the social work profession, which was a crucial bridge between Progressive Era and Popular Front generations of American Fabianism. The most important organization forming such a bridge was the ACLU, whose national board remained a who's who of liberal-left reform luminaries. Some Popular Front reformers, such as Jessie Lloyd O'Connor, Henry Demarest Lloyd's granddaughter, were linked to an earlier era of reform by family ties.[26] In the 1930s Jessie O'Connor became the leader of the Chicago branch of the League of Women's Shoppers, a group that, like the National Consumers' League, used the idea of moral consuming to unite middle- and working-class women and leftists with liberals. These women's groups carried the Gilded Age concept of the cross-class broad front into the era of the Popular Front.[27]

This reformer tradition had a clear WASP coloration, although it had featured a minor admixture of Jews starting in the early years of the twentieth century, mainly quite assimilated German American Jews. In the 1930s, the reformer element in the Popular Front featured a somewhat different look, as large numbers of Catholics and Jews appeared in important positions within trade unions that boasted newfound political heft, and in New Deal bureaus. Popular Fronters supported the New Deal but expected that someday it would exhaust its usefulness as a vehicle for progress toward a cooperative commonwealth. The newer Catholic and Jewish knowledge-class cadres of the Popular Front tended to envision a pacific process of qualitative change; the New Deal gave them faith in the potential for meaningful reform, even as they looked to a horizon beyond Roosevelt. Their political loyalties were cemented by gratitude to a president who had opened the doors of the state—and even of the nation—to their ranks for the first time in the country's history.[28]

The Popular Front reformers more likely to maintain a secret romance with revolution were those of northern European Protestant background, and those with long-standing ties to the earlier generations of Fabian-laborite reformers. This may seem ironic, since the ranks of the CP were dominated by the children of immigrant Jews and Catholics. But the strongly reformist tenor of the CP during its Popular Front phase is well known. The Fabian participation in the Popular Front is the final chapter in the tradition of those old-stock Americans who had pioneered the new liberalism in the Gilded Age. By the late 1930s, this constituency's lingering laborite and revolutionary sympathies found only a vicarious expression in their fervent and increasingly controversial support for the Soviet Union. No individual better exemplified the compartmentalized radicalism of the old-stock Fabians than Harry Ward. Like others with similar views, Ward would be red-baited and hounded from the position of prominence in American reform he had occupied for decades. His case illustrates how the influential tradition of which he was a part—one he inherited from Henry Demarest Lloyd, Jane Addams, Walter Rauschenbusch, and many others—met its end.

In 1934 Harry Ward was a professor of Christian ethics at Union Theological Seminary in New York and a leader of long standing in the social gospel's left wing. He had served continuously as the chairman of the national committee of the ACLU since the organization's founding in 1920, and he had been deeply involved in support work for the labor movement, especially for its radical wing, throughout the 1910s and the 1920s. In 1934, Roger Baldwin helped to persuade Ward to take over the chairmanship of the American League Against War and Fascism (ALAWF), which was rocked by conflict between its leading CP contingent and the CP's anti-Soviet rivals on the left. J. B. Matthews, who was, like Ward, a Methodist clergyman and also, unlike Ward, an SP member, had left the position vacant. (Matthews soon afterward became a professional anticommunist, working for the HUAC after its creation in 1938.) Ward thus commenced his role as one of the country's most prominent fellow travelers of the CP, meaning that he was as close an ally of the party as he could be without actually joining it; one journalist dubbed him "the model of a model fellow traveler." Under his leadership, the ALAWF became, by many accounts, the single most important Popular Front organization in the country. (It changed its name to the American League for Peace and Democracy [ALPD] in 1937.)[29] For decades, Ward had championed a long front of liberal reformers and leftist radicals, a broad front cemented by Enlightenment values and specifically by a belief in qualitative progress toward a society of greater equality and freedom. Ward remained open to a convulsive process of thoroughgoing political and social change, but he became very careful about expressing this openness. Under his leadership, the American League focused on foreign affairs, pressing for action against fascist aggression while at the same time voicing sharp reservations about going to war, but it also participated in militant action against American racism, which ALPD members perceived as the cutting edge of domestic fascism.

Ward appealed to American liberals of all stripes to support the Popular Front, but he and the American League harbored reservations about supporting the liberals' leader, Franklin Roosevelt, until at least 1935. Like many on the left, Ward at first viewed Roosevelt with great suspicion and found in the NRA an imitation of the "corporatist" approach to economic recovery undertaken in Italy and Germany. Ward, iterating the Marxist view that fascism was the form taken by efforts to save a decrepit capitalism, wrote, "For the present, the form of American fascism is to be discerned in the course of events under the Roosevelt Administration." Furthermore, "The whole program of the Roosevelt administration is permeated by preparedness for War," the ALAWF's "Manifesto and Program," adopted at its 1934 congress, charged, citing military appropriations and the NRA's military style. This manifesto asserted, "The imminent War danger is only another expression of the fundamental crisis of the capitalist system." The ALAWF condemned imperialism, "all[ying] itself with the masses in the colonial and semi-colonial countries . . . particularly . . . the Philippines and Cuba," thus including the United States among the imperialist powers.[30] It took changes in Roosevelt's foreign policy to really warm the ALAWF to him. After his famous "quarantine" speech in October 1937, the league began to quote Roosevelt in its publications and to fend off criticisms by stating that it was following his lead. However, that same year, with the league moving away from its simple pro-neutrality stance, toward a demand that the U.S. government discriminate between aggressors and victims in foreign conflicts, the league's materials continued to warn against giving the president too much power in setting foreign policy. At the league's 1937 congress, Reinhold Niebuhr, who was then emerging as an intellectual leader of the pro-intervention forces, nonetheless warned against idealizing the U.S. role in the world when he told the league's congress that "the democratic powers are the great capitalist powers and the capitalist forces within these nations are less interested in the preservation of democracy than in the preservation of capitalism."[31]

Despite the lingering echoes of an early-1930s radically anti-capitalist stance that Niebuhr's remarks carry, after mid-decade the trend for fellow travelers such as Harry Ward was toward a Popular Front stance of alliance with liberals. While Communists and anticommunists alike focused on the Popular Front's attachment to the Soviet Union, this coalition's rank and file viewed its least common denominator as the defense of democratic rights and the empowerment of ordinary citizens. While some liberals defined those rights strictly in terms of procedural fairness, Popular Front liberals saw democratic rights in terms of the liberty of labor and racial minorities to fight for equality. Ward cast fascism as the antithesis to the kind of people's democracy that the Popular Front wanted to realize in America. Whereas Communists in the early 1930s had stressed fascist repression of the left, the Popular Front insisted that the real fascist targets were democracy and reform. "Under the smoke screen of a defense against Communism, the Fascist International is an attack against Democracy, because Democracy leads to the kind of social change that the Fascists are opposed to," Ward argued in 1937. According to this view, those who favored the New Deal's current achievements and the preservation of traditional liberties should join forces with those who looked to the New Deal as the continuation of an evolution toward social democracy.[32]

But Ward held open the possibility of future social change, linking that possibility to the defense of political democracy. He called on liberals to return to the old Enlightenment vision of sequential historical change, rather than viewing the achievements of the present as the end of history. "The intellectual liberals . . . played a creative part in helping rising capitalism to smash feudalism." They were wrong if they thought their part in historic change was over. Ward argued, "[T]he liberals have a chance to discover that their middle road of 'democracy' . . . leads forward into radical change," and he urged a transcendence of "the capitalist-democratic" revolution that, in his view, had shaped American history.[33]

Despite differences over such large philosophical issues, and over the limits of various specific New Deal proposals, the issue of communism, in the late 1930s, began driving a wedge between Popular Front liberals and the others to whom Ward had appealed for unity. Conflicts over communism crystallized the differences between the branch of liberalism represented by Ward's advocacy of continuing sequential change in America and the branch that felt fundamental change was over. The opposition to the Popular Front was spearheaded by libertarians in the ACLU and anti-Soviet leftists, with both sets of individuals beginning to identify themselves through their rhetorical hostility to "progressive" politics, a term increasingly identified at this time with the Popular Front.[34] By 1939 the cause of anticommunism had made great strides in the United States, recovering from its earlier association with incredible right-wing zealots and from the Soviet Union's Depression-era allure.[35] Most leftists stuck with the Soviet Union until 1939. But the minority that had broken from the Popular Front earlier, or who had never joined it, became better organized after 1935. Anti-Soviet leftists such as Norman Thomas and Sidney Hook found their unexpected historic function in the campaign of the late 1930s to discredit progressives who would not condemn Communist parties and states along the lines they laid out.

They attacked the American League and Ward, focusing on his uncritical views on the Soviet Union. Hook organized the Committee for Cultural Freedom (CCF) in 1939, amassing an impressive list of signatories for his statement charging that the Soviet Union and Nazi Germany were essentially identical in their denial of liberty in intellectual as well as political matters. Ward added his name to a rejoinder produced by fellow travelers. They enumerated a set of differences between these two regimes—highlighting the fascist embrace of war for its own sake, in contrast to the Soviet use of war solely for instrumental purposes—defending the progressive nature of the Soviet Union, and criticizing the CCF for disrupting left unity in the face of fascism. Hook responded by escalating his letter-writing campaign against Ward—who was not an organizer of the anti-CCF statement—calling the clergyman an apologist for totalitarianism and a smear artist.[36]

How was Hook to gain traction for these rather familiar complaints? Anticommunists within the left hit upon the tactic of demanding some kind of a disavowal—either a renunciation of past politics by an individual, or a repudiation of that individual by his associates—as a way of keeping politically symbolic disputes alive. Several signers of the CCF's statement sat on the national executive board of the ACLU, and it was there that the showdown occurred. Norman Thomas and John Haynes Holmes were the foremost executive board members who supported Hook's call for Ward to resign from the position of chairman. They argued that it was "inappropriate" for the same person to chair the ALPD and the ACLU. This left the ACLU open to what Thomas called "legitimate" criticism that its agenda was not what it purported to be, but rather that it was manipulated by the same "alien" forces at work in the American League. (Of course, Thomas and Hook were doing more than anyone else to legitimate exactly the criticisms of which they now warned.)

This faction's growing anticommunism coincided with the mounting conflict within the ACLU's board between strict libertarianism and progressive advocacy. The most important dispute arose in 1937 over the question of defending the right of Henry Ford to circulate anti-union literature to his employees. The recently created National Labor Relations Board forbade this activity. Some on the ACLU's board found this offensive and wanted the organization to oppose the ruling. Holmes complained, "[W]e are allowing ourselves to become mere advocates of the rights of labor." His statement, with its misleading implication that the role of labor's advocate was something new for the ACLU, was representative of the new refrain sung by the libertarian, anticommunist faction on the board. The left-wing faction on the board, led by Mary van Kleeck, the lawyer Abraham Isserman, Ward, Elizabeth Gurley Flynn, and Robert Dunn, indeed was primarily concerned with defending the rights of labor. While this cleavage within the ACLU's board was openly discussed, the libertarian faction apparently determined that the way to break the back of its opposition was with the issues of pro-Sovietism and Communist influence, not by arguing for an abandonment of labor.[37]

In August 1939, the nonaggression pact linking Germany and the Soviet Union struck the political world like a tidal wave, providing support for those who had argued for the affinities between the two regimes and causing incalculable damage to those in the Popular Front who had spent years asserting that they were polar opposites locked in holy combat. The political fallout damaged the fellow travelers' position in every respect, on every issue. Roger Baldwin for one was "never so shaken" by anything else. He, along with uncounted others, resolved to distance himself from the CP and the Soviets. He resigned from the ALPD, stating that he saw no way the group, bound as by links of iron to a defense of the Soviet Union, could be of any further use in the changed world situation. He could no longer work with Communists, since they would demand a blackout on discussion of unfolding international events as the price of their cooperation. In September the Germans invaded Poland, and quickly the Soviets followed suit. Now the great champion of international peace was in the "aggressor" category so long denounced by the ALPD. In November it made things worse by invading Finland in the "Winter War," seeking a further territorial buffer zone against enemies.[38]

The endgame for the ALPD came swiftly. In October 1939 Ward testified before the HUAC, complaining of the committee's seizure of the ALPD's records and undergoing interrogation by Matthews. The heat was on for other groups in the Popular Front as well, such as the American Youth Congress, whose very public patronage by Eleanor Roosevelt came to an end. Under criticism for inaction, the ALPD condemned the Soviet invasion of Finland and called for an embargo on Soviet goods, but the ALPD still maintained that the Soviet Union should not be viewed as the moral equivalent of Germany or Japan. This was too little, too late. The defections came by the thousands, and the ALPD's raison d'être came into question. In early 1940 Ward and a handful of others simply disbanded the ALPD.[39]

The collapse of the ALPD symbolized the collapse of the whole Popular Front, and Ward's personal endgame followed quickly. It was played out within the ACLU's national leadership. Once the ALPD no longer existed, the "problem" created by Ward's dual chairmanships ostensibly had vanished as well. But Thomas and Holmes kept up the pressure for him to resign, and his support had thinned badly. The anticommunist faction battled with the progressive bloc over a series of resolutions designed to endorse the CCF's concept of totalitarianism and to bar from high ACLU office those who did not accept the new line on the Soviet Union. In February, the ACLU's governing bodies adopted a resolution stating that officers and staff must favor civil liberties "in all aspects and all places." While the resolution construed "support" of either fascism or communism as a violation of that principle, it offered an open-ended definition of such support. Membership in political organizations supporting foreign totalitarianism would count—the CP was named but others might qualify—as would "public declarations indicat[ing] . . . support" of totalitarianism. The board, besides barring

Communists from leading roles in the ACLU, was giving itself the power to inspect the political statements and activities of candidates for office within the group and to make its own judgments as to incriminating speech and behavior. The nation's premier advocates of free speech and conscience were establishing their own orthodoxy, one that went far beyond simple fealty to that cause. To put it differently, the ACLU embraced the official orthodoxy of cold war America before there was a cold war. Ward resigned from the chairmanship and the organization, likely fearing that the next step in the anticommunist agenda within the ACLU would be to expel him under the new rules.

Ward's fate foreshadowed the expulsion of the whole Popular Front from the ranks of respectable liberalism in the late 1940s. Revealingly, the board thanked him effusively for his long and unbending service to the ACLU's cause and for his "unqualified fairness" in his dealings as president. This was less curious than it seemed. The argument for ousting him was based only on a theoretical conflict of conscience on his part that was not borne out in his behavior. As with Hook's demand for public recantation, the conflict over communism among liberals and the left at this time set the future pattern for McCarthyism. What mattered was not observable and specific behavior, but one's loyalties. Ward's associations had become suspect to the inner circle of liberal activist leadership represented in the ACLU hierarchy, and he would not repudiate his past. This was what made him an un-person, to use a term coined by George Orwell in 1949 in his novel *1984*, and this—the issue of recantation to the proper authorities—would become the nub of each individual case of threatened or actual blacklisting in the 1950s.[40]

Of all of the Popular Front's constituencies, the exile of the Fabians was the most total, the interment of their many years of activism, and their one-time prominence, located in the farthest reaches of the pauper's graveyard of history. Besides Ward, there are other examples. One of these is that of Mary van Kleeck, the longtime head of the Social Science Division at the Russell Sage Foundation, a giant figure in the social work profession and the world of philanthropy between the 1910s and the 1930s. She, like Ward, became a fierce Soviet apologist; if anything, she was more militant than Ward in her criticism of the New Deal into the mid-1930s. Like Ward, she was pushed beyond the pale of respectability by 1940.[41] As with the Protestant clergy, some precincts of social work remained quietly friendly to leftists in the 1940s and 1950s. But, in both of these professions, the memory of radicalism became a source of embarrassment and fear, discussed only in whispers by those old enough to know this hidden history. From the Gilded Age until the end of the 1930s, American Fabians had entertained the question of social transformation as a normal and reasonable one, whatever position they ultimately took. Of the three major social bases of the Popular Front, the transformation of Fabianism during the Second Progressive Era was the most complete. It was crippled and all but killed.

The American Theory of Fascism

The diverse constituencies of the Popular Front joined forces because they shared a vision of qualitative progress that would emancipate the downtrodden and create a better world, and the threat that fascism posed to progress during the 1930s and 1940s made antifascism an especially strong unifying force. Antifascism always powerfully reminded Popular Front activists of what they were fighting for and against. The ALAWF anatomized fascism most systematically. American antifascists conjured an image of fascism that borrowed from formulations current within the international left, but that ultimately was a distinctively American image. They saw in fascism a noxious amalgam of hyper-nationalistic racism with extreme political violence directed particularly against organized labor, and they saw big business and financiers pulling the strings behind the scenes.

Following European antifascist rhetoric, American opponents of fascism discerned in this movement a determination by the forces of big capital to reverse through terror the gradual trend toward political and social democracy that had proved unstoppable over the course of the nineteenth century and the early twentieth. Harry Ward contended that fascism was a "gangsterized militarism," an effort by a dying capitalism to save itself through foreign conquests and by repressing the organized working class at home, finally disallowing all political opposition. Despite its pretensions, fascism was "a reactionary coup [d'état]. Not a revolution." It garnered support from a middle class that feared working-class empowerment, yet its gangsterism was quietly supported and probably bankrolled by big money, charged leftists and Popular Front liberals. Robert LaFollette's Senate investigation into anti-labor violence by large employers gave wide credence to Ward's claim that the brown shirts and the Black Shirts of European fascism had their American counterparts not in William Dudley Pelley's Silver Shirts and other marginal groups but rather in the "labor spy racket" and the large goon squads in Henry Ford's employ. "A Senate committee recently revealed," a league pamphlet announced, "that the same group of financial interests is supporting various anti-labor and anti-red organizations. . . . the same sort that financed Hitler . . . steel and munitions, and the bankers behind them." Ward wrote, "The country that has developed our physically brutal form of the 'third degree' has nothing to learn from Mussolini's Black Shirts or Hitler's Storm Troops."[42]

Popular Front antifascists conceded that an American fascism would differ from the European variety, but they found that cold comfort. "In the countries where democratic procedure is more deeply rooted and democratic tradition longer established," such as the United States, wrote Ward, fascism "proceeds more gradually, by the whittling away of representative controls and guarantees of freedom." The "repression" necessary for a fascist takeover, Ward said, might even "be accomplished by due process of law, under the form of an allegedly democratic state." It might occur that way because there was no militant socialist movement afoot in America that required violent suppression. A "completely repressive type of fascism will not find sufficient popular acclamation or toleration" under present conditions, he wrote in 1935. Only a war or a more total economic collapse would create such conditions. These differences in political behavior were finally secondary, Ward insisted, precisely because he agreed with the fundamental Marxist argument that such political forms were means to a socioeconomic end; the forms would vary from one country to another.[43]

Just as important, Popular Front antifascists contended that American fascists, rather than targeting Jews as a scapegoat for society's ills as in Germany, would build upon their nation's tradition of white supremacist violence against African Americans. Those who pointed with relief to the relative lack of anti-Semitic violence in America were barking up the wrong tree. Where European affairs were concerned, the American League stressed anti-Jewish actions and worked with Jewish groups to increase awareness of these phenomena. But the American parallel to European Jew-hatred was anti-black racism, and Ward and the league warned that Depression and fascism would bring a rise in lynching and other racist violence. When "racial ego mania" comes to the fore in America, Ward wrote, "it will be the Negro, as it has been and is, that will bear the brunt of that attack." Like other Popular Front groups, the American League persistently rang the tocsin against lynching and worked to make itself an interracial organization as well as part of an international solidarity movement. The league had a "sub-session" on "national and racial minorities," as it did for women's, labor, farm, youth, and religious groups, at the league's congresses. The league's actions in solidarity with people of African descent earned it a large store of credibility among African American activists. At the 1937 Pittsburgh conference, with fifty black delegates in attendance, white delegates organized a protest demonstration against hotels that would not house black customers. Roy Wilkins wrote in the *Amsterdam News*, "If the traditional prejudices can be battered down by the radical and liberal elements in their organizations such as the American League, the Negro will become a stalwart part of the movement for peace and democracy."

Perhaps most important, the league organized to protest the Italian invasion of Ethiopia when very few white Americans cared. In the summer of 1935, the ALAWF joined with Harlem's Provisional Committee for the Defense of Ethiopia to plan a march through Harlem in August to protest the invasion. At that time the Soviet Union was getting along with Mussolini's regime, but the league went its own way, speaking for interracial alliances based in principle and seeking to unite black and Italian American antifascists. Two parades, one led by Italians and the other by African Americans, met and merged to form a stream of twenty-five thousand people marching through Harlem. The league also organized a "Hands Off Ethiopia" rally of nine thousand at Madison Square Garden in September 1935 and a "People's March for Peace" of fifteen thousand in October, which the New York branch of the NAACP endorsed. In 1937, the ALAWF organized picket lines at the Italian consulate in New York.[44]

The prominence of racism in the American understanding of fascism was, in fact, the distinctive American contribution to analyzing this phenomenon. The location of radical racism at the core of fascism became familiar in the 1940s and afterward as a liberal theme. The Popular Front's antifascism crystallized into a single image of the fascist as everything opposed to the "democracy" that the Popular Front championed. But the most widely resonant connection that antifascism made with Americans was the link it made between Nazis in Germany and violent white supremacists in America. This was an enemy that liberal and radical Americans knew, and those who had done time in the trenches fighting against the political right also knew how racists and union-busting operatives tended to cooperate, south and north, west and east. To the North Carolina Communist Junius Scales, disaffected from the white southern culture in which he grew up, "Fascism meant the dominance of the know-nothing, bigoted, hateful brutality that I knew locally; were it to triumph on an international scale, it would make life intolerable."[45] In California, the lawyer and writer Carey McWilliams and others spoke of fascism as a force whose racism was directed at Latinos and Asian Americans as well as African Americans.[46]

The equation of German anti-Semitism and American racism did much to fix the energies of American antifascists on the exposure and destruction of white supremacy at home, but it also helps to explain the emergence of antifascism itself among American leftists and liberals. Antifascism was voiced earliest and most strongly, among both liberals and radicals, by those already enlisted in the none-too-wide ranks of antiracists. When, in 1934, Stephen Wise penned an article in DuBois's *Crisis* that was bluntly titled, "Parallel Between Hitlerism and the Persecution of Negroes," he surely was seeking to drum up support for Jewish opposition to the Nazi regime among the antiracist readership of this magazine; he did not need to convince readers that white supremacy in the United States was bad. DuBois, who was sometimes criticized for his allegedly friendly view of Japanese fascism before World War II, was a coruscating critic of Nazi anti-Semitism, sounding the alarm for Americans in the 1930s. Writing from Germany in 1936, DuBois testified that Nazi practices toward the Jews "surpass in vindictive cruelty and public insult anything" he had seen in his life, and he noted that he had "seen much." Like Ward and Wise, DuBois stated that Jews occupied a place in Germany corresponding to that of blacks in America. Upon his return home he wrote, "There has been no tragedy in modern times equal in its awful effects to the fight on the Jews in Germany." Reaching back deep into the stock of horrors contained in the Protestant-abolitionist memory, he continued, "It is an attack on civilization, comparable only to such horrors as the Spanish Inquisition and the African slave trade. It has set civilization back a hundred years."[47] The image of fascism as an inexplicable regression to primitive cruelty, as an eruption of sadistic and essentially irrational violence, proved more powerful in the American mind than any more historically specific or politically concrete understanding of this dreadful phenomenon. That image of fascism, as a descent into the violent spaces of the id, was rooted, for those who reported their horror at fascism's spectacle early on, in a visceral revulsion against racist violence. In 1944 Lester Granger, the executive secretary of the National Urban League, told students and faculty at Smith College, "We recognize Fascism . . . as being the same sinister creature, the same vicious enemy of mankind, no matter what its national garb or location. . . . [T]he anti-Negroism of Mississippi, Alabama and Georgia, and a half-dozen other states of the Union is first cousin to—no, the direct progenitor of—Fascism at its worst in Hitler's Germany."[48] Antifascism and antiracism would gain ground together in America. But these gains occurred only haltingly.

The cultural reversal that made racism seem like a violation of the American creed of equal opportunity, and that made "diversity" a touchstone for almost any American in public life, was a very long time coming, not complete until the twentieth century was at least three-quarters over. It was a hard-fought struggle on many fronts that ultimately would put racists on the cultural defensive for the first time in American history. During the 1920s, the white supremacism (and anti-Catholicism) of the Ku Klux Klan had been embraced by white middle-class Americans around the country as paradigmatically American. The beginnings of the struggle to overturn such attitudes in an openly political context lay in the Popular Front's antifascism and antiracism. The CP was the most aggressive in laying down markers for antiracism. Scales

Jim Crow vs. fascism

found the Communists he met in his college town of Chapel Hill "not remarkable" in intellect and talents. But they stood out from the crowd in their opposition to prejudice: "They would not tolerate white-chauvinist, anti-Semitic, or male-supremacist attitudes where they could do anything about them; they were passionate about the rights of working people; they hated the brutality of war and Fascism." Others in the Popular Front might find the Communists overly sensitive, but Communist zeal set a tone of celebrating ethnic diversity—and specifically of celebrating the historic contributions of African Americans to American life—that the entire Popular Front honored. In New York, white Communist schoolteachers became particularly well known as dogged advocates of racial equality and what was then called "inter-cultural" education, working with black teachers and parents to press for the observance of Negro History Week in the schools and giving special attention to black students to make sure they were not left behind educationally. In the spring of 1941, the International Workers' Order, a major Popular Front organization comprising divisions representing different ethnic groups, organized a pageant celebrating "the Negro in American life," featuring songs by Paul Robeson, as a way of expressing its enthusiasm for cultural pluralism and what it called the "unity of national groups." The "Ballad for Americans," performed by Robeson on the radio and then at the Republican National Convention in 1940, was the most famous invocation of this pluralist nationalism.[49]

Some today may find the rhetoric of ethnic "contributions" banal. But if so, they ought to consider how progressive such an idea was when compared to the attitudes of well-placed white racial liberals of the 1930s, such as the white southerner Will Alexander, who carefully attributed some of the problems faced by African Americans to their "inferiority complexes" and their "assumption of separateness," or Harold Ickes, who praised the "meek submission" that was supposedly "one of the great virtues of the Negro race as well as one of its great faults." These men were rightly viewed as among the best friends that African Americans had in Washington, sincere in their enmity to white supremacy. Yet such pioneers of white racial liberalism, along with the black social scientists E. Franklin Frazier and John Dollard, believed that black culture was defective and partly responsible for black suffering. In their view, African Americans hardly had much to contribute to American culture.[50]

Radicals such as Robeson formed the vanguard of a broader liberal interculturalism (which presaged the "multiculturalism" of later decades). One white Communist from the South wrote, in a striking formulation, that African Americans "are capable of giving the whites as much as the whites are capable of giving them. The Negro people form an integral part of America. Their cultural heritage is an American heritage. The American people have a right to this cultural heritage." Communists, "[b]y defining Black America's struggle for cultural recognition as a source of creative energy for the entire nation . . . helped give their white constituency a sense that they had a personal stake in black empowerment and that cultural interchange between the races represented a *defining* feature of the American experience. . . . In doing so, they helped give the struggle for racial equality the aura of a movement of cultural regeneration." In addition to the specific national value located in the African American cultural heritage, here germinated the more general idea that America's mongrel nature was something great, the source of a strength in which fascism would meet its match and its master. That idea eventually would be honored in Hollywood wartime pictures encapsulating American military resiliency in "multicultural" platoons of men from different, if stereotyped, backgrounds. As far as white Americans went, the former stress on the special value of the black experience remained more the province of radicals, as a kind of underground theme that resurfaced along with the repressed impulses of American rebellion starting in the late 1950s, when Norman Mailer and Jack Kerouac evoked the existential vitality of a politically ambiguous American negritude.[51]

During the 1940s, the most militant antiracists of all races framed their crusade for diversity as an essential part of the war against fascism. The class-oriented definition of fascism, the one that focused attention on the control of government by big business and the violent suppression of independent labor unions, was often invoked by American liberals and leftists throughout this decade. The pages of *PM*, the afternoon New York daily that served as the splashy venue for a nonsectarian Popular Front viewpoint between 1940 and 1948, were filled with warnings of just such a continuing fascist danger.[52] This and similar political outlets also railed against lynchings in the South during and after the war. Progressives thought that fascists were both anti-labor and anti-black, and that they used racial divisions to advance a plutocratic agenda. Yet the class-based aspect of fascism bore an uncertain relationship to the perhaps more emotionally potent equation of fascism with racist violence. In 1950, practically the last echo of Popular Front antifascism was heard in movie theaters across the country as the heroine of the sentimental film comedy *Born Yesterday*, played by the Popular Front activist Judy Holliday (who won an Academy Award for her role, shortly before her career was curtailed because of her political activities), screamed "Fascist!" at her erstwhile lover. He was a businessman in Washington seeking special favors from the government, and he had slapped her for her newfound insubordination. During and just after the war, liberals who worried about the "dollar-a-year" business executives manning government offices began to talk easily of a fascist danger in the District of Columbia. But there was nothing new in businessmen using government for their own purposes, bad as it was for the country. The fascist epithet, although it always would have special power, came to be used rather loosely. The common-sense picture of the fascist enemy at home during the 1940s differed little from the familiar patterns of the American right. The significance of fascism as a concept, certainly in its original European environment, lay precisely in its newness, in its difference from the traditional right. In the Second Progressive Era in America, "fascist" became a new word for the enemy one already knew. As it happened, the conception of fascism as government of, by, and for big business was not the one that would survive the convulsions of American politics in the late 1940s. As the liberal movement was transformed by the purging of its left wing during the red scare that followed World War II, the memory of antifascism survived only as a battle against racism, a battle rendered a matter of emotional and interpersonal struggle, a struggle shorn of its economic context.

The Emergence of Racial Liberalism

The most lasting legacy of Popular Front antifascism was its major contribution to the cultural pluralism that, by increasing degrees, came to dominate post–World War II American liberalism. Militant opposition to racism emerged as a prominent line of division between liberals and leftists, and between liberals in the Popular Front and those outside of it, in the 1930s and 1940s. Where blacks and whites came together in the Popular Front's organizations, virtually all black activists and white Communists challenged white liberals as never before to make antiracism part of their bottom line. This issue rose to the surface with a special clarity in the South because the issue of Jim Crow segregation made the question of one's position on racism inescapably specific; ambiguous answers became harder and harder to give. Southern liberals and leftists alike, during the Depression and after, acknowledged that the culture and politics of white supremacy formed the Achilles' heel of efforts to liberalize the South, to break the hold of the southern Democratic "barons" over the region's politics. But those identified as white liberals tended to shy away from a frontal assault on segregation and racism, feeling that the New Deal's program of regional development would raise living standards for black and white together (meaning separately) in the South, and that ultimately an enhanced horizon of economic opportunity would make way for a politics less mean in this region. They asserted that economic backwardness made the South fertile ground for the zero-sum intuitions of white racism—*if black Americans advance, I lose*—and that only a less straitened sense of well-being could change this. This was the perspective offered in the 1938 *Report on the Economic Conditions of the South,* which was produced by prominent white southern New Dealers with the blessing of the Roosevelt administration.

Thus, when pressed, southern white liberals during the 1930s and early 1940s tended to admit that they did not favor an outright challenge to Jim Crow. This was true initially within the Southern Regional Council (SRC), a moderate liberal group established in 1944. Many of the founding black members stated their opposition to segregation in principle, while indicating their willingness not to press for its abolition at that time, in the "Durham Manifesto," which was issued following a meeting in 1942 of distinguished black southerners in that North Carolina city. Some of the SRC's white members saw even this as too much and proceeded to declaim their lack of interest in the segregation issue.[53] Even the Southern Conference on Human Welfare (SCHW), the main southern Popular Front group, which was relentlessly red-baited from its founding in 1938, dealt with the segregation issue ambiguously. Inspired in part by the *Report on the Economic Conditions,* but including the active participation of Communists and fellow travelers, the SCHW gained notoriety by pledging not to hold segregated meetings after it was forced to comply with Jim Crow law at its founding conference in Birmingham. Yet it held back at first from taking a clear political position on Jim Crow. The Southern Conference Educational Fund, a group spun off from the SCHW, took an outspoken anti-segregation stance shortly after it was founded in 1946, and the SRC declared itself against Jim Crow in 1949, indicating that the late 1940s was the time when this dam broke among white liberals nationally.[54]

Before the late 1940s, interracial southern liberal groups experienced serious strains when black participants realized how fearful their white allies were of confronting the segregation question, and when the whites found to their shock that their black comrades planned to join the issue publicly. After World War II, Junius Scales, as a secret Communist, became active in the Committee for North Carolina (CNC), the state affiliate of the SCHW. At one point he intimated that the CNC should not support a proposal in the state legislature for a new teaching hospital at the University of North Carolina unless it were racially integrated and hired black doctors and nurses in decent numbers. Frank P. Graham, the president of the university, the first president of the SCHW, and a beloved figure among white southern liberals, disagreed. Raising this issue could kill the hospital entirely. "As I made my inquiry," remembers Scales, "I could see undisguised annoyance in the faces of several white liberals, who felt that I was being obstructionist and tiresome by raising the point." But Scales did not have to rebut Graham's position. Dr. David Jones did it instead. Jones was president of Bennett College, a black women's school in Greensboro, and a prominent supporter of Popular Front organizations. Jones practically exploded, saying, "My GOD! How LONG must my people wait until the first faltering word is spoken by white men of goodwill saying that segregation is *criminal*—that it is *destroying* my people?"[55]

Scales reflected that this dispute illustrated the difference between leftists and liberals, in a way not accounted for by textbook definitions of political ideology. "I found a gulf beginning to separate me from the majority of white liberals, who still clung to separate-but-equal delusions; were eager to avoid a confrontation on the 'race issue' . . . and were, all too often, ready to seek a 'solution' by promising a future fight which usually did not take place." Scales conceded that he expected much of his fellow southern whites. He knew how hazardous it was to oppose segregation in the South and conceded that "courageous" liberals such as Graham suffered opprobrium and intimidation from their fellow whites for going as far as they did.[56] Graham would be named to serve out a term in the U.S. Senate in 1949 and would be defeated in a vicious primary fight in 1950 by a Democratic opponent who accused him of promoting interracial sex—all of this against one of the South's more impressive sons, who by 1950 had come out in favor of *voluntary* desegregation only.[57] But Scales also knew that blacks risked life and limb, not high office, when opposing segregation, and he saw them willing to do so nonetheless. Here the interwar left critique of liberals recurred in a new context: the gaff was still too much for them to stand. In fact, this had become a non-content-based way of defining liberals and radicals. There always would be some issue of social justice on which most couldn't stand the gaff, but small numbers could. Viewed from the left, this moving boundary was the margin dividing liberals from radicals. In the middle decades of the twentieth century that margin hovered over the issue of "social equality" between black and white.

At least that was one view. Another was that standing up for the rights of African Americans was the essence of political liberalism. Even as radicals such as Scales lamented that liberals would not fight this battle, others began to define liberalism in terms of civil rights advocacy. This association would become axiomatic in American politics starting in the 1960s, when breakthrough civil rights legislation finally became part of U.S. law. It was in the 1940s that civil rights advocates began concerted efforts to establish that link. They asserted that true liberals, those who fulfilled the ideals of the New Deal and Franklin Roosevelt's leadership, would fight to apply the "Four Freedoms" that Roosevelt outlined in 1941—freedom of speech, of worship, from fear, and from want—to all

Americans regardless of race. This effort to extend a full serving of rights specifically to African Americans, and to argue that this was logically implied and even desired by Roosevelt himself, began even before Roosevelt died (after which time, of course, views that he never expressed—like these—were easily attributed to him). In this perspective, weakness such as that which Scales perceived in Graham's behavior appeared not as the failure of liberalism but as a betrayal of liberalism.

African American authors outlined this new concept of liberalism, one that had had no constituency when DuBois had tried it out in earlier years, in 1942 and 1943. Louis Martin wrote an article for *The Crisis* in 1942 titled "To Be or Not to Be a Liberal," in which he attached the wartime rhetoric of democracy to racial liberalism. In his rendition, racial liberalism was precisely nonracial liberalism, meaning that a true liberal acted on the basis of unqualified democratic principles, simply putting race aside. (Subsequently Martin was recruited to conduct publicity among black voters for the Roosevelt-Truman campaign in 1944, and in the 1960s he would work in the Democratic National Committee.)[58] In 1943 Thomas Sancton offered "A Southern View of the Race Question" in the *Negro Quarterly.* Striking a subtly different note, Sancton espied two different kinds of liberalism in American life. One was the old southern white moderation, as embodied in Frank Graham, that refused to challenge Jim Crow even while working to improve the lot of African Americans. To Sancton this was the "liberalism of yielding, yielding on points of justice rather than an active . . . effort to create justice and extend it through the whole broad field of race relations." Sounding a theme of disappointment that was actually less charitable than Scales's, Sancton explained the timidity of the old liberal by charging that he feared "the race of serfs which he hoped to lead gradually to a higher plane of freedom and welfare" might someday reject his leadership "and say 'the hell with you; I want democracy and I want it now.'" The new breed of liberal, in Sancton's view, would consciously reject the special exemption from the principles of democracy and freedom that the South had enjoyed during the First and Second Progressive Eras. In this formulation racial liberalism required an attack on racism, and specifically on the southern power structure.[59]

As this view gained adherents during World War II, taking strength from U.S. war propaganda that pitted American democracy against German and Japanese racism and dictatorship, racial liberalism elicited swift and powerful resistance from white defenders of racial privilege. Such conservatives always cast an eagle eye on the political landscape for emerging threats to their cherished ways of life, South and North. African Americans pressed for access to public housing in Detroit at this time and whites struck back both at the ballot box, electing truculent defenders of a whites-only policy on public housing, and in the streets, with vigilante violence.[60] As discussed below, southern Democrats ousted Henry Wallace from their party's national ticket in 1944 because they feared a new racial liberalism was coalescing around him.

During the 1940s southern segregation became a national political issue for the first time. African Americans and white Popular Fronters seized the opening offered by antifascist war propaganda to press their view, which had been very innovative when they had offered it prior to the attack on Pearl Harbor, that American democracy and pride in America's mongrel character were intimately related, and that racism was un-American. This "Double-V" campaign for victory over racism at home as well as abroad is well known; its Popular Front orientation is somewhat less widely appreciated.[61] The notion that opposition to bigotry was a baseline element specifically in American liberalism became securely anchored within the national leadership of the labor movement, despite the continuing racial exclusionism practiced by many AFL unions and the violent racism displayed by many white workers during the war, when "hate strikes" broke out on several occasions in response to a black presence on the shop floor. CIO activists pressed racial liberalism forward in the labor movement during the 1940s. In Los Angeles, they led a fight against restrictive covenants that barred African Americans from buying houses in various parts of Los Angeles, and they went so far as to organize defense committees for black families under attack from vigilantes who were trying to drive them from certain neighborhoods. The city's CIO Council also got involved in supporting the Sleepy Lagoon defendants, a group of Latinos convicted of crimes on weak evidence, as did many others in the California Popular Front, including Hollywood actors and actresses such as Rita Hayworth and Orson Welles and civil liberties lawyers such as Carey McWilliams. (The convictions were later overturned.) In 1944, Sidney Hillman told the annual convention of the left-wing United Electrical, Radio and Machine Workers of America Union (UE) that "Jew-baiting and red-baiting" were "two sides of the same coin" and implied that both were offensive to American values. It was more notable that two years later George Meany, then the secretary-treasurer of the AFL, saw fit to walk the CIO's line, saying, "Let there be no pussyfooting on the race issue. The American Federation of Labor is determined to bring in the fold of real free trade unionism all American workers of the South—white and black, Gentile and Jew, Protestant and Catholic."[62] Talk was cheap, and coming from the AFL, on this subject it was hard for knowledgeable listeners to take it very seriously. Yet it indicated the beginning of a period when anyone considered a liberal in good standing, and this now included the national leadership of the trade union movement, felt constrained to make some demonstration, convincing or not, of antiracism.

The growing cultural pluralism of the 1940s had sources other than the Popular Front. Communists and their allies were not the only Americans working for civil rights and tolerance of ethnic diversity during the Second Progressive Era. The other major sources feeding this widening freshet were the "intercultural" education movement and the push for interreligious tolerance and cooperation that Protestant, Catholic, and Jewish organizations made in the late 1930s and 1940s. Religious groups such as the National Conference of Jews and Christians, founded in 1927, reacted against the prevalence of racism and anti-immigrant feeling during the 1920s by initiating a long-term effort to educate the public out of anti-Semitism and anti-Catholicism, and the Service Bureau for Intercultural Education, established in 1934, broadened this new liberal front to a battle against ethnocentrism and racism in general. The "Tribal Twenties" had been an era whose atmosphere of ethnocentrism and nativism was embodied in the promulgation of federal legislation that severely restricted immigration, by the intense pressure for "Americanization" of immigrants and their children, pressure that had begun during the era of World War I, and by the rise of the second Ku Klux Klan, which was as much a movement to assert the continuing hegemony of "Anglo-Saxon" Protestant culture as it was an anti-black organization.

The emphasis in the intercultural movement was always on education. Logically enough, teachers were generally found in its forefront. In 1937, the Progressive Education Association, the major liberal educational group in America, formed the Commission on Intercultural Education, which in turn developed an "Education for Democracy" program that celebrated the "contributions" of various ethnic groups to American society. In the second half of the 1930s, the radical anti-Semitic program of the Nazi regime excited growing outrage around the world, America included. This outrage began to turn the tide, among those who thought themselves liberals, against the whole "Americanization" legacy of the 1910s and 1920s. During that earlier era, this assimilation program, which was directed against relative newcomers to the United States, had enjoyed wide support from participants in the first progressive movement. During the 1930s, Franklin Roosevelt and other prominent New Dealers by no means repudiated the memory of the push for Americanization. They continued to believe in the need for assimilation, but they preferred to pursue this goal through relatively gentle and welcoming methods. However, others in the New Deal coalition began to criticize the Americanizers more trenchantly.[63]

In the 1940s, the cultural pluralists really came into their own. As already discussed, in the decade's first half, wartime propaganda and popular culture seemed to validate their affirmation of unity-in-diversity.

Private organizations advanced their pluralistic agenda more aggressively in the late 1940s. Between 1945 and 1950, the number of organizations actively working in the United States to combat racial prejudice rose from about 300 to more than 1,350. In 1946 the Federal Council of Churches (FCC) adopted a resolution denouncing racial segregation and calling for a "non-segregated Church and a non-segregated society." The FCC had a reputation as a liberal organization before that time, but not as aggressively liberal as this on racial matters. It termed segregation "unnecessary and undesirable and a violation of the Gospel of love and human brotherhood."[64] This stark judgment stemmed from the work of a study commission the council had established in 1944 under the leadership of Will Alexander, a former Methodist minister in the vanguard of southern white liberalism since the 1910s. In the late 1940s liberal opponents of racism and ethnocentrism saw an opening and ran to daylight. They named their enemy "prejudice," a concept they popularized through their educational efforts. Cities and states established "human relations" councils and even "human rights" commissions, officially setting for government the task of reforming negative "attitudes" among the populace. Surely this was a new mission for government in America, and its novelty planted the seeds for a new source of resentment against government authority by some, even as it gave heart to others. "Attitude" itself was a rather recently developed conceptual tool among social scientists interested in "intergroup" relations at this time. Education was to be the antidote to prejudiced attitudes.

It was largely a matter of altering individual psychology. An emphasis on individual behavior and merit complemented the new liberal stress on eliminating bad attitudes among individuals. In the late 1940s the Governor's Interracial Commission of Minnesota recommended that citizens recite aloud the following pledge at gatherings of private organizations: "I will never by rumor or careless conversation indict a whole race or religious group by reasons of the delinquency of a few members. I will daily deal with every man in business, social, and political relations solely on the basis of his individual work."[65] Allard Lowenstein, a student at the University of North Carolina in the late 1940s who helped found a group called the National Conference of Students, gave a somewhat hyperactive rendition of similar views. On his stationery Lowenstein proclaimed the group's heroes (such as Frank Graham and the Roosevelts) and their political likes and dislikes: "WE DON'T GIVE A DAMN FOR Jim Crow, the Bosses . . . Franco . . . radicalism . . . Fascism (in all its forms, red and black); HURRAH FOR . . . intermarriage . . . God (whoever He may be)." Members had to sign a pledge reading, "I believe that men should be treated as individuals and judged accordingly. I can take no stock in selfish pride of race, color, or nationality. . . . I am opposed to discrimination, segregation, or any form of bigotry, as manifested in anti-Semitism, Jim Crowism—whether the object of the Jim Crow be Negro, immigrant, Mexican, Jew, Catholic, or Nisei—and in any concept of heightened racial, ethnic or religious nationalism."[66]

An American Dilemma, the massive study of race relations in America written and overseen by the Swede Gunnar Myrdal and published in 1944, which argued that racism contradicted a basic "American creed" of open opportunity and equality before the law, added new momentum to the ascendant force of liberal antiracism, even as it pulled racial liberalism away from its moorings in the Popular Front's antifascism.[67] Liberals who demanded the closure of the gap between ideal and practice quickly pointed to Myrdal's work for authority, and the concept of such a hiatus, and of the possibility of appealing to Americans' better angels as a civil rights strategy, set lasting terms for public discussion. *An American Dilemma* always encountered criticism from the left, over its hopefulness about the potential of education to break the cycle of self-reinforcing racist perceptions, and for its focus on the psychology of individual citizens rather than the need for collective action. These same criticisms could have been directed against the entire movement for intercultural education. Myrdal saw increased affluence as crucial to the alleviation of American racism, but he and his colleagues discerned in racism an independent factor that could not be eliminated indirectly. In this way he combined the perspective of the older white liberals who had preferred to combat white supremacy through economic progress with that of the newer liberals who wanted to tackle racism head-on. Since Communists and Popular Front liberals pressed the question of "white chauvinism" as a litmus-test issue in its own right for true progressives, complaints that Myrdal neglected "structural" issues sounded a bit hollow. He laid bare the principle of racial liberalism that the Popular Front itself promoted.

Myrdal did not neglect issues of economic class, but rather he addressed questions of class in a way likely to outrage Popular Front liberals. He was convinced that poorer whites, particularly in the South but also throughout the United States, were blacks' worst enemies, and that affluent whites were more likely to ally themselves with African Americans in working for racial equality. Myrdal, closely familiar with the work of Ralph Bunche and other left-leaning black academics, rejected as unrealistic their thesis that an interracial working-class alliance was the key to progress toward a nonracist democracy in America. That was a low-percentage play, in Myrdal's view. White workers were fiercely jealous of their caste superiority to African Americans and saw themselves as fighting with blacks to stay off the bottom rung of the social ladder. In contrast, in his view, "the Negro's friend—or the one who is least unfriendly—is still rather the upper class of white people, the people with economic and social security who are truly a 'noncompeting group.'"[68] Myrdal's elitist vision of progress toward civil rights threw down a blunt challenge before anyone who took a class line in American politics. Liberal cultural pluralism, with its focus on educational enlightenment, was implicated in that elitist vision, even if racial liberals often had difficulty acknowledging this. Those who resisted Myrdal's class analysis of white America and its racial politics would find much in the coming years to disturb them.

Women and Feminism

Far less prominent than racial liberalism during the 1940s was the push within progressive circles for equality between women and men. Yet a kind of Popular Front feminism began percolating among leftists and some liberals during this decade. In the 1910s, the concept of feminism had burst on the American political and cultural scene, and many of its cadres had been linked to the political left. As discussed in Chapter 2, this changed during the red scare that followed World War I; the organized feminist movement narrowed its agenda to escape political attack. In the 1920s and 1930s, the ambience of American dissent turned strongly masculine. The propaganda of the labor movement and the New Deal projected images of brawny working men, with stoic, nurturing mothers in the background.[69] Communist polemicists such as Michael Gold habitually depicted their enemies as milquetoasts, often in homophobic terms. The "rebel girl" from a working-class family remained a stock figure in the American left. On the other side of the class divide, novelists such as Dos Passos indelibly etched female characters, such as Mary French in his *The Big Money* (1936), who immersed themselves in social work among the proletariat and were tugged toward leftist commitment through their exposure to the shocking realities of class warfare.[70] Mary French's real-life counterparts continued to exist. Nonetheless, their prominence in current visions of social transformation and its mechanisms declined during the 1930s.

Things changed again in the 1940s, as women's activism and gender egalitarianism—feminism in everything but name—returned from the margins of political culture and became a visible element in Popular Front liberalism during its last years. In turn, the 1950s would be such an antifeminist period that when feminism abruptly reappeared in the 1960s it would seem, to many, to have been reinvented whole. Through its hidden Popular Front sources, post-1960 feminism had indirect links to the left tradition of sexual equality that many today still find hard to imagine.[71]

Popular Front feminism, shaped by antifascism, embedded its images of women's emancipation in a comprehensive vision of social change. In the 1930s, admirers of the Soviet Union counted the feminist aspect of its legal and social order—real enough when compared even to America, let alone to prerevolutionary Russia—among its progressive virtues. One such admirer was Dorothy Wolff Douglas, a politically active economist who wrote books on child labor in America and taught at Smith College. One student she influenced was Bettye Goldstein, later Betty Friedan, who attended Smith in the late 1930s. Douglas emphasized the stark contrast between women's participation in public life in the Soviet Union and in Nazi Germany, where severe gender conservatism and a celebration of "traditional" women's roles formed an integral part of the regime's fascist ideology. Antifascist politics suggested that American women should follow the (idealized) Soviet model, and freighted sexual conservatism with ominous associations, ones that Friedan made clear in her famous work, *The Feminine Mystique* (1963), where she called the suburban home of the 1950s a "comfortable concentration camp" for its female inmates.[72]

During the twentieth century's first half, different groups of activists envisioned American women's emancipation variously. Labor activists, social workers, and leftists opposed the proposed Equal Rights Amendment (ERA) to the Constitution—which most who actually called themselves "feminists" supported—as an elitist, pro-business proposal, and instead worked to extend "protective legislation" that, in their minds, would limit the exploitation of women and children by restricting their working hours and occupations and serve as an "entering wedge" for more comprehensive pro-worker reform. Many avowed feminists then, and almost all feminists after 1960, viewed such legislation as insulting and patriarchal, as it reinforced the idea that women were and ought to be—like children—a "dependent" class.[73] Up to the 1940s, champions of protective legislation, who accounted for most women's advocates who identified as either liberal or left, joined labor unions in pressing for a "family wage," that is for a wage paid to men that would be high enough to keep wives and children out of the dehumanizing world of wage labor. Thus they did position women as economic dependents.

Yet they were caught in a contradiction, for they also sympathized with the traditional Marxist view that women's departure from the unpaid world of household labor and their entry into the social sphere of production was a precondition of women's emancipation and society's progress. When the Communist thinker Mary Inman argued that housework should be viewed as productive labor, and that the aim of progressive forces should be to recognize its value and organize housewives, the CP rebuked her, unwilling to countenance a form of women's work that the left generally had deemed a vestige of feudalism. Communists during the Popular Front period tried to settle the issue by seeking broad left-liberal support for a "Women's Charter," an alternative to the ERA that would preserve protective legislation while guaranteeing women various rights. Similarly, the Congress of American Women (CAW), established as a Popular Front group in 1946, produced its own proposed Constitutional amendment that would ban all "discrimination" based on sex or marital status, but that added, "Nothing in this article shall be so construed to invalidate or prevent the passage of legislation improving the condition of women in their work or in their family status."[74] Debate over what improved the condition of women was impossible to resolve. But this formulation indicates the balance that the Popular Front sought to strike.

The war intensified both aspects of the Popular Front's gender politics. The rush of women into wage labor, and of wage-earning women into higher-paid jobs, encouraged the progressive tendency to affirm such activity and to demand equal pay and opportunities. At the same time, the customary work of homemakers, particularly the management of family consumption, gained enhanced respect as the government depicted it as part of the war effort. While the war was ongoing the CP was reluctant to press women's particular interests, just as it downplayed civil rights issues and supported labor's no-strike pledge, believing that nothing should detract from an all-out drive for victory over fascism. Without the CP's participation, no important progressive effort was going to be launched. Only when the war was over, in 1946, did Communists and their allies form the CAW, at the very moment when returning veterans were displacing women from many of the jobs they had gotten during the war.

This late-blooming Popular Front effort expressed the pent-up political demands of activists who felt that a corner had been turned in the emancipation of American women. Recognizing that women remained saddled with the major burden of housework and child-rearing duties, the CAW, like the CP, demanded publicly funded childcare facilities and school lunch programs. They also advocated a forty-hour work week and an old-age benefit program that would begin—for workers and for their wives who did not work outside the home—at age sixty. All this was appended to demands for full political and social equality for women and for the "right of all women to work; equal pay for equal work; equal training; upgrading and seniority with men in all occupations." (They still denounced the ERA and, paradoxically or not, stood by existing protective legislation.)[75] However, local chapters of the CAW in practice focused not on advancing the workplace interests of wage-earning women but rather on supporting homemakers and wives and mothers who were working the "second shift": they formed babysitting cooperatives, sought to preserve childcare facilities created during wartime, and protested the rising price of meat.[76] The organization was exceptional among women's political groups—but typical of Communist-led efforts—in its determined interracialism. One of its leaders was Claudia Jones, a prominent Afro-Caribbean Communist, and black women were active in local chapters around the country, even though their inclusion by the majority of white members could be awkward, as Gerda Lerner, a leader in the Los Angeles chapter, recounted in her memoir. The CAW's cultural activities featured an emphasis on celebrating American women's history, and African American women's experiences were included prominently, all of which put this popular history education effort decades ahead of professional historians; Lerner and Eleanor Flexner, two CAW activists (and CP members) who became pioneering American women's historians, were deeply affected by these efforts.[77]

Although the CAW saw the labor movement as the core of the nation's progressive forces, activists associated with it felt freed, with the war over, to criticize unions for their hostility to female workers. Elizabeth Hawes, a noted Popular Front writer who had worked for the UAW, described the discontent of homemakers in 1943 in her book *Why Women Cry*. But her book of three years later, *Hurry Up, Please, It's Time*, criticized the UAW. Like Communists and their allies, she derided Reuther's leadership and wrote, "If one believed in getting the union work done . . . one preferred the Communists to the Red-Baiters." Yet she distinguished the "Common Communists," who focused on worker concerns, from "Catechismic Communists," who seemed more concerned with defending the Soviet Union than the interests of American workers.[78] Such efforts to parse the different tendencies among Communists, with regard to gender politics or anything else, shortly would become hopeless, as fine distinctions were overwhelmed by a conflict that pitted all Popular Front progressives against anticommunist liberals.

Henry Wallace and the Shape of Cold War Dissent

The ostensible basis for the Popular Front was an alliance of all "democratic" forces against the threat fascism posed to them all. On the level of international diplomacy this meant an alliance of "democratic" or antifascist nations. This conception of the Popular Front was problematic because the Soviet Union was not a democracy. This wrinkle might be smoothed by arguing that either political or economic democracy qualified one for membership. Most liberals and leftists in the Popular Front who spoke of social or economic democracy referred to a system of social provision, and not to popular control over economic resources.

When they called the Soviet Union a social democracy they did not necessarily betray naïveté about who controlled what under Stalin. (Socialists and Trotskyists denied that the Soviets qualified on either count, but the Communists made sure their views didn't matter.) Popular Fronters might render the question of democracy moot by arguing, as Harry Ward did, that Soviet workers reported to him and other fellow travelers that they *felt* an "ownership" of the Soviet state, irrespective of elections and enforcement of the "Stalin Constitution" of 1936.[79] Few outside the ranks of committed fellow travelers seemed to take this seriously.

Many liberals did not buy the version of the Soviet Union that the fellow travelers were selling but still embraced an antifascist alliance with Stalin on pragmatic and qualified ideological grounds. They saw humanist ideals in the ideology of communism while also recognizing the ugly, brutal aspects of the Soviet regime, and they hoped that the better angels of Soviet life might be encouraged through the influence of Western democratic allies. They agreed that the United States could learn some things from the Soviets, too, and joined fellow travelers in saying that the best future would be one in which the two societies converged toward a fully democratic model, politically and socially. Many liberals who refrained from expressing unbridled enthusiasm for Stalin's Soviet Union still wanted to count themselves as progressives, with all that this implied. This intermediate position saved liberals from having to deny the simple fact that the Soviet Union was a dictatorship.

The easiest path was to leave the content of democracy vague, and that was the path most often taken by the progressives. Writers and activists influenced by the Popular Front spoke of democracy as the embodiment of a certain spirit, a populist ethos that celebrated the little people of the working class. Here was the imagery and rhetoric of the Popular Front, the defiant yet rather sunny mien of the broad left in the late 1930s and 1940s. No more the grim visage of the mob hungry for bread, the creaking of the tumbrels and the shadow of the guillotine; all of that was quite early-Thirties. There was reason for optimism; the future would be more "democratic." Usually the closest anyone came to defining this more vigorous democracy was to cite Roosevelt's Four Freedoms and to advocate enhanced strength, in the workplace and in politics, for industrial labor unions. Despite all the political conflict within the left and between the emerging camps of progressives and anti-progressive liberals, antifascists and anti-antifascists, and despite the nineteen-month departure of the Communists and their fellow travelers from the Popular Front during the period of the Nazi-Soviet alliance, this vision of an army of happy plebian warriors for a vaguely defined progress persisted among liberals and leftists from the late 1930s through the war years. The war itself, by giving the happy warriors an actual war to fight and more new allies than they could count, by suddenly rendering their rhetoric of democracy and freedom versus slavery and fascism the official rhetoric of U.S. government and society, seemed to make the image of the Popular Front the image of America.

This vagueness in defining democracy was due not only to the delicacy of "the Russian Question," as it was sometimes called. It also stemmed from the long history of American liberals and leftists moving away from transformative politics. That direction had been clear for some time, often with little acknowledgment that this was what progressives were up to. But the New Deal, and the fervent support that it generated by 1936 among those who now routinely called themselves liberals, made this process impossible to ignore. If Americans who called themselves either liberals or progressives continued to believe in the long-held ideals of the cooperative commonwealth and social democracy, and if during the 1930s and 1940s they came to treat Franklin Roosevelt's leadership and program as the embodiment of progress toward those goals, this spelled a drastic revision of those hoary ideals. For some, this was not a pleasant thing to admit.

Some progressives, such as Max Lerner and Freda Kirchwey, the editor of *The Nation*, sought to move the Popular Front's vision forward during the war by advocating a "democratic revolution" both in the United States and around the world. This phrase was exquisite in its ambiguity. It indicated support for New Deal–like programs around the world and for an embrace of the kind of "mixed economies" that took hold in western and central Europe after the war ended. No doubt Popular Front thinkers in America wished to see Communist parties involved in ruling coalitions after the war, since they joined in Communist-led efforts themselves. But were they calling for seizures of power anywhere? The evidence suggests that progressives in general saw such insurrectionary politics as legitimate in some parts of the "old world," and perhaps in the colonies of the European powers, but certainly not in America and almost surely not in western Europe. Kirchwey suggested during the war that, in eastern Europe, truly democratic forces—meaning forces, not necessarily Communists, representing workers and farmers—might gain power on the backs of Soviet might; few serious observers in the later war years expected an orderly, "normal" process to determine who held power in such lands. As the conflict between America and the Soviet Union developed in the late 1940s, the acceptability of revolution abroad would become a crucial point of division among American liberals, but it was not a serious controversy while the war was ongoing. Throughout the 1940s, the call for a global democratic revolution was a call for reform and evolution, not for revolution—at home, that is.[80]

The oddity of calling reform revolution was lessened by the awareness that Harold Laski—a strong influence on left-liberal thinkers in America during the 1930s and 1940s—and other British Labourites likewise called, during the war, for democratic revolution in their country. However, while counterparts on both sides of the Atlantic blurred the difference between revolution and evolution, in Britain the Labourites clearly were debating, as European socialists had done since the 1890s, the future of socialism. Without talk of socialism, and the embrace of class power and fundamental transformation that it conveyed, in America the call for a democratic revolution seemed a rhetorical flight of fancy.[81] But perhaps it was so in both countries. When the Labour party won power in Britain in 1945, it began to implement a welfare state far more comprehensive than anything gained or even specifically attempted by Democrats in America.[82] Nonetheless, the ambition of a comprehensive welfare state, one providing both security and a degree of redistributive justice, defined the horizons of both British democratic socialism and American liberalism. It would not be long before the Labourites, like their opposite numbers in some countries on the Continent, declared that they no longer constituted a class party.

The incoherence of the progressives' quasi-revolutionary rhetoric in the 1940s, and their genuine support for militant and expansive liberal reform in America, came clear as they rallied around the figure of Henry Wallace, former Republican, between 1944 and 1948. The story of the Wallace "movement" is not so much that of a rift opening between liberals and leftists as it is the story of a battle between two different varieties of liberalism. The ignominy of Wallace and his supporters in 1948 was deceptive, since at least some of their agenda survived and found broader acceptance in American life in the following twenty years. Somewhat unappreciated is the extent to which the militant liberalism of Wallace's 1948 campaign set the agenda for what came to be called "radicalism" or "the left" in America for the duration of the cold war.

Wallace became a rallying point for those forces within the Democratic party and among political liberals who clung to the progressive belief in ascension to a new stage of American history. Wallace made his first bid for national liberal leadership in his famous speech in May 1942, "The Price of Free World Victory." In a rejoinder to Henry Luce, the publisher of *Time,* who had declared that the twentieth century "must be an American century," Wallace called instead for a "century of the common man." Sounding much like other progressives during the war, he said he favored a "people's revolution" that would, building upon the legacies of political revolutions dating back to 1776 and 1789, solve the problem of poverty worldwide. Wallace's speech combined "the radical democratic and evolutionary positivist views of social progress, of linear development in history, punctuated by revolutionary epochs (the American and Russian revolutions and the Second World War) in which the people triumph over the forces of demagoguery and exploitation that seek to keep them in bondage."[83] Wallace, promoting a vision of jagged upward historical progress and enlisting all democratic movements in world history into that narrative, made himself a strong candidate to bear the standard of progressivism, to champion the cause of fundamental change in America.

Wallace chose to define the substance of the "century of the common man" by embracing racial liberalism. This would define the "people's revolution"—and it certainly would make it easier for the United States to lead such a global movement in the future. It also would furnish Wallace with cadres inside the Democratic party who would work to fulfill his own ambitions. By 1944, the issue of civil rights advocacy as it related to political liberalism had become truly pesky for Roosevelt and other party nabobs. After more than two years of war against fascism, African Americans and many others in the Popular Front wing of Roosevelt's coalition were pressing the matter, having come to believe that equal rights for all and the celebration of America's mongrel nature were baseline elements in their creed, which they now called liberalism.

Whether because he was looking for the main chance politically, or because his vision expanded with the passage of time, Wallace had undergone a stark change in his stance toward racial issues. As the secretary of agriculture, he had failed to support officials in his department who had drawn hostile attention by advocating fairness to African American farmers. In explanation he supposedly had said he did not believe black Americans should receive "special treatment." When Will Alexander served as head of the Farm Security Administration, Wallace was, in Alexander's view, "terribly afraid of this race issue."[84] Yet in 1943, after a race riot in Detroit, in which white workers pushed back against what they perceived as black incursions into privileged white space, economically and geographically, Wallace spoke to a labor gathering in that city and intoned, "We cannot fight to crush Nazi brutality abroad and condone race riots at home. . . . We cannot offer the blueprints and the skills to rebuild the bombed-out cities of other lands and stymie the rebuilding of our own cities. Slums have no place in America."[85] Soon Wallace explicitly echoed black activists' new formulation of liberalism as a creed of racial equality. Upon doing so, he sealed his fate as an outcast from the line of presidential succession, and he found himself the leader of a large dissident bloc among Democrats. At the party's nominating convention of 1944, the party "regulars," led by southern segregationists, succeeded in pushing Wallace out of the vice presidential slot that he had occupied for four years.[86]

Wallace's words in defeat at the convention were striking. He delivered the speech seconding Roosevelt's nomination, and in the process he defined liberalism as advocacy of "both political democracy and economic democracy regardless of race, color or religion." He said, "In a political, educational and economic sense, there must be no inferior races. The poll tax must go. Equal educational opportunities must come. The future must bring equal wages for equal work regardless of sex or race." One reporter wrote that southern Democrats "got a heaping dose of brine in their open wounds as Henry Wallace . . . rubbed the word 'liberal' eleven times in his brief platform appearance." Wallace continued to press his case for a new concept of political liberalism during the fall campaign, when he played the good soldier and worked for the ticket. He headed south, asserting, "A spirit of liberalism is abroad in the South." Furthermore, he announced, "If we are to have a great liberal party in this country the South must participate." African American activists were bitter over Wallace's ouster from the ticket. The black historian Rayford Logan called it a "tragic blow to the cause of liberalism and democracy," and he called for a new party comprised of "lovers of true democracy" from among the ranks of Democrats, Republicans, and Socialists.[87]

Change was indeed afoot in the South, but it was not so simply in the direction of liberalization. Black and white southern Popular Fronters were emboldened by the developments of the 1930s and 1940s, and African American veterans returned home to the South starting in 1945 and brought an additional dose of militancy to the fight for racial equality. But the backlash against this liberal movement overlapped with that movement's forward motion and, as in the ACLU's headquarters in New York, an anti-progressive countermovement began within the ranks of liberals. In the South as in the North, the issue of communism fueled this in-house showdown, while simply giving some a peg to hang their hat on. Because an anti-segregation stance, which was becoming nearly synonymous with liberalism, still seemed so perilous and radical to white southerners, and because of the attack on the Popular Front, the available space for political liberalism in the South was shrinking almost to the vanishing point.[88] According to Virginia Foster Durr, a white southerner highly active in Popular Front groups, the National Committee to Abolish the Poll Tax, a spin-off from the SCHW, ceased operations in 1948 when it ran out of backers and money; Durr was told clearly that money would continue to flow only if the committee cut ties with unions soon to be expelled from the CIO, which it would not do.[89] Once the Popular Front was destroyed in the South, there was almost nothing left for anticommunist liberals to work with there, and southern liberalism basically disappeared until it was revived by the civil rights movement after 1955.

In the South, the initial fight of liberals against liberals played out most prominently within the SCHW, and most spectacularly in the state of North Carolina. By 1943, the issue of Communist membership within the organization was causing turmoil. In that year, Charles Houston dissented from a new ACLU resolution denouncing the CP. He explained that the Communists were working against lynching, the poll tax, and Jim Crow and for an integrated labor movement, and that this was his agenda, too. Regardless of any disagreements he might have with them, they were working for "a broader base of democratic participation by the common people." Things got hotter after the war. In 1947, Americans for Democratic Action (ADA), a new organization of anticommunist liberals who now were determined to drive the Popular Front out of the Democratic party, moved into the South in an effort to compete with the SCHW. ADA tried without success to peel off prominent SCHW members, such as Governor Ellis Arnall of Georgia. The organization raided the CNC (an SCHW state affiliate) starting in late 1946, taking advantage of dissension over the issue of a racially integrated movement. Officials of the Textile Workers Union of America were pushing to restrict the participation of African Americans in the CNC. In 1947, Junius Scales revealed his secret CP membership to his fellow CNC activists, exciting tremendous anger among his colleagues and some defections to ADA. In May 1947, the HUAC issued a report smearing the SCHW as "perhaps the most deviously camouflaged communist-front organization" in America. This was just before a scheduled rally in support of Henry Wallace was to be held in Washington, to be sponsored by the Washington Committee of the SCHW. Despite these blows to the SCHW, ADA proved unable to capitalize on the opening that this created. It undertook no grassroots organizing and no "direct action" among workers or African Americans; it failed entirely to reach out to black activists. ADA "provided little more than a refuge for anti-Communist liberals. It never attempted to duplicate the work of the CNC by challenging the racial status quo in the South."[90]

Ostensibly ADA was hostile to Popular Front groups such as the SCHW because of differences over communism, not race. In 1947 Truman fired Wallace, who was still serving as the secretary of commerce (a consolation prize awarded him in 1944), over Wallace's public statements favoring continued friendly relations with the Soviet Union. To many people, this question of foreign policy seemed to be the prime source of the Truman-Wallace cleavage and of the longer rift within the Democratic party that came fully into public view in 1948. But the issue of civil rights, during the war, first crystallized the battle lines that formed again after the war. Both issues were vitally important in the showdown among the liberals, even though Truman sought to compromise on race and not on foreign policy. To those in ADA—such as Arthur Schlesinger, Jr., the newly deradicalized Reinhold Niebuhr, and others, such as Kirchwey, whose involvement might confound the standard image of the organization—communism had become, by 1947, the driving issue. Civil rights was an area in which to be flexible; it was a means to an end. If making liberalism anticommunist meant calling for civil rights in the North in order to win diverse and powerful working-class liberal cadres away from the Popular Front, and linking up with segregationist forces in the South in order to isolate a left that was closely identified with the cause of civil rights there, then that was acceptable. Some within the ADA camp, most famous among them Hubert Humphrey, at that time the mayor of Minneapolis, displayed genuinely strong feelings against racism and for civil rights. Nonetheless, their organization's raison d'être was to delegitimize communism and alliances with Communists, and to drive from every level of the Democratic party edifice, from the most local on up, not only Communists but those willing to work with Communists. Anything else was secondary.

The formation of the Progressive Citizens of America (PCA) in December 1946, and then the Progressive party (PP), was the reaction by those who either wanted to preserve the Popular Front or saw an anticommunist crusade as a distraction from the liberal agenda. The PP's announced platform reprised the old LaFollette Progressive agenda of public ownership of various and sundry institutions, but this seems more a token of ambitious liberal sentiment than a real plan of action that anyone saw as credible in 1948. The Progressives were signaling that they wanted Roosevelt's liberalism circa 1944 back—or at least Roosevelt's liberalism as they chose to remember it. This meant no cold war, either abroad or at home.

When the split among liberals over foreign policy broke fully to the surface, between 1946 and 1948, combining with the existing rift over whether or not to work with American Communists, the fight was exactly that: a fight between liberals. It was not primarily a struggle by liberals against a social-democratic left. Members of both the ADA and the PCA could lay claim to some variety of social-democratic ideal, and even the Soviet Union itself only gradually became a stark line of division between the two claimants to liberal leadership. Throughout the war Niebuhr, for one, resisted the idea that a U.S. conflict with the Soviet Union was inevitable and continued to insist that a fully democratic convergence of the best elements in the two social systems was possible.[91] But the liberals of ADA were united in having little use for American

Communists, and that did not change in 1941when the Communists returned to the antifascist fold. When the ADA liberals beat up the Progressive party, figuratively speaking, with the cudgel of anticommunism, the presence of Communists in the Progressive campaign was not all that alarmed them, and for some, the Communists were not in themselves even the greatest worry. Just as great a threat to the kind of liberal politics that ADA desired was the presence of so many liberals who were willing to work with Communists, and indeed to turn over leading positions in their coalition organizations to Communists. To an ADA activist in 1948, no sort of "proof" that the PP was a "true" Popular Front coalition and not a Communist front would have been meaningful, since in the anticommunist liberal view, there was no such thing as such a "true" coalition with Communists; in this view, Communists would only involve themselves in efforts that they could control. In any case, Wallace didn't need any Communist advisers to prod him to denounce "Hitlerite methods" in the U.S. government or to warn numerous times of a coming "fascist" danger from "Wall Street" control of that government. "The old parties are run basically by Wall Street and the Pentagon who are backing the killing of thousands of people abroad," he declaimed, sounding more, to our ears today, like a 1960s radical than a 1940s liberal.[92]

The point of division was one's willingness to work with Communists, not one's demonstration of intellectual independence from them; or, to put it differently, rapidly in the late 1940s, the refusal to work with Communists, and to work with anyone who worked with Communists, was becoming the only such demonstration considered serious and legitimate within the political mainstream. Lerner put his finger on the issue in a response of 1947 to Schlesinger's fierce anti–Popular Front communications: "You say that Wallace believes in the possibility of working with Communists. Does this mean that liberals are to organize a secondary boycott and exclude from their organization not only the Communists but also the genuine liberal who (however mistaken) may hold differing views of working with Communists?" This, of course, was exactly what Schlesinger and those who thought like him had in mind, and before long they would succeed in enforcing just such a "secondary boycott."[93]

Outside the world of letters, inside the hurly-burly of political organizing, the lines might be drawn less starkly. In Minnesota, Humphrey shrewdly worked to coopt fellow travelers in the new Democratic-Farmer-Labor (DFL) party (a result of a merger in 1944 between the old Farmer-Labor party and the previously weak state-level Democratic party), not to isolate or denounce them. He saved his invective specifically for Communists and continued to cultivate other Popular Front adherents, using honey instead of vinegar to win them to his side. At the same time, other ADA operatives in the state, led by Orville Freeman, developed extensive lists, at the most local precinct levels, of DFL members they deemed "O.K." or "B" (for "Bad"), to indicate whose side everyone was on. During 1948, in the complicated caucus-and-convention system used by the DFL party to endorse candidates, an army of activists, including many who would go on to national prominence, such as Freeman, Eugene McCarthy, and Walter Mondale, diligently worked to prevent the "Bs" from participating in the precinct caucuses that were the first step in the endorsement food-chain. The object was to exclude Communists and their allies from the party's machinery and break the Popular Front. The other side also had its "squeeze-out" lists, but turned out to be more poorly organized. The mobilization on the anticommunist side was formidable. Fourteen faculty members from the Catholic St. Thomas College in St. Paul went as delegates to the state party convention to vote against the Popular Front forces. At the end of the year the defeat of the Popular Front in Minnesota was stunningly complete.[94]

In the national campaign, race remained a major issue nationwide. Wallace took another turn through the South, refusing to speak at segregated venues and earning grudging respect even among his liberal enemies for his courage in facing down threatening white mobs at campaign stops. Truman responded affirmatively to the famous political advice of his aide, Clark Clifford, and offered a dramatic set of pro–civil rights proposals as the campaign season got underway. These included the establishment of a civil rights division within the Department of Justice, making the temporary Fair Employment Practices Commission permanent, eliminating the poll tax, and, doing what Roosevelt would not openly support, making lynching a federal crime. All of this was enough to cause Strom Thurmond of South Carolina to bolt the Democratic party and head a States' Rights party ticket—which did much better in the end than the PP—and to secure for Truman the lion's share of African American votes in northern cities. But Wallace's campaign laid down a marker, again, for Sixties-era dissidence that lay in the future, by seeking to make a personal confrontation with the country's internal devils the sign of true commitment. The PP did not speak of "putting your body on the line," but it might as well have. James Wechsler, a former Communist and, in his new identity as an anticommunist liberal, an energetic scourge of Wallace in 1948, covered Wallace's southern campaign and was given pause by what he saw. He derided Wallace as a Communist tool throughout the fall, but afterward he wrote, "The kind of ideological distinctions I talked about didn't seem to loom as large" in the context of southern racism and segregation.[95] Wechsler clearly wished to be on the progressive side of this fight, and he acknowledged, if only by implication, that ADA and its kind of liberal had not really joined in. Humphrey had denounced the old doctrine of states' rights at the Democratic convention, echoing Wallace in stating that getting the southern racists out of the national Democratic party was necessary to forge a "real, liberal Democratic party." His speech was the spark that pushed them out of the convention, even though the tinder had been laid by Truman months before with his civil rights program.[96] But as to throwing caution to the winds and confronting racism up close, the anti-progressives had left it to those they called "dupes" and "totalitarians." The ADA took its brief in the fall of 1948 to be exposing the collaboration between these two types, period. The same was true, in a minor way, for the Socialists and their candidate for president, Norman Thomas, whose campaign was dedicated to anticommunism. One supporter, John Roche (a future chairman of the ADA), told Thomas after the election, "We done our best—and kept the intellectuals away from Henry Wallace," with humorous exaggeration.[97]

When young American intellectuals set about reviving the political left, beginning about ten years later, the remnants of the SP and the ADA liberals together would form the political nexus to which that "new left" would look for initial sponsorship, and from which they quickly would become estranged. But Henry Wallace (who faded from public view almost immediately after his embarrassment in November, and who later renounced a good bit of what he had affirmed in 1948) would have his revenge upon the anti-antifascists. His program of, one, supporting civil rights and social equality for black Americans and, two, opposing the cold war, would, in broad terms, set the agenda for the American left for the duration of the conflict with the Soviet Union. The new left of the 1960s would not share the commitment to industrial unionism that characterized the progressive liberalism of the 1940s. This new generation of radicals also would nurture an alienation from the state that would set them apart from most liberals. Moreover, during the decade beginning in 1965, the expansion of the Vietnam War and the escalation of African American militancy would produce a temporary rebirth of revolutionary sentiment among radicalized youth. For all these departures from the politics of the Second Progressive Era, however, the most basic commitments of the "left" during the cold war would be the same as those that set progressive liberals in the 1940s apart from their liberal rivals: a militant stand for racial justice and opposition to anticommunist crusades, internationally and domestically. Just as the conflict between "liberals" and "progressives," between progressives and anti-progressives, in the late 1940s, was really a battle between different forms of liberalism, the new left would be, to a generally unrecognized extent, an expanded version of progressive liberalism that could not speak its own name. Meanwhile, the victorious anti-antifascist liberals of 1948 would find it hard to develop an agenda and vision that would inspire a new generation of Americans and replenish their own political movement. American liberals and radicals throughout the cold war would be the children of 1948.

Chapter 5
The Cold War Era

Relations between leftists and liberals were launched on a note of confusion and estrangement at the dawn of the cold war in the late 1940s. More than a half-century later, the same qualities marked their relations. The politics of the cold war, which began during the presidency of Harry S Truman (1945–53) and ended during that of George H. W. Bush (1989–93), shaped American liberalism and American radicalism decisively. During this period and afterward, liberals and radicals were mostly at loggerheads, often defining themselves against each other. Yet liberal and leftist political beliefs were often more compatible than many liberals and radicals would admit.

During the cold war, liberals expanded their agenda to include issues and demands that liberals rarely if ever had emphasized previously, while paradoxically abandoning the old liberal dream of a fundamentally changed society. Many liberal reformers, since the origins of the new liberalism in the late nineteenth century, had voiced piercing moral criticisms of American capitalism, even as they had worked within that society for incremental change. During the early years of the cold war, liberals at first accepted American capitalist democracy as a permanent framework for social improvement. Then, less ambiguously, they came to celebrate this society, while redefining liberalism as a movement for the inclusion of previously excluded groups in its bounties. The cold war also made liberalism an anti-revolutionary creed, plain and simple, where world politics was concerned, dispatching to the political graveyard earlier divisions of opinion among American reformers about revolution abroad.

Radicals, for their part, proclaimed themselves the true tribunes of the excluded and denounced cold war liberals as false prophets and handmaidens to America's ruling cliques. Leftists also extended a hand of friendship to radicals and revolutionaries abroad, setting themselves against U.S. foreign policy and U.S. world power. American radicals during this period oscillated between two different political identities. The first was that of the radical as militant reformer, the role that most leftists have enacted in modern America. The other was that of the prophet without honor in his own land. Since the opening of the cold war, American radicals frequently have forsaken strategies of power or influence in favor of harsh judgments on their society and a politics of personal integrity. While most American radicals were secular people during this period, they took on the religious function of prophecy, growing ever more politically estranged from their own society even as they continually helped to improve it—persisting, even if this was difficult for them to admit, in the work of liberalism.

The years between the middle 1940s and the middle 1960s were a conservative period in American life, dominated by the politics of anticommunism, although this began to change in the 1960s. This "classic" era of the cold war, as it might be called, was a time during which liberals were put back on their heels by conservatives; liberals responded to their narrowed fortunes, in part, by attacking those to their left to prove their own "reliability." Meanwhile, left-wing radicalism assumed a furtive, embattled posture. The cold war era became a period when American radicalism mutated, when obscure elements in dissident thought, including disenchantment with the organized labor movement and fear of state power, took on new importance. Some themes that earlier had had a place within the liberal political universe, particularly sympathy for convulsive social change abroad, seemed to migrate to the left, so that only radicals could embrace them. Moreover, a commitment to the elimination of racial caste inequality became a matter, alternately, of competition and cooperation between radicals and liberals, with both camps laying claim to the mantle of "civil rights" in different forms.

McCarthyism and the Great Rupture

In the years between 1946 and 1960, liberals and leftists were driven apart as never before by the red scare—the campaign to ostracize Communists and those allegedly sympathetic to them—creating a rift that proved impossible to bridge afterward. Conservatives such as Republican Senator Joseph McCarthy, who lent his name to the red scare, attacked liberals for, they charged, conspiring with Communists. Amid the escalating confrontation between the United States and the Soviet Union, liberals grew anxious to put daylight between themselves and anyone touched by the spreading contagion of accusation. The French left-wing writer Simone de Beauvoir, in America in early 1947, wrote in her journal, "Along with war psychosis, the 'red terror' is growing; every man on the Left is accused of being a communist, and every communist is a traitor."[1] One government employee was subjected to a loyalty investigation because he reportedly "[favored] peace and civil liberties," and was said to hold "convictions concerning equal rights for all races and classes" that "extend slightly beyond the normal feelings of the average individual"; such cases were legion.[2] In this atmosphere, repudiation—of one's own past, of one's associates—became the order of the day. The novelist James Baldwin returned to the United States in 1952 after living abroad and was shocked by what he found occurring among intellectuals in New York. "I had come home to a city in which nearly everyone was gracelessly scurrying for shelter, in which friends were throwing their friends to the wolves," he remembered. In later years Baldwin framed the lessons of the early 1950s in a way that illustrated the obstacles to a reconstructed progressive politics. He said that the red scare had taught him "something about the irresponsibility and cowardice of the liberal community."[3]

The anticommunists' hand in the liberals' civil war was greatly strengthened once the red scare began. Anticommunism was a matter of principle for many liberals and leftists. As discussed in Chapter 4, during the period of the Nazi-Soviet pact in 1939–41, anti-Soviet liberals and leftists had begun to redefine "liberalism" as anticommunist reformism and to cast aspersions upon "progressive" Popular Front politics as undemocratic and nearly treasonous. For such "vital center" liberals—the term was coined by Arthur Schlesinger, Jr. in the title of his 1949 book, which called on liberals to cleanse themselves of progressive affiliations—it was nothing new to denounce communism as "a political cancer in our society," as Hubert Humphrey did in 1952.[4] However, it reflected a changed climate when Walter Reuther, around the same time, called Communists "morally degenerated" "filth" who needed to be "fumigated."[5] This language of violence echoed that used by fascists and Communists against one another.

Several industrial unions were by far the biggest organizations in which the Communist-liberal coalition formula of the Popular Front continued to have purchase, and attacks against them, from within and without the union movement, escalated in the late 1940s. The biggest of the unions in question was the United Electrical, Radio and Machine Workers of America (UE). In 1948 James Lustig, a UE organizer, was arrested after he refused to furnish the HUAC with the records of the Joint Anti-Fascist Refugee Committee, a Popular Front organization. The union's president received a letter from a U.S. House committee requesting that he testify about whether or not the UE had "failed to set its house in order concerning its ideological aspects," an innovative way to frame the government's proper business. The UE saw its organizers beaten and run out of town in Virginia while police officers looked on.[6] In 1949 and 1950, the CIO, with the assent of its leader, Philip Murray, expelled the UE and ten other unions whose officials would not sign affidavits denying participation in the Communist movement, as outlined in a new law, the Taft-Hartley Act. CIO leaders embraced this provision of the law as an occasion to drop a growing political liability. These unions' exile into a political wilderness spelled the political liquidation of the Popular Front. Events in the trade-union movement snuffed out the light of a militant reformism that had provided most of the energy for an agenda of racial inclusion and equality in the labor movement. With the "amputation" of its left wing, labor became more conservative in the sense that it became more narrowly concerned with the pay and benefits of workers already organized into unions, and less with pressing a broad agenda of social progress.[7]

Some of the best-remembered dramas in this era of repudiation were enacted in the realm of popular culture, beginning with the theatrical hearings that the HUAC conducted in Hollywood in 1947, which were intended to expose Communist infiltration of the motion-picture industry.[8] After the "Hollywood Ten," a group of Communist screenwriters and directors, made a militant appearance at a HUAC hearing, liberals such as Humphrey Bogart, who had criticized the HUAC on civil liberties grounds, ran for cover. He now made sure to profess his hatred for communism and conceded that his earlier actions in solidarity with "the Ten" had been "ill-advised, even foolish."[9] (The "Ten" went to prison for contempt of Congress.) Carl Foreman, a former Communist, felt betrayed by Stanley Kramer, a filmmaker with whom Foreman coproduced *High Noon* (1952)—a movie often viewed as an oblique protest against McCarthyism—when Kramer bent to political pressures and pushed Foreman off the movie set and then denied Foreman his producing credit.[10] Kramer went on to make himself the most overtly liberal filmmaker in Hollywood, bringing to the screen sermons on the themes of racial brotherhood, peace, and intellectual freedom, respectively, in *The Defiant Ones* (1958), *On the Beach* (1959) and *Inherit the Wind* (1960). Those on the left no doubt felt that the moral elitism of well-placed liberals such as Kramer rested on a rotten foundation, with the liberals championing causes pioneered by leftists whom they had knifed in the back. The liberal approach to these issues, evident in Kramer's films, substituted smugness for populism and individual psychology for social context.

Besides labor and Hollywood, academia was a third arena where Popular Front politics had enjoyed a secure foothold and where McCarthyism followed. In 1949 a storm erupted at the University of California when faculty members were required to sign a "loyalty oath" to keep their jobs, outraging civil libertarians; in New York City the state-level Rapp-Coudert Committee did its best imitation of the HUAC by haling leftist schoolteachers into public hearings, causing many to be fired.[11] The HUAC induced prominent professors such as the historian Daniel Boorstin to name names and agree that communism was a menace in the faculty lounge. Out of the public eye, many faculty members made a clean breast of past political associations and named names of former associates to administrators who wished to keep the FBI and the HUAC off the campuses by doing their jobs for them. Those who refused to cooperate with such quiet investigations found themselves unemployed.[12] In California, dozens of colleges hired "security officers," typically former FBI agents, who were really political police. Their job was to compile dossiers on the faculty's politics, in imitation of "the Boss," J. Edgar Hoover, and then to make these files available to the state government.[13]

Present and former Communists were those in greatest jeopardy of being fired, but civil-liberties scruples about oaths or coerced testimony put liberals at risk, too. As critics routinely pointed out, a teacher who was actually a covert Soviet agent in America would not hesitate to lie and swear any oath mandated. Liberal idealism was not only an obvious reason why someone would refuse; it sometimes seemed the only reason. Sidney Hook, as ever, homed in on the fellow travelers. He argued that Communists were unfit to teach, but he conceded that "'progressive' intellectuals" who lined up with red initiatives ought not be fired. However, they should be harassed mercilessly. Such a person should "have his credentials to competent scholarship openly questioned by his peers."[14] These shunning tactics were designed precisely to drive the wedge between leftists and liberals ever deeper.

One historian, in 1977, conveyed the bitterness sown by these events when he asked, "[W]hat future historian who examines the vagaries of intellectuals during the period will fail to observe . . . that at a low ebb of American civil liberties Mary McCarthy wrote a novel about a faculty Machiavel who tries to save his job by *posing* as a victim of political persecution; that Robert Warshow and Leslie Fiedler wrote essays attacking the Rosenbergs and their sympathizers rather than the men who had just executed them . . . ?"[15] Another scholar's judgment in a 1985 study further reflects the damage done to the prospects for left-liberal entente. He wrote, "McCarthyism found its chief inspiration in the ideology of the cold war—an ideology that was constructed not by . . . conservative Republicans . . . but by liberal politicians and anti-Stalinist intellectuals."[16] To the generation of liberal and radical intellectuals who came of age in the 1960s, cold war liberals and anticommunist social democrats bore much blame for the carnage of the red scare. Most of that carnage was political and cultural but some of it, tragically, was mortal; beyond ignominy and desperation, there were suicides and other early deaths.

The derision heaped by many liberals and former radicals upon Ethel and Julius Rosenberg, who were executed in 1953 for supposedly helping the Soviet Union develop the atomic bomb through espionage, testifies to the tenor of the times. This becomes especially clear if one compares the widespread political abandonment of the unfortunate Rosenbergs with the reaction by reformers and radicals to the executions of Sacco and Vanzetti twenty-six years earlier. Those earlier defendants' involvement in the radical left had been just as clear as that of their later counterparts, yet few were the intellectuals who had sided with the judge and prosecutor in the earlier case. The Sacco-Vanzetti saga had had a radicalizing effect upon many liberal reformers, convincing them that America was "two nations," as Dos Passos put it: the powerful and the powerless, the big men and the little people. In the 1950s, liberals tended to view America through a different frame, an affirmative one, a frame that pictured their society as a place where the little people got adequate representation and where radical critics of society were emotionally unsound.[17] Dramas such as that of the Rosenbergs fit into and reinforced that view of America and continually pushed leftists and liberals away from the possibility of reconciliation.

For obscure reasons, the Popular Front–style links between liberals and leftists were not severed completely in California. The state legislature had instituted its own investigations into Communists and their allies starting in 1941, but that did not stop the growth of a vibrant Popular Front culture, which boasted a special glow because of the involvement of figures from the entertainment industry. Most progressive groups could not arrange award banquets, as the American Youth for Democracy did in Los Angeles in 1945, featuring Frank Sinatra and Ingrid Bergman. Dorothy Healey, a prominent Communist active in the Los Angeles CIO Council—which the national CIO shuttered in 1948 because of its red tinge—found liberals who would work with her, in defiance of the prevailing winds, through the late 1940s and into the 1950s. These included Robert Kenney, at one time the state attorney general, as well as ACLU activists in southern California. "The leaders of the Los Angeles ACLU were probably the kind of people that [Morris] Ernst was informing on," Healey noted acidly, referring to the national ACLU officer who was close to Hoover. She later reflected on the impression Kenney made on her. "For the first time I came to respect the politics of someone who was not in any way sympathetic to Communism but who was genuinely devoted to what we used to call 'bourgeois democratic' concepts. That is to say, he believed in the democratic process, civil liberties, and equality before the law without the slightest compromise or equivocation."[18] California Communists such as Healey remained less sectarian and more focused on the need for broad reformist coalitions than many of their opposite numbers elsewhere in the postwar years.

Despite principled exceptions such as Kenney, this era of conservatism reshaped liberalism, shifting it to the right. In the first half of the 1950s most liberals treated anyone with even a light reddish hue as a plague carrier. Liberal politicians such as Humphrey and Governor G. Mennen Williams of Michigan proffered "responsible" programs of policing subversives, disdaining special anticommunist authorities and augmenting the powers of the FBI and similar state-level agencies; the "professionalism" of Hoover, a fanatic without constitutional scruples, was the successful liberal's idea of a bulwark against tyranny.[19] In one of her occasional interludes of heresy, Mary McCarthy—who had associated herself with the anti-Soviet left since the late 1930s—in 1952 averred to a group of teachers that the red scare stemmed not merely from revulsion at "the crimes of Stalin," but also from a deeply conservative fear of "the original ideals of Communism," with its utopian egalitarianism. The "psychology of rich people" was taking over the country, she said. Americans had an uneasy "sense of being surrounded by an unappreciative world" filled with poor people, and the vindictive politics of McCarthyism were directed not merely against Soviet agents but against "'agitators'" of any kind who might rouse the have-nots against the haves, with whom an expanded middle class increasingly identified.[20]

As the 1950s drew to a close, some liberals and anti-Soviet leftists conceded that things had gotten out of hand. By 1956, Schlesinger, the sociologist David Riesman, the economist John Kenneth Galbraith, and the journalist James Wechsler had resigned from the American Committee for Cultural Freedom, a crown jewel of the postwar anticommunist propaganda apparatus. They said the group had gotten shrill and extreme, but the truth was that it had served its purpose and was no longer compelling.[21] Legal defense efforts for former Communists took on a higher profile by the end of the decade; the best-known case was that of Junius Scales, who went to prison in 1961 after a conviction under the Smith Act and, after a campaign for his release involving Wechsler, Norman Thomas, the iconoclastic radical Dwight Macdonald, the journalist Murray Kempton, and Reinhold Niebuhr, was set free at the behest of Attorney General Robert F. Kennedy in 1962.[22] Kennedy and his brother, then the president-elect, crossed an American Legion picket line in 1960 to see *Spartacus*, a movie that defied the Hollywood blacklist, as the star and producer, the ardent liberal Kirk Douglas, gave the screenwriting credit to Dalton Trumbo, one of the "Hollywood Ten."[23] Political repression was losing support. Yet liberals continued to reflect the "psychology of rich people." Certain that economic deprivation was no longer a matter for their urgent concern and cut loose from the ideological bearings that contact with a vital political left once had provided, reformers in the late 1950s searched for an agenda. They saw a public weary of President Dwight D. Eisenhower's (1953–61) conservatism and hungry for bold leadership, and they pondered how to frame a program of challenges for the affluent.

During the years 1957–60 the appearance of a new left-wing movement was widely anticipated. The Socialist party (SP) leader Michael Harrington found a warmer reception than in previous years when he spoke to college students. In 1959 he wrote a pamphlet entitled "The New Left: The Relevance of Democratic Socialism in America." The term "new left" had appeared earlier in Britain and France among former Communists disillusioned with Stalinism.[24] The pacifist radical A. J. Muste sought to get the American Forum for Socialist Education off the ground in 1957 as a way of gathering left-wing forces, but it fell victim to controversy over the involvement of former CP members, many of whom were seeking a new path of radicalism after Nikita Khrushchev's 1956 denunciation of Stalin's crimes.[25] A similar problem bedeviled the anti–nuclear weapons group SANE (short for Committee for a Sane Nuclear Policy), founded in 1957, which buckled under red-baiting pressures from the government in 1960 and agreed to purge its ranks of current and former Communists.[26] The reluctance of Socialists, pacifists, and liberals to reject McCarthyism limited their ability to attract the loyalty of dissident youth, who longed for a clean break with the politics of the 1950s.

Nonetheless, when a new left did arise in America, based initially in Students for a Democratic Society (SDS), a renamed offshoot of the SP, its sources reflected a hope that liberals and leftists could find common ground. The first SDS cadres were recruited from the Liberal Study Group within the National Student Association (NSA) beginning in the last years of the 1950s. The NSA's prevailing sentiment was a liberalism that was pro–civil rights and supported the cold war. (The NSA also was secretly funded by the CIA.)[27] SDS was augmented in the early going by members from the Student Peace Union, an anti–nuclear weapons group that had spread rapidly on the nation's campuses, and the FDR Four Freedoms Club, named for Franklin Roosevelt's 1941 statement of liberal principles that offered a blueprint for postwar visions of American social democracy. Longtime radicals frequently assumed the new left would mark the resumption of essentially familiar political tendencies that had been repressed for ten to fifteen years (except that it would be anti-Stalinist). This expectation failed to reckon with the alterations in liberal and radical thought that had taken place since the middle 1940s.

The Allure of "Radicalism"

A curious feature of the years between 1946 and 1960 was the recurring effort by writers of widely varying politics to affirm their own "radicalism," while avoiding the taint of communism and the Popular Front. "Radicalism" expressed a desire to maintain a stance of opposition to entrenched power. It borrowed against a familiar value of heroic individualism, in modes alternately stoic and insurgent, even as it projected the hope for a nurturing and empowering community of rebellion. "Radicalism" conveyed ambiguous and shifting meanings, sometimes contrasted with "liberalism" and sometimes with "progressivism." In every case it signified a rhetorical avoidance of the label "left." The radical identity, long on style and mutable on ideology, survived the period of the red scare to shape the thinking of a new generation of political rebels in the 1960s. The new left of that decade would find it difficult to reconstruct a broad front for progress with welfare-state liberals despite initial moves in that direction, in part because 1960s radicalism was heir to the disruptive strains of "radicalism" as they unfolded during the Truman and Eisenhower years.

An early salvo in the postwar battle to redefine radicalism was fired by Saul Alinsky, the community organizer, in his manifesto of 1946, *Reveille for Radicals*, which he opened by distinguishing "the radical" from "the liberal." Alinsky's anti-liberal polemics echoed the old refrain that liberals "couldn't stand the gaff" when conflict with powerful forces blocked the path of freedom. Yet Alinsky's indictment was more personal and less coherent than the left critique of liberalism had been in the hands of John Chamberlain or Lincoln Steffens. It remains somewhat puzzling that Alinsky, who never associated himself with the organized left, chose to define himself by using the figure of the liberal as a punching bag. Possibly he had in mind a certain kind of settlement-house worker when he derided "the liberal."[28] Whomever he had in mind, his passionate but muddled case that radicalism was noble and liberalism detestable foreshadowed, perhaps more strongly than the writings of any other author, crucial themes of radical politics throughout the post–World War II years.

Reveille for Radicals began with a paean to American diversity, in a tone of sentimental populism that showed the impact of the Popular Front on American letters. "The people of America are red, white, black, yellow, and all the shades in between. . . . Their face is the face of the future." Alinsky then explained that liberals do not "like people." His populist, ethnically diverse rendering of "the people" suggested that liberals lacked enthusiasm for cultural pluralism and racial equality. Making his point clearer, he wrote, "Liberals talk passionately of the rights of minority groups. . . . However, when these same liberals emerge from their meetings, rallies, and passage of resolutions and find themselves seated next to a Negro in a public conveyance they tend to shrink back slightly." Radicals, in contrast, truly felt an "identification" with the downtrodden and the different. They "like people, all people."[29]

Alinsky made a special point of criticizing the trade unions for having become inhospitable to radicalism, suggesting the "heresy" that labor had become a narrow-minded interest group rather than a force for social change. "In recent times it has become increasingly clear that the organized labor movement *as it is constituted today* is as much a concomitant of a capitalist economy as is capital," he wrote, arguing that a "monopolistic" economy in particular was welcomed by the industrial unions. Labor leaders foreswore allegiance to socialist ideology not only in response to political pressure, but out of sincere self-interest: "If the working classes were to assume political control of the economy and society, there would be little point in the continuation of the present type of labor unions." Alinsky denounced labor leaders for their timorousness in challenging racism within their ranks. "In the field of race relations the record of organized labor is sickeningly similar to that of organized business," he stated. This verdict, one that would echo loudly among black and white radicals in later years, was voiced by civil rights advocates as well as some leftists during the war. It also was stated matter-of-factly by Gunnar Myrdal in *An American Dilemma*, which Alinsky cited for support. Alinsky conceded "that it is not the whole labor movement itself that is the bride of big monopoly business, but rather it is the present reactionary labor leadership with its decadent philosophy which poisons the entire movement." This qualification of his indictment did little to blunt his basic message, which answered loudly in the negative, with respect to the unions, the question that titled this chapter of his book—"Where Is the Radical Today?"[30]

Overall the content of Alinsky's radicalism was unclear. The phrasing of his attack on organized labor suggested he favored socialism and a staunch anti-racism, but he pulled back from issuing such an agenda in favor of a personality-based concept of radicalism. He discerned a commodious radical tradition in America, in the style of Vernon Parrington (whom he cited) and Will and Ariel Durant, one that encompassed Patrick Henry and Thomas Paine, Thaddeus Stevens and Edward Bellamy, Wendell Phillips and John L. Lewis.[31] Liberals were those who claimed to be on the side of "the people" but who could not be counted on in a fight. Radicals were fighters.

Clearly there was nothing in Alinsky's political work that was truly alien to the messy political traditions of twentieth-century liberalism, and in time Alinsky and his disciples would find themselves criticized from their left for seeking "only" to improve the day-to-day lives of city dwellers. For example, Todd Gitlin, a prominent figure in the new left of the 1960s, lambasted Alinsky in 1971 for lacking an "ideology," a "transcendent vision of a society worth living in."[32] This may have seemed to be the case, since Alinsky continually insisted that community organizers should not impose a program on the neighborhoods they sought to organize, but rather should embrace whatever agenda neighborhood residents wished to pursue. He followed this line of thought faithfully in his stewardship of the Back of the Yards Neighborhood Council, based in the white "ethnic" Chicago neighborhood where he first made his mark, and for a time he came under criticism for his refusal (despite his own attack on organized labor over the question of white supremacy) to challenge the council's resistance to residential integration of the community.

Yet Alinsky had an ideology. He was a devotee of pluralist liberal social theory, as his habit of quoting Alexis de Tocqueville indicated. The liberal pluralists, such as the political scientist Robert Dahl, the sociologist Seymour Martin Lipset, and the economist Clark Kerr, became dominant in the American social sciences in the 1950s, arguing that, contrary to class-based visions of American society, the United States was fragmented into "interests" whose delegates fought their way into a process of political bargaining and compromise that was the essence of American democracy.[33] The pluralists had been a presence in the social sciences since the 1930s (Alinsky studied in the sociology department at the University of Chicago at that time), and they had appropriated as their intellectual forebears James Madison and de Tocqueville, who had emphasized the vitality of private groups operating in "civil society," as it came to be called, as the key to democratic freedom in America. Like the historian Charles Beard, Alinsky used rhetoric that suggested a two-class picture of U.S. society to those inclined toward such a picture, and as with Beard this rhetoric diverted attention from Alinsky's embrace of a pluralistic concept of American society and politics.[34] Alinsky's denunciation of the union movement for becoming merely an interest group that accepted society's basic structure was inconsistent with his own interest-group liberalism.

In the 1950s, politically minded social scientists such as Lipset, the sociologist Daniel Bell, and others used pluralist theory as a cudgel against Marxism, which the pluralists often simply conflated with the category of "ideology." Ideology in this meaning involved a vision of total social change, its adherents dangerous figures driven to find a sense of personal transcendence through the experience of revolution, a total break with the world as it exists, which Bell termed "chiliasm."[35] Since pluralists, in their anti-left polemics, defined themselves as nonideological, it was unsurprising that leftists would criticize pluralists for a lack of ideology.

While Alinsky's case provides one illustration of the confusion that surrounded the concepts of ideology, liberalism, and radicalism in the immediate postwar years, the inveterate naysayer Dwight Macdonald, also in 1946, offered clarity when he explained that a "Radical" was one who rejected "Progressive" politics. Alinsky had bypassed the harsh polemics over the Popular Front, but Macdonald wished to replay those debates. He did so in his famous article titled "The Root Is Man" in his journal *politics*, scoring "Progressives" for their willingness to see individual human beings sacrificed "as the price that must be paid to insure a desirable future." Clearly he was writing about Communists and their fellow travelers (despite his gesture toward a unifying critique of both the left and the right). He took the term "Progressive" seriously and rejected not only a belief in the Soviet Union but also the whole tradition of state-centered, science-driven action, taken in the name of human freedom and mastery over the world, that descended from the Enlightenment, a tradition in which the fellow-traveling intellectuals had located themselves. Appalled at the enormity of violence perpetrated during World War II by the use of modern technology and organization to kill millions, not only by the German state but also by his own government and by the Soviet Union, Macdonald called for an ethical politics. What he meant was a particular kind of ethics, one that judged means as well as ends and one that validated the Kantian dictum that the individual human being should be viewed always as an end, never as a means.[36]

This was what Macdonald called "Radicalism," and he discerned it among

> the as yet few individuals—mostly anarchists, conscientious objectors, and renegade Marxists like myself—who reject the concept of Progress, who judge things by their present meaning and effect, who think the ability of science to guide us in human affairs has been overrated. . . . They, or rather we, think it is an open question whether the increase of man's mastery over nature is good or bad in its actual effect on human life to date, and favor adjusting technology to man . . . rather than adjusting man to technology.

Always bold in his rhetoric, Macdonald explained that progressives had justified making people means, not ends, in the name of the future. He wrote that he stood on "the ground not of History but of those non-historical Absolute Values (Truth, Love, Justice) which the Marxists made unfashionable among socialists."[37]

The anti–Popular Front meaning of Macdonald's anti-progressivism was always clear. In 1947 and 1948 he went to great lengths to attack

Henry Wallace in print, going so far as to call him a "Fifth Columnist," the agent of a hostile foreign power. Macdonald saved his harshest venom for liberal allies of Communists rather than for the Communists themselves; this choice of targets paralleled anticommunist liberal tactics at that time, as discussed in Chapter 4.[38] For a time in the 1940s he leaned toward anarchism, writing in the aftermath of the atomic bombings in 1945, *"We must 'get' the national State before it gets us."* During the war he had been transfixed, like other Trotskyites, by the specter of an enveloping state power, whether "bureaucratic collectivism" in the Soviet Union or a "warfare state" in America. In this view, organized labor was simply a part of the state apparatus in America, just as it was under the Soviet and Nazi regimes. Macdonald derided Walter Reuther, seen by many "lib-labs" as a promising leader, as a "boy scout Labor-fakir." This punning epithet, a traditional barb directed at "labor barons" from the left, designated union leaders as stereotypical "oriental" potentates who held their minions in thrall while "faking" an embrace of democracy. Other writers who appeared in *politics* showed the same animus. For example, a youthful Daniel Bell wrote in 1944 that organized labor in America was making a "tragic" bargain with the state, agreeing to "behave themselves and accept an imperialist foreign policy" as the price of a share in continuing prosperity.[39] By 1950 Macdonald had cast aside his scornful neutrality toward warring state structures and "chose the West," as he put it, at the height of the cold war, siding with U.S. power rather than resisting the power of the state. Yet his disdain of labor and of traditional liberals lingered, even as he embraced the very warfare state he blamed such constituencies for abetting. When he moved left again in the 1960s, Macdonald showed how easily such prejudices could remain intact through a long series of political shifts.

In the 1960s Macdonald, like Alinsky, would be viewed by some young leftists as an inspiring elder and, his anti-authoritarianism on the upswing once again, he found himself embraced by many young dissidents who echoed his ethical absolutism of 1946, his simple humanism, and his criticism of the malign effects of science and technology. In 1962, for example, one journal of the new left featured an affirmation that "what is for us the ultimate and most irreducible value . . . is the person, the human being—not aspects, or parts or capacities of the human being, not systems or institutions . . . but the person, in his totality, in his freedom, in his originality and in his essential dignity."[40] This fiercely anti-ideological statement could have issued from Macdonald's pen. In 1972 Theodore Roszak, the author of *The Making of a Counter-Culture* (1969), wrote, "Had MacDonald's [*sic*] proposal [of 1946] become the ABC of postwar life, doubtless we should be living in a world of saner political discourse today."[41] Macdonald became a sort of godfather of the "Appropriate Technology" tendency; although few were probably aware of this in 1972, in 1946 he had suggested an early environmentalist sympathy when he put a photograph of industrial pollution on the cover of one of the *politics* issues that featured "The Root Is Man."[42] Macdonald's experiences in the 1940s, ancient history to young people in the 1960s, had led him to a renunciation of progress, a repudiation that suddenly found a widened vogue during the later years of another war, and which had fateful consequences for egalitarian thought in America.

By the middle 1950s, with the traditional left observing blackout conditions and with prominent social critics proclaiming that many of the precepts and goals of that left were outmoded, the meaning of radicalism was up for grabs. In 1954, Irving Howe and Lewis Coser, Trotskyites (thus the owners of sterling anticommunist credentials, to those in the know), began to publish *Dissent*, a journal of careful democratic socialism. In 1956, pacifists, including Bayard Rustin, David Dellinger, Paul Goodman, and Staughton Lynd, some of them socialists and some anarchists, started another publication, *Liberation*, whose sweeping anti-authoritarianism and Macdonald-like assertion of the absolute values of love, liberty, and the individual human's integrity, like its very name, would become common currency among the leftists of later generations.[43] Symbolizing the shifting concerns of political dissidents in the postwar era, the second issue of *Liberation* was devoted to the boycott of racially segregated city buses by the African American population of Montgomery, Alabama, which had begun in late 1955.

The members of both of these left circles had sat out World War II, honing their ideas about resistance in the face of enhanced state power, what later radicals would call, with a biblical flourish, the "new leviathan." The Trotskyites had never been able to stomach an alliance with the Soviet Union, but they had opposed war against fascism even during the period of the Nazi-Soviet pact, taking the ultra-left position that the war was a battle among rival imperialist powers, like World War I. The pacifists had gone to prison during the war for resisting the military draft. All of these radicals, the ones whose radicalism made it through the 1950s, had boycotted the entire antifascist movement. It is revealing of the nature of American politics during the 1950s that having opposed World War II was a less disabling political liability than having opposed fascism too early and with the wrong confederates. *Dissent* and *Liberation*, with their studied independence of all established political formations, were impressive accomplishments, not easily matched by the efforts of dissident thinkers during later conservative periods of American history. On the one hand, the impasse of leftist thought and organization at this time opened the door to fresh perspectives such as those found in *Libera-*

tion. On the other hand, all efforts to relaunch a politics of the left were hampered at this time by the murkiness of meaning that had resulted from the varying definitions of radicalism current in public life.

Liberation proved more influential with young radicals during the subsequent twenty years than did *Dissent*, because the *Liberation* editors were quicker to embrace the existing forces of political opposition, meaning civil rights agitation, anti–nuclear weapons protest, and antiwar activism, when they emerged, and because *Liberation* was more willing to break with the orthodox preoccupation of the 1950s, anticommunism. The thinker who best grasped the need to make this break if one wished to inspire an energetic new dissident movement was C. Wright Mills, who was close to neither publication. Mills rarely mentioned "radicalism" and before the 1960s his scholarship emphasized the impediments to rebellion. Yet Mills is an unavoidable presence in any discussion of how radicalism changed between the era of the Popular Front and that of the 1960s, so prominent a figure was he in the imagination of the new left. Particularly to white men among the radicals of the 1960s, Mills seemed to embody the radical identity. As his sociological work moved beyond his essays in *politics* during World War II and his ambivalent examination of labor leaders, *The New Men of Power* (1948), on to his study of the middle class, *White Collar* (1951) and his most famous book, *The Power Elite* (1956), Mills eliminated the consideration of progressive politics from his analysis, suggesting a growing resignation to the political nullity of the intellectual dissent that his own work represented.[44] Mills's dissent was a kind of time capsule for a future civilization to open and admire, its stoicism worth saluting by those who could, in the words of the great sociologist Max Weber—translated into English and presented to an American audience by Mills and his colleague Hans Gerth in 1946—"bear the fate of the times like a man."[45]

Mills's writings traced a long search for tools of political renewal. Only at the end of his life, in the early 1960s, did he discover rebel constituencies with which he could ally himself: college-educated youth and third-world revolutionaries. In the third world, revolutionary leaders *were* college educated and often young, as Mills noted. His 1960 derogation of tired liberals, with their smug pluralism and their hostility to protest, as "old men" and "old women" was more clearly an insult to the old than to women. But the crack about "old women" would linger, threatening, ultimately, in an era of feminism starting in the late 1960s, to overshadow Mills's polemical accomplishments in labeling cold warriors "NATO intellectuals" and denouncing the "crackpot realism" of thinkers who denied the realities of social injustice.[46] His words took on the connotations they did in part because of Mills's insistence on playing the role of cowboy in the groves of academe, and because of his own hero worship of Fidel Castro, rooted though his anti-imperialism was in a completely rational analysis of global history and society. Machismo played a prominent role at least in the form taken by U.S. activists' sympathy with the Cuban Revolution, if not in its motivation. The intellectual on the motorbike who ridiculed the old men and old women as he mused about taking to the hills to fight cut an indelible figure in the minds of young men who wanted, before and after all else, to rebel.[47]

The identities of radical and rebel threatened to come unmoored from specific political context in the cold war era and to appear instead as an atavistic individualism. This was the time when permanent ecstasy was conjured in sexualized visions of racial crossover by the novelists Jack Kerouac and Norman Mailer, when Robert S. McNamara, the president of the Ford Motor Company, picked *The Rebel*, by Albert Camus, as his contribution to his book group in Ann Arbor, and when Schlesinger termed his harshly anti-progressive liberalism "democratic radicalism."[48] One can only imagine the confusion that may have plagued the minds of curious young people.

It was in recognition of this predicament that the thinkers Paul Goodman and David Riesman—who coined the phrase "other-directed" in his masterwork of 1950, *The Lonely Crowd*—called explicitly for utopian thinking as early as the late 1940s.[49] While "utopian" was often a term of derision used by reformers against radicals, here it expressed a desire to escape the accretion of political labels and loyalties that clogged the path to an improved society, plus a new confidence that American capitalism had succeeded in transcending the world of economic scarcity, so that a spirit of play and human fulfillment might take center stage in social thought. Riesman called for a revival of the kind of small-scale collectivist experiment first derided as "utopian" by Karl Marx. Marxists always had deemed utopian socialism the fool's gold of the left because, in their view, perfect freedom could only be achieved under communism, and communism could only exist after capitalist development and a transitional stage of socialism had solved the problem of economic scarcity. Abundance such as had never existed was the precondition to utopia, and one could not walk straight to this kind of abundance from capitalism, in the Marxist view. Riesman and others concluded after World War II that the United States had done exactly that, bypassing socialism and opening the way to a postscarcity society. So it was logical to begin mapping the streets of utopia. The belief that scarcity had been transcended would spread far and wide in America as the years passed, finding expression in the title of Galbraith's 1958 book, *The Affluent Society*, and the 1960s would become a new golden age of intentional communities, often compared to the era of pre-Marxist radicalism in the

American 1830s and 1840s, the days of Brook Farm and the Oneida sect.[50]

As the 1950s ended and the 1960s began, the manifold attempts to validate and redefine "radicalism" had coalesced into three distinct tendencies in American political culture, and these vied for influence upon the baby-boom generation. These were a macho politics of insurgency, as embodied by Mills and Alinsky; a nonviolent politics of antistatism and personal liberation, expressed by the editors of *Liberation* and by Macdonald prior to his cold warrior phase; and anticommunist social democracy, espoused by SP activists, some "vital center" liberals such as Walter Reuther, and some in the *Dissent* circle. At the start of the 1960s, the initiators of a new left looked for patronage primarily to the last of these three tendencies. In 1962, when SDS held a retreat in order to produce a manifesto, it found a host in the UAW, which furnished SDS with its camp in Port Huron, Michigan. At early SDS gatherings in 1960, the invited speakers were Murray Kempton (an SP relic), Macdonald, Norman Thomas, Harrington, and James Farmer.[51] Harrington soon would become famous for writing *The Other America* (1962), an exposé of widespread poverty in the United States, Macdonald's review of which was widely credited with influencing President John F. Kennedy (1961–63) to consider a new antipoverty initiative.[52] Farmer was the leader of the Congress of Racial Equality (CORE), which had first imported Gandhian techniques of nonviolent resistance to power into the United States.[53]

The SDS leader Carl Oglesby later would ask, "Why not simply the *current* left? What makes it new?"[54] He got the question backward. The newness of the new left was clear; its members could find few immediate predecessors for the exact kind of politics they wanted to engage in. The better question was, What was left about it? The new left was attracted to the "radical" identity as it had been developed by writers since the middle 1940s. They wanted to be *fighters*—fighters against racism, against management of society by smug elites, against empire, and against a sense that history was over. What could this politics be called but left? It could have been called progressive liberalism; in the 1940s that is what it had been called. But that was unknown to most in the new left. Moreover, the fundamental issue that had defined the left for over a century had been not simply social inequality, but inequality as created by capitalism. Capitalism as such was an issue that radicals of the new left avoided for the first half of the 1960s, either because it seemed part of the dead wood of the past that they wished to transcend or because they harbored dreams at that time of influencing mainstream political figures, and talk of capitalism (and socialism) instinctively seemed, on the heels of the 1950s, politically disqualifying.[55] Thus it is curious that the young radicals identified with the category of the left, which they might have eschewed. One likely factor was the influence of Mills, who called the burgeoning student activism "the new left" in a widely circulated article of 1960.[56]

In the early 1960s there was good reason to think that SDS would develop as the youth wing of a revitalized liberal-labor push for social democracy, indirectly linked to both the SP and the Democratic party, notwithstanding the influence of macho insurgency and nonviolent resistance. Yet things would not work out that way. As the years passed, the second and third of these tendencies—macho insurgency and nonviolent resistance—would prove more appealing to the young dissidents of the 1960s than would the first—anticommunist social democracy. The Vietnam War would play a major role in determining that trajectory. But deeper factors in American life were at work as well. One of these factors was the perception of organized labor as a pillar of America's social and political structure, a perception that had simmered among radical thinkers since the World War II years, but one whose disruptive potential within liberal precincts was understood by few before the start of the 1960s. The feeling among middle-class thinkers that working-class immiseration was an outmoded expectation got stronger as the 1950s proceeded. *The Affluent Society* signaled the maturation of a post-scarcity or "qualitative" liberal politics in 1958, focused on enhancing health and beauty for those whose basic needs were already met, relegating the task of getting the basics for those without to the status of an unexciting mop-up operation. Schlesinger, who was Galbraith's comrade in ADA, promoted qualitative liberalism heavily. Both men perceived liberals in the Democratic party as needing a new agenda, and with the huge gains made by Democrats and liberals in the congressional elections of 1958, such thinkers saw an opening for liberals to chart a path up what the humanistic psychologist Abraham Maslow called the "hierarchy of needs."[57] It was a measure of the increasing detachment of many liberal intellectuals from the life of the American working class that so many of them failed to realize that these election results stemmed in large measure from the severity of the economic recession that had hit the country in 1957. The post-scarcity society had arrived only for some.

It had not arrived for African Americans, who in the 1950s intensified their push against the southern caste structure. The black liberation struggle, in which Farmer's CORE played a key early role, unlocked a portal that allowed the contending varieties of radicalism to rush into America's political life in unpredicted ways. This "civil rights movement" ended up settling the questions of how radicalism and liberalism each should be defined for a new era, and it seemed for a time to uncloud the vista of historical change, rebuking those who said history had ended.

Black Freedom and the Great Society Era: Requiem for Progress

Two different processes of coalition politics overlapped within liberal politics in the 1950s and 1960s. The first of these featured the construction of an inside-outside coalition joining the White House with black protest leaders, leading to historic political triumphs in 1964 and 1965; in dialectical fashion, this dynamic also featured the disillusionment of young African American activists with that coalition, which created deep fissures in it even before those triumphs. The second process was the ascendancy of a coalition that came neither from the most excluded sectors of society nor from the highest echelon of national power, but rather was driven by a multiracial, cross-class base of activists around the country who determined to revive and extend the New Deal's agenda. These activists were the Great Society liberals. The Great Society was a program of benefit to the middle class broadly defined, which is to say that it benefited many wage-earning Americans as well as salaried professionals and their families. The Great Society's agenda and sources of political support were not identical to those of the African American freedom struggle, but these agendas and constituencies overlapped.

Few foresaw how drastically the reintroduction of mass protest activities into American society by civil rights activists would alter the country's public life. The activism of the southern protesters ushered in a springtime for American reform. The black freedom struggle did not cause the promulgation of wide-ranging reform initiatives by Presidents John F. Kennedy and Lyndon B. Johnson (1963–69), but it generated the sense of a reopening of history that, in liberal circles, attached to the slogans of "the New Frontier" and "the Great Society." Johnson was the only president of this period who embraced the goals of the civil rights movement as one and the same in spirit with his agenda. Rhetoric was not substance, but nonetheless the entire period of ambitious liberal reform that stretched from the Montgomery boycott to the last civil rights act—outlawing racial discrimination in the sale and rental of housing—that Johnson signed into law, in 1968, and on to the regulatory reforms that a liberal-controlled Congress imposed upon President Richard M. Nixon (1969–74), can be viewed as the Great Society era of American liberalism.

The civil rights movement burst into national consciousness at an extremely conservative time, with the Montgomery bus boycott, in 1955–56.[58] The 1954 U.S. Supreme Court decision in *Brown* v. *Board of Education of Topeka, Kansas*, rejecting Jim Crow segregation as unconstitutional, had opened a door for political protest in the name of recognized constitutional rights that black activists eagerly stepped through. That happened as dramatically as it did only because of the presence of cadres who could make use of this opportunity. They came from diverse sources: long-standing civil rights constituencies such as the NAACP and a handful of reformist labor unions; and new ones such as the socially conscious clergy who included Martin Luther King, Jr., and radical pacifists such as Bayard Rustin, who sought out King in Montgomery and persuaded him that Gandhian nonviolence was the right path for the movement to take.

The coincidence of a new push for civil rights with the coldest years of the cold war was no mere coincidence. National political leaders saw that they were in a propaganda war with the Soviet Union in the third world and understood what a public-relations liability American apartheid was in Asia, Africa, and Latin America. This discernment led Presidents Truman and Kennedy to welcome either the perception or the reality of reform in the South (Eisenhower didn't much care).[59] NAACP leaders sought to separate racial reform from the Popular Front framework in which civil rights agitation had been couched in the years 1935–48. In 1946, *Time* published an article by Schlesinger claiming that the CP was "sinking tentacles" in the NAACP, triggering a frenzy within the black establishment to allay such concerns. In 1947, the national organization and its West Coast Regional Conference adopted resolutions formally excluding Communists, and pressure to eliminate fellow travelers as well continued until at least 1956.[60] DuBois, the NAACP's intellectual giant, started to become another of Orwell's "un-persons," a target of U.S. government prosecution for getting involved with the pro-Soviet Peace Information Center and failing to register with the U.S. attorney general's office as the "agent of a foreign power." His real "crime" was to lampoon U.S. leaders' claim that they, and not the Soviets, championed freedom in the world. DuBois was abandoned by the ACLU and most liberals, but he continued to enjoy popularity among politicized working-class black Americans, the people who needed to be mobilized if the direct-action tactics envisioned by some civil rights activists were to be tested.[61]

Despite DuBois's travails, overall the political left was far less isolated from the political mainstream of black America than from that of white America in the 1950s, and this was a factor in the capacity of African American activists to seize the day. African Americans often showed a "remarkable immunity" to McCarthyism.[62] Popular Front liberalism was never extirpated among African Americans. Mordecai Johnson, the president of Howard University (which depended heavily on congressional appropriations), resisted pressure to fire Inabel Lindsay, the dean of

Howard's School of Social Work, who had been involved in the Wallace campaign and other Popular Front activities; the white social work establishment provided little such protection to those, such as Mary van Kleeck, with similar political backgrounds.[63] When UE organizers, in 1950, came back to Pulaski, the Virginia city whence they had fled in terror the previous year, the only place in town where they could hold a meeting was the local NAACP hall; at the local level, this organization was less timorous about working with red-baited groups than were its national leaders.[64] Meanwhile, self-described progressives formed new civil rights organizations and maintained a toehold in the labor movement. The Civil Rights Congress and the National Negro Labor Council (NNLC) were creatures of the period 1946–56, bridging the interregnum between the Wallace campaign and the Montgomery movement.[65] The biggest stronghold of black progressive unionism was Detroit, where leftists clung to posts within certain UAW locals in the face of Reuther's efforts to dislodge them. Reuther went so far as to work against the campaign, conducted by his enemies in the UAW along with grassroots civil rights activists, to establish a state-level Fair Employment Practices Commission in Michigan, simply because they were the ones doing it. (Privately, Schlesinger called Reuther "always reliable.")[66] The presence of progressives in these precincts was revealed to the general public in 1952 when the HUAC held hearings in Detroit, supposedly to investigate Communist infiltration of defense industries. The hearings did not go as the committee members planned. One witness, the NNLC activist Coleman Young, turned the tables on the committee and offered an aggressive defense of militancy on behalf of racial equality, regardless of party affiliation; he challenged the members of the two major parties to show they were as committed to civil rights as Communists were. The HUAC had wanted to expose the continuing presence of Popular Front politics, and it had done so, but Young's performance showed how, when the issues of Jim Crow and civil rights were the focus, public discussion might serve to rehabilitate the politics of progressivism.[67]

It is fair to say that when a new wave of civil rights protest erupted starting in the middle 1950s, it came from outside the intellectual and organizational structure of liberalism.[68] Yet this was so only because liberalism had been redefined as "vital center" liberalism. Liberalism as it had been widely understood in 1945 would have accommodated civil rights protest far more easily than liberalism circa 1955. One of the aims of movement activists, notably the left-wing strategists who clustered around Rustin, was to remake white liberalism in the image of the more ideologically heterogeneous liberalism that persisted in black America during the Eisenhower period. This was part of what was denoted by the concept of "realignment," a vision of reconfiguring American politics into a clear contest between a social-democratic party and a right-wing party. This goal united Great Society liberals, new left radicals, and SP figures such as Rustin in the 1960s. The civil rights movement and its activist partners succeeded in this goal partway, forcing the question of legal caste restrictions into the center of the liberal agenda and making integrationism a line that politicians of both major parties eventually had to toe—even if only in token fashion—but appending matters of economic justice and universal opportunity only uncertainly to the agenda of liberals and of the party that housed most of them, the Democracy.

King voiced a desire not only to advance the interests of African Americans but also to transform American politics and society. He intoned in his first major public speech in Montgomery words that, with almost no alteration, he repeated many times afterward, saying, "[W]hen the history books are written in the future, somebody will have to say, 'There lived a race of people, a *black* people . . . who had the moral courage to stand up for their rights. And thereby they injected a new meaning into the veins of history and of civilization.'"[69] In a political context this figurative transfusion would mean, in part, making white America safe once again for radical perspectives, for left-influenced social criticism and aspiration. Prophetic social criticism once had had a home within white religious circles, with widely respected spokespersons such as Harry F. Ward. But the political conflicts of the 1940s had driven the liberal white clergy to the anticommunist center. King made his own anticommunism clear, as in his essay, published in 1963, titled "How Should a Christian View Communism?" There he stated, "Communism and Christianity are fundamentally incompatible," not only because of communism's atheism, but also because Christianity was offended by the way in which communism made the individual "little more than a depersonalized cog in the ever-turning wheel of the state." This was a familiar trope of liberal anticommunism.[70]

King added to this standard liberal argument a persistent moral critique of American capitalism (or "traditional capitalism," as he carefully put it). He concluded, "The Kingdom of God is neither the thesis of individual enterprise nor the antithesis of collective enterprise, but a synthesis which reconciles the truth of both." This was uncharted territory for all but a few of King's white contemporaries, who would have been hard pressed to identify "the truth" contained in collectivism. King argued that the United States would best the Soviet Union in the cold war if it showed the world that the freedom and justice embodied in the synthesis of individualism and collectivism truly flourished in America. "We must not engage in a negative anti-Communism, but rather in a positive thrust for democracy," he wrote. King made this argument, a kind of anti-anticommunism, consistently from the 1950s until his death in 1968.[71] King's familiarity with piercing social criticism, including the social gospel of Walter Rauschenbusch, Gandhian nonviolence, and Marxist-influenced analysis, went back to his undergraduate days at the historically black Morehouse College in Atlanta, headed by Benjamin Mays, a social gospel clergyman, and as a graduate student at Crozer Theological Seminary in Pennsylvania. Social critics who were on friendly terms with leftist knowledge under a ban at places such as Union Theological Seminary in the 1950s were still to be found by curious trainees for the African American clergy.[72]

By the early 1960s King was playing for high stakes, and he was willing to throw over his left-wing political advisers, Rustin and Stanley Levison, whose personal and political histories opened a path to blackmail. Both of them were former adherents of the Communist movement; Levison remained close to the CP, while Rustin long had been an anti-Soviet radical pacifist. Rustin was also gay.[73] But the very fact that King had left-wing advisers to jettison remains more striking than his concessions to red-baiters and gay-baiters. When Rustin first approached King in Montgomery he offered King a complete inventory of his political liabilities, and King responded by welcoming his help; King's wife, Coretta, had seen Rustin speak at her high school years before during his ceaseless evangelism for nonviolent change in America, and she greeted him warmly at her home.[74] Such responses by white reformers would have been unthinkable in 1956.

Some white liberals expressed grave concern about the danger of Communist influence over ingenuous civil rights activists well into the 1960s, despite all the evidence of American communism's extreme weakness. On one occasion in 1964, a group of civil rights activists came to Washington from Mississippi, where three of their comrades had disappeared in the lethally dangerous environment of the "Freedom Summer" campaign for black voter registration that the Student Nonviolent Coordinating Committee (SNCC)—the militant youth wing of the movement—and other groups had organized. The activists met with Senator Paul Douglas of Illinois, the academic in politics, a "liberal hero," to press for federal intervention in the South. One of them recalled, "I'll never forget this, [Douglas] said, 'you young people want to play you're great and . . . this is a wonderful thing you are doing, but,' he said, 'the main thing,' and he'd repeat this over and over again, 'is watch out for the Commies.' . . . That word is indelible in my memory; it was like something [from a] comic book . . . very sad and very disillusioning."[75] If there were few Communists around, there were some progressives—surviving remnants of the Popular Front, whom "vital center" liberals claimed were the entering wedge of totalitarian politics. Such liberals criticized southern activists for naïvely associating with wolves whose sheeps' clothing fooled only the foolish. The National Lawyers' Guild (NLG) and the Southern Conference Educational Fund (SCEF), Popular Front organizations that had survived the McCarthy period, assisted SNCC. White liberals pressed SNCC to break these ties, but the young activists refused. Allard Lowenstein, who had injected himself into the civil rights struggle in Mississippi, red-baited the NLG and SCEF inside the movement in 1963–64. He asserted, "You cannot expect liberals in this country to support the civil rights movement when you are using people who don't really believe in freedom."[76] Schlesinger reportedly told SNCC activist James Forman that it was "unpardonable" that he and his comrades should work with the NLG's lawyers. In 1964 C. Vann Woodward, the eminent historian of the South and long an enemy to southern inequality in all its forms, nonetheless worried to his colleague Staughton Lynd—who was deeply involved with SNCC—"Staughton, what are we going to do about the communists in SNCC?"[77]

Woodward may have been teasing Lynd with a joke. Even if so, the condescension embedded in his and Schlesinger's remarks—"what are we going to do?"—reflected not only a patronizing stance toward the black struggle for equality but also a broader attitude of elite distrust toward movements "from below," an elitism sewn lastingly into the fabric of liberal intellectual culture in the 1950s. Many liberal thinkers accepted the conservative claim that Joseph McCarthy spoke for America's heartland, for its "plain people" whose fierce anger was aimed at the country's cosmopolitan elites as much as at Communists. The former Marxists among them already felt let down by a proletariat who, in their view, had not risen to the occasion when fascism had reared its ugly head in Europe in the 1930s. Liberal scholars arranged McCarthyism, Hitlerism, and American agrarian populism in a single lineage of frightening political movements, steered by demagogues and fueled by the resentments of modest, provincial folk; many of these anti-populist scholars were Jewish and they were chilled to see a common thread of anti-Semitism running through all these movements. They had come to fear "the masses," and the masses were on the march in the South.[78]

Moreover, many intellectuals, in an era of expanding universities and other growth industries for people with their skills and connections, had become comfortable and now saw the "little people" as a threat to what they had secured. Some former leftist thinkers went all the way and considered themselves conservatives, but others maintained a liberal identity while embracing elitist views. The Hungarian historian John Lukacs, a conservative in a traditional European mold, immigrated to America in the late 1940s and was disquieted when several individuals told him that if he wanted to understand his new land he need only read "The

Lottery" by Shirley Jackson, a short story published in 1948 about humble townspeople who become a mob, in a yearly ritual, and murder one of their own number chosen at random. It surprised Lukacs that these "votaries of Liberalism" fervently embraced a story "incarnating a hatred and fear of The People."[79] In 1951 Alfred Kazin confided to his diary his disgust with the "[i]nsufferable" and "anxiously self-congratulatory" Jewish ex-radicals who staffed the liberal magazine *Commentary*. He wrote that "they have not the slightest interest . . . in poverty, in race hatred (except when 'they' turn on us), in workers found to be 'unemployable' by the latest technocratic revolution."[80] At times northern white liberals even seemed to swallow southern fairy tales about race relations in Dixie and to vest large doses of faith in the desire of white southern elites to reform their region from within. In the aftermath of the *Brown* decision, Reinhold Niebuhr—who, in his 1932 landmark work, *Moral Man and Immoral Society*, had recommended Gandhian nonviolent protest as a promising instrument of change for African Americans—warned against pushing the white South too far, for fear that a white backlash against outside interference might "arrest the promising organic growths of racial amity."[81] Some white liberals preferred any absurdity, it seemed, to "mass politics." An inability to identify with the African American protagonists of the southern struggle lingered in some liberal quarters into the 1960s.

Black activists, for their part, cared less about allegations of "anti-Americanism" than they did about racism and antiracism. King's very first piece of political journalism, ghostwritten by Rustin with King's collaboration, appeared in the first issue of *Liberation* in 1956. SNCC members acted baffled by tirades against their allies in the NLG and SCEF. Not only did these volunteers continually render whatever services they could give, but "when they volunteered their services, they agreed to take orders, not give them."[82] The bottom line was that SNCC couldn't afford to be picky about its friends in the Deep South, where it was undertaking the movement's most dangerous work. SNCC's policy of "non-exclusionism" represented a defiant break with the politics of the 1950s and heavily influenced the new left and the antiwar movement of the 1960s. That policy took shape because African American youth had been schooled to look over their shoulders for Klansmen, not for Communists.

Yet the African American and white activists in the southern movement found a lot of allies among white liberals, despite the warnings of the anticommunist and anti-populist chorus. Many whites saw in civil rights protest the basis for hopes of a new political beginning, of a revitalized liberalism on the side of the socially excluded and freed from the obsessions of the past. As one protégé of Rustin's said, "Now, suddenly, here was a movement for social justice" in the middle 1950s. "If you considered yourself a radical, then supporting that movement was the thing to do. You simply had to be there."[83] Many liberals had the same reaction, and a period of renewed left-liberal cooperation started to take off. "Liberals no longer had to content themselves with subscribing to *The Nation* or *Commonweal* and shaking their heads in dismay over the latest excesses of McCarthyism. Instead, they could donate money, attend a benefit concert, collect signatures on a petition, write their congressmen, march, picket, and in some cases even risk their lives in the South."[84] As the years passed, a national constituency of liberal support for the southern movement developed.

Lyndon Johnson and his lieutenants were aware of this development, and they feared a disastrous collision between their party's northern and southern wings at the Democratic National Convention in Atlantic City in 1964. There the Mississippi Freedom Democratic party (MFDP), a largely black organization of civil rights activists, challenged the "regular," segregationist, all-white state delegation, which was produced through a voting system that excluded African Americans and many whites, for the right to represent Mississippi at the convention. The MFDP had pledged its loyalty to Johnson, while the Mississippi regulars were expected to support the Republican nominee, Senator Barry Goldwater, because Goldwater opposed federal action on civil rights while Johnson supported it. Johnson feared that seating the MFDP would spur wider southern defections. The pressures placed on the MFDP—by Johnson, Humphrey, and Reuther, and by King and Rustin, who were by that time committed to a coalition with Johnson—to relent in its challenge and to accept a pledge of future reform were the cause of epic anger and disillusionment among young activists, black and white. Recollections of "Atlantic City" as a moment of mythic importance in the radicalization of these activists became standard fare in future memoirs. The SNCC activist Cleveland Sellers wrote that these events were "to the civil rights movement what the Civil War was to American history: afterward, things could never be the same. . . . After Atlantic City, our struggle was not for civil rights, but for liberation."[85] Stokely Carmichael, also of SNCC, announced, "This proves that the liberal Democrats are just as racist as Goldwater." White members of SNCC and SDS likewise viewed the 1964 Atlantic City imbroglio as the last straw as far as liberals were concerned. When Rustin tried to sell the MFDP on the compromise at an emotional meeting, the white SNCC worker Mendy Samstein felt emboldened to disregard Rustin's long history of sacrifice in the cause of social change and shout, "You're a traitor, Bayard, a traitor! Sit down!" Todd Gitlin wrote, "The very name [Atlantic City] became synonymous with liberal betrayal. To the New Left, Atlantic City discredited the politics of coalition—between militants and the liberal-labor establishment, between whites and blacks, between youth and elders." Up to that time, "liberalism posed a dilemma" for SDS. "After, it was an obstacle."[86]

Yet these lamentations over the alleged betrayal of radicals-in-the-making by establishment liberals have obscured the severity of the rift that opened *among* Democratic party activists at the convention. Without the breaking of these ranks, the MFDP's challenge never could have gone as far as it did. Before the convention, nine state delegations and twenty-five Democratic members of Congress had committed themselves to the insurgents. The MFDP claimed that California Governor Pat Brown, not one to rock his party's boat in quixotic causes, had "said the traditional Mississippi Party was so far out of tune with the national Democratic Party that it should not be allowed near the convention hall."[87] The MFDP's point man before the convention's Credentials Committee was the redoubtable Joseph Rauh, who was prominent in the national Democratic party, the main lawyer for the UAW, and the national chairman of ADA, a group whose embrace of the civil rights cause had become warmer since the calculations of 1948. Fannie Lou Hamer's televised testimony to the committee, in which she related details of the beating she suffered at the hands of Mississippi police for her voter-registration work, elicited hundreds of telegrams from around the country to the White House urging that the MFDP be seated.

The red-baiting tactics of old failed to undermine support for the militants among white liberals. Lowenstein showed hostility toward Ella Baker, who headed up the MFDP's actions in Washington, ostensibly because of her Popular Front activism during the 1930s and 1940s. (Even Rauh, burned by MFDP's criticism at the convention after he urged the activists to accept the offered compromise, lapsed into old-style ADA tactics, privately writing Humphrey, "Communist influence was, of course, evident at the Convention.")[88] But Johnson had to use strong-arm tactics to coerce members of the Credentials Committee into switching their votes—he got Brown and many other prominent liberals to assist him—and bringing the number of supporters below the threshold required to send the matter before the whole convention.[89] In January 1965, the seating of five white Congressmen from Mississippi was challenged on the floor of the House of Representatives, based on the illegitimacy of the voting procedures in that state. Black activists denounced liberals and Democrats for not supporting nonracial democracy when this challenge was defeated. Yet it received an impressive 143 votes in support (to 228 against).[90]

A restive wing of the liberal coalition wished to break decisively with southern segregationist forces, executing the realignment strategy. This strategy would encourage the departure of right-wing southerners from the Democratic party and into the Republican party. Liberal Republicans and the newly activated political forces would join the Democrats. Johnson had reservations, aware that his support for civil rights might exact a frightful cost for his party. Earlier in 1964, after he had signed the Civil Rights Act—which made employment discrimination and de jure Jim Crow segregation illegal—Johnson had commented privately that he had "delivered the South to the Republican party for a long time to come."[91] Johnson tried in Atlantic City to blunt the immediate political force of black protest. This brought the alienation of some promising young cadres from his party, and it did not placate segregationist voters, who deserted him en masse. For him, the one dark cloud on election day in 1964 formed over the Deep South, where Goldwater won a bloc of five states. By 1965 Johnson may have realized that continued compromise on the voting rights issue held little hope of maintaining the old New Deal coalition. One constituency or another would have to go from his camp, and since white southerners were already leaving, the choice had been made for him. After several more months of protest and violent response in the South, Johnson pushed a Voting Rights bill through Congress, seeking to minimize his party's overall political losses by enfranchising African Americans in the South and giving heart to liberals nationwide.

The strength of liberal forces had been building since the late 1950s, their agenda well defined and tested at the state level. The elections of 1958 not only swept Democrats into power in Congress; they also brought Pat Brown into the governor's mansion in Sacramento, an important event in liberalism's history. "A turning point in California political history, 1958 marked the beginning of an eight-year period during which the Democratic Party, organized labor, and the NAACP solidified an electoral bloc that placed California ahead of the national curve in its embrace of a postwar liberalism that prefigured the Great Society." This "bloc" had its several organizational nuclei: the "amateur Democrats," white and generally professional-class activists gathered in Democratic Clubs in the state's big cities and coordinated statewide in the California Democratic Council (CDC); NAACP chapters and other black organizations; local branches of the Community Service Organization (CSO), which had been founded by Alinsky and his protégés and was a major force in organizing working-class Mexican Americans to vote and to press for decent government services in their communities; and union locals. The unions, like the CSO, often focused on local issues, while the CDC and similar club networks in other states were strongly oriented toward national and international issues. But all these groups could agree on a set of state and national policy goals.[92]

Sacramento provided a boatload of new funds for a massive expansion of higher education—which resulted in California's world-famous public university system, with schooling offered tuition-free to state residents—better public health and unemployment insurance, and a ceaseless march of major public works projects. To the frustration of conservatives and the delight of liberals, this enormous public investment made the state's economy surge. Civil rights also had become a cause dear to the heart of a new generation of liberal activists, and in California they got a fair-employment law signed by Brown in 1959 and a fair-housing law in 1963 (which was then overturned through referendum in 1964, in the same election in which the state's voters gave a big majority to Lyndon Johnson). These California initiatives offered a clear foretaste of Johnson's Great Society agenda. It amounted to a revival of the New Deal, refitted to include racial groups that had been categorically excluded from the benefits of the previous wave of reform in the 1930s, plus a new emphasis on state and federal money for education.

In other states around the country, the common coin was a desire to complete what was seen as the unfinished business of the New Deal. In some places, such as Minnesota, where the breakthrough Democratic election year was 1954, and in Michigan, where a potent organization rooted in UAW locals kept G. Mennen Williams in the governorship throughout the 1950s, the reform agenda was prosecuted by the party faithful. In New York, self-identified "Reform" or "Independent" Democratic Clubs placed themselves in a lineage of genteel anti-machine politics going back to the days of Theodore Roosevelt. Such reformers idolized Eleanor Roosevelt for her pro–civil rights stance (which had weakened in the 1950s as her anticommunism waxed) and Adlai Stevenson, who was no crusader for human rights, for his eloquence and appearance of integrity.[93] Whether the new liberal Democratic activists thought sound policy could be pursued by the party regulars or required a break with the back-room boys, whether local activists emphasized bread-and-butter liberalism or procedural reform, these activists generally embraced a consistent liberal program. Great Society liberals marked themselves off from the New Deal with their emotional embrace of civil rights for people of all races, while they demanded not the preservation but the expansion of the New Deal welfare state.[94] The Democratic party's national platform in 1960, on which John Kennedy ran for president, reflected the new balance of forces in that party well enough. "Kennedy ran for office committed to a liberal wish list of bold initiatives; if elected, and true to these promises, he would raise the minimum wage, improve the conditions of farm workers, secure passage of national health insurance for the elderly, and launch a 10-year campaign to eliminate urban slums."[95] This came in addition to the party's surprisingly strong embrace of civil rights—calling, for example, for an end to poll taxes and for Jim Crow school districts to submit concrete desegregation plans by 1963.[96]

When Democratic presidents returned to the White House in 1961 after eight years of Eisenhower, their liberal claimants had plenty of ideas about how presidential power ought to be used. In office, Kennedy was chary of the liberal agenda; the storied vigor that he wished to inject into government was almost entirely focused on fighting the cold war more effectively. Johnson was a horse of a different color. His circumstances were also different, certainly after the 1964 elections. He was freed to be as liberal a president as he chose by his party's huge majorities in both houses of Congress and the predominance of liberals in the Democratic caucuses.

In the event, Johnson wanted to be very liberal, far more so than most observers had expected. Johnson did not wait for 1964 to signal his intentions. He told Roy Wilkins of the NAACP in December 1963 that he was "[f]ree at last, free at last. Thank God almighty, I'm free at last" to support civil rights legislation, gently mimicking Martin Luther King, Jr. Three days after Kennedy's murder, Johnson told Walter Heller, the chairman of the White House Council of Economic Advisers, that he should tell his "liberal friends . . . to lay off . . . to quit lobbying. I'm for them. I know they have good programs. . . . They don't need to waste my time. . . ." In January 1965, when Vice President Hubert Humphrey said, "[T]he issues are . . . set out already; they include war on poverty, economic growth, world peace, security and medicare, human dignity, human rights, education, opportunity for the young . . . building a better America," Johnson congratulated him on putting it so well.[97]

Johnson placed himself in the context of previous liberal reform. According to his aide Bill Moyers, Johnson's embrace of the slogan "Great Society," which he launched in the spring of 1965, was rather tepid. "He didn't like it as much as he liked the New Deal. That's really what he saw himself doing." "He kept saying to Moyers, 'I'm going to be President for nine years and so many days, almost as long as FDR' or second only to FDR, and he saw it as a chance to finish what Roosevelt had begun." Soon after taking over from Kennedy, Johnson said, "Everything on my desk today was here when I first came to Congress" in the 1930s. When he signed Medicare and Medicaid into law in 1965 he did so on Harry Truman's front porch in Independence, Missouri, with the older man sitting close by. This was the sentimental gesture of a leader who saw his society returning to the track of upward progress after years of wasted time. The theme of fulfillment or completion drew Johnson strongly. He also was wont to say, "I'm going to be the president who finishes what Lincoln began."[98]

The phrase "Great Society" announced a post-scarcity agenda. In the lofty phrases of Johnson's speech at the University of Michigan in May 1964, when he first offered this term publicly, he asserted that the new challenge facing American society, now that it had produced enormous wealth through "unbounded invention and untiring industry," was "to use that wealth to enrich and elevate our national life, and to advance the quality of our . . . civilization." Johnson claimed that "material progress is only the foundation on which we will build a richer life of mind and spirit." The dangers facing America in 1964 included "soulless wealth" and the "boredom and restlessness" of increased leisure time without creative purpose.[99] The words that framed Johnson's policy proposals might have been written by the psychological theorist Abraham Maslow.

Yet this post-scarcity packaging always has been misleading, for Johnson's Great Society program operated largely within the world of scarcity. Highway beautification (his wife's personal concern) did answer complaints about ugliness amid plenty, ones that Galbraith had voiced in *The Affluent Society.* And clean air and water regulations that Johnson secured were conceived as health measures that Americans could afford now that they had accumulated wealth, implying that a country not (yet) wealthy had to put up with deadly pollution. These were landmark laws, which laid the groundwork for later protections. More clearly nonmaterial in their benefits were the cultural enhancement organizations that Johnson and Congress created, the National Endowments for the Arts and Humanities and public television. Most of Johnson's program, however, was clearly aimed at improving the material circumstances of Americans. Medical insurance and expanded Social Security benefits eased the burdens of both poor and middle-class Americans. Urban renewal—for all its defects—and rural development were framed as antipoverty and economic revival programs. Massive aid to education at all levels, primary through college and beyond, was not a post-scarcity concept either. Educational improvement was universally understood then, as now, as a way of strengthening the country's "human capital." From the perspective of individual students, a better education system was supposed to provide a staircase toward better earnings, not edification for unexpected leisure time.

The rhetoric of the Great Society suggested that Johnson wished to establish the functional equivalent of a ministry of culture, helping Americans learn how to live meaningfully in a world beyond work. But, except for the few cultural programs mentioned above, which accounted for a small fraction of the Great Society programs' expenditures, that was not what the Great Society was about at all. Johnson was right to see it instead as the fulfillment of the New Deal's unfinished business. He knew better than many liberal intellectuals that the American public, or at least his target voters, were not clamoring for a program to satisfy the psychology of rich people. Johnson shared more with King than a Protestant postmillennial vision of creating a better society. The two leaders both aimed to satisfy the aspirations of people who had more than their parents had had, but who did not feel secure.

However, there was one important sense in which the Great Society program was a post-scarcity liberal program. Johnson insisted there was no need to rob Peter to pay Paul. He was not only a budget hawk who repeatedly balanced government expenditures with revenues; he also was an enemy of soaking the rich and a friend to big business. As Walter Lippmann commented on Johnson's antipoverty program, "A generation ago it would have been taken for granted that a war on poverty meant taxing money away from the haves and turning it over to the have nots. . . . But in this generation a revolutionary idea has taken hold. The size of the pie can be increased by intention, by organized fiscal policy and then a whole society, not just one part of it will grow richer."[100] Lippmann seemed unaware of how regressive the tax basis of the New Deal had been.[101] Nonetheless, he was correct to see that, under Johnson, the rhetoric of liberalism put aside criticism of big business and the rich. Johnson's chosen method for increasing the "size of the pie" was the same as Kennedy's had been: a big tax cut aimed at business and the wealthy. (The stimulative impact of spending on the Vietnam War was a by-product of Johnson's foreign policy, not its intention.) The insistence on this regressive version of Keynesianism, and Johnson's unwillingness to discomfit powerful interests when push came to shove, are well known. Johnson ruled out any public sector job creation from the start as part of the War on Poverty, even though common sense dictated, and experience proved, that his preferred method of training young men from high-unemployment populations for nonexistent jobs was not going to generate jobs for them. Johnson seemed to think that everyone's needs could be met with no one's ox getting gored.

This laid the basis for an estrangement between Johnsonian liberals and critics to their left who, in the course of the 1960s, came to see either big business or American capitalism itself as the enemy of progress. These critics included avowed leftists, both white and black, but also ardent liberals who saw the needs of farm workers, minority youth, and consumers in conflict with the business establishment. Two different visions of progress were at work in American society at this time, one consonant with Great Society liberalism and one that posed a sharp challenge to it. The first was a gradualist, postmillennial vision of continual reform. This idea of progress maintained a powerful hold on Great Society liberals. Many of them thought that eventually American society would be transformed through an accretion of reforms bringing greater equity, security, wealth, and beauty. Americans' very moral lives would grow more sensitive as fewer person-hours were required in dirty physical labor, and those still required to do that kind of work would receive improved care and compensation. This was a vision of completing the New Deal and continuing on what was perceived as a blocked path toward European-style social democracy. Although the Great Society was not itself a post-scarcity program, it would pave the way toward a post-scarcity form of capitalism. If enough laws were passed in Washington and in state capitals around the country, eventually America would be Sweden. These liberal true believers could be very critical of big business, but such criticism did not betoken hostility toward the economic system. Great Society liberals tended to believe in American capitalism. Most of them remembered the Great Depression and had shared in the postwar boom. Their vision of peaceful transformation was a vision of transforming capitalism, not leaving it behind. They thought that its excesses had to be curbed and that it had to be supplemented by a more robust and larger public sphere. Capitalism could be humanized.

Johnson and similar political animals who wished to tap the energies of Americans fired with such a vision, while still staying on the good side of powerful interests, had to tread a careful path toward Stockholm. But it was possible. Officeholders could continue to choose from a wide array of potential reforms to deliver. Rhetorically, they could embrace this vision with a fair degree of political safety in the 1960s, so long as they did not mention Europe or socialism. Johnson managed this challenge masterfully. He would have maintained the loyal support of most such liberals who leaned a bit to the left had it not been for the Vietnam War. Even with the war, he kept the support of many of them.

The more radical anticapitalism that bloomed during these years, by contrast, was virtually impossible for the political system as then constituted to accommodate. Some of those on the left gradually shucked off their reluctance to call capitalism their enemy. In early 1965, at the first large demonstration against the Vietnam War in the nation's capital, SDS president Paul Potter called on his peers to "name that system" that they found oppressive and that they opposed, but he refrained from naming that system capitalism or imperialism.[102] A few years later, many called for socialism as a way out of the domestic and foreign repression they associated, by then, with American capitalism. In 1968 John and Barbara Ehrenreich concluded, "We have . . . come to call the system—'capitalism.'" (Perhaps the quotation marks indicated a continuing ironic distance from the very concept.) They embraced the idea of socialism, whose object, in their words, was "a truly human society," one in which "human needs take priority over all others."[103] This marked a blunt return to an older perspective on historical change.

Although the Vietnam War brought liberals and leftists almost to blows, the seeds of such conflict had already been planted. Perhaps the conflict would not have mushroomed as it did in the absence of the war, but in that case serious strains still would have been present. Left-wing disgust with the obsessive anticommunism of "vital center" liberals, disillusionment with organized labor, sympathy for insurgency by downtrodden groups at home and abroad, and ambivalence about state power, all tendencies that germinated within radical thought between the 1940s and the early 1960s, each played a role in ensuring that, as Gitlin stated it poignantly, "it wasn't liberalism that reaped the harvest of the young's growing disgruntlement" in 1960s America. Cold war liberals became "fathers who lost their political children."[104]

While each of these issues was important in its own right, the early history of the 1960s left was rooted specifically in a deep sense of solidarity with the African American movement. The movement's authority attached particularly strongly to those engaged in hazardous direct-action work, which meant that SNCC—a direct pipeline to SDS—generated a powerful mystique. The unhappiness of SNCC and other black activists with white liberals in the 1960s, which broke into public view in the aftermath of the conflict in Atlantic City, affected budding radicals of all races powerfully. The regularity with which young black activists criticized "white liberals" made a disdain of such figures de rigueur in the new left, creating a field of rhetoric more reminiscent of the CP's militant "third period" polemics in the early 1930s than of the Popular Front.

It is not always noted how early expressions of frustration with white liberals issued from the black movement. It did not begin with Atlantic City. As early as 1958, King had criticized the "quasi-liberalism" of northern white liberals when he had reflected on the school integration crisis in Little Rock.[105] Clearly he meant "white liberal" when he said "liberal." He implied that liberals failed to fulfill their own creed, not that their creed itself was defective. In his famous "Letter from Birmingham Jail" in 1963, King criticized "the white moderate" in disquieting terms not unlike those Malcolm X directed toward white liberals. "I have almost reached the regrettable conclusion," King wrote, "that the Negro's great stumbling block in his stride toward freedom is not the White Citizen's Counciler or the Ku Klux Klanner, but the white moderate . . . who constantly says: 'I agree with you in the goal you seek, but cannot agree with your methods of direct action'; who paternalistically believes he can set the timetable for another man's freedom. . . ."[106] King did not equate "moderate" with "liberal," yet he amplified the very terms of criticism that were coming to haunt white liberals. After the famous protests in Birmingham and the violent counterattack by "Bull" Connor and his henchmen in the spring of 1963, Langston Hughes published a poem called "Northern Liberal: 1963," in which he sarcastically mimicked liberal fears that protest would bring conflict and violence. In the voice of the white liberal, he wrote: "Dogs have vindicated me—/I knew that it would come."[107] In the heyday of the civil rights movement white liberals were charged with resisting the conflict that was a necessary part of progress, with paying lip service to the value of change while exhibiting a deep bias for order, and with wishing to reap political dividends from black emancipation while maintaining control over the grassroots movement.

As the years passed in the 1960s, these criticisms settled into a kind of shorthand, a set of refrains about the untrustworthiness of white liberals. In the fall of 1963 Lowenstein brought SNCC representatives and others to Yale University to recruit volunteers for Freedom Summer. As part of this effort Marian Wright, then a law student and supposedly not a militant firebrand, announced to an audience, "We can see the subtle bigotry beneath the veneer of liberalism, and so we wonder whom we can really trust as a friend."[108] Around the same time James Baldwin said, "There is no role for the white liberal, he is our affliction," and he derided liberals' "missionary complex" in dealing with black Americans.[109] The Atlantic City events in 1964 added high-strength fertilizer to seeds already sprouting. Charles Sherrod of SNCC said afterward that, if the MFDP had accepted the compromise offered by Johnson's allies, "It would have said to blacks across the nation and the world that we share the power, and that is a lie! The 'liberals' would have felt great relief for a job well done. The Democrats would have laughed again at the segregationist Republicans and smiled that their own 'Negroes' were satisfied."[110] In February 1965 John Lewis, who embodied the spirit of Christian interracialism within SNCC, told a staff meeting that the group could not rely on "white liberals and the so-called affluent Negro leader. . . . They will sell us down the river for the hundredth time in order to protect themselves."[111] After mid-decade the rhetoric became cruder. At CORE's convention in 1966, Stokely Carmichael, Lewis's successor at the helm in SNCC, said simply, "We don't need white liberals." One black Harlem activist said in 1967, "The quicker we get white liberals out of the black community, the better off we'll be. White liberals are the slimiest snakes on earth."[112]

Yet for all these provocative comments, none was more disturbing than the remarks made by Kenneth Clark, the eminent social psychologist who had worked with Myrdal on the preparation of *An American Dilemma* in late 1963. Clark said that "so far as the Negro is concerned, the ethical aspect of American liberalism . . . is primarily verbal." The liberal, he asserted, "in relation to the Negro . . . has never been as liberal as he likes to profess." He left open the question of whether he, like the black activists of the World War II years, saw liberals failing to live up to liberal values, or whether he saw liberal values themselves as defective on issues of race. But clear and devastating was Clark's comment, "I must confess bluntly that I now see white American liberalism primarily in terms of the adjective 'white.'" For liberal politics, this perception represented a regression to the years before 1935. Echoing King's comments on "the white moderate" earlier that year, Clark called the white liberal "a curious and insidious adversary—much more insidious than the out-and-out bigot." From an avatar of liberal interracialism, in 1963, this comment should have proved sobering.[113]

Young militants, both black and white, became alienated politically from liberal political forces in the 1960s, and this estrangement can be traced to the deep and evidently ineradicable mistrust of white liberals by African American civil rights activists. This is not to say that this mistrust was the only cause of that alienation; but it was a highly emotional source of this generational rift, and it appeared earlier than did the Vietnam War as an issue.

At mid-decade Rustin advocated a shift in movement strategy toward a broader understanding of coalition politics, essentially urging activists for racial justice to align the inside-outside coalition with the Great Society coalition, and to turn, as he phrased it, "From Protest to Politics." On the merits Rustin had a strong case in arguing that the black movement could not advance toward its unfulfilled economic goals on the basis of African American political strength, and that only a program that benefited large numbers of whites as well as blacks could garner the support required to fulfill the program of "jobs and freedom." Rustin called this program "revolutionary" and argued, in a contrarian vein indebted to his Marxist intellectual training, that the arduous struggles just finished had represented the *easy* part of the movement's journey. Jim Crow laws and barriers to voting, largely southern phenomena, had represented the detritus of an earlier stage of social development, according to Rustin, and such vestiges had found few defenders outside the South. Jim Crow had seemed irrational and backward to whites in other regions. This was not so with the largely unregulated capitalist labor market and the loss of good manufacturing jobs through automation, phenomena that Rustin identified as the impediments to further progress toward social equality. Only a mighty political coalition could tackle these problems, for this would mean fundamental changes to the way in which economic decisions were made and the economic surplus distributed in America.

Rustin's failure to attract young cadres from the African American movement toward his vision says much about the prospects for such a traditional social-democratic program in postwar America. He had been a mentor for black activists gathered at Howard University at the start of the 1960s. One of them, Michael Thelwell, said, "We adopted his view that the integration of American society required a radical coalition of social and interracial forces. . . . We became Bayard Rustin people." Five years later, they were no longer. The drive to get free of management by white liberals became overwhelmingly powerful within SNCC. Long afterward, Rustin commented, "A few years after the 1964 convention, SNCC collapsed. Its grand design for transforming Southern politics had failed. It found it could not build a political movement consisting exclusively of poor people."[114]

The important point is not to pay tribute to Rustin's analytical acumen, impressive though it was. Rather, the point is that in the 1960s, the traditional politics of social democracy, with economic goals to be achieved through electoral coalition politics, even when these goals and strategies were broadcast prominently by such an able exponent, left the most talented young American radicals and militants cold. Black power, instead, took black activists by storm, fueled by their frustration with the inability of liberal political structures—which figured large in Rustin's prescription—to meaningfully enhance economic opportunities for working-class African Americans.[115] Black leaders within the political system began talking of a need to create public-sector jobs, something the nation's political leaders simply were not going to do on a large scale.[116] To white militants, the "radical" identity, nurtured through the conservative period since the demise of the Popular Front by a small number of writers and activists, proved more appealing than the hope of apprenticeship to Great Society liberals.

The Great Society's achievements were many and often lasting, but the career of Great Society liberalism ended sooner than many anticipated. As African American militants were bailing out, white voters were turning right with a vengeance. The elections of 1966 put an end to the dominance of Great Society politics in Washington. The residual vision of progress left over from the New Deal era, a vision of transforming America through gradual reform into a clean capitalist paradise with plenty for all, had no champion who could navigate it through the several outbursts of long-festering sores in the body politic that occurred during the 1960s. It would be a bit extreme to say that "in reality the liberals were a rather small group, who succeeded, just barely, and for a few years only, to pass a few bills," or that "though liberalism was a vigorous ideology, it never had broad support. Its years of success were few and difficult." Nevertheless, such chastened judgments do capture the essential truth of the liberals' tenuous hold on power.[117] The halls of power proved a tricky place for Great Society liberals to reside. Left-liberal coalition efforts seemed more promising when leftists and liberals alike were forces of opposition.

In the 1960s, as the classic period of the cold war drew to a close amid accelerating turbulence, both domestically and abroad, both liberals and leftists once again were notable factors in American politics. The 1960s and 1970s witnessed what remains, in the early twenty-first century, the most significant left-wing movement to appear in American life since the 1940s. Yet in the mid-1960s, new left activists were poised for a period of conflict with liberals that would extend the estrangement between reformers and radicals that had begun in the 1940s and worsened in the 1950s, and that would threaten to bury still deeper in American history the memory of a broad left-liberal front for progressive social transformation.

Chapter 6

Vietnam and After

The years between the mid-1960s and the mid-1970s formed the last era of vitality and effectiveness for liberals and leftists in American history. The escalation of the Vietnam War exacerbated preexisting differences between these two groups and launched many reformers and radicals on trajectories of alienation and mutual suspicion. The political strength, even the political relevance, of both groups dwindled after the mid-1970s. At the same time, in some areas of political life, notably among feminists, reconciliation between liberals and radicals followed an initial period of animosity. Yet that example of rising comity could not prevent the persistence of alienation between self-identified radicals and liberals in general. The developments of the cold war era, particularly McCarthyism, had severed the threads of historical knowledge that might have given pause to leftists and liberals who thought their goals were widely divergent and could not be otherwise. Virtually no memories of left-liberal cooperation for broad objectives were evident in the Vietnam generation.

The long Vietnam War's corrosive effects on American life included frightful damage to the idea that determined state action and advanced technology were instruments of progress in American hands. Liberals either supported the war as a necessary anticommunist venture or opposed it in the name of decency and reason. Radicals saw in their government's policy a reactionary effort to stop the global forces of progress, forces that radicals glimpsed in the shape of third-world revolution. The war made it harder than it already had been for either liberals or leftists to talk about progress in America; certainly progress of the transformative kind that had inspired earlier generations of liberals and leftists seemed nowhere on the American horizon. The national political environment, shaped by the rising strength of the political right—which reacted against Great Society liberalism, against African American militancy, and against the culture and politics of youth radicalism—contributed greatly to the lingering infirmity of ideas of progress in American life. Liberals ever more focused their energies on salvaging past accomplishments. Leftists increasingly saw America as a reactionary society harboring few and powerless progressive elements, and with the passing years they turned toward efforts to carve out livable spaces for themselves within what they perceived as a hostile or indifferent country. In the wake of the Vietnam War, fewer liberals and leftists than ever before believed that the future belonged to them.

Circumstances for liberals and radicals in the United States remained less than propitious in the decades between the mid-1970s and the early twenty-first century. By the turn of the century, liberals found themselves much on the defensive within one major political party, the Democrats, but completely alien to the other, the Republicans—and hence locked inside the former. The radical left existed entirely outside the formal system of two-party politics and governmental representation, even as many who still embraced the critical values and transformative dreams of the left enjoyed comfortable and prestigious places in America's cultural apparatus, and even as new dissident coalitions arose to protest social inequities and military adventures. All the while, other forces for progressive change, forces that did not identify themselves primarily in ideological terms, worked to advance an egalitarian agenda. The most successful such force in the years since the Vietnam era was feminism, which resurfaced in American life in the early 1960s after a period of absence, but which became a formidable force within both radical and liberal precincts only later in that decade.

The Re-feminization of Dissent

In the decades between World War II and the end of the twentieth century, activism in behalf of women's equality with men reflected notable ideological ambiguity and, experiencing repeated reversals within the left, feminism eventually influenced liberalism perhaps more than it did radicalism. After the brief rise of Popular Front feminism in the 1940s, feminism all but disappeared from public life, a victim of both a conservative cultural trend and the red scare. The Congress of American Women (CAW), discussed in Chapter 4, and other Popular Front women's advocates gravitated toward Henry Wallace's presidential campaign of 1948 and toward the Communist-linked unions of the CIO, and the CAW was destroyed along with these other manifestations of late-1940s progressivism. In this period, Betty Friedan worked for *UE News,* a paper published by the left-wing electrical workers' union, and for the Federated Press news service, which was aligned with the Popular Front, hailing progressive unions and writing about the continuing need to resist "the reactionary pattern that is fascism." She covered the founding meeting of the Progressive party in Philadelphia in 1948 with great enthusiasm, highlighting the diversity of the delegates in attendance. In her articles and others in *UE News* from around this time, "The villains . . . were Truman, Hubert H. Humphrey, Nixon, Walter Reuther, HUAC, and American capitalists. The heroes included Wallace, Roosevelt, and union leaders." Wallace's humiliation on election day in 1948 and the expulsion of the UE and the other left-wing unions from the CIO left a deep imprint on Friedan. She developed a nearly-pathological fear of revealing her youthful leftist involvements decades after McCarthyism had passed. In the immediate aftermath of the CAW's liquidation in 1950 such fears were well founded. The HUAC investigated the CAW, the Justice Department placed it on the attorney general's list of subversive organizations, and finally the State Department demanded that it register with the U.S. government as the agent of a foreign power. This its leaders refused to do and, believing they could not win a legal fight over this requirement, they decided on a mercy killing.[1]

While it is not true that Friedan and her writings revived feminism single-handed in the 1960s, she came about as close to doing so as any individual could for any movement, and while the impact of 1940s progressivism on her politics is visible in retrospect, she made every effort to obscure that lineage. Friedan had read writings by Friedrich Engels, Thorstein Veblen, and Simone de Beauvoir on women and gender relations as she researched and wrote *The Feminine Mystique*, but these thinkers went unacknowledged, presumably for political reasons. Other women involved in the National Organization of Women (NOW), which Friedan and others founded in 1966, had similar political histories, notably Kathryn Clarenbach, who in the 1940s had put her energies into various progressive causes in Madison, Wisconsin and had worked on Wallace's presidential campaign. NOW drew on what Friedan once called "the seething underground of women in the Government, the press and the labor unions" who had toiled for women's interests in obscurity for years, who truly knew the meaning of Max Weber's dictum that politics is "the slow boring of hard boards." Many of them probably knew something of progressive liberalism and the presence of women's advocates in it, almost occult knowledge in the 1950s and 1960s.[2]

Women's advocates in the early 1960s showed the impatience for change characteristic of idealistic liberals and radicals during the Kennedy years. Friedan's words uncannily resembled those of Mario Savio, the hero of 1964's Free Speech Movement at the University of California at Berkeley, when she wrote of the need for history to move forward. Both Friedan and Savio lambasted politicians—such as Kennedy—and social scientists who declared that the grand debates over the nature of the good society lay in the past and that all future changes would be minor adjustments. In *The Feminine Mystique*, Friedan wrote that to view "occupation housewife" as the "model for all women" "presupposes that history has reached a final and glorious end in the here and now, as far as women are concerned." She was having none of that. In an essay titled "An End to History," Savio predicted that students and African Americans "will not accept an end to events, this historical plateau, as the point beyond which no change occurs."[3] This expectation of and demand for qualitative change represented a startling revival of the historical consciousness that had been pervasive among leftists and many liberals during the sixty years prior to the mid-1940s. In the 1950s and 1960s, liberal social scientists who charted a supposedly universal process of "modernization" in third-world countries identified a trend toward "sex egalitarianism" as an essential feature of that multifaceted phenomenon, and Friedan echoed such views to the degree that she presented women's emancipation as coextensive with historical progress in America. Cold war liberals displaced subdued feminist values abroad but no longer presented other lands as holding lessons for the United States. Friedan and other feminists in the 1960s sought to bring the idea of progress back to America through the avenue of changing gender relations.[4]

The early-1960s frustration with ideological dead-enders had a more concrete political analogue in the efforts by SNCC and SDS to put aside McCarthy-era conflicts over the Communist issue. As already discussed, the symbolic action these groups took to signal their impatience was to embrace the stance of nonexclusionism, to refuse to demand anticommunist bona fides from those who sought to join their causes. The other important group that did the same was Women Strike for Peace (WSP), which was organized in 1961 and which protested nuclear weapons testing and cold war brinkmanship. With Communists and former Communists in their organization, WSP's leaders, having seen SANE defanged as it bowed its head before a red-baiting U.S. senator, resisted an identical fate. The HUAC summoned WSP's founder, Dagmar Wilson, and others before it in 1962, and the witnesses refused to toe the committee's line, deftly turning aside accusations of softness toward reds. WSP was not a feminist organization, and indeed its skillful use of "maternal" politics helped it avoid penalty of any kind. It also would provoke derision from young feminists when they joined WSP's antiwar protest by American women in 1968. But WSP signaled early on the determination of many American women to bid farewell the cultural conservatism of the 1950s, which had held that their place was in the home.[5]

By 1965, antifeminist conventions, like anticommunist ones, had sustained damage. In what was perceived as a new era, organized feminism participated in the ongoing reconstruction of political liberalism. NOW made itself the unquestioned leading women's rights group in America soon after its establishment, and it quickly closed the old debate over the ERA versus protective legislation in favor of the ERA. By 1970 its position expressed a consensus among feminists.[6] A proposal long associated with anti-union elitists and racists became closely linked with Great Society liberalism. Friedan's and NOW's vocal support for the cause of racial equality, which no doubt owed much to the Popular Front experiences of Friedan, Clarenbach, and others, helped seal this association. (Many other female activists of the 1950s and 1960s who did not identify primarily, if at all, with the feminist movement worked ceaselessly for racial equality within the YWCA and other organizations.)[7]

Friedan's proposals for change displayed an ambiguity characteristic of middle-class left-liberal politics in the 1960s. *The Feminine Mystique* was a post-scarcity analysis of middle-class society; the limited social applicability of her discussion offered easy fodder for criticism. She spoke as the delegate of affluent women, a psychologically downtrodden group within a privileged class. She envisioned a "conscience coalition" that would remake society; this term, much in use in the years 1965–75, usually referred to a gathering of comfortable liberals, to which African Americans and some progressive labor unions would be appended. In the 1970s Friedan said that women (presumably liberal women such as those in NOW) "in coalition with students, Blacks and intellectuals can build real change in society." An emphasis on wages and job opportunities for women, sometimes with a distinctly social-democratic orientation, consistently marked Friedan's political vision. That was far from a post-scarcity agenda. Yet she fell out with the National Women's Political Caucus, which she had helped found, when she advocated supporting female candidates for office regardless of party or ideology.[8]

Friedan also got out of step with the mainstream of liberal feminism as, under the influence of younger women in the post-1968 years, it embraced open lesbians and the cause of sexual liberation. She never completely opposed "personal politics" as an element in feminism. She urged changes in personal life and individual psychology. In the middle 1960s NOW embraced the cause of abortion rights, a classic instance of taking a "personal" issue, meaning one traditionally kept very quiet, public. *The Feminine Mystique* promised sexual liberation—within marriage—quite clearly. But Friedan did not think this promise should become a plank in a political platform. When she said, in 1969, "the gut issues of this revolution involve employment and education and new social institutions and not sexual fantasy," she used sensational language to exaggerate a real distinction between her and radical feminists. The difference was that she confined personal liberation to a private sphere of intimate relations and accepted heterosexuality as a social norm. Young women who identified as radicals made public issues of both sexuality and power relations within personal relationships, and the most theoretically minded of their number came to argue that the very distinction between public and private was an essential feature of liberal ideology, one worth discarding.[9]

The difference in public ideals between the radical refrain of liberation and liberal conceptions of equality and freedom was the crux of the theoretical difference between radical and liberal feminisms. During the late 1960s and 1970s the differences were real but appeared greater than they were, partly because of differences in generational style, partly because of the controversy over lesbianism's acceptability, and partly because many of the young firebrands embraced radical positions on American capitalism and foreign policy. Of those sources of conflict, only the question of sexuality appears, in retrospect, to have any possible bearing on the intrinsic radicalism or liberalism of different varieties of feminism. At least equally as important were the general question of treating personal life as part of public politics and the related questions of whether or not men oppressed women and how far the conventions of family life should be rethought. This last issue was a point of stark difference between liberal feminists, who called for greater equity between wives and husbands, and radicals, who not uncommonly advocated replacing the nuclear family with other arrangements.

The question of male oppression was to some extent a matter of rhetorical delicacy or indelicacy. To cite an overused analogy, African Americans fighting for racial equality did not always use the language of group oppression, but their struggle really presupposed that such a relation of oppression existed. The extent and depth of personal ties between women and men made this a sensitive point to raise in terms of gender relations. When Casey Hayden and Mary King, two activists working for racial justice, circulated a memorandum in 1965 terming gender relations a "caste" system, this marked a breakthrough in public discussion.[10] But even for Friedan and other liberals, their struggle made little sense if women were not an oppressed class. While Friedan did not propose that men submit to scrutiny from their wives for evidence of "male chauvinism," as Communists authorities had demanded in the late 1940s and 1950s, she clearly knew there was such a thing. (This very term, as well as "women's liberation," had originated in the Communist movement, as young feminists of the 1960s who had grown up as "red-diaper babies" were aware.)[11] Her preferred stance toward men, which emphasized the need for "partnership" with women, was a matter of tactics and strategy. But it also at times appeared as a point of principle, for she could not embrace the radical view that men as a class oppressed women, even though some portions of *The Feminine Mystique* pointed to such a conclusion. Diplomacy played the largest role in the notion that "the system," rather than the privileged class or caste, oppressed them. In *The Feminine Mystique,* Friedan moved back and forth between these two analytical stances, while also asserting that women shared in the responsibility for their own oppression by accepting this fate, a note that many radical feminists sounded as well.

Feminists known as "radicals," in fact, were "steeped in liberal tradition." It is close to an impossible task to arrange the various forms of feminism that have existed in cold war America—including "radical," "socialist," "cultural," and "postmodern" feminisms—neatly "on a liberal-left continuum." As well, it was untrue that liberal feminists fought only for the right of affluent, highly educated women to enter sanctums of male privilege. Incidents such as Friedan's celebrated "integration" of the males-only bar at the famous Plaza Hotel in New York made it appear that liberal feminists embraced an elitist agenda. But NOW, the Women's Equity Action League, and other groups agitated for anti-discrimination and affirmative-action measures in the workplace that mainly benefited working-class women. Both "liberals" and "radicals" fought for the rights of individual women and for the equality of women with men as a group.[12] When the 1977 International Women's Year Conference in Houston—an enormous, unifying event for American feminists—endorsed a "Plan of Action" supporting the ERA, abortion rights, and lesbian rights and stressing the continuing significance of racial inequality, "any sharp division between liberals and radicals no longer made any sense."[13]

The revival of feminism in the 1960s was a signal feature of the Great Society era, and feminism outlasted the Great Society, maintaining a more durable broad base of support than ever before in American history. Like the African American struggle, it offered a sphere of activism in which the division between leftists and liberals might appear irrelevant. Whereas the politics of the broad front could not be lastingly revived by the civil rights movement because militant African Americans, white leftists, and white liberals all became alienated from one another in the context of racial politics, the limits of feminism's ability to revitalize a comprehensive left-liberal alliance stemmed from different sources. Feminists on the whole would have been pleased to see their cause embraced by almost anyone. The new left had difficulty doing so, while liberals largely proved able to; this determined the ideological direction of the feminist movement.[14] Of course, feminists aimed specifically to advance the interests of a particular social group—albeit one that comprised slightly over half the population—not to promote an ideology as a cause in itself. Neither they nor the advocates of any other group's welfare could bridge the divide between champions of liberal and left ideologies, one that broke wide open in the 1960s following decades of subterranean strains.

The "Numerous Bases of Division": The Vietnam War and Corporate Liberalism

We have become a nation of young, bright-eyed, hard-hearted, slim-waisted, bullet-headed make-out artists. A nation—may I say it?—of beardless liberals.

—Carl Oglesby, 1965

Franklin Roosevelt had said that the generation of the 1930s had a rendezvous with destiny. So did the generation of the 1960s. But their meeting with destiny came in a far-off place, Vietnam. The basis for dissension between new left radicals and cold war–Great Society liberals during the 1960s was present from the start, but the war ensured that their disagreements grew salient and bitter. The growing liberal-left division focused on international affairs but also featured the new left's derision toward liberal reform as the radicals understood it. The new left developed a highly critical concept of contemporary reform that they came to call "corporate liberalism." During this period it became unsurprising for left intellectuals to refer to "the menace of liberal scholarship" or "the banality of liberalism."[15] The war added powerful fuel to animosities already smoldering because of conflicts over race. "Verbal violence"—accusations of moral incompetence and intellectual dishonesty—became the common currency of political debate among liberals and leftists.[16]

Between 1960 and 1965 the new left moved away from its initial support for a realigned Democratic party, to be led by a revitalized bloc consisting of liberals, labor unions, and civil rights supporters, and toward a more definite protest stance, one of outsiders, not insiders. Ambiguities about the defects of the insiders suffused early new left thought. In 1963 SDS issued "America and the New Era" (ANE), a manifesto that identified a conservative "Establishment" of interlocking national elites straight out of *The Power Elite.* It criticized the Kennedy administration for a bias in favor of closed-door management of social problems by this establishment, which allowed select members of less august social groups, particularly organized labor, into its deliberations. Kennedy's "active and managerial" vision of government's role in social conflict was distinguished from Eisenhower's "subservience to narrow military-industrial interests." This presumably was what ANE indicated with its one reference to "the capture of liberal rhetoric and the liberal political base by the *corporate liberalism* of the New Frontiersmen" (italics added).

The document developed briefly the notion that the institutional structure of power in America was changing, calling the Kennedy administration's ideal "the 'corporate state'" as seen in "such countries as France and West Germany, in which government and business recognize that national planning by central bodies and strong programs of social welfare are necessary." This was one meaning of corporatism or "corporate liberalism"—a new ideology for a new regime, a variant on postwar liberal ideas of pluralist power sharing.[17]

New left analysts saw this as bad, not good. In their view, "[E]fforts to dampen social conflict and prevent popular upsurge limit drastically the possibilities for real reform and innovation." They thought street politics and open conflict formed the true path to progress, and they lamented that sincere liberals in the unions and elsewhere had abandoned "protest marches, local reform movements, and independent bases of power" in favor of "cocktail parties and seminars." Liberalism had a laudable "populist and progressive" heritage that featured "militant rhetoric" in the service of social change, but contemporary liberals had forsaken activism for lobbying, an outside role for an inside one. They had been captured, perhaps bought. Beyond the practical effect of this cooptation, ANE lamented its psychological impact. The document characterized liberal pluralism as "an attempt . . . to *manipulate* and control conflict" (italics added), a process that "robs men of their initiative and autonomy."[18] The political and moral "autonomy" of "men" was a key value for the new left from the start, and throughout the 1960s, thinkers associated with the new left would describe as manipulation what their befuddled liberal elders thought were concessions and important gestures of inclusion toward insurgents. Others widened the indictment beyond the New Frontiersmen. "Manipulative and managerial," went the new left indictment, "twentieth-century liberalism has adapted itself without difficulty to the corporation's need to soften conflicts and to reconcile the apparently irreconcilable forces . . . to which it has given rise."[19] This critique of liberal reform as the velvet glove surrounding the iron fist of corporate power would spread deep and wide among American radicals. The thesis of elite manipulation easily shifted from anti-establishment polemics to anti-populist jeremiads, as radicals found themselves isolated from an increasingly conservative public following the Vietnam era.

Charges of manipulation and cooptation formed a different critique than that of corporate liberalism as a new establishment ideology. ANE identified "the labor movement and organized liberalism" as separate from the "Establishment," implying that the administration was not composed of genuine liberals, that its "corporate liberalism" was merely a pose, an attempt by conservatives to fool liberals into thinking they had friends in power. The two different concepts of corporate liberalism at work here—as the ideology of a truly reformist but quietly authoritarian corporate state and as a reformist mask for essentially unreconstructed corporate and military power—would continue to coexist in new left thought. But in either case the conclusion was that "the hope for real reform lies not in alliances with established power, but with the re-creation of a popular left opposition." In 1963 SDS hoped that many liberals outside the government would join this opposition.[20]

Increasingly liberals became the objects of new left ire. Gradually "the liberal establishment" became a trope current on the left as well as the right. Between 1962 and 1964 SDS activists conducted community organizing drives among poor Americans in locales across the country, and while these projects failed to lead to the leftist political insurgency the radicals had hoped for, they fueled a rising sense of disgust with the political establishment. Many of the cities where SDS conducted these projects, such as Chicago and Newark, were run by Democratic party machines linked to the national party; this circumstance, and the ascendancy of Kennedy and Johnson in national politics, led the new left increasingly to blur its earlier distinction between "the Establishment" and "the labor movement and organized liberalism," as well as that between liberals and Democrats. Beginning with the Free Speech Movement at the University of California at Berkeley in the fall of 1964, student radicals initiated a long-lasting campaign against America's university administrators who, they charged, were prostituting their schools, selling research and future employees to industrial and military "clients" at the heart of everything the new left was against. Many of these administrators, such as Clark Kerr at Berkeley, were proud liberals, and these men had entangled their institutions with the "military-industrial complex." Liberals such as Kerr were part of the broader national establishment, seeing business corporations and the military as no threat to the good society's realization and depicting protest and dissidence as outmoded and antisocial.[21] The radical indictment of liberals as establishment adornments who shilled for corporate and military power commanded more evidence in the universities than anywhere else.

Some national leaders in SDS continued at mid-decade to avert open conflict between liberals and the left, but they saw that this was becoming more difficult. In early 1965 Paul Potter, then SDS president, wrote that his comrade Tom Hayden—who spent the mid-1960s living in the Newark project—"seems to be moving closer and closer to a position that the liberal establishment (if not all liberals) constitutes the most dangerous enemy we confront." Potter noted that "that point of view . . . stands in direct and polar opposition to the public attitude of SDS in the past. We have tried to be fraternal critics of liberal institutions and organizations. . . . [W]e have searched for common ground and not the numerous bases of division."[22]

Starting in 1965 the common ground became harder to see, as both of the new left's concepts of corporate liberalism were framed ever more critically. In 1966 Todd Gitlin denounced "the sham of pluralism," arguing that nonelite groups had no representation in essential decision making. He echoed the "state capitalism" idea, asserting that "a tightly planned corporate complex . . . dominates the economy" and that the military-industrial complex formed "a pattern of industry-government symbiosis."[23] Richard Flacks assailed the "liberal corporatism" of the establishment, arguing that the "process of consultation among a national elite," including union representatives, was real. But in his view liberal corporatism was lamentable because it "tends toward the *co-optation* of dissent and reform" if not "their suppression." The establishment's actual concessions to equalization of wealth were paltry. Sounding more than a bit like Galbraith, Flacks charged that corporate power's prerogatives went unchallenged in the Great Society coalition, which consequently mandated "the maintenance of less than full employment, a decidedly impoverished public sector, a very strong emphasis on private consumption, and the use of public funds to subsidize private interests."[24] Gitlin, too, sounded notes consistent with the "qualitative liberalism" of the late 1950s, but with a more ominous undertone. "The liberal faith in additive progress mistakes quantity for quality," he stated. Middle-class Americans were supposed to accept payment for their disempowerment in the form of material goods, but they also suffered "meaningless work . . . empty politics and spectator culture."[25] This dark picture of American life pointed to a cul-de-sac; even as the new left and other insurgent forces grew in numbers and militancy, tools for changing America remained unavailable according to the left's more analytical thinkers.

The picture no doubt would have appeared less gloomy had the Vietnam War not been ongoing for many years already. After the introduction of large-scale U.S. ground combat forces in the spring of 1965, a sense of crisis pervaded liberal elements; Kennedy and Johnson had made this a Democrats' war, and the stakes for the future of reform politics were high. As to the new left, from its start it had advocated an "open door for revolutions" in the third world, with Castro's Cuba foremost in mind.[26] This created the basis for alienating the new left's mentors in the SP and the Democratic party, whose anticommunism was not confined to Europe and the United States. Norman Thomas, Reuther, and others favored the Truman doctrine of fighting enemies of "freedom"—which in practice was equated with U.S. power—in wars and civil conflict around the world. In 1959, scholars at the University of Wisconsin in Madison began a scholarly journal, *Studies on the Left*, that promulgated the concept of corporate liberalism and framed it with detailed accounts of how famous "liberals" in American history—these historians paid little attention to the actual historical use or non-use of this term—had pioneered the imposition of U.S. power on foreign lands in order to protect established U.S. economic interests. *Studies on the Left* forged an iron link between what it characterized as U.S. economic imperialism and the history of domestic liberal reform. Its authors argued that U.S. leaders sought to control markets and resources in third-world countries as a way to expand the economic pie in America, so that the slices given to different groups in American society would not have to be reapportioned. Economic empire was an alternative to redistribution; the editors of *Studies on the Left*, led by James Weinstein and deeply influenced by the Madison professor William Appleman Williams, called for socialism in America, asserting that this was the only way to forsake the path of empire abroad. They were influential in the left.[27]

Early SDS statements struck an uncertain note on Kennedy's foreign policy. In 1962 the new left's anticommunist elders forced SDS to stiffen its denunciation of Communist regimes as the group composed its original manifesto, the Port Huron Statement; the young activists considered crusading anticommunism largely irrelevant to their foreign-policy concerns and a definite problem in American politics. A year later, ANE gave a brief account of the cold war's origins that emphasized almost exclusively how, after World War II, "America moved quickly to assert its power and influence in every area" of the globe. But ANE stressed the U.S. imperative of global stability, seeing in Kennedy a leader who sought détente with the Soviets and who accepted the validity of "the anti-colonial revolution" and neutrality in the cold war among third-world nations. This took Kennedy's anti-colonial rhetoric too seriously. The administration welcomed anti-colonial revolutions in the third world so long as they were eighteenth-century revolutions. Constitutional republics open to foreign trade and investment and U.S. security ties were celebrated, called "peaceful revolution"; attempts at social democracy were viewed grimly.[28] Any emerging nation whose leaders sought to nationalize economic resources long controlled by foreign interests or to establish close ties with the Soviet Union or the People's Republic of China risked being labeled by U.S. officials and their minions as dangerously "imperiled" by Communist plotting. Covert operations, or, in rare cases such as Vietnam and the Dominican Republic, U.S. invasion, might follow if the United States thought it could get away with it. This was Kennedy's policy, as it had been Eisenhower's.

In October 1965 Carl Oglesby gave a widely circulated speech at an antiwar gathering that neatly combined anti-liberal themes that had developed in preceding years among radicals. He assumed that the establishment was a liberal establishment and he recognized the continuity in U.S. foreign policy since Truman's day. Thus he laid not only the Vietnam War but the whole postwar history of U.S. attempts to suppress third-world aspirations at liberalism's doorstep. He called Truman "a mainstream liberal," Eisenhower "a moderate liberal," and Kennedy "a flaming liberal." In contrast to his shaky grasp of political history, Oglesby's knowledge of U.S. foreign policy was impressive, as he demonstrated with his recollection of U.S. involvements in third-world turmoil. He told the assembled crowd about the CIA's part in ousting moderate, elected nationalist governments in Guatemala and Iran in the 1950s, and in British Guiana under Kennedy; he told them about Johnson's quick congratulation to a rightist regime in Brazil after it seized power in a coup in 1964; he told them about Johnson's invasion of the Dominican Republic in 1965, which the president and his supporters justified with fabricated tales of Communist violence to maintain in power a right-wing junta that had overthrown an elected government. This last episode was particularly sordid, as leading Democratic figures in Washington had personal stakes in sugar companies operating in the Dominican Republic, as Oglesby related.[29] He had the goods on U.S. interference, often violent, in third-world affairs, and he explained it simply: the U.S. military sat at the disposal of American corporate and financial power. It had nothing to do with communism, except insofar as any leftist government in the third world might threaten the prerogatives of U.S. capital. But a government didn't have to be leftist at all to provoke U.S. aggression; it just had to declare economic independence. This was history straight out of Smedley Butler, the early twentieth-century commandant of the U.S. Marine Corps whose conversion to anti-imperialism had led him to confess his sins publicly and whose denunciations of U.S. foreign policy were rediscovered in the Vietnam era.[30] The difference was that, to Oglesby, the men who had thus served capital in the White House and the state department since 1933 had been liberals.

Oglesby held out hope of peeling liberals away from the awful power structure they too often supported, but the hope seems empty in retrospect. He ventured a distinction between "corporate liberals" and "humanist liberals," and invited the latter to come over to the opposition. He asserted that there really was something decent in liberalism that should have rebelled against Vietnam and similar wars. "Corporatism or humanism: which? For it has come to that. Will you let your dreams be used? Will you be a grudging apologist for the corporate state? Or will you help try to change it . . . in the name of simple human decency and democracy . . . ?" But Oglesby explained at length that he thought liberalism and U.S. imperialism fitted together tightly. If his account of history was right, why should liberals side with SDS and not with Lyndon Johnson? Oglesby clung to the idea that humanist liberals had been duped, but those who had duped them did not appear to be false liberals; rather the corporate liberals understood liberalism's imperial needs all too well. He was in a corner. He repudiated suspicions of anti-Americanism, saying, "Don't blame *me* for *that!* Blame those who mouthed my liberal values and broke my American heart."[31] His heart wished to see liberals come over to the anti-imperialist camp, but his mind consigned liberals to the enemy camp. Within two years Oglesby was calling for an anti-imperial, libertarian alliance between the new left and elements of the political right.[32] This strategy, while politically inert, was more consistent with his analysis.

Oglesby identified liberalism with cold war liberalism, skewing liberalism to the right, and this war-fueled perception fed a widening comedy of generational misperception that was captured in a priceless interaction between the journalist I. F. Stone and the folksinger Phil Ochs at a crucial antiwar rally in Washington in the spring of 1965. Stone published *I. F. Stone's Weekly*, a newsletter whose close scrutiny of the U.S. government's actions made it a crucial source of information for early new left radicals. SDS leaders had invited Stone to their national council in December 1964, where he had argued that they should become more active on the antiwar front. Having prodded the young radicals to organize the rally, Stone appeared on the stage during the gathering to make a key speech. Ochs preceded Stone and sang "Love Me, I'm a Liberal," a classic anthem of youthful condescension. More vicious than Bob Dylan's "The Times They Are a-Changin'" because its criticisms were more specific, Ochs's song, written in the voice of a liberal elder lecturing a young listener, telegraphed repeatedly the message that liberals claimed to root for the underdog but, when push came to shove, sided with the forces of order. Ochs sang, "The people of old Mississippi/ Should all hang their heads in shame/ . . . But if you ask me to bus my children/I hope the cops take down your name." The climax to the song suggested Ochs was familiar with the left sympathies that once had moved some cold war liberals—and that he had heard such liberals justify themselves by referring to their youth:

> Once I was young and impulsive
> I wore every conceivable pin
> Even went to the socialist meetings
> Learned all the old union hymns
> But I've grown older and wiser
> And that's why I'm turning you in.

"I. F. Stone didn't like it. He'd been a liberal himself all these years, he told the crowd. . . . 'I've seen snot-nosed Marxist-Leninists come and go,' said Stone."[33]

Stone was a walking vestige of progressive liberalism, a Popular Front liberal who nonetheless avoided taking an uncritical stance toward the CP and the Soviet Union. With the red scare at fever pitch, he had called on progressives to openly advocate a democratic, liberal form of socialism in America, and he had argued that, in many third-world countries, "The situation calls for the kind of clean sweep only a revolution can provide."[34] A true independent, he did not think his social-democratic leanings put him outside the reach of liberal ideology. It is unclear what the SDS leaders thought he was, but they thought highly of him at a time, 1965, when many liberals and social democrats, including Rustin and Thomas, widened the breach with the new left by attacking SDS for allowing a Communist youth group to join in the planning for this antiwar rally. That year was a pivot; afterward, an insurgent, anti-imperialist liberal such as Stone was increasingly hard for young radicals to imagine.

The question remains whether Stone or any other liberal was right to resist the course of empire on liberal grounds. Stone represented a liberal tradition of humanism and of fidelity to the principle of self-determination for all peoples. During the Spanish-American War, surviving nineteenth-century liberals had had good reason to oppose empire. But could liberals of the mid-twentieth century sustain the principles of the Enlightenment without shifting left and favoring social reconstruction at home? According to the new left's analysis of corporate liberalism, an American liberal would have to abandon liberalism to abandon empire. A liberal might oppose a particular war while maintaining a commitment to empire (and thus to liberalism). Even if liberalism required global hostility to socialist revolution, it would not follow that the United States would be obliged to wage war against every assertion of third-world nationalism; any particular counterinsurgency war was a matter of choice. Yet some self-identified liberals went much further and questioned the whole cold war stance of the United States toward third-world nationalism.

The radical conviction that liberalism led to empire in twentieth-century America rested on both a restrictive concept of liberalism and a narrow concept of socialism. The new left viewed the two categories as mutually exclusive, which historically they were not. The historians of *Studies on the Left* made a powerful point in arguing that a new social contract involving a more equal distribution of wealth in American society was the alternative to economic empire and the garrison state required of such an empire. Yet they were wrong to insist that such an anti-imperialist course could only be pursued by those who called themselves socialists and not by avowed liberals. The point was redistribution and social justice. In theory, social-democratic politics could flow from liberal individualism adjusted to an industrial world. In practice, plenty of progressive liberals had favored such a policy and opposed empire abroad. When new left radicals forced the rhetoric of socialism back into American life, it represented a victory for them. Such terms had been banished from public life in America for a long time. But what had been repressed during the McCarthy era returned as a fetish. If one thought that socialism meant violent revolution, the line between socialists and liberals was rigid. But in the 1960s the only new left radicals who asserted that socialist commitment must lead to insurrection were the small groups, such as the Weather Underground, that emerged from the break-up of SDS at the decade's end. Yet their avowals of socialist commitment lacked content; these were declarations of revolt, not demands for reconstruction. As a rule, those new left radicals who were most serious about socialism were uninterested in insurrection, and the converse also was true.

In the second half of the 1960s there was ever less discussion of a united front joining liberals and leftists. The terms of alienation were established and little of substance was added to them after mid-decade. Antiwar candidates with left sympathies ran against pro-war Democrats. The best-known such race prior to 1968 was the effort, in 1966, by the journalist Robert Scheer to unseat Jeffrey Cohelan, the U.S. representative for the Berkeley area. After the primary—which Cohelan won but in which Scheer polled 45 percent of the vote—Scheer led a serious effort to get liberals to boycott the general election, in which Governor Pat Brown was up for reelection. Brown supported the war and had forced Si Casady out of his position at the head of the California Democratic Council—which comprised the leading cadres of Great Society liberalism in the state—because Casady opposed the war. Scheer sought to lead a group called Californians for Liberal Representation (CLR), which worked to reorganize liberal forces independent of Brown's control, in an antiwar direction. CLR represented a revival of Popular Front liberalism, including Communists as well as a broad spectrum of African American, Chicano, antiwar, and education activists. "It was the first time since the late 1930s that you had so many people, both the Left and liberals, together in the same room at a statewide conference," according to Dorothy Healey. The question of boycotting the elections of 1966 divided the nascent coalition. Scheer's position won out, prompting "the people who represented genuine mass organizations, like the united Farmworkers," to leave. They "were under no illusions" about what a victory of Brown's opponent, the Republican Ronald Reagan, would mean for the people they represented.[35] Reagan defeated

Brown and launched his career in national politics. Although the margin was too wide to attribute it to antiwar liberals who had stayed home on election day, the result left bitter traces within the state Democratic party and offered a foretaste of 1968's legacy.

Some liberals came over to the side of opposition to the liberal Democratic regime in Washington. This left-liberal opposition tended to focus specifically on the war. Antiwar petitions signed by a legion of the nation's premier intellectuals, ranging from poets to scientists, became a familiar feature of American letters after 1965, with an acceleration in 1967. The antiwar "March on the Pentagon" in October 1967 brought out seventy thousand protesters, prominently featuring writers, including leftists such as Noam Chomsky and Norman Mailer and those such as Mary McCarthy and Robert Lowell whose politics were harder to pin down. The group Clergy and Laity Concerned formed in 1965 and channeled the energies of liberal Christian and Jewish activists around the country into cautious, dignified antiwar protest. The presence of such elements in antiwar ranks emboldened liberals and those hovering between liberalism and the left. Even when liberal war opponents expressed anguish over their government's behavior around the world and called America a menace, they generally hewed to moral outrage and shied from systematic analysis of the U.S. role in the world. A classic indictment came from Susan Sontag, who stated in 1967 that America "has become a criminal, sinister country—swollen with priggishness, numbed by affluence, bemused by the monstrous conceit that it has the mandate to dispose of the destiny of the world." American intellectuals, she said, needed to "confront the bloodstained face of America." The antiwar movement "failed to establish a theoretically coherent movement for revolutionary change," as some new left radicals hoped it would. Yet it "educated thousands of Americans about U.S. 'imperialism.'"[36] Sontag's coruscating moral criticism of America's government and people went rather far and reflected the morally exacting, socially critical spirit that the Vietnam experience and the influence of a revived left released into American intellectual life in the 1960s.

As early as 1967, the forces of the new left found themselves swamped within the antiwar movement by the swelling tide of liberals and others who did not draw radical inferences from their objection to the war. Liberals and radicals marched and worked together for peace in all corners of America. The massive Moratorium protests in the fall of 1969 were organized by liberals who had worked in Eugene McCarthy's campaign in 1968 and who sought, rather successfully, to legitimize antiwar protest within the political mainstream. Famous radicals continued to try to influence the political system occasionally, as when Tom Hayden and Jane Fonda organized seminars for congressional staff personnel in

Washington through their Indochina Peace Campaign in the early 1970s. But overall, left-liberal estrangement grew increasingly poisonous in a period of campus violence and left-wing identification with third-world revolutionaries. With the left failing to maintain leadership within the antiwar movement, many radicals abandoned attempts at coalition, increasingly advocating victory by the Vietnamese revolutionaries over U.S. forces. A small faction conducted property destruction and bombings to increase the costs of the war and in the hope of sparking an insurrectionary uprising among alienated youth. This activity, exemplified in the Weather Underground, comprised a tiny segment of the new left. Political radicals and counterculture activists—hippies—constructed alternative institutions and began to spend much of their time in "hip" enclaves where they had little contact with the "straight" world. Liberals and leftists had less reason to explain their mutual disdain. Left-liberal collaboration, where it occurred, was a partnership that hardly dared speak its name. The terms of alienation held intellectual sway.

A limited left-liberal reconciliation occurred in the area of legal defense for political dissidents during the decade from 1965 to 1975. This became a new golden age of civil-liberties defense work within the American bar. The National Lawyers' Guild (NLG) and the ACLU experienced revivals, and the latter organization finally cast off its cold war tendency to defer to the government's demands for limits on citizen freedoms. Celebrated cases of antiwar protesters repeatedly brought forth a solid front of liberals and leftists united against state tyranny; the Watergate revelations about the presidential abuse of power strengthened libertarian commitments. Yet the cases of Benjamin Spock, the Chicago Eight, and many others did not help foster a lasting left-liberal coalition, as the Sacco-Vanzetti case had. Many liberals became more aggressive advocates of political freedom and some liberal lawyers were radicalized by what they saw in courtrooms and court documents. But this emboldened constitutional coalition, salutary—and temporary—though it was, reflected agreement only on what the government ought not to do, not on agreement about what the future of the country ought to be.

When the issue of Vietnam subsided within American politics, as it did in the early 1970s, even before the war ended, the years of left-liberal strife had made such a deep impact as to prevent a turn back to domestic issues as a sphere for sustained left-liberal coalition. The "bases of division" had been amplified too high. African American disillusionment with the social-welfare measures of the Great Society reinforced preexisting doubts within the new left about the adequacy of the liberal welfare state. In 1967 Hayden said he saw "little evidence to justify the view that the social reforms of the past thirty years actually improved the quality of American life in any lasting way . . . many of the reforms gained were illusory or token." Left-liberal estrangement had gone beyond rational analysis. In 1968 Richard Rothstein, another SDS activist, neatly rolled up all of the new left's criticisms of liberalism, stating that he and his comrades had become "enemies of welfare state capitalism, with little faith or desire that the liberal-labor forces within this system be strengthened vis-à-vis their corporatist and reactionary allies. We view those forces—and the social 'reforms' they espouse—as being incompatible with a non-interventionist world policy and as no more than a manipulative fraud perpetrated upon the dignity and humanity of the American people."[37] Radicals spoke of the War on Poverty as a confidence game that mainly enriched social workers and enterprising academics who won government grants, not the poor; this criticism of the "poverty industry" was used to assail liberals by enemies left and right. What meager benefits the poor received were intended to buy their quiescence, said critics on the left.

Still, rebellion should be supported, for only this would bring concessions from the establishment. The new left so firmly believed that liberals ruled America and was so committed to a view of the liberal reform tradition as a series of cunning stratagems for maintaining order by a sophisticated power elite, that it failed to anticipate the right-wing reaction that the protests of the late 1960s helped to cause. Too many of them thought a united establishment would respond with dollars, not with clubs and bullets. Radicals maintained a faith that the liberal elders they so detested would prevent disaster and impose a peaceful settlement on an increasingly polarized society. In 1967 Dorothy Healey debated Robert Scheer in California on the question, "Which Way for the Left?" In Healey's words, "I warned against the mistaken optimism so prevalent on the New Left that the country's ruling circles had made a permanent decision to rule through the cooptive politics of liberalism rather than the coercive politics of reaction. Bob's position was, basically, that the Old Left had nothing to teach the New Left."[38] Events sustained Healey's perspective.

The liberals lost their hold on power, although a new generation of reformers entered public life in the 1970s. Antiwar protest was dampened after 1970, but liberal Democrats who had stayed loyal to Johnson felt freer after Nixon's election to voice opposition to the war. As conservatives never tired of pointing out, the trauma of the Vietnam experience resulted in a reflexive reluctance to make war in the third world among a generation of liberals. Their antiwar or anti-imperial impulses never took the coherent form that left-wing ideology furnished to radicals, but they did inhibit the warrior inclinations of a series of presidents, most notably Reagan, whose range of war-making action in Central

America during the 1980s was constricted by Democrats in Congress, and by the wide ranks of anti-intervention activists, who remembered Vietnam.

The new liberals were linked uncertainly to Great Society liberalism, which had taken a rhetorical beating from all sides. Reform measures pressed by longtime liberals, including the establishment of the Occupational Safety and Health Administration (OSHA), were passed by Congress and signed into law by Nixon. Only a few years later President Gerald Ford moved to weaken OSHA; the winds had shifted in American politics. Organized labor "protested vehemently. No other group did, for who among the 'liberals' that emerged from the peace and youth movements ever had heard of OSHA?"[39] Many Democratic liberals worked during 1968 and afterward to displace the party regulars with a congeries of reformers who, according to some overexcited observers, represented a Trojan horse for the new left. Often this agglomeration, which included feminist, antiwar, civil rights and consumer activists, as well as those who simply thought it was a new generation's turn for power, was promoted as "the new politics." Oddly, fervent opponents of war and advocates of racial equality gathered under this rubric with reform-oriented ex-supporters of Adlai Stevenson (who was dead and could not protest).[40] Advocates of this "new politics" often said that the time had come, in an affluent society, when a "conscience coalition," noted earlier, of African Americans and white liberals was big enough to take power. How wrong they were.

Arnold Kaufman, the philosopher at the University of Michigan who was credited with the phrase "participatory democracy" and who involved himself with the "new politics," called his stance "radical liberalism." This name resonated with a distinguished Anglo-American tradition running from John Stuart Mill to John Dewey but one that neither Kaufman nor anyone else succeeded in connecting firmly to an actual program of the moderate left in the 1960s or 1970s. In the heyday of the new left, rare was the radical who proclaimed that his or her favorite program of redistribution and social justice was designed ultimately to empower the individual. Powerlessness and empowerment were key themes in new left thought, but an explicit individualism seemed retrograde.

The main activists looking for a new vehicle came from the professional, college-educated middle class. But by the 1960s they were severed from the memory of the Fabian and laborite traditions that had shaped the social-democratic tendencies within this class up to 1940. Now they were just freelancers, lacking a firm grounding in doctrine, program, or historical vision to guide them with any consistency. One year it might be labor-backed redistributive social democracy, and antistatist slow-growth bohemianism the next. This was the unstable politics of middle-class radicals without allies, oscillating between grandiose schemes for majority coalitions and efforts to meet the needs and desires of their own class. The inconsistency of vision among those searching for political renewal, for a change of direction in their society, during the era of the Great Society is as striking as the rough consistency of vision among their predecessors during the days of the broad front for progress between the 1880s and the 1940s.

Prophets and Professors

After the mid-1970s neither liberals nor leftists in the United States had much to celebrate. Occasionally they parried a thrust by the resurgent forces of the political right; victories were largely a matter of holding ground already gained. Liberals and leftists might join forces to work for important discrete goals, such as consumer-protection measures, increases in the minimum wage, or preventing a threatened war, but the terms of alienation established in the 1960s kept them from forming general alliances or reconsidering their categories. Handfuls of radicals found niches in the more progressive labor unions, where they worked as militant labor advocates, imitating their Communist forebears. Many more established themselves within what C. Wright Mills called "the cultural apparatus," the edifice of intellectual production that included the universities and the publishing industry. In the 1980s rightists rang the tocsin to warn the people of the "tenured radicals" in their midst, dangerous creatures who held the nation's future leaders captive, fifty minutes at a time.[41] Many college professors proudly called themselves radicals. Marxism was openly discussed in the academy as nowhere else in American life. But this was only one aisle in a supermarket of intellectual radicalisms, including several kinds of feminist, literary, and philosophical analysis, full of jargon impenetrable to all but the initiated. These exclusive churches became associated with the catch-all phrase "theory." The radicalism of these doctrines was assumed by many and obscure to others. A small minority of the professors concerned with "theory" engaged in radical political activity recognizable as such to non-professors. In practice, most were liberals, much though they derided liberalism.

Academic radicals tended to view American society as immoral, exploitative, and dehumanizing—to criticize it on both material and cultural grounds—but they saw little way to eradicate the structures that so oppressed the people. Therefore they proceeded along several avenues of avoidance. Some embraced liberal reformism as the best that could be hoped for. Some retreated into pure prophecy, denouncing America's iniquities and looking to a day of reckoning, either from U.S. society's internal contradictions or from "the wretched of the earth" who one day might play the Huns or the Vandals to the new Rome. Others insisted that cultural analysis was a means to personal transformation, for it gave one new eyes to see the world; like old-time evangelists, these avatars of "theory" believed that society could be saved one soul at a time.

Whatever the approach taken, members of the academic left aspired to live in communities of people with similar sensibilities. They viewed university towns and districts as enclaves of dissidence, enclaves intoxicating to the young of the professional and business classes. Gradually, in the 1980s and 1990s, these areas were drained of their bohemian elements and became increasingly the sites of high-taste boutiques and eateries. It became harder to deny that such enclaves were actually part and parcel of a broader professional-class culture, often liberal in politics and cultural attitudes and alienated from the life of the working and lower-middle classes, whose culture was largely defined by purchases made at different sorts of retail chain-outlets and distinctive forms of enjoyment. Most academic radicals and liberals reserved their heartfelt sympathies for members of historically downtrodden groups in America; wage-earning Americans might be included in this list, but most easily if they were not white or if they were poor enough that they could not participate in the gross culture of the suburban majority. The gentrification of university life was a key event in the emergence of what the conservative commentator David Brooks cuttingly termed "bourgeois bohemians."[42] It was not difficult to poke fun at Volvo-driving, Starbucks-frequenting scourges of capitalism. In truth, most of them would have been happy to live in Sweden, with capitalism humanized, not eliminated.

Together the comfortable absorption of the academic left into the cultural apparatus and the prophetic tendency of academic left commentary on American life formed a paradox. Yet this was not the contradiction it at first appears. There was an organic link between the esthetic and moral judgments delivered on the main thrust of American life. Both rested on a feeling of great distance from the imagined "average" American; neither variety of condemnation was much present in the Popular Front period, when a sentimental identification with "America" marked the left. In the 1960s, the historian Christopher Lasch commented, "Since the First World War, the social critic in America, deprived of the advantages of the sustained tradition of criticism that would have evolved in connection with a broad movement for radical change, tends to present his ideas 'as extremely personal judgments upon the state of society.'"[43] He was wrong to date this deprivation so early; it did not occur until the late 1940s, and it went into abeyance in the 1960s. But that reprieve did not last. The continually expressed hope on the left that the 1960s might recur represented a commentary on the isolation and helplessness that most radicals, like many liberals, experienced in later years—and on their ever weaker sense that the future was on their side.

In the 1990s a brief dust-up over the virtues of the Enlightenment spotlighted some opposing forces within the "academic left." Todd Gitlin, Arthur Schlesinger, and Michael Tomasky authored books lamenting the declension of liberalism and the left into what many called "identity politics," meaning an emphasis on race, gender, and sexual identity as the basis of political organization. To Gitlin and Tomasky, progressive politics ought to speak to a universal human identity; they also criticized leftists since the 1960s for neglecting issues of economic inequality, which they thought had the capacity to surmount American society's racial, gender, and cultural antagonisms and to unite a majority for liberal goals. For Schlesinger, American liberals in particular ought to stress the "Unum" in the national motto "E Pluribus Unum"—"Out of Many, One"—as against the selfish individualism that he associated with the political right. All three viewed non-universal identities as a basis for division more than for progressive mobilization.[44]

Such views raised hackles among intellectuals on the left. The historian Martin Duberman criticized what he viewed as the effort by straight, white, male liberals and leftists to "bring back the Enlightenment," as did the historian Robin D. G. Kelley. The writer Barbara Ehrenreich—significantly, not an academic—disputed claims that left activists neglected issues of class or derided Enlightenment values. Duberman asserted that an engagement with "theory" could lead to personal transformation of a sort that Gitlin and Tomasky did not imagine. Kelley cited devastating academic studies of the supposedly universal values of humanity and progress associated with the Enlightenment, which—all seemed to agree—was the source of liberal and left universalism. Such studies revealed Enlightenment thought as tainted fatally by the racism and sexism of eighteenth-century European thinkers. The images of freedom, humanity, and progress etched by such thinkers were based on contrasts with necessarily unfree and supposedly backward segments of the human family. One could not simply pluck the nice words out of the context of their origins, said Kelley, and clean them off for a truly universal application. Kelley also emphasized that as a practical matter, racial and gender politics were nothing new for liberals and leftists, that progressives long had stressed concerns specific to members of particularly downtrodden groups—and not just to the proletariat. He pointed out that the vibrant sectors of the labor movement had embraced the very identity politics that some (straight, white, male) leftists derided, building upon anti-racist and feminist initiatives when seeking popular support for pro-worker efforts. This was where the actual left was, Kelley argued, and it was leaving many left intellectuals behind.[45]

Kelley and Ehrenreich demonstrated their superior knowledge of what was occurring on the American left at the fin-de-siècle. Yet Duberman and Kelley failed to topple the basic Enlightenment values of universal human freedom and identity that they chided Gitlin, Tomasky, and others for yearning to see affirmed. Critics of the Enlightenment who derided that tradition as a basis for progressive politics at the twentieth century's end invariably echoed the Enlightenment tradition themselves. They generally agreed that identity politics could be divisive, and they pointed out that African Americans, women, and others who organized politically as members of such groups frequently affirmed the Enlightenment's values. Ehrenreich humorously quoted a conversation she had with Katha Pollitt, a feminist commentator: "'And the Enlightenment,' I asked her, 'did you ever say a mean thing about that?' Of course not, she said. 'In fact, I think we ought to try it.'"[46]

The real disagreements pertained to strategy rather than to ultimate values. "Neo-Enlightenment" authors tended to write as if they were attempting to construct a progressive appeal that might command majority support among the U.S. public. Their critics were unconcerned with gaining majority support and instead scoured the land for the existing building blocks of an energetic reform movement that might place egalitarian change on the nation's political agenda.[47] Academic arguments that criticized the Enlightenment as a source of progressive values and promoted theory as an agent of personal transformation cluttered the debate and obscured the true bases of agreement and disagreement. The anti-universalist, anti-humanist views that Gitlin and Tomasky lambasted were not dominant among thinkers on the left, but such views were more likely to be met with wry humor than forceful rebuttal among intellectuals. This decreased the likelihood that a clear and explicit concept of progress would return to liberal or radical politics in America. Adherents of academic theory could scarcely think of a dirtier word than "meta-narrative," meaning the kind of grand story of human history necessary for any coherent idea of progress. It was left to a conservative, the sociologist Robert Nisbet, to observe, "If the idea of progress does die in the West, so will a great deal else that we have long cherished in this civilization."[48]

Progressivism without Progress?

Historically speaking, the essential point to make about the old belief in qualitative progress is not that it was good or bad, or that its confidence in the direction of history was or was not justified. In an important sense this special belief in progress was simply what there was in a significant piece of the American political landscape. Without it, much of liberal and left politics in America would have made no sense and perhaps could not have existed. Nothing replaced it. The Great Society borrowed against the intellectual and moral capital of previous generations, but by the start of the twenty-first century that had been spent.

"Progressive" became a popular term once again starting in the 1990s, but it was a label used to avoid controversy, not to name a doctrine. Or, rather, the term named so many different doctrines and political identities that its ambiguity facilitated an avoidance of ideological debate. The supreme irony of this term's proliferation was that liberals and leftists alike had lost their claims on the future, once a powerful motor driving each tendency forward. They might name new benefits they wished the state to provide its citizens—single-payer universal health care, tighter environmental regulations, and other things—but they found it difficult to name the better society they hoped to create. It is hard to make progress absent a belief in progress.

Obama's Hope?

The Great Society itself provided the faith for a disempowered church of liberals, a group durable in size but spurned by the political elites to which they looked for leadership, and a stranger to the left.[49] Beginning in 1988, "liberal" became a political swear word, an epithet so damaging that candidates for public office soon began running from it—a new generation's "red." Michael Dukakis, the Democratic presidential candidate in that year, faced withering Republican criticism over his membership in the ACLU, among other things. Embracing a technocratic perspective, Dukakis proclaimed his administrative competence and eschewed emotional calls for social justice. The congressional Democratic leader Thomas "Tip" O'Neill, a liberal in the tradition of the New Deal and the Great Society, held a press conference, apparently intended to help his party's nominee, where O'Neill mused, "Do I consider Mike Dukakis a liberal of my stripes? Absolutely not. He's a progressive. He's a leader who's a technician."[50] Others soon began to call themselves progressives, harking back to the 1900–1917 era, thinking this term suggested a managerial stance safely distant from the dangerous classes and unpopular minorities. Anti-elitist economic politics, which had been closely associated with liberalism in earlier times, had come to seem outlandish even to many who disdained conservatism. Political figures who urged lower income tax rates, even for wealthy individuals and corporations, and deregulation of industry and finance might be considered liberals if they toed the line on other issues. When Ralph Nader ran for president on minor-party tickets in 2000 and 2004, protesting what he termed a bipartisan plutocratic policy regime in

Washington, it was difficult for many to recognize him as a largely unreconstructed 1960s liberal. Still, disquiet with the rightward drift of the entire party system was evident among liberals, and a small number supported Nader because he was "the real liberal" on the ballot. (It was cold comfort to Nader's supporters to observe that he, unlike Wallace in 1948, broke the 2.5 percent barrier nationwide.)[51]

In the 1990s and after, those located on the border between liberalism and the left, including many who were drawn to the Nader campaigns, also began to call themselves "progressives," but they meant something very different from a cool technocratic stance. They echoed not the managerial reformers of the 1900–1917 era, but rather the new left of the 1960s and 1970s, and—whether they were aware of it or not—the insurgent liberals and radicals of the Second Progressive Era of 1924–48. (Little was known of the new liberals of the late Gilded Age and the Progressive Era.) Often alienated from the two-party system, these left-progressives saw themselves, in the manner of the new left, as outsiders. They thought of liberals as insiders who cut deals with the power elite and tended to betray "the people." In the 1990s and after, both varieties of "progressivism" foundered on a kind of class antagonism—expressed in terms of antagonistic cultural identities, not economic interests—that many liberals and leftists found hard to comprehend.[52] The closing years of the 1990s witnessed the unheralded return of the economic within left-progressive politics, as young anti-sweatshop activists and environmentalists joined forces with dissident elements in organized labor to oppose, sometimes militantly, the new transnational institutions of a laissez-faire trade and investment regime known as "globalization"—a regime whose advocates were called "neoliberal" everywhere outside the United States, and who inside the United States included both conservatives and some liberals, Republicans and Democrats.[53] This dissident coalition made a spectacular debut on the public stage with its disruptive protests during the meeting of the World Trade Organization in Seattle in 1999, a meeting that Bill Clinton had hoped to host in triumph.[54] Scarcity had made a comeback in the social imagination; capitalism's automatic beneficence once again was questioned. The opposition to laissez-faire globalization was itself politically ambiguous, its ultimate goals indistinct, and thus it held the potential for a renewed alliance between leftists and liberals still attached to notions of economic equity.

Left-progressives were loath to say that they were liberals, even though many of them would have been hard-pressed to dissent from most traditional liberal priorities; the reluctance was often a matter of attitude and identity, not one of program. Socialism was not a label that many of them embraced, either. This was not the result of the fall of the Communist regimes in eastern Europe. The tumultuous events of 1989–91 had a less than profound impact on American leftists, a confirmation of their long-standing claim that they did not follow the Soviet star. At most, the obituaries delivered on the Marxist utopia in the 1990s shined a bright light on the absence of any coherent social ideal among American radicals. In the early twenty-first century there remained no progressive consensus on the meaning of progress, and little thought was devoted to the matter. The "waning of the sense of historical time," the loss of a sense of connection to both the past and the future, was a phenomenon that afflicted radicals and liberals along with many others.[55] Those interested in composing a "radical tradition" often treated the record of America's past as a cafeteria serving line, from which individual items could be plucked and combined in the most appetizing way. This was not the same as feeling connected to a vital coalition or movement for change.

The events of the early twenty-first century excited yet another burst of interest in the term "progressive," this time among people who had grown up after the 1960s—sometimes long afterward—and who were united by their opposition to the foreign and domestic policies of President George W. Bush (2001–). In this case the ambiguities of the term were patent. Definitions proliferated on the computer networks of the Internet, where many youthful activists who felt at home within the medium of the World Wide Web established "web logs," or "blogs," to record their thoughts and communicate with like-minded people about current events. Some of these Internet-based cadres—the "netroots," as they sometimes called themselves—defined their progressivism in terms indistinguishable from the liberalism of the New Deal and the Great Society; some were drawn to the "neoliberalism" of the post–Great Society era and to the managerialism of the 1900–1917 period; yet others identified with the left-progressivism that descended from the insurgencies of the 1960s. Some declined to define their political creed in substantive terms at all, preferring to emphasize a political style marked by a willingness to confront the political right and the Republican party. These new progressives found the Bush administration's domestic policies—on economic, social, and civil-liberties matters—extreme and alarming; they tended to oppose, as foolish or unjust, the administration's war and occupation in Iraq, launched in 2003 ostensibly as part of a broad response to threats against the United States exemplified in the terrorist attacks of 11 September 2001. "Netroots" progressives channeled much of their energies into partisan efforts to replace Republican officeholders with Democrats, and that emphasis on partisan battles accommodated both variety and lack of clarity about the meaning of this new progressive politics.[56]

Left-progressives also fervently opposed the Iraq War and forged new coalitions to protest against it. These were coalitions in the tradition of the new left's anti-imperialism, but they were more diverse in terms of race, gender, and ethnicity than any previous antiwar activism in U.S. history.[57] However, this left-progressive antiwar movement and the highly partisan "netroots" progressives, who made a bid for influence within the Democratic party, had few points of contact. The alienation between antiwar or anti-imperialist progressives and Democratic liberals that had accreted during the cold war and Vietnam eras had created barriers of mutual suspicion, even of fear and loathing, which automatically rose again between the new formations of the post-"9/11" years. The idea that the two constituencies ought to cooperate would have seemed absurd to a great many in each.

When traditions are disrupted, self-knowledge is lacking and confusion abounds. Some left-progressives influenced by academic theory indulged in "the anarchist sublime," reiterating the dream, recurrent among American radicals since World War II, of jumping straight to the libertarian utopia of communism while bypassing the authoritarian stage of state socialism.[58] Yet that tendency obscured the deep roots that tied broader ranks of left-progressives to the American tradition of liberal ideology. Avowed liberals and "netroots" progressives, similarly, had difficulty seeing their kinship with the actually existing left and its largest traditions. The politics of transformation had a good run in American life, emboldening several generations of reformers and radicals to feel that they were on the upward side of history and to repel conservative and rightist efforts as reactionary. This tradition's decline and afterlife were protracted, and it shows little prospect of revival. A maligned tradition's resuscitation is anything but inevitable. It remains possible that leftists or liberals—progressives of any stripe—might advance once again a vigorous idea of progress toward a new, better stage of American history. Reformers and radicals could, either separately or together, work to create that new America. They could, like many of their counterparts in the past, picture themselves striding forward toward a future consonant with their values. If the historian's job is not to predict the future, it also is not to offer a counsel of despair. However, honesty requires the admission that possibilities based more in hope than in evidence are not usually the stuff of which history is made.

Notes

Introduction

1. In Peter Berkowitz, ed., *Varieties of Progressivism in America* (Palo Alto, Calif.: Hoover Institution Press, 2004), authors representing or sympathetic to Clintonian "New Democrats"—such as the political philosopher William A. Galston and the journalist Franklin Foer—as well as more liberal figures—such as the civil-liberties champion David Cole—lay claim to the mantle of progressivism. While liberals and leftists most commonly use the term, this example indicates the plasticity of the category with special vividness.

2. Michael Tomasky, *Left for Dead: The Life, Death, and Possible Resurrection of Progressive Politics in America* (New York: The Free Press, 1996), and E. J. Dionne, Jr., *They Only Look Dead: Why Progressives Will Dominate the Next Political Era* (New York: Simon and Schuster, 1997) were published a decade ago.

3. See E. J. Dionne, Jr., *Why Americans Hate Politics* (New York: Simon and Schuster, 1991), chapter 1.

4. There are recent exceptions: the roundtable published in *Radical History Review* 71 (spring 1998) entitled "Liberalism and the Left: Rethinking the Relationship," featuring essays by Eric Foner, Blanche Wiesen Cook, Amber Hollibaugh, and Manning Marable, and commentary by Sara Evans, Gerald Horne, and Robert Westbrook; Eric Foner, *The Story of American Freedom* (New York: W. W. Norton & Co., 1998); Michael Kazin, "What Liberalism Owes to the Left," in *Liberalism for a New Century*, ed. Neil Jumonville and Kevin Mattson (Berkeley: University of California Press, 2007); and recent publications by Howard Brick, including his essay "The Postcapitalist Vision in Twentieth-Century American Social Thought," in *American Capitalism: Social Thought and Political Economy in the Twentieth Century*, ed. Nelson Lichtenstein (Philadelphia: University of Pennsylvania Press, 2006), 21–46, and his book *Transcending Capitalism: Visions of a New Society in Modern American Thought* (Ithaca, N.Y.: Cornell University Press, 2006).

5. Staughton Lynd, *Intellectual Origins of American Radicalism* (New York: Pantheon Books, 1968); Mari Jo Buhle, Paul Buhle, and Harvey J. Kaye, eds., *The American Radical* (New York: Routledge, 1994); Timothy Patrick McCarthy and John McMillian, eds. *The Radical Reader: A Documentary History of the American Radical Tradition* (New York: The New Press, 2003).

6. Important work along these lines includes Gabriel Kolko, *The Triumph of Conservatism: A Re-interpretation of American History, 1900–1916* (New York: Free Press of Glencoe, 1963); James Weinstein, *The Corporate Ideal in the Liberal State, 1900–1918* (Boston: Beacon Press, 1968); R. Jeffrey Lustig, *Corporate Liberalism: The Origins of Modern American Political Theory, 1890–1920* (Berkeley: University of California Press, 1982); and Colin Gordon, *New Deals: Business, Labor, and Politics in America, 1920–1935* (Cambridge: Cambridge University Press, 1994).

7. Richard Hofstadter, *The Age of Reform: From Bryan to F. D. R.* (New York: Vintage Books, 1955), framed the "age of reform" similarly, setting its start and end dates at about 1890 and 1940.

8. See the comments in Edward A. Purcell, Jr., "Social Thought," *American Quarterly* 35, nos. 1–2 (spring–summer 1983): 81.

9. See Charles A. Beard's introduction to J. B. Bury, *The Idea of Progress: An Inquiry into Its Origin and Growth* (New York: Macmillan, 1932), specifically xxxii–xl; Arthur A. Ekirch, Jr., *The Idea of Progress in America, 1815–1860* (1944; New York: P. Smith, 1951); Boyd C. Shafer, "The American Heritage of Hope, 1865–1940," *Mississippi Valley Historical Review* 37, no. 3 (December 1950): 427–50; Rush Welter, "The Idea of Progress in America: An Essay in Ideas and Method," *Journal of the History of Ideas* 16, no. 3 (June 1955): 401–15; Clarke A. Chambers, "The Belief in Progress in Twentieth-Century America," *Journal of the History of Ideas* 19, no. 2 (April 1958): 197–224; and Joyce O. Appleby, *Capitalism and a New Social Order: The Republican Vision of the 1790s* (New York: New York University Press, 1984). For a more general discussion of concepts of progress, see Bury, *The Idea of Progress*; Robert A. Nisbet, *Social Change and History: Aspects of the Western Theory of Development* (New York: Oxford University Press, 1969); and Robert A. Nisbet, *History of the Idea of Progress* (New York: Basic Books, 1980).

10. See Michael Kazin, *The Populist Persuasion: An American History* (New York: Basic Books, 1995), 36–37, as well as the classic discussion in Hofstadter, *The Age of Reform.*

11. Kathryn Kish Sklar, *Florence Kelley and the Nation's Work: The Rise of Women's Political Culture, 1830–1900* (New Haven, Conn.: Yale University Press, 1995), 132–33; John Dewey, "Academic Freedom" [1902], in *Middle Works, 1899–1924,* ed. Jo Ann Boydston (Carbondale: Southern Illinois University Press, 1976–83) 2:59, quoted in Robert B. Westbook, *John Dewey and American Democracy* (Ithaca, N.Y.: Cornell University Press, 1991), 92; Joseph Freeman, *An American Testament: A Narrative of Rebels and Romantics* (New York: Farrar & Rinehart, 1936), vii.

12. Opinions varied as to whether the new society would be a "postcapitalist" one, to use Howard Brick's term, or a new and drastically different phase of capitalist society. See Brick, *Transcending Capitalism.*

13. On Lippmann, who worked for a reform-oriented Socialist mayor of Schenectady, New York in his youth and later criticized the New Deal from its right, while never really straying from the broad confines of the new liberalism, see Ronald Steel, *Walter Lippmann and the American Century* (Boston: Little, Brown, 1980); and Barry D. Riccio, *Walter Lippmann: Odyssey of a Liberal* (New Brunswick, N.J.: Transaction Books, 1994). On Berle, see Jordan A. Schwarz, *Liberal: Adolf A. Berle and the Vision of an American Era* (New York: The Free Press, 1987), a good example of a book that takes one individual as a paradigm for a sprawling, diverse political tendency.

14. See Alan Brinkley, *The End of Reform: New Deal Liberalism in Recession and War* (New York: Alfred A. Knopf, 1995).

15. Christopher Lasch argued that the American left became estranged from mass movements representing a true popular base of support during the World War I era. Christopher Lasch, *The Agony of the American Left* (New York: Alfred A. Knopf, 1969). While the middle-class origins of many radicals has complicated the question of class loyalty and solidarity with the majority for the American left for a long time, I think the full estrangement of the left from popular bases of support and from majoritarian, populist sentiment occurred later.

16. Works I have found useful regarding the history of liberalism on an international basis include Guido de Ruggiero, *The History of European Liberalism*, trans. R. G. Collingwood (1927; Boston: Beacon Press, 1959); Dorothy Ross, "Liberalism," in *Encyclopedia of American Political History: Studies of the Principal Movements and Ideas*, ed. Jack P. Greene (New York: Charles Scribner's Sons, 1984), 750–63; J. G. Merquior, *Liberalism, Old and New* (Boston: Twayne Publishers, 1991); Pierre Manent, *An Intellectual History of Liberalism*, trans. Rebecca Balinski (Princeton, N.J.: Princeton University Press), 1994; John Gray, *Liberalism*, 2nd ed. (Minneapolis: University of Minnesota Press, 1995); Ira Katznelson, *Liberalism's Crooked Circle: Letters to Adam Michnik* (Princeton, N.J.: Princeton University Press, 1996); Alan Sykes, *The Rise and Fall of British Liberalism, 1776–1988* (London: Addison Wesley Longman, 1997); and Alan S. Kahan, *Liberalism in Nineteenth-Century Europe: The Political Culture of Limited Suffrage* (Houndmills: Palgrave Macmillan, 2003).

17. See Thomas Frank, *What's the Matter with Kansas? How Conservatives Won the Heart of America* (New York: Metropolitan Books, 2005).

18. On the use of "liberalism" as a foil by sympathetic historians of militant civil rights politics during the cold war, see the recent exchange between Robert O. Self and Matthew J. Countryman, discussing Countryman's fine book, *Up South: Civil Rights and Black Power in Philadelphia* (Philadelphia: University of Pennsylvania Press, 2006). Robert O. Self, "Matthew Countryman's *Up South* and Urban Political History," *Pennsylvania Magazine of History and Biography* 130, no. 4 (October 2006): 393–98; Matthew J. Countryman, "Response," ibid., 407–14.

Chapter 1

1. Richard Hofstadter, *Social Darwinism in American Thought, 1860–1915* (Philadelphia: University of Pennsylvania Press, 1944) emphasizes this doctrine as the key justification for Gilded Age conservatism. Robert C. Bannister, *Social Darwinism: Science and Myth in Anglo-American Social Thought* (Philadelphia: Temple University Press, 1979) provides a revisionist view. Mike Hawkins, *Social Darwinism in European and American Thought, 1860–1945: Nature as Model and Nature as Threat* (Cambridge: Cambridge University Press, 1997) offers a rejoinder to the revisionists.

2. The most comprehensive detailed study of this protracted battle remains Sidney Fine, *Laissez-Faire and the General-Welfare State: A Study of Conflict in American Thought, 1865–1901* (Ann Arbor: University of Michigan Press, 1956). Much of the historical work charting the overall development of statist reform during the Gilded Age and Progressive Era dates from 1930–65, and most of it embraces the same overall "progressive" framework of interpretation, one that projects back into the Gilded Age the conflict between twentieth-century liberals and conservatives. See Eric F. Goldman, *Rendezvous with Destiny: A History of Modern American Reform* (New York: Alfred A. Knopf, 1952); Ray Ginger, *Altgeld's America: The Lincoln Ideal versus Changing Realities* (New York: Funk & Wagnalls Co., 1958); and Ray Ginger, *The Age of Excess: The United States from 1877 to 1914* (New York: Macmillan, 1965). This work may seem naïve or ahistorical to today's scholars. Yet it is not surpassed by later work taking up these matters directly, largely because there is so little of it. For work in a similar vein focusing on the Progressive Era (1900–1917), see note 4, below. Richard Hofstadter, *The Age of Reform: From Bryan to F.D.R.* (New York: Vintage Books, 1956), is the major exception to the progressive interpretation descending from this era of histor-

ical work. For a welcome recent return to this subject, see Nancy Cohen, *The Reconstruction of American Liberalism, 1865–1914* (Chapel Hill: University of North Carolina Press, 2002). The most notable treatments from recent decades are Nell Irvin Painter, *Standing at Armageddon: The United States, 1877–1919* (New York: W. W. Norton & Co., 1987); and Alan Dawley, *Struggles for Justice: Social Responsibility and the Liberal State* (Cambridge, Mass.: Harvard University Press, 1991). Both Painter and Dawley seek to revive the basic outlines of the progressive interpretation, while taking account of subsequent scholarship in a host of areas.

David Green, *The Language of Politics in America: Shaping Political Consciousness from McKinley to Reagan* (Ithaca, N.Y.: Cornell University Press, 1987), 21–43, contends that the "conservative" camp was not truly antigovernment—that it benefited greatly from state favoritism—and that therefore the egalitarian attack on laissez-faire missed the point. There is an element of truth in Green's analysis, but it is too sweeping.

As my remarks indicate, I endorse the contention in Robert Crunden, *Ministers of Reform: The Progressives' Achievement in American Civilization, 1889–1920* (New York: Basic Books, 1982), that a specifically Protestant sense of social mission lay at the heart of the post-1890 reform leader cohort, the "progressives" who grew up during the later Gilded Age. I see this old-stock, mainly Republican cohort as the group who established the lasting framework of Progressive Era reform. At the same time, urbanites, immigrants and their children, and Democrats were crucial participants in the progressive movement(s). Elizabeth Sanders, *Roots of Reform: Farmers, Workers, and the American State, 1877–1917* (Chicago: University of Chicago Press, 1999), argues forcefully that the Democrats were the party of egalitarian reform at the national level throughout the Gilded Age and Progressive Era. See John D. Buenker, *Urban Liberalism and Progressive Reform* (New York: Charles Scribner's Sons, 1973), on the urban reform scene; James J. Connolly, *The Triumph of Ethnic Progressivism: Urban Political Culture in Boston, 1900–1925* (Cambridge, Mass.: Harvard University Press, 1998), updates this emphasis. Like most of the historical literature in this area, Buenker, while establishing links between early twentieth-century progressivism and New Deal liberalism, does not make clear who was first called a "liberal" in this sense and when.

3. This description of "social politics" as the exclusion of things from the market is offered in Daniel T. Rodgers, *Atlantic Crossings: Social Politics in a Progressive Age* (Cambridge, Mass.: Belknap Press of Harvard University Press, 1998), 29–30, following Gøsta Esping-Andersen, *Politics Against Markets: The Social Democratic Road to Power* (Princeton, N.J.: Princeton University Press, 1985).

4. See Sanders, *Roots of Reform*, for a rousing requiem, replete with factual support, for an older historical literature connecting Gilded Age farmers' and workers' movements to Progressive Era achievements. For examples of that older work, see John D. Hicks, *The Populist Revolt: A History of the Farmers' Alliance and the People's Party* (Minneapolis: University of Minnesota, 1931); Harold U. Faulkner, *The Quest for Social Justice, 1898–1914* (New York: Macmillan, 1931); Theodore Saloutos and John D. Hicks, *Agricultural Discontent in the Middle West, 1900–1939* (Madison: University of Wisconsin Press, 1951); and Harold U. Faulkner, *The Decline of Laissez-Faire, 1897–1917* (New York: Rinehart, 1951). The best summary of the outpouring of scholarship during the 1960s and 1970s on the various reform movements of the Progressive Era is Daniel T. Rodgers, "In Search of Progressivism," *Reviews in American History* 10, no. 4 (December 1982):

113–32. Rodgers makes clear what most historians of progressivism today realize: that there was no single progressive agenda.

5. See Ronald D. Rotunda, *The Politics of Language: Liberalism as Myth and Symbol* (Iowa City: University of Iowa Press, 1986), chapter 4, and Green, *Language of Politics in America*, chapters 4–5.

6. Important titles include Peter Clarke, *Liberals and Social Democrats* (Cambridge: Cambridge University Press, 1978); Michael Freeden, *The New Liberalism: An Ideology of Social Reform* (Oxford: Oxford University Press, 1978); Stefan Collini, *Liberalism and Sociology: L. T. Hobhouse and Political Argument in England, 1880–1915* (Cambridge: Cambridge University Press, 1979); and Peter Weiler, *The New Liberalism: Liberal Social Theory in Great Britain, 1884–1914* (New York: Garland Publishing, 1982).

7. For many years almost the only focused effort to address this problem was a section of *The Age of Reform* titled "From the Mugwump to the Progressive." Hofstadter, *Age of Reform*, 164–73; on the problem more generally, see ibid., 131–73. In two long essays, Mary O. Furner has sought to rectify this neglect. Mary O. Furner, "The Republican Tradition and the New Liberalism: Social Investigation, State Building, and Social Learning in the Gilded Age," in *The State and Social Investigation in Britain and the United States*, ed. Michael J. Lacey and Mary O. Furner (Cambridge: Woodrow Wilson Center Press and Cambridge University Press, 1993), 171–241; and Mary O. Furner, "Knowing Capitalism: Public Investigation and the Labor Question in the Long Progressive Era," in *The State and Economic Knowledge: The American and British Experiences*, ed. Mary O. Furner and Barry Supple (Cambridge: Woodrow Wilson International Center for Scholars and Cambridge University Press, 1990), 241–86. For a brief history of American liberalism in all its varieties, see Dorothy Ross, "Liberalism," in *The Encyclopedia of American Political History: Studies of the Principal Movements and Ideas*, ed. Jack P. Greene (New York: Charles Scribner's Sons, 1984), 750–63. Anne Kornhauser, "Liberalism," in *Poverty in the United States: An Encyclopedia of History, Politics, and Policy*, ed. Gwendolyn Mink and Alice O'Connor (Santa Barbara, Calif.: ABC-CLIO, 2004), 439–45, is a recent, succinct discussion.

8. John G. Sproat, *"The Best Men": Liberal Reformers in the Gilded Age* (New York: Oxford University Press, 1968), 143.

9. See Karl Polanyi, *The Great Transformation* (New York: Farrar & Rinehart, 1944); Weiler, *The New Liberalism*, 14–15.

10. Historians have filled bookshelves debating whether liberalism or republicanism was the dominant ideology of early America, and when liberalism displaced republicanism. As my remarks in the main text suggest, I think these ideological traditions cohabited nicely for much of American history, at least into the Gilded Age. The works that started this conversation in earnest are Louis Hartz, *The Liberal Tradition in America: An Interpretation of American Political Thought Since the Revolution* (New York: Harcourt, Brace, 1955); and Bernard F. Bailyn, *The Ideological Origins of the American Revolution* (Cambridge, Mass.: Belknap Press of Harvard University Press, 1967). For reliable guides to the outpouring of works on both sides of the argument and in-between, see Ross, "Liberalism"; James T. Kloppenberg, "The Virtues of Liberalism: Christianity, Republicanism, and Ethics in Early American Political Discourse," *Journal of American History* 74, no. 1 (June 1987): 9–33; Daniel T. Rodgers, "Republicanism: The Career of a Concept," *Journal of American History* 79, no. 1 (June 1992): 11–38; and Joyce O. Appleby, *Liberalism and Republicanism in the Historical Imagination* (Cambridge, Mass.: Harvard University Press, 1992).

11. The phrase comes from Charles A. Beard and Mary R. Beard, *The Rise of American Civilization* (New York: Macmillan, 1935).

12. Robert H. Wiebe, *The Search for Order, 1877–1920* (New York: Hill and Wang, 1967), 9.

13. Ibid., 7.

14. Kathryn Kish Sklar, *Florence Kelley and the Nation's Work: The Rise of Women's Political Culture, 1830–1900* (New Haven, Conn.: Yale University Press, 1995), 107; David R. Roediger and Philip S. Foner, *Our Own Time: A History of American Labor and the Working Day* (New York: Greenwood Press, 1989). For an account that attributes lasting significance to the "Great Upheaval" of the 1880s, see Painter, *Standing at Armageddon.*

15. Laurence Gronlund, *The Cooperative Commonwealth*, ed. Stow Persons (1884; Cambridge, Mass.: Belknap Press of Harvard University Press, 1965). On Gronlund, see Mark Pittenger, *American Socialists and Evolutionary Thought, 1870–1920* (Madison: University of Wisconsin Press, 1993), chapter 3.

16. See Peter J. Rachleff, *Black Labor in the South: Richmond, Virginia, 1865–1890* (Philadelphia: Temple University Press, 1984); and Susan Levine, *Labor's True Women: Carpet Weavers, Industrialization, and Labor Reform in the Gilded Age* (Philadelphia: Temple University Press, 1984).

17. Michael Kazin notes that the pages of the AFL's publications, up to World War I, were open to all manner of reformers and radicals. Michael Kazin, *The Populist Persuasion: An American History* (New York: Basic Books, 1995), 62.

18. This in itself is no insult. Leon Fink, the Knights' most important recent historian, is correct to caution against the "overvaluation of intellectual coherence as a test of political and cultural authenticity." Leon Fink, "The New Labor History and the Powers of Historical Pessimism: Consensus, Hegemony, and the Case of the Knights of Labor," in *In Search of the Working Class: Essays in American Labor History and Political Culture* (Urbana: University of Illinois Press, 1994), 91.

19. Dorothy Ross, "Socialism and American Liberalism: Academic Social Thought in the 1880's," *Perspectives in American History* 11 (1977–78): 13.

20. Rodgers, *Atlantic Crossings*, 100.

21. Steven J. Hahn, *A Nation Under Our Feet: Black Political Struggles in the Rural South from Slavery to the Great Migration* (Cambridge, Mass.: Belknap Press of Harvard University Press, 2003), 431–40, offers a sober evaluation of interracialism and its limits in populism. Lawrence Goodwyn, *Democratic Promise: The Populist Moment in America* (New York: Oxford University Press, 1976), the most romantic account, coined the term "movement culture" in this context.

22. John L. Thomas, *Alternative America: Henry George, Edward Bellamy, Henry Demarest Lloyd and the Adversary Tradition* (Cambridge, Mass.: Belknap Press of Harvard University Press, 1983), 314.

23. Robert D. Johnston, *The Radical Middle Class: Populist Democracy and the Question of Capitalism in Progressive Era Portland, Oregon* (Princeton, N.J.: Princeton University Press, 2003), 76–77, 88–89, features a nice discussion of this "political economy," quoting James Livingston. James Livingston, *The Federal Reserve System: Money, Class, and Corporate Capitalism, 1890–1913* (Ithaca, N.Y.: Cornell University Press, 1986).

24. The first of these views was buried under so much rhetorical overkill in subsequent decades that it is almost forgotten. It was associated with Hicks, *The Populist Revolt.* Sanders, *Roots of Reform*, is a rousing requiem for this view. Hofstadter, *The Age of Reform* is the classic expression of the liberal critique of populism. Norman Pollack, *The Populist Response to Industrial America: Midwestern*

Populist Thought (Cambridge, Mass.: Harvard University Press, 1962), offers the last major revision, which Pollack refined in further works and which received a new twist in Goodwyn, *Democratic Promise.* For accounts that transcend the old arguments, see Bryan Palmer, *"Man over Money": The Southern Populist Critique of Industrial Capitalism* (Chapel Hill: University of North Carolina Press, 1980); and Thomas Goebel, "The Political Economy of American Populism from Jackson to the New Deal," *Studies in American Political Development* 11 (spring 1997): 109–48.

25. See Sanders, *Roots of Reform*; and Michael Kazin, *A Godly Hero: The Life of William Jennings Bryan* (New York: Alfred A. Knopf, 2006), 55–56, 148–64.

26. See Chester M. Destler, *American Radicalism, 1865–1901: Essays and Documents* (New London, Conn.: Connecticut College, 1946), chapters 8–9.

27. Donald Read, *Cobden and Bright: A Victorian Political Partnership* (London: Edward Arnold Publishers Ltd., 1967); L. T. Hobhouse, *Liberalism* (New York: Henry Holt and Company/London: Williams and Norgate, 1911), chapters 3–4; Elie Halevy, *The Growth of Philosophic Radicalism* (London: Faber and Faber, 1934). For those interested in such matters, the "History of Economic Thought Website" produced at the New School in New York and found at http://cepa.newschool.edu/het offers a fine introduction.

A somewhat different view of the mugwumps' social doctrines is offered in John Tomsich, *A Genteel Endeavor: American Culture and Politics in the Gilded Age* (Stanford, Calif.: Stanford University Press, 1971), chapters 4–5. Cohen, *The Reconstruction of American Liberalism* stresses the mugwump approval of elite social administration.

28. Rogers Smith points out that the term "liberalism" did not appear in the United States before the Gilded Age. Rogers M. Smith, "Liberalism and Racism: The Problem of Analyzing Traditions," in *The Liberal Tradition in American Politics: Reassessing the Legacy of American Liberalism*, ed. David F. Ericson and Louisa Bertch Green (New York: Routledge, 1999), 15.

29. Sproat, *"The Best Men"*; Michael E. McGerr, *The Decline of Popular Politics: The American North, 1865–1928* (New York: Oxford University Press, 1986), chapter 3; Michael E. McGerr, "The Meaning of Liberal Republicanism: The Case of Ohio," *Civil War History* 28, no. 4 (December 1982): 307–23; Eric Foner, *Reconstruction: America's Unfinished Revolution, 1863–1877* (New York: Harper & Row, 1988), 488–511; Ari A. Hoogenboom, *Outlawing the Spoils: A History of the Civil Service Reform Movement, 1865–1883* (Urbana: University of Illinois Press, 1961); and Thomas L. Haskell, *The Emergence of Professional Social Science: The American Social Science Association and the Nineteenth-Century Crisis of Authority* (Urbana: University of Illinois Press, 1977). The *Chicago Tribune* is quoted in Heather Cox Richardson, *The Death of Reconstruction: Race, Labor, and Politics in the Post–Civil War North, 1875–1901* (Cambridge, Mass.: Harvard University Press, 2001), 108.

30. The question of whether there was a difference between liberals and conservatives in the Gilded Age is a tricky one. James P. Young resurrects the idea of a conflict between humanitarian, socially minded liberals and "laissez-faire conservatives" during this period. But those known at this time as liberals believed in laissez-faire perhaps more honestly than these "conservatives" did. James P. Young, *American Liberalism Reconsidered: The Troubled Odyssey of the Liberal Idea* (Boulder, Colo.: Westview Press, 1996), 127–36. Sidney Fine notes that laissez-faire economists of the Gilded Age "tended to identify themselves with either the Liberal Republican-mugwump faction of the Republican party or the Samuel Tilden-Grover Cleveland wing of the Democratic party." Fine, *Laissez-Faire and the General-Welfare State*, 51.

There is a small historical literature on "conservatism" in the Gilded Age, all of which dates back to the 1950s. None of it grapples with the problem of anachronism in the use of language, nor does it suggest any difference between Gilded Age conservatism and mugwump liberalism. Robert G. McCloskey, *American Conservatism in the Age of Enterprise, 1865–1910: A Study of William Graham Sumner, Stephen J. Field and Andrew Carnegie* (Cambridge, Mass.: Harvard University Press, 1951); Clinton Rossiter, *Conservatism in America: The Thankless Persuasion*, 2nd ed. (1955; New York: Alfred A. Knopf, 1966), chapter 5. Rossiter, *Conservatism in America*, 159, counts Godkin as a conservative.

31. Cleveland's adherence to the gold standard placed him on the same side of affairs as did his free trade and anti-union positions. For a most sympathetic view of Cleveland, see Robert Kelley, *The Transatlantic Persuasion: The Liberal-Democratic Mind in the Age of Gladstone* (New York: Alfred A. Knopf, 1969), 293–350. Kelley is critical of what he calls the "historical stereotypes" that have led most historians of this period to view the policies favored by Tilden-Cleveland Democrats as "conservative," and he goes so far as to term them the leaders of "the left center"; ibid., 289n9, 323. These remarks in themselves tell us quite a lot about the confusion that has reigned among historians of liberalism in the Gilded Age. In any case, Kelley makes a large claim for the mugwumps' influence on Cleveland; ibid., 302.

32. *The Nation*, 40 (1885), 91, quoted in Alan Pendleton Grimes, *The Political Liberalism of the New York Nation, 1865–1932*, The James Sprunt Studies in History and Political Science, vol. 34 (Chapel Hill: University of North Carolina Press, 1953), 31.

33. Lincoln Steffens, *The Autobiography of Lincoln Steffens* (New York: Harcourt, Brace & World, 1931), 180.

34. This is the compelling argument of Richardson, *The Death of Reconstruction.*

35. Quoted in Grimes, *Political Liberalism*, 9. On Douglass's belief in self-reliance, see David W. Blight, *Frederick Douglass' Civil War: Keeping Faith in Jubilee* (Baton Rouge: Louisiana State University Press, 1989), 203–6.

36. Richardson, *The Death of Reconstruction*, 143; *The Nation*, 42 (1886), 745–6, quoted in Grimes, *Political Liberalism*, 10.

37. Godkin, *Unforeseen Tendencies of Democracy*, 224, quoted in Grimes, *Political Liberalism*, 40. Haskell, *The Emergence of Professional Social Science*, stresses old liberal intellectuals' perceptions of social complexity and interdependence.

38. Robert H. Wiebe, *Self-Rule: A Cultural History of American Democracy* (Chicago: University of Chicago Press, 1995) argues that during the Progressive Era the middle and upper classes were able to "sink the lower class." If he is even partly right, Godkin's anxiety seems overblown.

39. Charles Francis Adams, Jr., and Henry Adams, *Chapters of Erie, and Other Essays* (Boston: J. R. Osgood and Company, 1871); Godkin quoted (from 1873) in Richard L. McCormick, "The Discovery That Business Corrupts Politics: A Reappraisal of the Origins of Progressivism," in *The Party Period and Public Policy: American Politics from the Age of Jackson to the Progressive Era* (New York: Oxford University Press, 1986), 325.

40. Sproat, *"The Best Men,"* 68, 128.

41. Ibid., 121; Kristin L. Hoganson, *Fighting for American Manhood: How Gender Politics Provoked the Spanish-American and Philippine-American Wars* (New Haven, Conn.: Yale University Press, 1998), 23.

42. Rebecca Edwards, *Angels in the Machinery: Gender in American Party Politics*

from the Civil War to the Progressive Era (New York: Oxford University Press, 1997), 32.

43. Oswald Garrison Villard, *Fighting Years: Memoirs of a Liberal Editor* (New York: Harcourt, Brace and Company, 1939), 119–20.

44. Quoted in Guido de Ruggiero, *The History of European Liberalism*, trans. R. G. Collingwood (1927; Boston: Beacon Press, 1959), 106.

45. Edwards, *Angels in the Machinery*, 121, 156; Hoganson, *Fighting for American Manhood*, 18, 20–21; Kazin, *A Godly Hero*, 89.

46. Robert L. Beisner, *Twelve Against Empire: The Anti-Imperialists, 1898–1900* (New York: McGraw-Hill, 1968); Kazin, *A Godly Hero*, 91–92.

47. On the Dominican controversy see Foner, *Reconstruction*, 494–97.

48. Villard, *Fighting Years*, 82–83.

49. Ibid., 4–5. Villard was correct about his grandfather's economic views; see John L. Thomas, *The Liberator: William Lloyd Garrison* (Boston: Little, Brown, 1963), 298–99, 371. On Villard generally, see Michael Wreszin, *Oswald Garrison Villard: Pacifist at War* (Bloomington: Indiana University Press, 1965); on Storey, see William B. Hixson, *Moorfield Storey and the Abolitionist Tradition* (New York: Oxford University Press, 1972).

50. Thomas, *Alternative America*, 51.

51. Walter Rauschenbusch, quoted in Michael McGerr, *A Fierce Discontent: The Rise and Fall of the Progressive Movement in America, 1870–1920* (New York: The Free Press, 2003), 66. McGerr compiles a long list of similar comments, most of them from the 1890s, by social gospel and new liberal thinkers; ibid., 58–59, 66.

52. For a recent analysis of the Cleveland scene, see Shelton Stromquist, "The Crucible of Class: Cleveland Politics and the Origins of Municipal Reform in the Progressive Era," *Journal of Urban History* 23, no. 2 (January 1997): 192–220.

53. The developments in New York are discussed in Richard L. McCormick, *From Realignment to Reform: Political Change in New York State, 1893–1910* (Ithaca, N.Y.: Cornell University Press, 1981), and those in California in Philip VanderMeer, "Hiram Johnson and the Dilemmas of California Progressivism," in *The Human Tradition in the Gilded Age and Progressive Era*, ed. Ballard C. Campbell (Wilmington, Del.: Scholarly Resources, 2000), 169–86. The railroads were the leading reform issue in many rural areas of the country as well.

54. Rodgers, *Atlantic Crossings*, 64–65. An American Fabian League existed briefly at the end of the nineteenth century. Established in 1895 under the leadership of William D. P. Bliss, also the founder of the Society of Christian Socialists (1889), its journal, the *American Fabian*, only lasted until 1900. See Fine, *Laissez-Faire and the General-Welfare State*, 193. But such formal affiliation with the Fabian movement is not required for inclusion in the more diffuse political environment I am designating American Fabianism.

55. Chester M. Destler, *Henry Demarest Lloyd and the Empire of Reform* (Philadelphia: University of Pennsylvania Press, 1963), 142, 159. For a somewhat abstract discussion of Lloyd's thought, see David W. Noble, "The Paradox of Progressive Thought," *American Quarterly* 5, no. 3 (autumn 1953): 204–7; and David W. Noble, *The Paradox of Progressive Thought* (Minneapolis: University of Minnesota, 1958), 138–56.

56. Destler, *Henry Demarest Lloyd*, 225.

57. Herbert G. Gutman, "Protestantism and the Labor Movement: The Christian Spirit in the Gilded Age," in *Work, Culture and Society in Industrializing America* (New York: Vintage Books, 1977), 115. See Robert H. Craig, *Religion and*

Radical Politics: An Alternative Christian Tradition in America (Philadelphia: Temple University Press, 1992), 13–14. Craig faults even Rauschenbusch for embracing an overly idealistic vision of social change. Older works on the social gospel make this same point. See Charles H. Hopkins, *The Rise of the Social Gospel in American Protestantism, 1865–1915* (New Haven: Yale University Press, 1940); and Henry F. May, *Protestant Churches in Industrial America* (New York: Harper & Brothers, 1949). Like Gutman, Craig recovers a remarkable range of very different Christian social thought from the working-class milieux of the Gilded Age; Craig, *Religion and Radical Politics*, 17–45

58. Destler, *Henry Demarest Lloyd*, 251; Sklar, *Florence Kelley*, 227. However, Thomas, *Alternative America*, 327, states that Lloyd nonetheless privately referred to the Civic Federation as a promising development, "one of Fabianism's surest allies"!

59. Stromquist, "The Crucible of Class," 205.

60. James Gilbert, *Designing the Industrial State: The Intellectual Pursuit of Collectivism in America, 1880–1940* (Chicago: Quadrangle Press, 1972), 33. Gilbert goes too far in casting Fabianism as the dominant intellectual tendency among reform intellectuals during the Progressive Era. However, his is one of the most original attempts to summarize the developments in political and social thought in that period. On the "vanguardism" that Gilbert sees at work among both liberal reformers and socialists, see ibid., 65–69.

61. Rodgers, *Atlantic Crossings*, 52.

62. Ibid., 70–74. Sometimes this broad front was known as "progressivism" in England, where the term was first used in the context of London city politics in the 1890s. Weiler, *New Liberalism*, 54, 23, 88; Rodgers, *Atlantic Crossings*, 52.

63. Quoted in Thomas, *Alternative America*, 209.

64. Ibid., 280.

65. Ibid., 349.

66. Destler, *Henry Demarest Lloyd*, 250. Lloyd's mention of a "right . . . to wife" was no misstep. On the importance of a husband's property in his wife to nineteenth-century American liberal ideology, see Amy D. Stanley, *From Bondage to Contract: Wage Labor, Marriage, and the Market in the Age of Slave Emancipation* (Cambridge: Cambridge University Press, 1998), chapter 5.

67. Quoted in Fine, *Laissez-Faire and the General-Welfare State*, 209–10.

68. Ross, "Socialism and American Liberalism"; Mary O. Furner, *Advocacy and Objectivity: A Crisis in the Professionalization of American Social Science, 1865–1905* (Lexington: University Press of Kentucky, 1975).

69. Quoted in Weiler, *New Liberalism*, 152.

70. De Ruggiero notes, instructively, that George's ideas about nationalizing land values had their basis in the classical liberal writings of the economist David Ricardo. "Rent was not a gift of nature," according to Ricardo. "[T]he deduction of a positive programme of expropriation finds a solid foundation in Ricardo's theory, and was in the future to be the basis of democratic and proletarian claims." De Ruggiero, *History of European Liberalism*, 110, 111. While a great many people on both sides of the Atlantic were captivated by the leveling radicalism of George's proposals, he himself retained a keener awareness of their liberal roots.

71. Quoted in Sklar, *Florence Kelley*, 132–33.

72. Ibid., 215.

73. Victoria Bissell Brown explains that the political legacy that Addams received from her father, an active Republican whom she revered, was not a

Quaker-abolitionist one, as many have thought. Rather, John Addams was a moderate antislavery Republican who was especially enthusiastic about the Whig party's program of government-sponsored economic development, which the Republicans embraced in practice (while never relinquishing the myth of the self-made man). Victoria Bissell Brown, *The Education of Jane Addams* (Philadelphia: University of Pennsylvania Press, 2004), 21–22. See Crunden, *Ministers of Reform*, 5, on Addams as "the most extreme example" of the reverence for Lincoln and the GOP among early progressive leaders. According to Eldon J. Eisenach, *The Lost Promise of Progressivism* (Lawrence: University Press of Kansas, 1994), 49–51, in the "real" progressive view the Republican party alone was a suitable vehicle for national renewal.

74. See Crunden, *Ministers of Reform*, 65–66.

75. Jean Bethke Elshtain, *Jane Addams and the Dream of American Democracy: A Life* (New York: Basic Books, 2002) emphasizes that Addams and her collaborators did not view the urban poor as "clients" in need of welfare services. Despite Elshtain's insistence on contrasting Hull House with the welfare programs of the Great Society in the 1960s, Addams and her colleagues enacted, *avant le lettre*, the War on Poverty's principle of allowing the recipients of aid the "maximum feasible participation" in designing and administering social welfare programs.

76. Brown, *The Education of Jane Addams*, 195, 245.

77. Ibid., 245–46. Also see Nan Enstad, *Ladies of Labor, Girls of Adventure: Working Women, Popular Culture, and Labor Politics at the Turn of the Twentieth Century* (New York: Columbia University Press, 1999).

78. Quoted in Weiler, *New Liberalism*, 46.

79. Robyn Muncy, *Creating a Female Dominion in American Reform, 1890–1930* (New York: Oxford University Press, 1991), 35; Ellen Carol DuBois, *Harriot Stanton Blatch and the Winning of Woman Suffrage* (New Haven, Conn.: Yale University Press, 1997), 93–101.

80. Sklar, *Florence Kelley*, 176, 277.

81. *Citizen* is the title of yet another recent biography of Addams. Louise W. Knight, *Citizen: Jane Addams and the Struggle for Democracy* (Chicago: University of Chicago Press, 2005). The complexity of Addams's views on questions of class can prove vexing. Shelton Stromquist, *Reinventing "The People": The Progressive Movement, the Class Problem, and the Origins of Modern Liberalism* (Urbana: University of Illinois Press, 2006) argues that Addams and other new liberals wished to banish class from American politics. My view is different.

82. On her personality, see Brown, *The Education of Jane Addams*, 10, 226.

83. DuBois, *Harriot Stanton Blatch*, 115. DuBois goes on to explain that bourgeois women, despite their pretensions on this point, dominated American suffrage organizations; ibid., 117–21. Also see Sarah Deutsch, "Learning to Talk More Like a Man: Boston Women's Class-Bridging Organizations, 1870–1940," *American Historical Review* 97, no. 2 (April 1992): 379–404. Deutsch prefers the term "class-bridging" over "cross-class," arguing that the former term indicates the "middle-class dominance" within these organizations; ibid., 381n10.

84. Nancy F. Cott, *The Grounding of Modern Feminism* (New Haven, Conn.: Yale University Press, 1987), 24–25, 34.

85. Maureen A. Flanagan, *Seeing with Their Hearts: Chicago Women and the Vision of the Good City, 1871–1933* (Princeton, N.J.: Princeton University Press, 2002), 46–51, 59–70, 118. Flanagan presses this interpretation vigorously in her study.

86. Mari Jo Buhle, *Women and American Socialism, 1870–1920* (Urbana: University of Illinois Press, 1981), 81. See Ruth Bordin, *Women and Temperance: The*

Quest for Power and Liberty, 1873–1900 (New Brunswick, N.J.: Rutgers University Press, 1990).

87. Sklar, *Florence Kelley*, 236.

88. Works in this vein include Henry F. May, *Protestant Churches in Industrial America* (New York: Harper & Brothers, 1949); Robert Bremner, *From the Depths: The Discovery of Poverty in the United States* (New York: New York University Press, 1956); Clarke A. Chambers, *Seedtime of Reform: American Social Service and Social Action, 1918–1933* (Minneapolis: University of Minnesota Press, 1963); Roy Lubove, *The Professional Altruist: The Emergence of Social Work as a Career, 1880–1930* (Cambridge, Mass.: Harvard University Press, 1965); and Allen F. Davis, *Spearheads for Reform: The Social Settlements and the Progressive Movement, 1890–1914* (New York: Oxford University Press, 1967).

89. This is often known as the "social control" thesis. Fewer books than one might think have advanced this interpretation. These include Joseph R. Gusfield, *Symbolic Crusade: Status Politics and the American Temperance Movement* (Urbana: University of Illinois Press, 1963); David J. Pivar, *Purity Crusade: Sexual Morality and Social Control, 1868–1900* (Westport, Conn.: Greenwood Press, 1973); Paul Boyer, *Urban Masses and Moral Order in America, 1820–1920* (Cambridge, Mass.: Harvard University Press, 1978); and Riva S. Lissak, *Pluralism and Progressives: Hull House and the New Immigrants, 1890–1919* (Chicago: University of Chicago Press, 1989). The introduction to Peggy Pascoe, *Relations of Rescue: The Search for Female Moral Authority in the American West, 1874–1939* (New York: Oxford University Press, 1990) offers a useful summary and critique of the social control thesis.

90. Ellen Fitzpatrick, *Endless Crusade: Women Social Scientists and Progressive Reform* (New York: Oxford University Press, 1990); Muncy, *Creating a Female Dominion*; the essays in Noralee Frankel and Nancy S. Dye, eds., *Gender, Class, Race and Reform in the Progressive Era* (Lexington: University Press of Kentucky, 1991); and Sklar, *Florence Kelley* locate the settlement house workers primarily in the context of women's history.

91. Sklar, *Florence Kelley*, 148–51; DuBois, *Harriot Stanton Blatch*, 91–92.

92. Florence Kelley, quoted in Sklar, *Florence Kelley*, 303. See also Muncy, *Creating a Female Dominion*, 31–33.

93. Wiebe, *The Search for Order*, 166 is the source of this elegant, justly influential formulation.

94. Rodgers, "In Search of Progressivism," 127n1; McGerr, *A Fierce Discontent*, 280; Richard L. McCormick, "Progressivism: A Contemporary Reassessment," in McCormick, *The Party Period and Public Policy*, 263.

95. Eisenach, *The Lost Promise of Progressivism*, presents this nationalist, centralist tendency as "true" progressivism. Perhaps needless to say, Lloyd does not figure in his account. He includes Addams and Kelley but gives a rather partial presentation.

96. Gary Gerstle, "The Protean Character of American Liberalism," *American Historical Review* 99, no. 4 (October 1994): 1043–73, argues for the importance of ethnicity and race in progressivism, and indeed for the prominence of an egalitarian embrace of diversity among the progressives. On Balch's pluralism, see Alan Dawley, *Changing the World: American Progressives in War and Revolution* (Princeton, N.J.: Princeton University Press, 2003), 116–17. Manning Marable, *W. E. B. DuBois: Black Radical Democrat* (Boston: Twayne Publishers, 1986), 66, 78–81, recounts Villard's efforts to undermine DuBois.

Horace Kallen, discussed extensively in Gerstle, "The Protean Character of

American Liberalism," and elsewhere, is the most famous exponent of ethnic pluralism in pre–World War I America. Randolph Bourne, the author of the phrase "transnational America," moved the discussion to a rather different plane, calling for a transcendence of ethnic differences, not a mutual appreciation of them. Kallen and Bourne were members of a younger generation than those I am discussing here; the younger liberals who came to the fore in the 1910s were less restrained than the original new liberals in their embrace of diversity. See David A. Hollinger, "Ethnic Diversity, Cosmopolitanism, and the Emergence of the American Liberal Intelligentsia," in *In the American Province: Studies in the History and Historiography of Ideas* (Baltimore, Md.: Johns Hopkins University Press, 1989), 56–73.

97. See Adolph L. Reed, Jr., *W. E. B. DuBois and American Political Thought: Fabianism and the Color Line* (New York: Oxford University Press, 1997), chapter 2.

98. Marable, *W. E. B. DuBois*, 87.

99. Ibid., 126.

100. Kevin K. Gaines, *Uplifting the Race: Black Leadership, Politics, and Culture in the Twentieth Century* (Chapel Hill: University of North Carolina Press, 1996), 24, 93–96.

101. Joseph J. Huthmacher, *Senator Robert F. Wagner and the Rise of Urban Liberalism* (New York: Atheneum, 1968); Melvin I. Urofsky, *Louis D. Brandeis and the Progressive Tradition* (Boston: Little, Brown, 1981); Philippa Strum, *Louis D. Brandeis: Justice for the People* (Cambridge, Mass.: Harvard University Press, 1984); Buenker, *Urban Liberalism and Progressive Reform*; and Connolly, *Triumph of Ethnic Progressivism*.

102. Strum, *Louis D. Brandeis*, 108, 181–82.

103. For an exhaustive treatment of these intellectual developments, see James T. Kloppenberg, *Uncertain Victory: Social Democracy and Progressivism in European and American Thought, 1870–1920* (New York: Oxford University Press, 1986).

104. Furner writes, "The historical project of the long Progressive Era, stretching *from the 1880s through World War I*, was the reconstruction of American liberalism or, more precisely, the formation of an American 'New Liberalism.'" She is correct: it took that long. I emphasize that not until late in this process did many Americans think of the project upon which they were embarked as the reconstruction of liberalism. Furner, "Knowing Capitalism: Public Investigation and the Labor Question in the Long Progressive Era," in *The State and Economic Knowledge*, ed. Furner and Supple, 242, emphasis added. Furner's emphasis in this essay, as in Furner, "The Republican Tradition and the New Liberalism," on "social investigation" is somewhat different from mine.

105. Herbert D. Croly, *The Promise of American Life* (New York: Macmillan, 1909); Edward A. Ross, *Social Control* (New York: Macmillan, 1901).

106. John Chamberlain, *A Farewell to Reform: The Rise, Life and Decay of the Progressive Mind in America* (1932; Gloucester, Mass.: Peter Smith, 1958), calls Progressive Era activists who cared earnestly about social justice the "neo-democratic" progressives; Don S. Kirshner, "The Ambiguous Legacy: Social Justice and Social Control in the Progressive Era," *Historical Reflections* 2 (1975): 69–88 follows this usage.

107. For a recent statement of this point, see Fareed Zakaria, *The Future of Freedom: Illiberal Democracy at Home and Abroad* (New York: W. W. Norton & Co., 2003).

108. Quoted in John Milton Cooper, Jr., *The Warrior and the Priest: Woodrow Wilson and Theodore Roosevelt* (Cambridge, Mass.: Belknap Press of Harvard University Press, 1983), 114, emphasis in the original.

109. Martin J. Sklar, "Woodrow Wilson and the Political Economy of Modern United States Liberalism," *Studies on the Left* 1, no. 3 (fall 1960), reprinted in *For a New America: Essays in* Studies on the Left, *1959–1967*, ed. James Weinstein and David W. Eakins (New York: Vintage Books, 1970), 48–51, 87–88, notes Wilson's knowledge of both of these intellectual traditions and suggests that Wilson was particularly attached to a conservative evolutionary view of economy and society, making him complacent about the corporate reorganization of American life. Sklar's landmark work on Wilson and the Progressive Era receives its fullest airing in Martin J. Sklar, *The Corporate Reconstruction of American Capitalism, 1890–1916: The Market, the Law, and Politics* (Cambridge: Cambridge University Press, 1988).

110. Quoted in De Ruggiero, *History of European Liberalism*, 151.

111. Louis Galambos, "AFL's Concept of Big Business: A Quantitative Study of Attitudes toward the Large Corporation, 1894–1931," *Journal of American History* 57, no. 4 (March 1971): 856.

112. See Julie Greene, "Dinner-Pail Politics: Employers, Workers, and Partisan Culture in the Progressive Era," in *Labor Histories: Class, Politics, and the Working-Class Experience*, ed. Eric Arnesen, Julie Greene, and Bruce Laurie (Urbana: University of Illinois Press, 1998); and Julie Greene, *Pure and Simple Politics: The American Federation of Labor and Political Activism, 1881–1917* (Cambridge: Cambridge University Press, 1998). Greene's work revises the view, long orthodox among labor historians, that the AFL under Samuel Gompers's leadership eschewed partisan activity for most of this period.

113. See John P. Enyeart, "Revolution or Evolution: The Socialist Party, Western Workers, and Law in the Progressive Era," *Journal of the Gilded Age and Progressive Era* 2, no. 4 (October 2003): 377–402.

114. Gilbert, *Designing the Industrial State*, 94.

115. Ibid., 84–90.

116. The CIR has attracted much attention recently from historians, including Clarence E. Wunderlin, Jr., *Visions of a New Industrial Order: Social Science and Labor Theory in America's Progressive Era* (New York: Columbia University Press, 1992); Furner, "Knowing Capitalism"; Shelton Stromquist, "Class Wars: Frank Walsh, the Reformers, and the Crisis of Progressivism," in *Labor Histories*, ed. Arnesen, Greene, and Laurie; and Leon Fink, *Progressive Intellectuals and the Dilemmas of Democratic Commitment* (Cambridge, Mass.: Harvard University Press, 1997), 80–113.

117. On the wage question, see Furner, "Knowing Capitalism," 263–65.

118. This is Mary Furner's apt phrase. Ibid., 281, 282.

119. This is specifically true of Stromquist, "Class Wars."

120. Fink, *Progressive Intellectuals*, 97–104, recounts these exchanges in some detail.

121. See Lewis L. Gould, *Reform and Regulation: American Politics, 1900–1916* (New York: John Wiley & Sons, 1978), 12, 133.

122. George W. Wickersham to Charles D. Nagel, quoted in Gould, *Reform and Regulation*, 142.

123. In Sklar's view, the tariff reduction that Wilson signed into law (the Underwood tariff) actually benefited large industrial exporters more than it did farm interests. M. Sklar, "Woodrow Wilson," 82–85.

124. Quoted in Cooper, *The Warrior and the Priest,* 180.

125. See Gould, *Reform and Regulation,* 162.

126. Quoted in Cooper, *The Warrior and the Priest,* 253.

127. Ibid., 168.

128. See Joseph A. McCartin, *Labor's Great War: The Struggle for Industrial Democracy and the Origins of Modern American Labor Relations, 1912–1921* (Chapel Hill: University of North Carolina Press, 1997).

129. Quoted in Cooper, *The Warrior and the Priest,* 264.

130. Frederic C. Howe, *The Confessions of a Reformer* (New York: Charles Scribner's Sons, 1925), 250, 279.

131. Cott, *The Grounding of Modern Feminism,* 35.

132. Quoted in ibid., 43.

133. See Buhle, *Women and American Socialism,* 257–59.

134. Steffens recalled that Lippmann first introduced the crowd at Mabel Dodge's salon to psychoanalysis, which Steffens had no trouble in assimilating to his cynical belief that appearances are always deceiving. While many on the political left always have maintained that Freudianism represented a reactionary, bourgeois diversion from social issues, Steffens saw it differently, writing, "The new psychology was a feather in the cap of the red who had always held that to change men's minds one must first change their environment." Steffens, *Autobiography,* 656. Regardless of whether he got Freud right, a good many reds might have seen it this same way.

135. Howe, *The Confessions of a Reformer,* 279.

136. See Charles Forcey, *The Crossroads of Liberalism: Croly, Weyl, Lippmann, and the Progressive Era, 1900–1925* (New York: Oxford University Press, 1961), 178.

137. Chamberlain, *A Farewell to Reform,* 278–79.

138. Max Eastman, *Enjoyment of Living* (New York: Harper, 1948).

139. David M. Rabban, in a discussion that salvages this strain of American activism from the dustbin of history, mentions the National Liberal League (which existed since at least as early as 1878), the Kansas Liberal League, and the Manhattan Liberal Club. David M. Rabban, *Free Speech in Its Forgotten Years* (Cambridge: Cambridge University Press, 1997), 38, 42, 46.

140. Quoted in Henry F. May, *The End of American Innocence: A Study of the First Years of Our Own Time* (New York: Alfred A. Knopf, 1959), 314.

141. For a recent, quite elegant commemoration, see Christine Stansell, *American Moderns: Bohemian New York and the Creation of a New Century* (New York: Metropolitan Books, 2000).

142. Ibid., 306.

143. Quoted in Elizabeth Gurley Flynn, *The Rebel Girl: An Autobiography—My First Life (1906–1926)* (New York: International Publishers, 1973), 76.

144. May, *The End of American Innocence,* 302.

145. Quoted in Cooper, *The Warrior and the Priest,* 137.

146. Chamberlain, *A Farewell to Reform,* 278; May, *The End of American Innocence,* 333.

Chapter 2

1. Lucille Milner, *Education of an American Liberal* (New York: Horizon Press, 1954), 137–39.

2. Ibid., 51.

3. Paul L. Murphy, *World War I and the Origin of Civil Liberties in the United States* (New York: W. W. Norton & Company, 1979), 170; Robert C. Cottrell, *Roger Nash Baldwin and the American Civil Liberties Union* (New York: Columbia University Press, 2000); and Peggy Lamson, *Roger Baldwin, Founder of the American Civil Liberties Union: A Portrait* (Boston: Houghton Mifflin, 1976).

4. Baldwin's "philosophical anarchism," which was well known to his associates from that time, offers an obscure link to the anticommunism that oriented the ACLU's individualist agenda in later years. But even so, this is quite a different kind of individualism from that which a later generation might have expected to see present at the ACLU's founding—more new left than cold war liberal.

5. David M. Rabban, *Free Speech in Its Forgotten Years* (Cambridge: Cambridge University Press, 1997). Although Rabban is more explicit on this point, his discussion of the political legacy of World War I follows in the tradition of Murphy, *World War I and the Origin of Civil Liberties.*

6. Murphy, *World War I and the Origin of Civil Liberties*, 174, presents the ACLU as a group of individualist liberals, and definitely not radicals, from the start, at one point terming Villard, for example, a classical liberal. This mischaracterization rests on a citation of an unreliable essay in Ronald Radosh, *Prophets on the Right: Profiles of Conservative Critics of American Globalism* (New York: Simon and Schuster, 1975). For a nuanced view of this period, see C. Roland Marchand, *The American Peace Movement and Social Reform, 1898–1918* (Princeton, N.J.: Princeton University Press, 1972).

7. Milner, *Education of an American Liberal*, 38.

8. Quoted in Marchand, *The American Peace Movement and Social Reform*, 223.

9. Lillian D. Wald to miscellaneous, n.d. [August or September 1914], in Paul U. Kellogg Papers, Social Welfare History Archives, University of Minnesota (hereafter Kellogg Papers), Box 32, Folder 308.

10. John Haynes Holmes, *I Speak for Myself: The Autobiography of John Haynes Holmes* (New York: Harper & Brothers, 1959), 171.

11. James Weinstein, *The Decline of Socialism in America, 1912–1925* (New York: Vintage Books, 1969), documents this political success.

12. Emily Greene Balch to Paul U. Kellogg, 12 October 1914, Kellogg Papers, Box 32, Folder 308; Mornay Williams to Paul U. Kellogg, 26 January 1915, Kellogg Papers, Box 32, Folder 308; Reinhold Niebuhr, *Moral Man and Immoral Society* (New York: Scribner's, 1932). In this book Niebuhr chastised religious liberals specifically for failing to come to grips with class conflict, and he sanctioned the use of violence to achieve a just settlement of that conflict. Only later in the 1930s did he focus his attention on the need for the use of force in international affairs, easily transferring his critique of sentimental liberalism to that sphere. He continued to deploy this critique against those to his left during the cold war. See Richard W. Fox, *Reinhold Niebuhr: A Biography* (New York: Pantheon, 1985). In 1946, Balch won the Nobel Peace Prize.

13. "Towards the Peace That Shall Last," *The Survey* 33, no. 23 (6 March 1915).

14. See Marchand, *The American Peace Movement and Social Reform*, 206.

15. Florence Kelley to Paul U. Kellogg, "Lincoln's Birthday," 1915, Kellogg Papers, Box 32, Folder 308.

16. [Julia C.] Lathrop to Paul U. Kellogg (telegram), 1 March 1915; Felix Adler to Paul U. Kellogg, 27 February 1915; Owen R. Lovejoy to Paul U. Kellogg, 23 February 1915; Louis D. Brandeis to Paul U. Kellogg, 16 February 1915, all in Kellogg Papers, Box 32, Folder 308.

17. Crystal [Eastman] to Paul U. Kellogg, 8 December 1915, Kellogg Papers, Box 32, Folder 310.

18. On Holmes and Balch, see Marchand, *The American Peace Movement and Social Reform,* 231–32.

19. See Harriet Hyman Alonso, "Nobel Peace Laureates, Jane Addams and Emily Greene Balch: Two Women of the Women's International League for Peace and Freedom," *Journal of Women's History* 7, no. 2 (summer 1995): 9–13, for a clear account. The countries whose leaders were visited by WPP delegations were Austria-Hungary, Belgium, Denmark, England, France, Germany, Italy, the Netherlands, Norway, Russia, Sweden, and Switzerland.

20. Oswald Garrison Villard, speech introducing Jane Addams, 9 July 1915, Kellogg Papers, Box 32, Folder 309.

21. See Nancy F. Cott, *The Grounding of American Feminism* (New Haven, Conn.: Yale University Press, 1987), 64–65.

22. Marchand, *The American Peace Movement and Social Reform,* 221, 219. The authors of the criticisms were, respectively, Fannie Garrison Villard and Lucia Ames Mead.

23. These numbers come from Blanche Wiesen Cook, "Introduction," in Crystal Eastman, *On Women and Revolution,* ed. Blanche Wiesen Cook (New York: Oxford University Press, 1978), 13.

24. Villard, speech introducing Jane Addams.

25. Holmes, *I Speak for Myself,* 176.

26. Ibid., 185–86; Fosdick quoted in Marchand, *The American Peace Movement and Social Reform,* 369. See also Ray H. Abrams, *Preachers Present Arms* (New York: Round Table Press, 1933).

27. For the most extensive treatment of the People's Council, see Harriet Hyman Alonso, "Gender and Peace Politics in the First World War: The People's Council of America," *International History Review* 19, no. 1 (February 1997): 83–102; see also Alan Dawley, *Changing the World: American Progressives in War and Revolution* (Princeton, N.J.: Princeton University Press, 2003), 167–69. Alonso states that the People's Council existed until 1919, but her own account documents no organizational activity after 1917, nor does any other.

28. See David M. Kennedy, *Over Here: The First World War and American Society* (New York: Oxford University Press, 1980), 15, 21. The author of this commentary was John Sharp Williams, a Democrat of Mississippi. Williams merely said of Norris's commentary, "If it be not treason, it grazes the edge of treason." Dawley, *Changing the World,* 137.

29. Oswald Garrison Villard, *Fighting Years: Memoirs of a Liberal Editor* (New York: Harcourt, Brace and Co., 1939), 372.

30. See Charles Chatfield, "World War I and the Liberal Pacifist in the United States," *American Historical Review* 75, no. 7 (December 1970): 1932; and Marchand, *The American Peace Movement and Social Reform,* 292.

31. Louis P. Lochner, *Always the Unexpected: A Book of Reminiscences* (New York: Macmillan, 1956), 68, notes the civil libertarian element in the conference's agenda and obscures somewhat the peace terms the conference advanced by stating that the terms called simply for "an early, general, and democratic peace." The conference's list of demands included a call for "freedom of speech, and of the press, right of assembly and right to petition the government," the seventh item out of ten. See *Revolutionary Radicalism: Its History, Purpose and Tactics, with an Exposition and Discussion of the Steps Being Taken and Required to Curb It* (a Report of the Joint Legislative Committee Investigating

Seditious Activities, Filed April 24, 1920, in the Senate of the State of New York) (Albany: J. B. Lyon Co., 1920), *part 1: Revolutionary and Subversive Movements Abroad and at Home,* vol. 1, 1072. This compendious report is known as the Lusk Committee report, after Clayton R. Lusk, the chairman of the New York State Senate committee whose investigations produced it. The main author of the report was Archibald E. Stevenson.

32. Chatfield, "World War I and the Liberal Pacifist," 1934. On the "lay congress" concept, see Alonso, "Gender and Peace Politics in the First World War," 90.

33. Alonso, "Gender and Peace Politics in the First World War," 94.

34. Donald Johnson, *The Challenge to American Freedoms: World War I and the Rise of the American Civil Liberties Union* (Lexington: University of Kentucky Press, 1963); and Chatfield, "World War I and the Liberal Pacifist," respectively, advance these interpretations.

35. Quoted in Dana Frank, *Purchasing Power: Consumer Organizing, Gender, and the Seattle Labor Movement, 1919–1929* (Cambridge: Cambridge University Press, 1994), 39.

36. *Revolutionary Radicalism,* part 1, vol. 1, 1040.

37. See Allen F. Davis, *American Heroine: The Life and Legend of Jane Addams* (New York: Oxford University Press, 1973), 263–64; Davis reproduces a spiderweb chart on 265.

38. See *Revolutionary Radicalism,* part 1, vol. 1, 1031.

39. Villard, *Fighting Years,* 323.

40. Lillian D. Wald to Crystal Eastman, 28 August 1917, Survey Associates Records: Editorial Records, Social Welfare History Archives, University of Minnesota (hereafter Survey Associates Records), Box 67, Folder 499.

41. See Marchand, *The American Peace Movement and Social Reform,* 259–62; Wald quoted on 259.

42. Addams quoted in Davis, *American Heroine,* 247.

43. Allen F. Davis details these accomplishments in his article, "Welfare, Reform and World War I," *American Quarterly* 19, no. 3 (fall 1967): 516–33.

44. Cott, *The Grounding of Modern Feminism,* 66–74. Eastman herself opposed the proposal of 1921 to place the NWP in support of disarmament, thinking it wiser for members to pursue that goal through other organizations. But she supported the broad feminist agenda that the party's convention rejected.

45. Works that detail the political repression of the war years include H. C. Peterson and Gilbert C. Fite, *Opponents of War* (Madison: University of Wisconsin Press, 1957); Harry N. Scheiber, *The Wilson Administration and Civil Liberties* (Ithaca, N.Y.: Cornell University Press, 1960); William Preston, *Aliens and Dissenters: Federal Suppression of Radicals, 1903–1922* (Cambridge, Mass.: Harvard University Press, 1963); Joan Jensen, *The Price of Vigilance* (Chicago: Rand McNally, 1968); Frederick C. Luebke, *Bonds of Loyalty: German-Americans and World War I* (DeKalb: Northern Illinois University Press, 1974); and Christopher Capozzola, "The Only Badge Needed Is Your Patriotic Fervor: Vigilance, Coercion, and the Law in World War I America," *Journal of American History* 88, no. 4 (March 2002), 1354–82; as well as the other works cited in this chapter, among many other books and articles.

46. Johnson, *The Challenge to American Freedoms,* 104–7, tells this sorry tale.

47. Davis, *American Heroine,* 226–31, details the uproar over her remarks.

48. Walter Nelles, *A Liberal in Wartime: The Education of Albert DeSilver* (New York: W. W. Norton & Co., 1940), 129.

49. Many of these incidents are recounted in an effective section of Murphy, *World War I and the Origins of Civil Liberties*, 128–32. Many of them were listed earlier, in Lochner, *Always the Unexpected*, 73–75.

50. See Elizabeth Gurley Flynn, *The Rebel Girl: An Autobiography—My First Life (1906–1926)* (New York: International Publishers, 1973), 239–40, for a memorable account. On the O'Hare and Stokes cases, see Kathleen Kennedy, *Disloyal Mothers and Scurrilous Citizens: Women and Subversion During World War I* (Bloomington: Indiana University Press, 1999), chapters 2 and 4. O'Hare served eighteen months of her sentence and was freed by President Wilson; Stokes saw her conviction nullified by the U.S. Supreme Court in 1920, and the U.S. Department of Justice declined to retry her. Ibid., 31, 65.

51. A. J. Muste to Eugene Lyons, Workers' Defense Union, 10 January 1920, Elizabeth Gurley Flynn Papers, 1917–1923, Immigration History Research Center, University of Minnesota (hereafter Flynn Papers). Muste wrote specifically of the deportations of aliens deemed undesirable by the federal government, but his comment pertained to the entire climate of repression.

52. Quoted in Johnson, *The Challenge to American Freedoms*, 110.

53. Caroline A. Lowe to Elizabeth Gurley Flynn, organizer, Workers' Defense League, Flynn Papers.

54. See Johnson, *The Challenge to American Freedoms*, 154–55.

55. Workers' Defense Union to Frederic C. Howe, 22 July 1919, 1; Frederic C. Howe to Eugene Lyons, publicity manager, Workers' Defense Union, 8 August 1919, 5; both in Flynn Papers.

56. Frederic C. Howe, *The Confessions of a Reformer* (New York: C. Scribner's Sons, 1925), 257; Dawley, *Changing the World*, 158–59.

57. Quoted in Joseph P. Tumulty, *Woodrow Wilson as I Know Him* (Garden City, N.Y.: Doubleday, Page & Company, 1921), 505.

58. Johnson, *The Challenge to American Freedoms*, 182.

59. Villard, *Fighting Years*, 465.

60. So Villard wrote in February 1919. Ibid., 402.

61. John Dos Passos, *U.S.A.* vol. 2: *1919* (New York: The Library of America, 1996), 619.

62. Quoted in Johnson, *The Challenge to American Freedoms*, 198–99.

63. Quoted in Nelles, *A Liberal in Wartime*, 141.

64. Williams to Kellogg, 26 January 1915, Kellogg Papers, Box 32, Folder 308.

65. Quoted in Nelles, *A Liberal in Wartime*, 97.

66. "Towards the Peace That Shall Last," statement of the AUAM in *The Survey*, March 1915.

67. The advertisement, which ran on 22 June 1918, is reproduced in *Revolutionary Radicalism*, part 1, vol. 1, 1094–95. Other signatories besides the ones previously mentioned included Walter Weyl and James Harvey Robinson.

68. Quoted in Johnson, *The Challenge to American Freedoms*, 198.

69. Quoted in ibid., 146.

70. Biedenkapp, treasurer, Workers' Defense Union, to "Dear Comrade," 20 March 1920, Flynn Papers.

71. "Civil Liberty: A Statement defining the position of the American Civil Liberties Union on the issues in the United States to-day," a pamphlet reproduced in *Revolutionary Radicalism*, part 1, vol. 1, 1985.

72. Flynn, *The Rebel Girl*, 246.

73. Steven J. Hahn, *A Nation Under Our Feet: Black Political Struggles in the Rural South from Slavery to the Great Migration* (Cambridge, Mass.: The Belknap Press of

Harvard University Press, 2003), 431–40, provides a realistic, up-to-date assessment of populism's racial politics. Peter J. Rachleff, *Black Labor in the South: Richmond, Virginia, 1865–1890* (Philadelphia: Temple University Press, 1984), remains the foremost work on race and the Knights of Labor. On Afro-Caribbean radicals, see Winston James, *Holding Aloft the Banner of Ethiopia: Caribbean Radicalism in Early Twentieth-Century America* (London: Verso, 1998).

74. Barbara Foley, *Spectres of 1919: Class and Nation in the Making of the New Negro* (Urbana: University of Illinois Press, 2003), 13, 18, 40–44, 83–84. See Theodore Kornweibel, *"Seeing Red": Federal Campaigns against Black Militancy, 1914–1925* (Bloomington: Indiana University Press, 1998).

75. On the antiracist Socialists in New York and elsewhere, see Foley, *Spectres of 1919*, 36–40, 82, 85–87. On Harrison, see Jeffrey B. Perry, ed., *A Hubert Harrison Reader* (Middletown, Conn.: Wesleyan University Press, 2001).

76. Max Eastman, *Love and Revolution: My Journey Through an Epoch* (New York: Random House, 1964), 255.

77. Ibid., 137.

78. Theodore Draper, *The Roots of American Communism* (New York: Viking Press, 1957) remains the most detailed and incisive discussion of this trajectory.

79. Elizabeth Gurley Flynn, for the WDU, to "all amnesty and defense organizations throughout the country," 25 March 1919, Flynn Papers.

80. Eastman, *Love and Revolution*, 21.

81. Bertrand Russell, "Socialism and Liberal Ideals," *Living Age* 306, no. 3966 (10 July 1920): 117 (reprinted from *The English Review*).

82. The left-wing journalist Mary Heaton Vorse and the prominent socialist editor Abraham Cahan actually traveled to Hungary at the behest of Herbert Hoover. They and Eastman were thrilled by what they saw. Dawley, *Changing the World*, 225.

83. See Dawley, *Changing the World*, 175–78, on what he calls "progressive realism" as a basis for liberal acceptance of the Bolshevik regime's legitimacy. Dawley terms this stance a "lost alternative." Ibid., 177. I see it as a stance with a rather persistent history, even if one muddied with ambivalence and liberal self-doubt, in interwar America.

84. Daniel T. Rodgers, *Atlantic Crossings: Social Politics in a Progressive Age* (Cambridge, Mass.: Belknap Press of Harvard University Press, 1998), 299. Also see Clarke Chambers, *Paul U. Kellogg and the* Survey: *Voices for Social Welfare and Social Justice* (Minneapolis: University of Minnesota Press, 1971).

85. *Revolutionary Radicalism*, part 1, vol. 1, 1020.

86. Marchand, *The American Peace Movement and Social Reform*, 376–77.

87. Norman Thomas, for the *World Tomorrow*, to Eugene Lyons of the WDU, 6 January 1920, Flynn Papers.

88. Henry Neumann, for the Brooklyn Society for Ethical Culture, to Eugene Lyons of the WDU, 8 January 1920, Flynn Papers. He referred specifically to the U.S. government's deportations of alien radicals.

89. Russell, "Socialism and Liberal Ideals," 118.

90. Emma Goldman, *My Disillusionment in Russia* (Garden City, N.Y.: Doubleday, Page & Co., 1923).

91. Christopher Lasch, *The American Liberals and the Russian Revolution* (New York: Columbia University Press, 1962), 149.

92. Quoted in Nick Salvatore, *Eugene V. Debs: Citizen and Socialist* (Urbana: University of Illinois Press, 1982), 290–91.

93. Hillquit, in *From Marx to Lenin* (New York: The Hanford Press, 1921),

quoted in Seymour Martin Lipset and Gary Marks, *It Didn't Happen Here: Why Socialism Failed in the United States* (New York: W. W. Norton, 2000), 198–99.

94. Quoted in Salvatore, *Eugene V. Debs,* 331.

95. Quoted in ibid., 336.

96. Eastman, *Love and Revolution,* 160.

97. See Michael H. Hunt, *Ideology and U.S. Foreign Policy* (New Haven, Conn.: Yale University Press, 1987).

98. Baldwin to Lochner, 21 May 1917, quoted in *Revolutionary Radicalism,* part 1, vol. 1, 1057.

99. William Nye Doty to Harry Weinberger, 14 November 1920; Harry Weinberger to Elizabeth Gurley Flynn, 1 September 1920; both in Flynn Papers.

100. *Revolutionary Radicalism,* part 1, vol. 1, 1076. This opposition to the pursuit of individual clemency was not a singular case. Other radicals caught up in the red scare took a similar position, for instance Mollie Steimer, whose case Kathleen Kennedy analyzes. Kennedy, *Disloyal Mothers and Scurrilous Citizens,* 37.

101. *Revolutionary Radicalism,* part 1, vol. 1, 1076.

102. Harold Stearns, "Liberalism Invincible," *Dial* 66 (19 April 1919): 409.

103. Quoted in Lasch, *Liberals and the Russian Revolution,* 143.

104. John Chamberlain, *A Farewell to Reform: The Rise, Life and Decay of the Progressive Mind in America* (1932; Gloucester, Mass.: Peter Smith, 1958), 323.

105. Howe, *The Confessions of a Reformer,* 334.

106. Chamberlain, *Farewell to Reform,* 304–5, 203. He borrowed the term "economic fundamentalism" from the popular economist George Soule.

107. Lincoln Steffens, *The Autobiography of Lincoln Steffens* (New York: Harcourt, Brace & World, 1931), 831, 743.

108. Will Durant, "The Future of American Socialism," *Dial* 66 (17 May 1919): 495.

109. Steffens, *Autobiography,* 797–98. Steffens made his famous comment to Bernard Baruch, and in his *Autobiography* wished to set the record straight, complaining of the many ways in which he had been misquoted. It made little difference. Ibid., 799.

110. Ibid., 525.

111. Ibid., 526; Chamberlain, *Farewell to Reform,* 42, 67–73.

112. Chamberlain, *Farewell to Reform,* 201.

113. Howe, *The Confessions of a Reformer,* 322.

Chapter 3

1. An alternative view is offered in David A. Horowitz, *Beyond Left and Right: Insurgency and the Establishment* (Urbana: University of Illinois Press, 1997). Horowitz eschews farmer-laborism as a category, instead depicting the Upper Midwest progressives as part of a small-producer tradition that transcended the categories of left and right. He sees these "insurgents" as hostile to big business, big labor, and big government alike, at least after the midwestern progressives were estranged from the New Deal in 1938. For a more conventional (and persuasive) view, see Ronald A. Mulder, *The Insurgent Progressives in the United States Senate and the New Deal, 1933–1939* (New York: Garland, 1979).

2. Micah L. Sifry, *Spoiling for a Fight: Third-Party Politics in America* (New York: Routledge, 2003); Lisa Jane Disch, *The Tyranny of the Two-Party System* (New York: Columbia University Press, 2002); and David Reynolds, *Democracy Unbound: Progressive Challenges to the Two Party System* (Boston: South End Press, 1997).

3. "Progressives and Socialists," *New Republic* 56 (7 November 1928): 316.

4. Edmund Wilson, *The American Jitters: A Year of the Slump* (1932; New York: Books for Libraries/Arno Press, 1980), 113–20. For a presentation of Hoover's bona fides, see Joan Hoff-Wilson, *Herbert Hoover, Forgotten Progressive* (Boston: Little, Brown, 1975).

5. Edmund Wilson, "An Appeal to Progressives," *New Republic* 65 (14 January 1931): 238. This appeared two months before the Progressive Conference occurred.

6. Arthur M. Schlesinger, Jr., *The Age of Roosevelt,* vol. 3: *The Politics of Upheaval* (Cambridge, Mass.: The Riverside Press/Boston: Houghton Mifflin, 1960), 137–38.

7. For Wheeler's own account of his disillusionment, see Burton K. Wheeler, "My Years with Roosevelt," in *As We Saw the Thirties: Essays on Social and Political Movements of a Decade,* ed. Rita James Simon (Urbana: University of Illinois Press, 1967), 190–215.

8. As Otis L. Graham, Jr. pointed out, if the social work progressives, those most likely to support LaFollette and later Franklin Roosevelt, are removed from the Bull Moose lists, Theodore Roosevelt's supporters take on quite a conservative profile. Otis L. Graham, Jr., *An Encore for Reform: The Old Progressives and the New Deal* (New York: Oxford University Press, 1967), 169n6.

9. Louis Galambos's content analysis of labor publications found that 1924 marked the high point of negative opinions published concerning big business during the years 1894–1931. This coincidence may have given left-liberal activists a false impression of organized labor's stance toward America's economic elites. Louis Galambos, "AFL's Concept of Big Business: A Quantitative Study of Attitudes toward the Large Corporation, 1894–1931," *Journal of American History* 57, no. 4 (March 1971): 859.

10. James Weinstein, *The Corporate Ideal in the Liberal State: 1900–1918* (Boston: Beacon Press, 1968), 150, 152. Weinstein refers to LaFollette's abortive presidential candidacy in 1912, but his analysis, which casts LaFollette as constitutionally unable to come to terms with "corporate" capitalism, would apply in 1924 as well. Weinstein's ironclad interpretation of LaFollette's midwestern progressivism, so reminiscent of John Chamberlain's view of "reform," makes impossible any rational explanation of big business opposition to LaFollette. John Chamberlain, *A Farewell to Reform: Being a History of the Rise, Life, and Decay of the Progressive Mind in America* (New York: Liveright, 1932).

11. David Burner, "Election of 1924," in *History of American Presidential Elections, 1789–1968,* ed. Arthur M. Schlesinger, Jr. and Fred L. Israel (New York: Chelsea House, 1971), 3:2480.

12. "Where Are the Pre-War Radicals: A Symposium," *The Survey* 55 (1 February 1926): 556–64.

13. Samuel Blythe, quoted in Russel B. Nye, *Midwestern Progressive Politics: A Study of Its Origins and Development, 1870–1958* (East Lansing: Michigan State University Press, 1959), 298.

14. Quoted in Nye, *Midwestern Progressive Politics,* 306; Donald Young, ed., *Adventure in Politics: The Memoirs of Philip LaFollette* (New York: Holt, Rinehart and Winston, 1970), 87.

15. James R. Barrett, "Boring from Within and Without: William Z. Foster, the Trade Union Educational Leagues, and American Communism in the 1920s," in *Labor Histories: Class, Politics, and the Working-Class Experience,* ed. E. Arnesen, J. Greene, and B. Laurie (Urbana: University of Illinois Press, 1998), 314.

16. See Molly Ladd-Taylor, "Hull-House Goes to Washington: Women and the Children's Bureau," in *Gender, Class, Race, and Reform in the Progressive Era*, ed. Noralee Frankel and Nancy S. Dye (Lexington: University Press of Kentucky, 1991), 110–26; and Gwendolyn Mink, *The Wages of Motherhood: Inequality in the Welfare State, 1917–1942* (Ithaca, N.Y.: Cornell University Press, 1995), chapter 3.

17. Clarke A. Chambers, *Seedtime of Reform: American Social Service and Social Action, 1918–1933* (Minneapolis: University of Minnesota Press, 1963), details these activities.

18. The scholarship on the Sacco-Vanzetti case is surprisingly thin. Michael M. Topp, *The Sacco and Vanzetti Case: A Brief History with Documents* (Boston: Bedford/St. Martin's, 2005); and Jerome H. Delamater and Mary Anne Trasciatti, eds., *Representing Sacco and Vanzetti* (New York: Palgrave Macmillan, 2005), offer recent views.

19. Ronald Edsforth, "Made in the U.S.A.: Mass Culture and the Americanization of Working-Class Ethnics in the Coolidge Era," in *Calvin Coolidge and the Coolidge Era: Essays on the History of the 1920s*, ed. John Earl Haynes (Washington, D.C.: Library of Congress/Hanover, N.H.: University Press of New England, 1998), 247; Michael A. Bernstein, "The American Economy of the Interwar Era: Growth and the Transformation from the Great War to the Great Depression," in ibid., 195. This is not to say that American workers did not frequently struggle to keep up with expenses in this era, enjoying little bargaining power on the job during a low period for labor unions. And income and wealth disparities widened in the 1920s. Nonetheless, the U.S. working class saw concrete benefits from the increased wealth of the period, with many employers making the eight-hour day standard in the country for the first time; as Edsforth points out, increased household expenditures on health care and food also helped bring about a seven-year increase in life expectancy in the United States between the 1910s and the 1920s (from 51.8 years to 58.7). Edsforth, "Made in the U.S.A.," 248.

20. Michael Denning, *The Cultural Front: The Laboring of American Culture in the Twentieth Century* (London: Verso Books, 1997), argues that Dos Passos's vision of the "Lincoln republic" was obsolescent by the 1920s. Although I agree that it failed to shape the hegemonic ideals of any substantial political movement, I think Denning underestimates the lingering power of that vision's poignancy.

21. John Dewey, "Academic Freedom" [1902], in *Middle Works, 1899–1924*, ed. Jo Ann Boydston (Carbondale: Southern Illinois University Press), 2:59, quoted in Robert B. Westbook, *John Dewey and American Democracy* (Ithaca, N.Y.: Cornell University Press, 1991), 92. See Peter Gay, *The Enlightenment: An Interpretation, The Rise of Modern Paganism* (New York: W. W. Norton & Co., 1966), 31–71.

22. Matthew Josephson, *Infidel in the Temple: A Memoir of the Nineteen-Thirties* (New York: Alfred A. Knopf, 1967), 108–9; Harry F. Ward, "Italian Fascist Revolution," p. 4, Harry F. Ward Papers, Burke Library, Union Theological Seminary, New York (hence Ward Papers), Series III: Subseries A: Box 2: Folder 12: [Revolution?] I—n.d.; Wilson, *The American Jitters*, 312–13; Joseph Freeman, *An American Testament: A Narrative of Rebels and Romantics* (New York: Farrar & Rinehart, 1936), vii, 667; George H. Soule, *The Coming American Revolution* (New York: Macmillan, 1934), quoted in Richard H. Pells, *Radical Visions and American Dreams: Culture and Social Thought in the Depression Years* (New York: Harper & Row, 1973), 90.

23. Frederic C. Howe, *The Confessions of a Reformer* (New York: C. Scribner's Sons, 1925).

24. On this intellectual background the definitive work is James T. Kloppen-

berg, *Uncertain Victory: Social Democracy and Progressivism in European and American Thought, 1870–1920* (New York: Oxford University Press, 1986).

25. John Dewey, *Individualism Old and New* (New York: Minton, Balch & Co., 1930); John Dewey, *Liberalism and Social Action* (New York: G. P. Putnam's Sons, 1935). On the development of Dewey's ideas in this vein, see Westbrook, *John Dewey and American Democracy,* 42–51, 93–94, 165–66, 363–64, and (on the discussion of his writings of the 1930s, which reflected a decades-long philosophical consistency) 429–39.

26. John Dewey, "The Future of Liberalism," *Journal of Philosophy* 22, no. 9 (1935): 225–30, reprinted in Howard Zinn, ed., *New Deal Thought* (Indianapolis: Bobbs-Merrill, 1966), 30–31.

27. Ibid.; Schlesinger, *The Politics of Upheaval,* 192. See Sidney Hook, *Towards the Understanding of Karl Marx: A Revolutionary Interpretation* (New York: The John Day Co., 1933); and Christopher Phelps, *Young Sidney Hook: Marxist and Pragmatist* (Ithaca, N.Y.: Cornell University Press, 1997). Schlesinger celebrated the harmony he saw between Franklin Roosevelt's "pragmatism" and Dewey's, but Dewey, in frustration, dissented from that view during the 1930s, insisting that his pragmatism, applied to national policy, required a far more systematic and sustained program than Roosevelt ventured.

28. Sonnichsen quoted in Kathleen G. Donohue, *Freedom from Want: American Liberalism and the Idea of the Consumer* (Baltimore, Md.: Johns Hopkins University Press, 2003), 144. Sonnichsen was an official with the Co-operative League of the United States. On the cooperatives in Seattle, see Dana Frank, *Purchasing Power: Consumer Organizing, Gender, and the Seattle Labor Movement, 1919–1929* (Cambridge: Cambridge University Press, 1994), chapter 2. Frank sees the absence of a nationwide labor party in the United States as limiting the radical potential of cooperatives, which was more fully realized in Europe. Donohue contends that American cooperative thought inevitably moved away from radicalism and toward liberalism because of its tendency to emphasize consumption and to ignore the reality that many consumers were producers, too. In these respects she too contrasts American cooperative thinkers with their European counterparts. Donohue, *Freedom from Want,* 144–49. Cooperatives in the Upper Midwest were for producers as well as consumers, and more the former than the latter; this did not make them radical.

29. Wilson, *The American Jitters,* 313.

30. Max Eastman, "Motive-Patterns of Socialism," *Modern Quarterly* 11 (fall 1939), quoted in Pells, *Radical Visions and American Dreams,* 355. The two other camps Eastman identified were the economic planners and the rebels against all authority, who were drawn to socialism's promise of human equality.

31. Harry F. Ward, "Progress or Decadence?" in *Recent Gains in American Civilization: By a Group of Distinguished Critics of Contemporary Life,* ed. Kirby Page (New York: Harcourt, Brace & Co., 1928), 299–300.

32. Ward, "Progress or Decadence?" 300. Donald Meyer, *The Protestant Search for Political Realism, 1919–1941,* 2nd ed. (Middletown, Conn.: Wesleyan University Press, 1988), criticizes Ward harshly for his antimodernism. At one point Meyer goes so far as to refer to Ward's "totalitarianism" (144). It is unclear whether he refers to Ward's totalizing social and spiritual vision or simply, in the style of cold war anticommunists, to his loyalty to the Soviet Union. Hal Draper also takes derisive note of Ward's longing for unity, which Draper terms "communism" (presumably different from "Communism"). Hal Draper, "The Two Souls of Socialism," *New Politics* 5 (Winter 1966): 17–18.

33. Sherwood Eddy, *Russia Today: What Can We Learn from It?* (New York: Farrar & Rinehart, 1934), 179, 177. These quotes are used to great effect against Eddy and Ward in Meyer, *The Protestant Search for Political Realism,* 186–99. See Frank A. Warren III, *Liberals and Communism: The "Red Decade" Revisited* (Bloomington: Indiana University Press, 1966), 23–33, on the importance of the idea of planning among liberals during the 1930s.

34. Harry F. Ward, "Impending Changes in the United States," p. 7, Ward Papers, Series III: Subseries A: Box 2: Folder 13: [Revolution?] II—n.d.

35. Graham, *An Encore for Reform,* 31n12.

36. Kenneth S. Davis, *FDR: The New Deal Years 1933–1937* (New York: Random House, 1986), 56.

37. Schlesinger, *The Politics of Upheaval,* 414. Harold L. Ickes, *The Secret Diary of Harold L. Ickes,* vol. 1: *The First Thousand Days* (New York: Simon & Schuster, 1953), 363 and Davis, *FDR: The New Deal Years,* 508–13 emphasize the May meeting. James MacGregor Burns, *Roosevelt: The Lion and the Fox* (New York: Harcourt, Brace & Co., 1956), 222, 224–26 gives a less momentus account, consistent with the disparaging account that Schlesinger, *The Politics of Upheaval* renders of the Senate progressives.

38. Mulder, *The Insurgent Progressives in the United States Senate and the New Deal,* 301, 274–76; Horowitz, *Beyond Left and Right,* 159.

39. Call for meeting quoted in Millard L. Gieske, *Minnesota Farmer-Laborism: The Third Party Alternative* (Minneapolis: University of Minnesota Press, 1979), 125–26; Westbrook, *John Dewey and American Democracy,* 445–47; and R. Alan Lawson, *The Failure of Independent Liberalism, 1930–1941* (New York: G. P. Putnam's Sons, 1971), 44.

40. Quoted in Gieske, *Minnesota Farmer-Laborism,* 139, 153.

41. Quoted in Nye, *Midwestern Progressive Politics,* 331.

42. Donohue, *Freedom from Want,* 192–95. Donohue also argues that thinkers in the LIPA strongly associated these categories with political liberalism.

43. Schlesinger, *The Politics of Upheaval,* 112.

44. Bingham quoted in Donald L. Miller, *The New American Radicalism: Alfred M. Bingham and Non-Marxian Insurgency in the New Deal Era* (Port Washington, N.Y.: Kennikat Press, 1979), 127, 96; Alfred M. Bingham, *Insurgent America: The Revolt of the Middle-Classes* (New York: Harper, 1935), 104–5, 125–26, 177–79. Lawson, *The Failure of Independent Liberalism,* stresses the LIPA's focus on consumers as a constituency.

45. Miller, *New American Radicalism,* 107; Stuart L. Weiss, "Maury Maverick and the Liberal Bloc," *Journal of American History* 57, no. 4 (March 1971): 884n19.

46. Amlie quoted in Miller, *New American Radicalism,* 112; Thomas quoted in Lawson, *The Failure of Independent Liberalism,* 43; Muste quoted in Donald R. McCoy, *Angry Voices: Left-of-Center Politics in the New Deal Era* (Lawrence: University of Kansas Press, 1958), 10. The incident that inflamed Muste was Dewey's public invitation, in late 1930, to Senator George Norris to take over the leadership of the LIPA and the third-party movement. Muste wanted no part of a movement so focused on individual leaders, and certainly not on Republicans or Democrats. The rhetorical flourishes of 1933 did not bring Muste back. Westbrook, *John Dewey and American Democracy,* 447–48.

47. Schlesinger, *The Politics of Upheaval,* 422.

48. See David Brody, "On the Failure of U.S. Radical Politics: A Farmer-Labor Analysis," *Industrial Relations* 22, no. 2 (spring 1983): 141–63.

49. McCoy, *Angry Voices*, 76–77; Schlesinger, *The Politics of Upheaval*, 143–44; Weiss, "Maury Maverick and the Liberal Bloc," 880–95. Gieske, *Minnesota Farmer-Laborism*, 207, states that the second meeting of the caucus, which decided to send out the call for the Chicago conference, included "no senators and only half the congressmen" who had been at the first gathering.

50. Dewey quoted in Nye, *Midwestern Progressive Politics*, 333.

51. One, the American Labor party (ALP), had even been organized at the White House's instigation as a way of gaining support from dissidents in the SP.

52. McCoy, *Angry Voices*, 80.

53. Gieske, *Minnesota Farmer-Laborism*, 188–92; Rexford G. Tugwell, *The Industrial Discipline* (1933), quoted in Paul Douglas, "Rooseveltian Liberalism," in Zinn, *New Deal Thought*, 55. My discussion of the Minnesota party's fortunes draws heavily on Gieske's account and on Richard M. Valelly, *Radicalism in the States: The Minnesota Farmer-Labor Party and the American Political Economy* (Chicago: University of Chicago Press, 1989). Valelly's book is the most sophisticated look at this party, drawing on all the important primary and secondary sources; it takes a more credulous attitude toward the party's "radicalism" than does Gieske's.

54. George H. Mayer, *The Political Career of Floyd B. Olson* (Minneapolis: University of Minnesota Press, 1951), 139–40, 177. The Minnesota state government under Olson's leadership outlawed "yellow-dog" contracts and anti-strike court injunctions; both devices had been targets of union ire for decades. Minnesota also limited women's work hours on industrial jobs to fifty-four hours per week, a measure that today will seem retrograde but which was widely hailed by labor advocates, including many women, at that time as progressive. (In addition to labor-oriented measures and old-age insurance, Olson's administration passed laws aimed at conserving natural resources such as forests.)

55. Floyd B. Olson, "My Political Creed," *Common Sense* 4 (April 1935): 6–7; reprinted as "A New Party to Challenge Capitalism," in Zinn, *New Deal Thought*, 394, 395, 397 (italics in original); Miller, *New American Radicalism*, 121.

56. Gieske, *Minnesota Farmer-Laborism*, 220; Burns, *Roosevelt*, 202. Olson had desired such an arrangement with the national Democratic party in 1932 and according to George H. Mayer so had Roosevelt, but in that year they succeeded only partway in bringing it off. Mayer, *The Political Career of Floyd B. Olson*, 97–102.

57. Ronald Edsforth, *The New Deal: America's Response to the Great Depression* (Malden, Mass.: Blackwell Publishers, 2000), 172, 174–75; Brody, "On the Failure of U.S. Radical Politics."

58. Valelly, *Radicalism in the States*, 117–18, 119–20; Mayer, *The Political Career of Floyd B. Olson*, 250. Even in 1932 Olson experienced defections among the more prosperous farmers of southern Minnesota. Ibid., 116. Olson's share of the vote went from 59.3 percent to 50.6 percent to 44.6 percent, according to Valelly; his analysis reveals that the erosion of his support between 1930 and 1934 occurred largely in rural Minnesota.

59. Gieske, *Minnesota Farmer-Laborism*, 220–22; Schlesinger, *The Politics of Upheaval*, 549. Fine was well known for his study, *Labor and Farmer Parties in the United States* (New York: Rand School of Social Science, 1928).

60. LaFollette's effort, discussed below, was called the National Progressives of America (NPA). My interpretation of the limits of farmer-laborism's viability is quite different from that of Valelly, *Radicalism in the States.* I greatly respect Valelly's work, but I do not see how, in concrete terms, the New Deal "nationalized" American reform politics in a way that prevented the continuation of farmer-laborism in the states where it had been strongest. Part of my difference

with Valelly here is that he leaves unquestioned the "radicalism" to which his book's subtitle refers. Just as important, I conclude that the Roosevelt administration took much of the wind out of farmer-laborism's sails by appeasing the farm half of that movement. One can say that the farmers were paid off to settle down, or one can say that this pacification indicates the bourgeois character of agrarian grievances from start to finish. In either case, this effect has little to do with formal competition between national and state-level political institutions.

61. LaFollette, a plurality winner in each of his three-way gubernatorial general election victories, got 36.2 percent of the vote in 1938, down from 41.2 percent in 1934, and 47.6 percent in 1936. John E. Miller, *Governor Philip F. LaFollette, the Wisconsin Progressives, and the New Deal* (Columbia: University of Missouri Press, 1982), 159–60. (He was first elected governor in 1930 while running as a Republican; the tough race then was in the primary, and he won the general election easily against a weak Democratic opponent. Ibid., 11–12.)

62. Miller, *Governor Philip F. LaFollette,* 81, 85–86, 113; Schlesinger, *The Politics of Upheaval,* 107.

63. See Hyman Berman, "Political Antisemitism in Minnesota during the Great Depression," *Jewish Social Studies* 38, nos. 3/4 (summer/fall 1976): 247–64.

64. Henry A. Wallace, "The New Farm Act: Balanced Abundance for Farm and City," *Vital Speeches of the Day* 4 (15 March 1938): 338–40, reprinted as "A Defense of the New Deal Farm Program" in Zinn, *New Deal Thought,* 238. For more detail on farm policy, see Theodore Saloutos, "New Deal Agricultural Policy: An Evaluation," *Journal of American History* 61, no. 2 (September 1974): 394–416; and Anthony J. Badger, *The New Deal: The Depression Years, 1933–40* (New York: Hill and Wang, 1989), chapter 4. On NRA code restrictions on production, see Ellis W. Hawley, *The New Deal and the Problem of Monopoly: A Study in Economic Ambivalence* (Princeton, N.J.: Princeton University Press, 1966), 60–61. The NRA's actual success in reining in production is a somewhat murkier matter.

65. Miller, *Governor Philip F. LaFollette,* 134.

66. Davis, *FDR: The New Deal Years,* 606.

67. Schlesinger, *The Politics of Upheaval,* 519–23, 563.

68. Murray Kempton, *Part of Our Time: Some Ruins and Monuments of the Thirties* (1955; New York: Dell, 1967), 337.

69. Irving Howe, *Sherwood Anderson* (n.l.: William Sloane Associates, Inc., 1951), 219.

70. Bingham quoted in Miller, *New American Radicalism,* 133.

71. Michael J. Webber, *New Deal Fat Cats: Business, Labor, and Campaign Finance in the 1936 Presidential Election* (New York: Fordham University Press, 2000), 114–15; David Plotke, *Building a Democratic Political Order: Reshaping American Liberalism in the 1930s and 1940s* (Cambridge: Cambridge University Press, 1996), 98–99, 152, 154–55; William E. Leuchtenburg, *Franklin D. Roosevelt and the New Deal, 1932–1940* (New York: Harper & Row, 1963), 188. The most complete accounting of labor contributions to the Democrats in 1936 is in Webber, *New Deal Fat Cats*; he states that over $470,000 of the industrial union movement's total contribution came from the UMWA (116). Plotke, *Building a Democratic Political Order* argues that support within the labor movement of the 1930s for a radical restructuring of the U.S. economy and society was modest, and that the New Deal that Roosevelt offered to labor fit well with dominant working-class demands.

72. Miller, *Governor Philip F. LaFollette,* 153. The best discussions of the indus-

trial expansion bill are in Schlesinger, *The Politics of Upheaval*, 215–18; and Miller, *New American Radicalism*, 139–41.

73. Edsforth, *The New Deal*, 280–81; Burns, *Roosevelt*, 360–64. Curiously, Burns states that the GOP gained eighty-two seats in 1938, while Leuchtenburg, *Franklin D. Roosevelt and the New Deal*, 271, gives the number as eighty-one. One thing of which we can be certain is that the Republicans saw an increase of seventy-five. The Republicans had secured 117 seats in the lower chamber in the 1932 elections, 103 in 1934, and an embarrassing 89 in 1936. Edsforth, *The New Deal*, 72, 76; Leuchtenburg, *Franklin D. Roosevelt and the New Deal*, 116.

74. Edsforth, *The New Deal*, 153, figure 7.2; Leuchtenburg, *Franklin D. Roosevelt and the New Deal*, 271n57.

75. Lucille Milner, *The Education of an American Liberal* (New York: Horizon Press, 1954), 193; Burns, *Roosevelt*, 270; Schlesinger, *The Politics of Upheaval*, 597. Wald and Peabody, a philanthropist, were co-chairmen of the Good Neighbor League, which supposedly existed in twenty states.

76. Plotke, *Building a Democratic Political Order*, 114 (and see 114n54), 158–61.

77. An early statement of this view was offered in Paul H. Douglas, "Rooseveltian Liberalism," the LIPA leader's review of Rexford G. Tugwell, *The Industrial Discipline*, in *The Nation* 136 (21 June 1933), reprinted in Zinn, *New Deal Thought*, 54–55. John Kenneth Galbraith, *American Capitalism: The Concept of Countervailing Power* (Boston: Houghton Mifflin, 1952) is a later elaboration.

78. See Badger, *The New Deal*, 245–83.

79. Burns, *Roosevelt*, 202; Schlesinger, *The Politics of Upheaval*, 422; Leuchtenburg, *Franklin D. Roosevelt and the New Deal*, 190. Schlesinger, *The Politics of Upheaval*, 346–52, 375–80; and Plotke, *Building a Democratic Political Order*, 136–38, 140, analyze Roosevelt's failings as a party leader. Badger argues there was little Roosevelt could do to remake his party. See Badger, *The New Deal*, 298, for a clear statement.

80. Frances Fox Piven and Richard A. Cloward, *Poor People's Movements: Why They Succeed, How They Fail* (New York: Vintage Books, 1979), 41–95.

81. Schlesinger, *The Politics of Upheaval*, 15–180, passim.

Chapter 4

1. Quoted in Sanford Lakoff, *Max Lerner: Pilgrim in the Promised Land* (Chicago: University of Chicago Press, 1998), 100.

2. Corliss Lamont, *You Might Like Socialism: A Way of Life for Modern Man* (New York: Modern Age Books, 1939).

3. Ronald Edsforth, *The New Deal: America's Response to the Great Depression* (Malden, Mass.: Blackwell Publishers, 2000), 255.

4. Bruce Nelson, *Workers on the Waterfront: Seamen, Longshoremen, and Unionism in the 1930s* (Urbana: University of Illinois Press, 1988), 253.

5. Mark Naison, "Remaking America: Communists and Liberals in the Popular Front," in *New Studies in the Politics and Culture of U.S. Communism*, ed. Michael E. Brown, Randy Martin, Frank Rosengarten, and George Snedeker (New York: Monthly Review Press, 1993), 49; Roger Keeran, "The Communist Influence on American Labor," in ibid., 181, 182. Naison's excellent essay is the best short survey of the Popular Front.

6. Naison, "Remaking America," 52–53, 54.

7. Keeran, "The Communist Influence," 178.

8. Ronald L. Filippelli and Mark D. McColloch, *Cold War in the Working Class:*

The Rise and Decline of the United Electrical Workers (Albany: State University of New York Press, 1995), 85. They offer the one-third figure, adding the memberships of eighteen CIO unions that, they state, Communists "led or were dominant partners in the leadership of." Keeran, "The Communist Influence," 190, citing David Milton, *The Politics of U.S. Labor* (New York: Monthly Review Press, 1982), yields the one-half figure, splitting that proportion evenly between "Communist-controlled unions" and those "where the Communists had substantial influence."

9. Mark Naison, "Remaking America," 67–68; Dorothy Healey and Maurice Isserman, *Dorothy Healey Remembers: A Life in the American Communist Party* (New York: Oxford University Press, 1990), 74.

10. This is the argument of Steve Fraser, *Labor Will Rule: Sidney Hillman and the Rise of American Labor* (New York: Free Press, 1991), and is expressed concisely in Steve Fraser, "The 'Labor Question,'" in *The Rise and Fall of the New Deal Order, 1930–1980,* ed. Steve Fraser and Gary Gerstle (Princeton, N.J.: Princeton University Press, 1989), 55–84.

11. See Kevin Boyle, *The UAW and the Heyday of American Liberalism, 1945–1968* (Ithaca, N.Y.: Cornell University Press, 1995), 29–31 for a concise account.

12. Local studies such as Robin D. G. Kelley, *Hammer and Hoe: Alabama Communists during the Great Depression* (Chapel Hill: University of North Carolina Press, 1990); Michael K. Honey, *Southern Labor and Black Civil Rights: Organizing Memphis Workers* (Urbana: University of Illinois Press, 1993); Robert R. Korstad, *Civil Rights Unionism: Tobacco Workers and the Struggle for Democracy in the Mid-Twentieth-Century South* (Chapel Hill: University of North Carolina Press, 2003); Rick Halpern, *Down on the Killing Floor: Black and White Workers in Chicago's Packinghouses, 1904–1954* (Urbana: University of Illinois Press, 1997); and Daniel Letwin, *The Challenge of Interracial Unionism: Alabama Coal Miners, 1878–1921* (Chapel Hill: University of North Carolina Press, 1998) establish the general picture. Judicious overviews can be found in Eric Arnesen, "Passion and Politics: Race and the Writing of Working-Class History," *The Journal of the Historical Society* 6, no. 3 (September 2006): 323–56; Eric Arnesen, "Following the Color Line of Labor: Black Workers and the Labor Movement before 1930," *Radical History Review* 55 (winter 1993): 53–87; and Bruce Nelson, *Divided We Stand: American Workers and the Struggle for Black Equality* (Princeton, N.J.: Princeton University Press, 2001).

13. Quoted in Richard Iton, *Solidarity Blues: Race, Culture, and the American Left* (Chapel Hill: University of North Carolina Press, 2000), 119. Iton argues that this sentiment represents an elitism that boded ill for the CP's ultimate prospects among African Americans.

14. See Donald H. Grubbs, *Cry from the Cotton: The Southern Tenant Farmers' Union and the New Deal* (Chapel Hill: University of North Carolina Press, 1971).

15. See Nelson Lichtenstein, *The Most Dangerous Man in Detroit: Walter Reuther and the Fate of American Labor* (New York: Basic Books, 1995), 208–11.

16. Quoted in Walter A. Jackson, *Gunnar Myrdal and America's Conscience: Social Engineering and Racial Liberalism, 1938–1987* (Chapel Hill: University of North Carolina Press, 1990), 237.

17. Quoted in David Levering Lewis, *W. E. B. DuBois: The Fight for Equality and the American Century, 1919–1963* (New York: Henry Holt and Company, 2000), 246. Smith had backed out of an agreement he had made with the NAACP leadership to take a vocal position in favor of civil rights in exchange for the group's support in the presidential election. DuBois ended up supporting Norman Thomas.

18. Jonathan Scott Holloway, *Confronting the Veil: Abram Harris Jr., E. Franklin Frazier, and Ralph Bunche, 1919–1941* (Chapel Hill: University of North Carolina Press, 2002), 95, 96, 103. Harris probably had been a CP member somewhat earlier. Abram Harris, Jr. and Sterling D. Spero, *The Black Worker: The Negro and the Labor Movement* (New York: Columbia University Press, 1931).

19. Lewis, *W. E. B. DuBois*, 29, 254–55, 250.

20. Holloway, *Confronting the Veil*, 59–60.

21. See the account offered in Holloway, *Confronting the Veil*, 67–75.

22. Mark Naison, *Communists in Harlem during the Great Depression* (New York: Grove Press, 1983), 177–81, 188.

23. John B. Kirby, *Black Americans in the Roosevelt Era: Liberalism and Race* (Knoxville: University of Tennessee Press, 1980), 166–70, offers a trenchant analysis of the NNC's thwarted hopes. See Beth Tompkins Bates, "A New Crowd Challenges the Old Guard in the NAACP, 1933–1941," *American Historical Review* 102, no. 2 (April 1997): 340–77.

24. Naison, *Communists in Harlem*, 292, 295–97, 310–12; Lawrence S. Wittner, "The National Negro Congress: A Reassessment," *American Quarterly* 22, no. 4 (winter 1970): 883–901.

25. See Mario T. García, *Mexican Americans: Leadership, Ideology, and Identity, 1930–1960* (New Haven, Conn.: Yale University Press, 1989), chapter 6; and Zaragosa Vargas, *Labor Rights Are Civil Rights: Mexican American Workers in Twentieth-Century America* (Princeton, N.J.: Princeton University Press, 2005).

26. See Jessie Lloyd O'Connor, Harvey O'Connor, and Susan M. Bowler, *Harvey and Jessie: A Couple of Radicals* (Philadelphia: Temple University Press, 1988).

27. See Meg Jacobs, *Pocketbook Politics: Economic Citizenship in Twentieth-Century America* (Princeton, N.J.: Princeton University Press, 2005), 156–58; and Landon R. Y. Storrs, *Civilizing Capitalism: The National Consumers' League, Women's Activism, and Labor Standards in the New Deal Era* (Chapel Hill: University of North Carolina Press, 2000).

28. See Gary Gerstle, *American Crucible: Race and Nation in the Twentieth Century* (Princeton, N.J.: Princeton University Press, 2001), chapter 3.

29. Walter Goodman, *The Committee: The Extraordinary Career of the House Un-American Activities Committee* (Baltimore, Md.: Penguin Press, 1969), 70. In the main text, at times I refer to the American League rather than to the ALAWF or the ALPD; despite the name change in 1937, the two groups were identical.

30. Harry F. Ward, "The Development of Fascism in the United States" (pamphlet published by the American League against War and Fascism, 1937), 3, American League for Peace and Democracy Papers (hereafter ALPD Papers), Swarthmore College Peace Collection, Swarthmore College, Swarthmore, Pa. Ward's pamphlet was a reprint of his article of the same title, which appeared in the *Annals of the American Academy of Political and Social Science* 180 (July 1935). Also see Harry F. Ward to L. H. Keeble, 26 October 1934, in Harry F. Ward Papers, Series II: Subseries A: Box 3: Folder 3: General Correspondence—1933–35. "Manifesto and Program of the American League against War and Fascism," Second U.S. Congress against War and Fascism, Chicago, Illinois, 28, 29, and 30 September, 1934, ALPD Papers.

31. *Proceedings, People's Congress for Democracy and Peace, Pittsburgh, Nov. 26–28, 1937: Fourth National Congress, American League for Peace and Democracy*, 13, 9; "Neutrality Legislation: Where We Stand and Why," *Critical Issues*, 1, American League against War and Fascism, both in ALPD Papers.

32. *Proceedings, Fourth National Congress*, 12, ALPD Papers.

33. Harry F. Ward, "Liberalism at the Crisis," *Christian Century* 53, no. 1 (25 March 1936), 463; "Italian Fascist Revolution," 4, in Ward Papers, Series III: Subseries A: Box 2: Folder 12: [Revolution?] I—n.d.; "Impending Changes in the United States," 7, in Ward Papers, Series III: Subseries A: Box 2: Folder 13: [Revolution?] II—n.d. Also see Donald Meyer, *The Protestant Search for Political Realism, 1919–1941*, 2nd ed. (Middletown, Conn.: Wesleyan University Press, 1988), 187.

34. Ward, "Liberalism at the Crisis," 465, 463.

35. Ellen Schrecker, *Many Are the Crimes: McCarthyism in America* (Boston: Little, Brown, 1998). Richard Gid Powers, *Not without Honor: The History of American Anticommunism* (New Haven, Conn.: Yale University Press, 1998), strives mightily to raise the profile of left anticommunists in the interwar period. Yet the far larger grassroots constituency for anticommunism lay on the right.

36. "The Green Light for Liberals," *Christian Advocate* (Pacific edition) 88, no. 52 (28 December 1939), 1244, in Ward papers, Series II: Subseries A: Box 3: Folder 5: General Correspondence—1939–40. This editorial in a Methodist journal attacked Ward very strongly. Ward stressed differences between the Nazis and the Soviets regarding war in his testimony of April 1939 to the U.S. House Committee on Un-American Activities. Harry F. Ward, testimony to the House Committee on Un-American Activities, 3 April 1939, transcript, 25; in Ward Papers, Series II: Subseries A: Box 3: Folder 5: General Correspondence—1939–40.

37. Samuel Walker, *In Defense of American Liberties: A History of the ACLU*, 2nd ed. (Carbondale: Southern Illinois University Press, 1999), 103; on the controversies of the middle 1930s, see ibid., 101–3, 115–18.

38. Ibid., 129; Roger Baldwin to National Committee, American League for Peace and Democracy, 17 October 1939; Roger Baldwin to Harry F. Ward, 6 July 1961. Both in Ward Papers, Series II: Subseries A: Box 3: Folder 16: General Correspondence—Roger Baldwin.

39. August Raymond Ogden, *The Dies Committee: A Study of the Special House Committee for the Investigation of Un-American Activities, 1938–1944* (Washington, D.C.: Catholic University of America Press, 1945), 153–54; Walker, *In Defense of American Liberties*, 129; Robert Cohen, *When the Old Left Was Young: Student Radicals and America's First Mass Student Movement, 1929–1941* (New York: Oxford University Press, 1993), 228–29, 298–304. After Ward's appearance, the HUAC publicized the membership list of the ALPD's Washington, D.C. chapter, which included many U.S. government officials; this action provoked criticism of the committee's excesses. Alson J. Smith, "Death of a League," *New Republic* 102, no. 12 (18 March 1940): 373–74, by the ALPD's last director of religious work, gives a clear account of the ALPD's whimpering demise. See Junius I. Scales and Richard Nickson, *Cause at Heart: A Former Communist Remembers* (Athens: University of Georgia Press, 1987), 118, on the American Peace Mobilization.

40. Walker, *In Defense of American Liberties*, 131–32. Baldwin, Holmes, and Morris Ernst were among the signers of the tribute. George Orwell, *Nineteen Eighty-Four, A Novel* (New York: Harcourt, Brace, 1949).

41. Mary van Kleeck, "Our Illusions Regarding Government," in *Proceedings of the 61st Annual Conference of Social Work* (Chicago: University of Chicago Press, 1934), 473–85, is the text of the famous speech she gave denouncing the New Deal before an audience of social workers in 1934. Van Kleeck still awaits the historian who wishes to tell this story. John Earl Haynes, "The 'Rank and File Movement' in Private Social Work," *Labor History* 16 (winter 1975): 78–98, an

anticommunist account, and Guy Alchon, "Mary van Kleeck and Social-Economic Planning," *Journal of Policy History* 3, no. 1 (1991): 1–23, with a different focus, are the most serious treatments. Mary Ann Brenden, "Mary van Kleeck: Social Worker and Leader," in *From Vision to Action: Social Workers of the Second Generation*, ed. Janice Andrews (St. Paul, Minn.: College of St. Catherine/University of St. Thomas, 1992), 75–88, is laudatory but not deeply analytical.

42. "Fascism: What Is It?" (January 1937), 1, 3, ALPD Papers; "The German Fascist Revolution," 2, Ward papers, Series III: Subseries A: Box 2: Folder 13: [Revolution?] II–n.d.; Ward, "The Development of Fascism," 7. On the importance of the LaFollette committee's work, see Michael Denning, *The Cultural Front: The Laboring of American Culture in the Twentieth Century* (London: Verso Press, 1996), 13–14, 104, 261–62; and Leo Huberman, *The Labor Spy Racket* (New York: Modern Age Books, 1937).

43. Ward, "The Development of Fascism," 8; "Italian Fascist Revolution," 3, Ward papers, Series III: Subseries A: Box 2: Folder 12: [Revolution?] I—n.d. Frank A. Warren, *Liberals and Communism: The "Red Decade" Revisited* (Bloomington: Indiana University Press, 1966), discusses the different theories of fascism that circulated in the 1930s; also see Denning, *The Cultural Front*, 126–27, 375–77; and Arthur M. Schlesinger, Jr., *A Life in the Twentieth Century: Innocent Beginnings, 1917–1950* (Boston: Houghton Mifflin, 2000), 230. In fact, few writers conformed to the pure "Marxist" theory.

44. Ward, "Development of Fascism," 3; Proceedings of the Second U.S. Congress against War and Fascism, Chicago, Ill., Sept. 28–30, 1934, 12, ALPD Papers; *Proceedings, People's Congress for Democracy and Peace, Pittsburgh, Nov. 26–28, 1937: Fourth National Congress, American League for Peace and Democracy*, 29–30, ALPD Papers; Denning, *The Cultural Front*, 13–14; Naison, *Communists in Harlem*, 198, 155–57, 174–75, 195–96. One should not exaggerate the degree of interracialism practiced in the American League, whose top leadership was almost all white (Patterson was an Afro-Caribbean leftist). Still, there was more genuine interracialism and militant antiracism here, and in other organizations of the Popular Front, than was to be found among any of the other largely white liberal groups. Harold Cruse, *The Crisis of the Negro Intellectual* (New York: William Morrow, 1967), argues that the Popular Front was out of touch with African American life.

In March 1937, the American League's national bureau laid plans "to cooperate with the Jewish Peoples Committee for United Action Against Fascism and Anti-Semitism in protesting against the attack upon the Jews in Poland." National Bureau Minutes, American League against War and Fascism, March 22, 1937, 1, ALPD Papers. This was merely one among several issues on which the American League worked in solidarity with domestic and foreign groups concerning foreign oppression. Spanish, Chinese, and Japanese activists typically spoke at the league's annual congresses.

45. Scales and Nickson, *Cause at Heart*, 61.

46. See Dan Geary, "Carey McWilliams and Antifascism, 1934–1943," *Journal of American History* 90, no. 3 (December 2003): 912–34.

47. Stephen Wise, "Parallel Between Hitlerism and the Persecution of Negroes," *Crisis* (May 1934): 127–29; Lewis, *W. E. B. DuBois*, 398, 399, 400.

48. Michael Reisch and Janice Andrews, *The Road Not Taken: A History of Radical Social Work in the United States* (Philadelphia: Brunner-Routledge, 2001), 109.

49. Scales and Nickson, *Cause at Heart*, 66; Naison, *Communists in Harlem*, 216, 303.

50. Ruth Feldstein, *Motherhood in Black and White: Race and Sex in American Liberalism, 1930–1985* (Ithaca, N.Y.: Cornell University Press, 2000), 37, 38. Ickes surely was also concerned to frame proposals for government assistance to African Americans in a way that would disarm white opposition.

51. Naison, *Communists in Harlem*, 216–17. On intercultural education and its links to later multicultural thought, see Stuart Svonkin, *Jews against Prejudice: American Jews and the Fight for Civil Liberties* (New York: Columbia University Press, 1997), chapter 3; and Daryl Scott, "Postwar Pluralism, *Brown v. Board of Education*, and the Origins of Multicultural Education," *Journal of American History* 91, no. 1 (June 2004): 69–82.

52. Paul Milkman, *PM: A New Deal in Journalism, 1940–1948* (New Brunswick, N.J.: Rutgers University Press, 1997). *PM* articulated a no-enemies-to-the-left position but, while it was red-baited consistently, it was not under the CP's thumb, as the timing of its establishment indicates. It started publishing during the time of the Nazi-Soviet pact, and combined Popular Front advocacy with an interventionist stance on the war at a moment when the CP was in its "peace" phase. See Mark L. Kleinman, *A World of Hope, a World of Fear: Henry A. Wallace, Reinhold Niebuhr, and American Liberalism* (Columbus: Ohio State University Press, 2000); and Geary, "Carey McWilliams and Antifascism" for good discussions of the concept's currency among liberals at this time.

53. Morton Sosna, *In Search of the Silent South: Southern Liberals and the Race Issue* (New York: Columbia University Press, 1977), 116–20. In 1944 a volume entitled *What the Negro Wants* was published, consisting of essays by black thinkers and activists involved in or inspired by the meeting in Durham. Rayford W. Logan, ed., *What the Negro Wants* (Chapel Hill: University of North Carolina Press, 1945). According to David R. Goldfield, W. T. Couch, the director of the University of North Carolina Press and a noted white liberal, "persuaded Logan to tone down his introduction and published the work . . . with a minimum of publicity." Goldfield, *Black, White, and Southern: Race Relations and Southern Culture, 1940 to the Present* (Baton Rouge: Louisiana State University Press, 1990), 42. Sosna notes that Couch actually penned a "publisher's introduction" for *What the Negro Wants*, in which he wrote that desegregation would be "disastrous for everyone and more so for the Negro than the white man." Sosna, *In Search of the Silent South*, 111.

54. Sosna, *In Search of the Silent South*, 146–49, 163; Goldfield, *Black, White, and Southern*, 50–51.

55. Scales and Nickson, *Cause at Heart*, 170, 172.

56. Ibid., 172.

57. See William H. Chafe, *Never Stop Running: Allard Lowenstein and the Struggle to Save American Liberalism* (New York: Basic Books, 1993), 88–92; Samuel Lubell, *The Future of American Politics*, 3rd ed. (New York: Harper Colophon, 1965), 106–13.

58. Louis Martin, "To Be or Not to Be a Liberal," *Crisis* 49 (1942): 285, quoted in Patricia Sullivan, *Days of Hope: Race and Democracy in the New Deal Era* (Chapel Hill: University of North Carolina Press, 1996), 166; Transcript, Louis Martin Oral History Interview I, 14 May 1969, by David G. McComb, Internet Copy, Lyndon Baines Johnson Library, 2–3.

59. Thomas Sancton, "A Southern View of the Race Question," *Negro Quarterly* (January 1943): 197–206, quoted in Sullivan, *Days of Hope*, 166.

60. See Thomas J. Sugrue, "Crabgrass-Roots Politics: Race, Rights, and the Reaction against Liberalism in the Urban North, 1940–1964," *Journal of American History* 82, no. 2 (September 1995): 551–78.

61. See Eric Foner, *The Story of American Freedom* (New York: W. W. Norton & Co., 1998), 236–47.

62. Dorothy Healey and Maurice Isserman, *Dorothy Healey Remembers: A Life in the American Communist Party* (New York: Oxford University Press, 1990), 91; Geary, "Carey McWilliams and Antifascism"; Filippelli and McCulloch, *Cold War in the Working Class*, 75; Iton, *Solidarity Blues*, 66.

63. Walter A. Jackson, *Gunnar Myrdal and America's Conscience: Social Engineering and Racial Liberalism, 1938–1987*, 279–80; Gerstle, *American Crucible*, chapter 4. Also see Svonkin, *Jews against Prejudice*, and Lawrence A. Cremin, *The Transformation of the School: Progressivism in American Education, 1876–1957* (New York: Alfred A. Knopf, 1961).

64. Jackson, *Gunnar Myrdal and America's Conscience*, 281.

65. Ibid., 281.

66. Chafe, *Never Stop Running*, 43–44.

67. Gunnar Myrdal, *An American Dilemma: The Negro Problem and Modern Democracy* (New York: Harper & Brothers, 1944).

68. Jackson, *Gunnar Myrdal and America's Conscience*, 130.

69. Elizabeth Faue, *Community of Suffering and Struggle: Women, Men, and the Labor Movement in Minneapolis, 1915–1945* (Chapel Hill: University of North Carolina Press, 1991); Barbara Melosh, *Engendering Culture: Manhood and Womanhood in New Deal Public Art and Theater* (Washington, D.C.: Smithsonian Institution Press, 1991).

70. John R. Dos Passos, *The Big Money* (New York: Harcourt, Brace, 1936). See Elizabeth Gurley Flynn, *The Rebel Girl: An Autobiography—My First Life (1906–1926)* (1955; New York: International Publishers, 1973), for information on the most famous "rebel girl," for whom Joe Hill wrote the song of that title.

71. Daniel Horowitz, *Betty Friedan and the Making of* The Feminine Mystique: *The American Left, the Cold War, and Modern Feminism* (Amherst: University of Massachusetts Press, 1998); Kate Weigand, *Red Feminism: American Communism and the Making of Women's Liberation* (Baltimore, Md.: Johns Hopkins University Press, 2001); Daniel Horowitz, "Feminism, Women's History, and American Social Thought at Midcentury," in *American Capitalism: Social Thought and Political Economy in the Twentieth Century*, ed. Nelson Lichtenstein (Philadelphia: University of Pennsylvania Press, 2006), 191–209.

72. Horowitz, *Betty Friedan*, 50–53; Betty Friedan, *The Feminine Mystique* (1963; New York: Dell Publishing, 1964), chapter 12.

73. For the story of one feminist who rejected these choices, see Ellen Carol DuBois, *Harriot Stanton Blatch and the Winning of Woman Suffrage* (New Haven, Conn.: Yale University Press, 1997). Nancy Woloch, ed., *Muller v. Oregon: A Brief History with Documents* (Boston: Bedford Books/St. Martin's Press, 1996), offers a fine overview of the debates over protective legislation.

74. Weigand, *Red Feminism*, 31, 58.

75. Ibid., 73–74. The quotation is from a pamphlet written in 1947 by Elizabeth Gurley Flynn for the CP; according to Weigand, her list of demands was identical to that advanced by the CAW.

76. Weigand, *Red Feminism*, 60.

77. Gerda Lerner, *Fireweed: A Political Autobiography* (Philadelphia: Temple University Press, 2002), 233–34, 258–61, 323–24; Ellen C. Du Bois, "Eleanor Flexner and the History of American Feminism," *Gender and History* 3 (spring 1991): 81–90.

78. Horowitz, *Betty Friedan,* 129. Elizabeth Hawes, *Why Women Cry* (New York: Reynal & Hitchcock, 1943); Elizabeth Hawes, *Hurry Up, Please, It's Time* (New York: Reynal & Hitchcock, 1946).

79. See Ward's introduction to Pat Sloan, *Russia without Illusions: Seven Years in the Soviet Union* (New York: Modern Age Books, 1939).

80. Frank A. Warren, *Noble Abstractions: American Liberal Intellectuals and World War II* (Columbus: Ohio State University Press, 1999), 192–93.

81. Ibid., 166–69.

82. See James T. Kloppenberg, *The Virtues of Liberalism* (New York: Oxford University Press, 2000), chapter 7.

83. Norman D. Markowitz, *The Rise and Fall of the People's Century: Henry A. Wallace and American Liberalism, 1941–1948* (New York: The Free Press, 1973), 48–49.

84. Quoted in Kirby, *Black Americans in the Roosevelt Era,* 52.

85. Warren, *Noble Abstractions,* 79.

86. A memorable fictionalized version of the shenanigans at the convention is provided in Gore Vidal, *The Golden Age: A Novel* (New York: Doubleday, 2000). Vidal may get that part of the story right, but his insistence that Wallace was Roosevelt's only genuine legatee represents a rather surprising triumph of sentimentality over accuracy.

87. Sullivan, *Days of Hope,* 183, 187, 186.

88. Sosna, *In Search of the Silent South,* 165.

89. Virginia F. Durr, *Outside the Magic Circle: The Autobiography of Virginia Foster Durr,* ed. Hollinger F. Barnard (University: University of Alabama Press), 190–91.

90. Sullivan, *Days of Hope,* 240, 242–43. This effort to compete with the SCHW in the South was rather odd, since in Washington and New York it was clearly understood that the ADA was conceived as an organization of well-placed politicos and intellectuals, not as a mass-based pressure group.

91. Warren, *Noble Abstractions,* 111, 194, 200.

92. Steven M. Gillon, *Politics and Vision: The ADA and American Liberalism, 1947–1985* (New York: Oxford University Press, 1987), 33; Markowitz, *The Rise and Fall of the People's Century,* 294. Kleinman, *A World of Hope, a World of Fear,* observes the prominence of the theme of fascism in the rhetoric of Wallace and the Progressive party.

93. Warren, *Noble Abstractions,* 242; Lakoff, *Max Lerner,* 144. Even at that time, Lerner worried about "Communist control" over Popular Front groups, and he became increasingly critical of Wallace's relationship with CP cadres in 1948. He voted for Norman Thomas for president in that year.

94. Jennifer A. Delton, *Making Minnesota Liberal: Civil Rights and the Transformation of the Democratic Party* (Minneapolis: University of Minnesota Press, 2002), 138–43, 153; Lubell, *The Future of American Politics,* 200–201.

95. Quoted in Sullivan, *Days of Hope,* 271.

96. Gillon, *Politics and Vision,* 48–50. Jennifer Delton notes that this was another attempt at cooptation of the near left by Humphrey, for in Minnesota many would have noticed that the rhetorical formula "civil rights over states' rights" echoed the Farmer-Labor party's old slogan "human rights over property rights." Humphrey thus suggested that he had that old-time religion while shifting the issue from capitalism to racism. Delton, *Making Minnesota Liberal,* 120.

97. Markowitz, *The Rise and Fall of the People's Century,* 296.

Chapter 5

1. Simone de Beauvoir, *America Day by Day,* trans. Carol Cosman (Berkeley: University of California Press, 1999), 42.

2. Quoted in Robbie Lieberman, *The Strangest Dream: Communism, Anticommunism, and the U.S. Peace Movement, 1945–1963* (Syracuse, N.Y.: Syracuse University Press, 2000), 39.

3. Quoted in Carol Polsgrove, *Divided Minds: Intellectuals and the Civil Rights Movement* (New York: W. W. Norton & Co., 2001), 89.

4. Arthur M. Schlesinger, Jr., *The Vital Center: The Politics of Freedom* (Boston: Houghton Mifflin, 1949); Humphrey quoted in Ellen Schrecker, *Many Are the Crimes: McCarthyism in America* (Boston: Little, Brown, 1998), 144.

5. Nelson Lichtenstein, *The Most Dangerous Man in Detroit: Walter Reuther and the Fate of American Labor* (New York: Basic Books, 1995), 309.

6. Ronald L. Filippelli and Mark D. McColloch, *Cold War in the Working Class: The Rise and Decline of the United Electrical Workers* (Albany: State University of New York Press, 1995), 121–22, 147.

7. Nelson Lichtenstein, *State of the Union: A Century of American Labor* (Princeton, N.J.: Princeton University Press, 2002), 117. See Patrick Renshaw, *American Labor and Consensus Capitalism, 1935–1985* (Jackson: University Press of Mississippi, 1991); Steven Rosswurm, ed., *The CIO's Left-Led Unions* (New Brunswick, N.J.: Rutgers University Press, 1992); and Robert H. Zieger, *The CIO, 1935–1955* (Chapel Hill: University of North Carolina Press, 1995).

8. The most memorable treatment remains Victor S. Navasky, *Naming Names* (New York: Viking Press, 1980).

9. Schrecker, *Many Are the Crimes,* 327.

10. On *High Noon,* see Paul Buhle and Dave Wagner, *Radical Hollywood: The Untold Story Behind America's Favorite Movies* (New York: The New Press, 2002), 416–21.

11. See M. J. Heale, *McCarthy's Americans: Red Scare Politics in State and Nation, 1935–1965* (Athens: University of Georgia Press, 1998), chapters 1–2.

12. Schrecker, *Many Are the Crimes,* 97; Ellen Schrecker, *No Ivory Tower: McCarthyism and the Universities* (New York: Oxford University Press, 1986).

13. Richard H. Pells, *The Liberal Mind in a Conservative Age: American Intellectuals in the 1940s and 1950s* (New York: Harper & Row, 1985), 288.

14. Pells, *The Liberal Mind in a Conservative Age,* 291; Sidney Hook, *Heresy, Yes: Conspiracy, No!* (New York: J. Day Co., 1953).

15. Morris Dickstein, *Gates of Eden: American Culture in the Sixties* (New York: Basic Books, 1977), 29.

16. Pells, *The Liberal Mind in a Conservative Age,* 338.

17. Andrew Ross, *No Respect: Intellectuals and Popular Culture* (New York: Routledge, 1989) offers a rigorous analysis of the campaign against the Rosenbergs within the liberal-left intelligentsia.

18. Dorothy Healey and Maurice Isserman, *Dorothy Healey Remembers: A Life in the American Communist Party* (New York: Oxford University Press, 1990), 105, 108, 113, 147.

19. William W. Keller, *The Liberals and J. Edgar Hoover: Rise and Fall of a Domestic Intelligence State* (Princeton, N.J.: Princeton University Press, 1989); Heale, *McCarthy's Americans,* chapter 6.

20. Pells, *The Liberal Mind in a Conservative Age,* 294. The novel McCarthy had

written satirizing the alleged victims of (Joseph) McCarthyism was *The Groves of Academe* (New York: Harcourt, Brace, 1952). On Mary McCarthy, who had begun as a Trotskyist and would lean once again to the left during the Vietnam War, see Carol Brightman, *Writing Dangerously: Mary McCarthy and Her World* (New York: C. Potter, 1992).

21. Pells, *The Liberal Mind in a Conservative Age*, 343–44.

22. Junius Irving Scales and Richard Nickson, *Cause at Heart: A Former Communist Remembers* (Athens: University of Georgia Press, 1987), xxiii, 357–58, 368.

23. Stephen J. Whitfield, *The Culture of the Cold War*, 2nd ed. (Baltimore, Md.: Johns Hopkins University Press, 1996), 219.

24. Maurice Isserman, *The Other American: The Life of Michael Harrington* (New York: Public Affairs, 2000), 146, 168–69.

25. John D'Emilio, *Lost Prophet: The Life and Times of Bayard Rustin* (New York: Free Press, 2003), 251–52; Jervis Anderson, *Bayard Rustin: Troubles I've Seen: A Biography* (New York: HarperCollins, 1997), 202–5. On such efforts generally, see Maurice Isserman, *If I Had a Hammer . . . : The Death of the Old Left and the Birth of the New Left* (New York: Basic Books, 1987).

26. See Lieberman, *Strangest Dream*, chapter 6.

27. Ever since a young Allard Lowenstein, in the early 1950s, had crusaded successfully to align the NSA with the U.S. government's foreign policy regarding the cold war, the CIA had viewed the group as a useful tool in propaganda combat with the global left, and as a recruiting ground for idealistic and ambitious young people, such as Gloria Steinem, whom it could use as assets. Maurice Isserman and Michael Kazin, *America Divided: The Civil War of the 1960s*, 2nd ed. (New York: Oxford University Press, 2004), 54–55; William H. Chafe, *Never Stop Running: Allard Lowenstein and the Struggle to Save American Liberalism* (New York: Basic Books, 1993), 92–108, 254–56.

28. During World War II, Alinsky's Back of the Yards Neighborhood Council pursued a heated conflict with a traditional social-work settlement house, the University of Chicago Settlement, over control of social-service resources. In the course of this battle Alinsky expressed contempt for conventional social-work liberals, calling them elitist "do-gooders" who wished to improve urban working people rather than to stand in true solidarity with them. This explanation of the anti-liberal antipathy expressed in *Reveille* is speculation. The biography by Sanford Horwitt, the only substantial study of Alinsky, does not seek to explain this matter.

A social-work "do-gooder" presumably would have offered a contrast with the politically engaged social workers of the 1930s, who included Alinsky's wife, Helene. She had been the president of a social workers' union during the Great Depression and a member of the American League for Peace and Democracy, and perhaps she influenced him. But he always maintained a safe distance from such controversial groups and efforts, one reason why later efforts to red-bait him failed. (His friendship with important officials of the Roman Catholic Church in Chicago protected him as well.) Sanford D. Horwitt, *Let Them Call Me Rebel: Saul Alinsky, His Life and Legacy* (New York: Vintage Books, 1989), 46, 63, 130, 135–43.

29. Saul D. Alinsky, *Reveille for Radicals* (1946; New York: Vintage Books, 1989), 3, 6, 13, 19.

30. Ibid., 24, 26–27, 29, 33–34.

31. Alinsky became close to Lewis starting in the late 1930s and wrote an admiring biography of him, published in 1949. Saul Alinsky, *John L. Lewis: An*

Unauthorized Biography (New York: G. P. Putnam's Sons, 1949). Despite the book's subtitle, Lewis cooperated extensively with Alinsky during the writing of the biography. Vernon L. Parrington, *Main Currents in American Thought: An Interpretation of American Literature from the Beginnings to 1920* (New York: Harcourt, Brace and Co., 1930); Will Durant and Ariel Durant, *The Story of Civilization* (New York: Simon and Schuster, 1935–75).

32. Horwitt, *Let Them Call Me Rebel*, 535. The book under review was Saul D. Alinsky, *Rules for Radicals: A Practical Primer for Realistic Radicals* (New York: Random House, 1971), Alinsky's effort to remain current.

33. Robert A. Dahl, *Who Governs?: Democracy and Power in an American City* (New Haven, Conn.: Yale University Press, 1961); Clark Kerr, *Industrialism and Industrial Man: The Problems of Labor and Management in Economic Growth* (Cambridge, Mass.: Harvard University Press, 1960); and Seymour Martin Lipset, *Political Man: The Social Bases of Politics* (Garden City, N.Y.: Doubleday, 1960), are pluralist classics. See Howard Brick, *Age of Contradiction: American Thought and Culture in the 1960s* (Ithaca, N.Y.: Cornell University Press, 2000), 18–22; Lichtenstein, *State of the Union*, 148–56; and Pells, *The Liberal Mind in a Conservative Age*, 142–47, 178, 243–44. See Dorothy Ross, *The Origins of American Social Science* (Cambridge: Cambridge University Press, 1991), chapters 9–10, on the earlier period.

34. Charles A. Beard, *An Economic Interpretation of the Constitution of the United States* (New York: Macmillan Co., 1913); Charles A. Beard and Mary R. Beard, *The Rise of American Civilization* (New York: Macmillan, 1933).

35. Daniel Bell, *Marxian Socialism in the United States* (1952; Ithaca, N.Y.: Cornell University Press, 1996); Daniel Bell, *The End of Ideology: On the Exhaustion of Political Ideas in the Fifties* (Glencoe, Ill.: The Free Press, 1960); Howard Brick, *Daniel Bell and the Decline of Intellectual Radicalism: Social Theory and Political Reconciliation in the 1940s* (Madison: University of Wisconsin Press, 1986).

36. Dwight Macdonald, "The Root Is Man," *politics* 3 (July 1946): 97–115; Dwight Macdonald, "The Root Is Man, Part Two," *politics* 3 (October 1946): 194–214. See Gregory D. Sumner, *Dwight Macdonald and the* politics *Circle: The Challenge of Cosmopolitan Democracy* (Ithaca, N.Y.: Cornell University Press, 1996).

37. Quoted in Michael Wreszin, *A Rebel in Defense of Tradition: The Life and Politics of Dwight Macdonald* (New York: Basic Books, 1994), 177.

38. Ibid., 200–01. Macdonald wrote a two-part article on Wallace in *politics* in 1947. Dwight Macdonald, "Henry Wallace," *politics* 4 (March/April 1947): 33–44; Dwight Macdonald, "Henry Wallace," *politics* 4 (May/June 1947): 96–117. He published the articles as a pamphlet in 1948. Dwight Macdonald, *Henry Wallace, the Man and the Myth* (New York: Vanguard Press, 1948).

39. Wreszin, *A Rebel in Defense of Tradition*, 114, 138, 161.

40. Gabriel Breton, "The Ideology of the Person," *New University Thought* 2 (1962), quoted in Kevin Mattson, *Intellectuals in Action: The Origins of the New Left and Radical Liberalism, 1945–1970* (University Park: Pennsylvania State University Press, 2002), 249. New left thought shifted back and forth between disdain of ideology, reflecting liberal thought of the 1950s, and statements of the need for an ideology.

41. Theodore Roszak, *Sources: An Anthology of Contemporary Materials Useful for Preserving Personal Sanity While Braving the Great Technological Wilderness* (New York: Harper Colophon Books, 1972), ix; Theodore Roszak, *The Making of a Counter-Culture: Reflections on the Technocratic Society and Its Youthful Opposition* (New York: Doubleday, 1969).

42. Wreszin, *A Rebel in Defense of Tradition,* 176.

43. Isserman, *If I Had a Hammer . . .*, chapters 3–4, discusses these left groupings splendidly. Also see Irving Howe, *A Margin of Hope: An Intellectual Autobiography* (San Diego, Calif.: Harcourt Brace Jovanovich, 1982); and David T. Dellinger, *From Yale to Jail: The Life Story of a Moral Dissenter* (New York: Pantheon Books, 1993).

44. See Dan Geary, "The 'Union of the Power and the Intellect': C. Wright Mills and the Labor Movement," *Labor History* 42, no. 4 (2001): 327–45. As Geary discusses, Mills during the 1940s worked to forge or maintain a dissident labor-led movement. I see Mills as less than sanguine about the potential fruits of these efforts even then, despite his political efforts at that time. Geary's forthcoming study, *C. Wright Mills* (Berkeley: University of California Press), finally will give us a full-length intellectual biography worthy of his subject.

45. Max Weber, "Science as a Vocation," in *From Max Weber: Essays in Sociology,* ed. H. H. Gerth and C. Wright Mills (New York: Oxford University Press, 1946), 155. Of course, Weber described those who "cannot" do what these moral sympathizers with Mills could. According to this volume's preface, Gerth did the translation, Mills the editing of the English-language text. Ibid., vii. C. Wright Mills, *The New Men of Power: America's Labor Leaders* (New York: Harcourt, Brace, 1948); C. Wright Mills, *White Collar: The American Middle Classes* (New York: Oxford University Press, 1951); C. Wright Mills, *The Power Elite* (New York: Oxford University Press, 1956).

46. C. Wright Mills, "Letter to the New Left," *New Left Review,* 5 (September–October 1960): 18–23.

47. Van Gosse, *Where the Boys Are: Cuba, Cold War America, and the Making of a New Left* (London: Verso, 1993).

48. David Halberstam, *The Best and the Brightest* (New York: Fawcett Crest Books, 1973), 291; on Schlesinger's use of the term "radicalism," see Kyle A. Cuordileone, *Manhood and American Political Culture in the Cold War* (New York: Routledge, 2005), 29–31.

49. Percival Goodman and Paul Goodman, *Communitas: Means of Livelihood and Ways of Life* (Chicago: University of Chicago Press, 1947); David Riesman with Nathan Glazer and Reuel Denney, *The Lonely Crowd: A Study of the Changing American Character* (1950; New Haven, Conn.: Yale University Press, 1961), 304–7; David Riesman, "Some Observations on Community Plans and Utopia," in *Selected Essays from* Individualism Reconsidered (Garden City, N.Y.: Doubleday/Anchor Books, 1955), 67–104.

Riesman himself moved from the American Committee for Cultural Freedom to genteel peace advocacy in the late 1950s, using as a vehicle the Committees of Correspondence, named with a patriotic flourish, which he helped to establish in connection with the American Friends Service Committee. On Riesman and *The Lonely Crowd,* see the superb discussion in Wilfred M. McClay, *The Masterless: Self and Society in Modern America* (Chapel Hill: University of North Carolina Press, 1994), 236–57, 265–68.

50. John Kenneth Galbraith, *The Affluent Society* (Boston: Houghton Mifflin, 1958). For an early serious effort to link the two eras, see Laurence R. Veysey, *The Communal Experience: Anarchist and Mystical Counter-Cultures in America* (New York: Harper & Row, 1973).

51. Kevin Boyle, *The UAW and the Heyday of American Liberalism, 1945–1968* (Ithaca, N.Y.: Cornell University Press, 1995), 158–60; Peter B. Levy, *The New Left and Labor in the 1960s* (Urbana: University of Illinois Press, 1994); Wreszin, *A Rebel in Defense of Tradition,* 371–74.

52. Michael Harrington, *The Other America: Poverty in the United States* (New York: Macmillan, 1962).

53. In 1947, CORE embarked on the "Journey of Reconciliation," sending biracial groups of riders on interstate bus lines in the South to protest continuing segregation in the transportation system. James Farmer, *Lay Bare the Heart: An Autobiography of the Civil Rights Movement* (New York: Arbor House, 1985); and D'Emilio, *Lost Prophet*, 54–56, 62–63, 133–40.

54. Quoted in Todd Gitlin, *The Sixties: Years of Hope, Days of Rage* (New York: Bantam, 1987), 79.

55. Paul Potter, the president of SDS at mid-decade, argued for the first of these explanations. Paul Potter, *A Name for Ourselves* (Boston: Little, Brown, 1971), 101.

56. Mills, "Letter to the New Left."

57. Abraham H. Maslow, *New Knowledge in Human Values* (New York: Harper, 1959); Abraham H. Maslow, *Toward a Psychology of Being* (Princeton, N.J.: Van Nostrand, 1962); Carl R. Rogers, *On Becoming a Person* (Boston: Houghton Mifflin, 1961). See Daniel Horowitz, *The Anxieties of Affluence: Critiques of American Consumer Culture, 1939–1979* (Amherst: University of Massachusetts Press, 2004); and Ellen Herman, *The Romance of American Psychology: Political Culture in an Age of Experts* (Berkeley: University of California Press, 1995).

58. For a new chronology and conceptualization of the civil rights struggle, see the summation and analysis of recent scholarship in Jacquelyn Dowd Hall, "The Long Civil Rights Movement and the Political Uses of the Past," *Journal of American History* 91, no. 4 (March 2005), 1233–63.

59. Recent scholarship confirms this. Gerald Horne, *Black Liberation/Red Scare: Ben Davis and the Communist Party* (Newark: University of Delaware Press, 1994); Mary L. Dudziak, *Cold War Civil Rights: Race and the Image of American Democracy* (Princeton, N.J.: Princeton University Press, 2000); Thomas Borstelmann, *The Cold War and the Color Line: American Race Relations in the Global Arena* (Cambridge, Mass.: Harvard University Press, 2001); Penny M. Von Eschen, *Satchmo Blows Up the World: Jazz Ambassadors Play the Cold War* (Cambridge, Mass.: Harvard University Press, 2004).

60. Joanne Grant, *Ella Baker: Freedom Bound* (New York: John Wiley & Sons, 1998), 98–99. Wilson Record, *The Negro and the Communist Party* (Chapel Hill: University of North Carolina Press, 1951); and Wilson Record, *Race and Radicalism: The NAACP and the Communist Party in Conflict* (Ithaca, N.Y.: Cornell University Press, 1964) remain the most detailed accounts, ones in full sympathy with the NAACP leadership's resolve on this matter. Also see Carl T. Rowan, *Dream Makers, Dream Breakers: The World of Justice Thurgood Marshall* (Boston: Little, Brown & Co., 1993); Juan Williams, *Thurgood Marshall: American Revolutionary* (New York: Times Books, 1998); and Mark V. Tushnet, *Making Civil Rights Law: Thurgood Marshall and the Supreme Court, 1936–1961* (New York: Oxford University Press, 1994).

61. David Levering Lewis, *W. E. B. DuBois: The Fight for Equality and the American Century, 1919–1963* (New York: Henry Holt and Company, 2000), 526, 548–55; Gerald Horne, *Black and Red: W. E. B. DuBois and the Afro-American Response to the Cold War, 1944–1963* (Albany: State University of New York Press, 1986).

62. Lichtenstein, *The Most Dangerous Man in Detroit*, 317.

63. Michael Reisch and Janice Andrews, *The Road Not Taken: A History of Radical Social Work in the United States* (Philadelphia: Brunner-Routledge, 2001), 88.

64. Filippelli and McColloch, *Cold War in the Working Class*, 147.

65. Gerald Horne, *Communist Front? The Civil Rights Congress, 1946–1956* (Rutherford, N.J.: Fairleigh Dickinson University Press, 1988).

66. Lichtenstein, *The Most Dangerous Man in Detroit*, 317, 357. Schlesinger, writing in the early 1960s, was addressing issues of foreign policy; but his comment carried a broad indictment. For a sympathetic treatment of the UAW's civil rights work, see Boyle, *The UAW and the Heyday of American Liberalism*, chapter 4.

67. See Martin Halpern, "'I'm Fighting for Freedom': Coleman Young, HUAC, and the Detroit African American Community," *Journal of American Ethnic History* 17, no. 1 (fall 1997): 19–38. See Robert O. Self, *American Babylon: Race and the Struggle for Postwar Oakland* (Princeton, N.J.: Princeton University Press, 2003), 76–82, for a discussion of another locality—Oakland, California—during these years, which shows Popular Front progressivism to have had a somewhat weaker hold on African American politics during the late 1940s and early 1950s.

68. This is the argument of David L. Chappell, *A Stone of Hope: Prophetic Religion and the Death of Jim Crow* (Chapel Hill: University of North Carolina Press, 2004), chapters 1–2.

69. Martin Luther King, Jr., "Address to the First Montgomery Improvement Association (MIA) Mass Meeting," in *A Call to Conscience: The Landmark Speeches of Dr. Martin Luther King, Jr.*, ed. Clayborne Carson and Kris Shepard (New York: IPM/Warner Books, 2001), 12.

70. Martin Luther King, Jr., "How Should a Christian View Communism?" in *Strength to Love* (1963; Philadelphia: Fortress Press, 1981), 97, 100. This essay first took oral form, in a sermon King delivered in 1962. Martin Luther King, Jr., "Can a Christian Be a Communist?" Sermon delivered at Ebenezer Baptist Church, 30 September 1962, Atlanta, Ga., in *The Papers of Martin Luther King, Jr.*, vol. 6: *Advocate of the Social Gospel, September 1948–March 1963*, ed. Clayborne Carson et al. (Berkeley: University of California Press, 2007), 445–54. The reformist and prophetic elements in white American Protestantism were resuscitated in the 1960s as well. See James F. Findlay, *Church People in the Struggle: The National Council of Churches and the Black Freedom Movement, 1950–1970* (New York: Oxford University Press, 1993); and Mitchell K. Hall, *Because of Their Faith: CALCAV and Religious Opposition to the Vietnam War* (New York: Columbia University Press, 1990).

71. King, "How Should a Christian View Communism?," 103, 104, 105.

72. Taylor Branch, *Parting the Waters: America in the King Years, 1954–63* (New York: Simon and Schuster, 1988), 62, 69–80; Lawrence Edward Carter, Sr., ed., *Walking Integrity: Benjamin Elijah Mays, Mentor to Martin Luther King Jr.* (Macon, Ga.: Mercer University Press, 1998). Branch, *Parting the Waters*, 80, notes that King received critiques of his early anticommunist preaching from Melvin Watson, the chairman of the Morehouse School of Religion, who was a sympathetic student of Marxist thought.

A new book by Thomas F. Jackson, *From Civil Rights to Human Rights: Martin Luther King, Jr., and the Struggle for Economic Justice* (Philadelphia: University of Pennsylvania Press, 2006), argues vigorously that King, from early in his career, was a Christian socialist of sorts.

73. According to John D'Emilio, Rustin's ouster from King's inner circle in 1960 stemmed from conflict between Rustin and Levison, on the one hand, and tension with the NAACP, on the other. Roy Wilkins, the head of the NAACP, spurred Congressman Adam Clayton Powell, Jr. to publicly red-bait the two advisers to King, and Powell then privately threatened to claim that King and Rustin

were lovers. In the face of King's consternation, Rustin offered to resign from the staff of the Southern Christian Leadership Conference (SCLC), and King accepted. D'Emilio, *Lost Prophet*, 293–99.

74. Anderson, *Bayard Rustin*, 187. According to D'Emilio, a brain trust that included Rustin's longtime associates A. Philip Randolph and James Farmer and the leaders of In Friendship and the War Resisters League (Rustin's employer) decided to send Rustin to Montgomery to seek influence with Martin Luther King, Jr. D'Emilio, *Lost Prophet*, 226–28.

75. Doug McAdam, *Freedom Summer* (New York: Oxford University Press, 1988), 130.

76. Chafe, *Never Stop Running*, 191.

77. Polsgrove, *Divided Minds*, 232, 233.

78. See Michael Paul Rogin, *The Intellectuals and McCarthyism: The Radical Specter* (Cambridge, Mass.: MIT Press, 1967); Isserman, *Other American*, 156. The locus classicus of the tendency is Daniel Bell, ed., *The Radical Right* (Garden City, N.Y.: Doubleday, 1955).

79. McClay, *The Masterless*, 264–65.

80. Polsgrove, *Divided Minds*, 88.

81. Ibid., 46.

82. Chafe, *Never Stop Running*, 191; Schrecker, *Many Are the Crimes*, 394.

83. D'Emilio, *Lost Prophet*, 224–28; Anderson, *Bayard Rustin*, 212.

84. Isserman, *Other American*, 156.

85. Cleveland Sellers with Robert Terrell, *River of No Return: The Autobiography of a Black Militant and the Life and Death of SNCC* (New York: William Morrow & Co., 1973), 111.

86. Isserman, *Other American*, 246; Gitlin, *The Sixties*, 151–62; and Nick Kotz, *Judgment Days: Lyndon Baines Johnson, Martin Luther King Jr., and the Laws that Changed America* (Boston: Houghton Mifflin, 2005), chapter 8, provide the most detailed accounts of the Atlantic City events I have found.

Some historians have echoed this story of youthful disillusionment with liberals, also focusing on the treatment of the MFDP in 1964 as a convenient point of departure. See, for example, Winifred Breines, "Whose New Left?" *Journal of American History* 5, no. 2 (September 1988): esp. 537–40.

87. Clayborne Carson, *In Struggle: SNCC and the Black Awakening of the 1960s* (Cambridge, Mass.: Harvard University Press, 1981), 124; Grant, *Ella Baker*, 171; Kotz, *Judgment Days*, 203.

88. Chafe, *Never Stop Running*, 199; Boyle, *The UAW and the Heyday of American Liberalism*, 196.

89. Kotz, *Judgment Days*, 216–17.

90. Kwame Ture and Charles V. Hamilton, *Black Power: The Politics of Liberation* (1967; New York: Vintage Books, 1992), 94–95.

91. Robert Dallek, *Flawed Giant: Lyndon Johnson and His Times, 1961–1973* (New York: Oxford University Press, 1998), 120.

92. Self, *American Babylon*, 92. Also see Walton Bean, *California: An Interpretive History*, 3rd ed. (New York: McGraw-Hill, 1978), 396–400. According to James Q. Wilson, the club Democrats in Los Angeles, like those in New York City, were strongly white, often Jewish, and definitely upper middle class. In his view, these clubs were unattractive to members of racial minority groups and labor unions. Wilson, *The Amateur Democrat: Club Politics in Three Cities* (Chicago: University of Chicago Press, 1966), 13–6, chapter 9. Self's book is a study of Oakland, a city Wilson did not examine. Alan Ware, *The Breakdown of Democratic Party Organiza-*

tion, 1940–1980 (Oxford: Oxford University Press, 1985), which does examine the East Bay area (comprising Oakland, Berkeley, and other cities) as well as New York and Denver, generally accepts Wilson's profile of club membership and presents African American political organization in the East Bay as rather weak. On the California activities of the CSO, see Margaret Rose, "Gender and Civic Activism in Mexican American Barrios in California: The Community Service Organization, 1947–1962," in *Not June Cleaver: Women and Gender in Postwar America, 1945–1960,* ed. Joanne Meyerowitz (Philadelphia: Temple University Press, 1994), 177–200.

93. Eleanor Roosevelt was close to Stevenson, who was known for moderation on the civil rights issue. In advance of the 1956 Democratic National Convention she worked on a moderate civil rights plank for the party platform that would be sufficiently gradualist to keep white southerners from bolting. John F. Martin, *Civil Rights and the Crisis of Liberalism: The Democratic Party, 1945–1976* (Boulder, Colo.: Westview Press, 1979), 145.

94. Kevin Boyle, *The UAW and the Heyday of American Liberalism, 1945–1968* (Ithaca, N.Y.: Cornell University Press, 1995); Wilson, *The Amateur Democrat.*

95. Isserman and Kazin, *America Divided,* 60.

96. Martin, *Civil Rights and the Crisis of Liberalism,* 169. Isserman and Kazin, *America Divided,* depict the party's stance on civil rights in 1960 as more equivocal.

97. Dallek, *Flawed Giant,* 60, 63, 80, 113.

98. Ibid., 63, 83, 112.

99. Lyndon B. Johnson, "Remarks at the University of Michigan, May 22, 1964," in *Lyndon B. Johnson and American Liberalism: A Brief Biography with Documents,* by Bruce J. Schulman (Boston: Bedford Books/St. Martin's Press, 1995), 174, 177.

100. Quoted in Dallek, *Flawed Giant,* 75.

101. See Mark H. Leff, *The Limits of Symbolic Reform: The New Deal and Taxation, 1933–1939* (Cambridge: Cambridge University Press, 1984).

102. Paul Potter, "The Incredible War," in *The New Left: A Documentary History,* ed. Massimo Teodori (Indianapolis: Bobbs-Merrill, 1969), 248.

103. John and Barbara Ehrenreich, "From Resistance to Revolution," in Teodori, *The New Left,* 459, 465.

104. Gitlin, *The Sixties,* 58, 60.

105. Polsgrove, *Divided Minds,* 61.

106. Martin Luther King, Jr., *Why We Can't Wait* (New York: Mentor, 1964), 84.

107. Polsgrove, *Divided Minds,* 175.

108. Chafe, *Never Stop Running,* 183–84.

109. This remark, and those of Kenneth Clark, quoted below, come from the accounts in Walter A. Jackson, *Gunnar Myrdal and America's Conscience: Social Engineering and Racial Liberalism, 1938–1987* (Chapel Hill: University of North Carolina Press, 1990), 299–300, and Polsgrove, *Divided Minds,* 201–5, of a panel discussion held in New York City. This roundtable discussion appeared in print in *Commentary* in March 1964 ("Liberalism and the Negro: A Round-Table Discussion: James Baldwin, Nathan Glazer, Sidney Hook, Gunnar Myrdal").

110. Carson, *In Struggle,* 128.

111. Ibid., 151.

112. D'Emilio, *Lost Prophet,* 449.

113. Jackson, *Gunnar Myrdal and America's Conscience,* 299–300; Polsgrove, *Divided Minds,* 201–5.

114. Anderson, *Bayard Rustin*, 280, 237, 317–18.

115. See Self, *American Babylon*; and Matthew J. Countryman, *Up South: Civil Rights and Black Power in Philadelphia* (Philadelphia: University of Pennsylvania Press, 2005) for detailed accounts of this process.

116. Self, *American Babylon*, 179, 236–37.

117. Martin, *Civil Rights and the Crisis of Liberalism*, 229.

Chapter 6

1. Daniel Horowitz, *Betty Friedan and the Making of* The Feminine Mystique: *The American Left, the Cold War, and Modern Feminism* (Amherst: University of Massachusetts Press, 1998), 136, 137; Gerda Lerner, *Fireweed: A Political Autobiography* (Philadelphia: Temple University Press, 2002), 272–74. On the UE, see Susan M. Hartmann, *The Other Feminists: Activists in the Liberal Establishment* (New Haven, Conn.: Yale University Press, 1998), chapter 2.

2. Horowitz, *Betty Friedan*, 200–201, 251, 327n53. See Hartmann, *The Other Feminists*; and Dorothy Sue Cobble, *The Other Women's Movement: Workplace Justice and Social Rights in Modern America* (Princeton, N.J.: Princeton University Press, 2004). Friedan omitted all mention of Engels's work—the single most important influence on left-feminist thought in the twentieth century—and of Veblen's. She mentioned *The Second Sex*, by de Beauvoir, once in passing. Betty Friedan, *The Feminine Mystique* (1963; New York: Dell, 1964), 14. George Cotkin remarks on the shallowness of Friedan's appreciation of de Beauvoir's perspective, noting that Friedan echoed the voluntarism that she detected in French existentialism while eschewing de Beauvoir's materialism and anti-capitalism, thus ignoring the French writer's "theoretical structure" and "essential interpretive thrust." George Cotkin, *Existential America* (Baltimore, Md.: Johns Hopkins University Press, 2003), 253. Also see Sandra Dijkstra, "Simone de Beauvoir and Betty Friedan: The Politics of Omission," *Feminist Studies* 6 no. 2 (summer 1980): 290–303.

3. Howard Brick noted the similarity between Friedan and Savio. Howard Brick, *Age of Contradiction: American Thought and Culture in the 1960s* (Ithaca, N.Y.: Cornell University Press, 2000), 53. Mario Savio, "An End to History" was originally published in *Humanity* in December 1964. It is reprinted in Massimo Teodori, ed., *The New Left: A Documentary History* (Indianapolis, Ind.: Bobbs-Merrill, 1969), 158–61.

4. Brick, *Age of Contradiction*, 49–51.

5. Amy Swerdlow, *Women Strike for Peace: Traditional Motherhood and Radical Politics in the 1960s* (Chicago: University of Chicago Press, 1993); Robbie Lieberman, *The Strangest Dream: Communism, Anticommunism, and the U.S. Peace Movement, 1945–1963* (Syracuse, N.Y.: Syracuse University Press, 2000), chapter 7; Sara M. Evans, *Tidal Wave: How Women Changed America at Century's End* (New York: The Free Press, 2003), 27–28.

6. Representatives of the UAW departed NOW in 1967 over the issue of the ERA and protective legislation, but three years later they returned, the UAW having reversed its traditional stance on the issue. So had other groups that were previously opposed, including the YWCA, the American Association of University Women, and the League of Women Voters. Evans, *Tidal Wave*, 65.

7. The key source here is Susan Lynn, *Progressive Women in Conservative Times: Racial Justice, Peace, and Feminism, 1945 to the 1960s* (New Brunswick, N.J.: Rutgers University Press, 1992).

8. Horowitz, *Betty Friedan*, 232. Those who spoke of a conscience coalition frequently mentioned the United Auto Workers as an important partner; often the UAW was the only union named. See Kevin Boyle, *The UAW and the Heyday of American Liberalism, 1945–1968* (Ithaca, N.Y.: Cornell University Press, 1995), chapter 7.

9. Horowitz, *Betty Friedan*, 232. See Jean Bethke Elshtain, *Public Man, Private Woman: Women in Social and Political Thought* (Princeton, N.J.: Princeton University Press, 1981); and Nancy Fraser, *Justice Interruptus: Critical Reflections on the "Postsocialist" Condition* (New York: Routledge, 1997).

10. Casey Hayden and Mary King, "Sex and Caste," reprinted in Sara Evans, *Personal Politics: The Roots of Women's Liberation in the Civil Rights Movement and the New Left* (New York: Vintage Books, 1980), 235–38.

11. Kate Weigand, *Red Feminism: American Communism and the Making of Women's Liberation* (Baltimore, Md.: Johns Hopkins University Press, 2001), 149.

12. For ample detail, see Nancy MacLean, *Freedom Is Not Enough: The Opening of the American Work Place* (Cambridge, Mass.: Harvard University Press, 2006).

13. Sara M. Evans, "Comment," *Radical History Review* 71 (spring 1998): 43; Evans, *Tidal Wave*, 141.

14. On the advance of feminism in liberal institutions, see Hartmann, *The Other Feminists*.

15. Noam Chomsky, "The Menace of Liberal Scholarship," *New York Review of Books*, 2 January 1969; Christopher Lasch, "The Banality of Liberalism," *New York Review of Books*, 9 December 1965.

16. The term comes from David L. Schalk, *War and the Ivory Tower: Algeria and Vietnam* (New York: Oxford University Press, 1991), 164.

17. "America and the New Era," in *The New Left*, ed. Teodori, 175, 176, 179. The concept of a corporate state has a rich history; many thinkers rendered this idea more ominous than did ANE. James Burnham, *The Managerial State* (New York: John Day, 1941) represents one milestone in this intellectual history. On a specifically anti-Soviet version of the concept associated with a left-wing thinker, see Christopher Phelps, "C. L. R. James and the Theory of State Capitalism," in *American Capitalism: Social Thought and Political Economy in the Twentieth Century*, ed. Nelson Lichtenstein (Philadelphia: University of Pennsylvania Press, 2006), 157–74.

18. "America and the New Era," 177, 180.

19. Christopher Lasch, *The Agony of the American Left* (New York: Vintage Books, 1969), 10–11.

20. Ibid., 175, 181.

21. See Paddy Riley, "Clark Kerr: From the Industrial to the Knowledge Economy," in Lichtenstein, ed., *American Capitalism*, 71–87, for a good discussion of a figure misunderstood by his young enemies in some ways, and in others understood only too well.

22. Todd Gitlin, *The Sixties: Years of Hope, Days of Rage* (New York: Bantam, 1987), 166.

23. Todd Gitlin, "Power and the Myth of Progress," in *The New Left*, ed. Teodori, 189, 188.

24. Richard Flacks, "Is the Great Society Just a Barbecue?" in *The New Left*, ed. Teodori, 192, 193.

25. Gitlin, "Power and the Myth of Progress," 190.

26. The phrase comes from the most famous work by the historian William Appleman Williams, *The Tragedy of American Diplomacy* (Cleveland: World Publishing Co., 1959).

27. Kevin Mattson, "Between Hope and Despair: Revisiting *Studies on the Left*," in *The New Left Revisited*, ed. John McMillian and Paul Buhle (Philadelphia: Temple University Press, 2003), 28–47, is a good brief account of the journal's history.

28. The term was Arthur M. Schlesinger, Jr.'s. Quoted in Michael E. Latham, *Modernization as Ideology: American Social Science and "Nation Building" in the Kennedy Era* (Chapel Hill: University of North Carolina Press, 2000), 9.

29. Carl Oglesby, "Trapped in a System," in *The New Left*, ed. Teodori, 182. In 1966 Allard Lowenstein and Norman Thomas would be enlisted to ensure that a badly flawed election ratifying the coup would pass international muster. William H. Chafe, *Never Stop Running: Allard Lowenstein and the Struggle to Save American Liberalism* (New York: Basic Books, 1993), 256–60.

30. See Smedley D. Butler, *War Is a Racket: The Anti-War Classic by America's Most Decorated General* (Los Angeles: Feral House, 2003); and Hans Schmidt, *Maverick Marine: General Smedley D. Butler and the Contradictions of American Military History* (Lexington: University Press of Kentucky, 1998).

31. Oglesby, "Trapped in a System," 185, 187.

32. Carl Oglesby, "Vietnamese Crucible: An Essay on the Meanings of the Cold War," in *Containment and Change: Two Dissenting Views of American Foreign Policy*, by Carl Oglesby and Richard Shaull (New York: Macmillan, 1967), 164–68. Oglesby's long essay in this volume was an extended reprise of the interpretation of U.S. foreign policy advanced by Williams and *Studies on the Left*.

33. Gitlin, *The Sixties*, 183. Ochs was no more a Marxist-Leninist than Stone was a cold war liberal.

34. I. F. Stone, "The Horrid Word 'Socialism'" (published 3 March 1950), in *The Truman Years, 1945–1952* (Boston: Little, Brown, 1972), 170–72; I. F. Stone, "Justice Douglas and the Peasant Revolution" (published 16 May 1952), in ibid., 221.

35. Dorothy Healey and Maurice Isserman, *Dorothy Healey Remembers: A Life in the American Communist Party* (New York: Oxford University Press, 1990), 202–03.

36. Sandy Vogelgesang, *The Long Dark Night of the Soul: The American Intellectual Left and the Vietnam War* (New York: Harper & Row, 1974), 33, 73. Sontag noted the importance of making "emotional" appeals that could shake Americans out of their habitual "chauvinism." Ibid., 102.

37. Hayden quoted in Frank Annunziata, "The New Left and the Welfare State: The Rejection of American Liberalism," *Southern Quarterly* 15, no. 1 (October 1976): 42; Richard Rothstein, "Evolution of the ERAP organizers," reprinted in *The New Left: A Collection of Essays*, ed. Priscilla Long (Boston: Porter Sargent Publishers, 1969). Both quoted in Maurice Isserman, *The Other American: The Life of Michael Harrington* (New York: PublicAffairs, 2000), 278.

38. Healey and Isserman, *Dorothy Healey Remembers*, 203.

39. John F. Martin, *Civil Rights and the Crisis of Liberalism: The Democratic Party, 1945–1976* (Boulder, Colo.: Westview Press, 1979), 249.

40. Kevin Mattson, *Intellectuals in Action: The Origins of the New Left and Radical Liberalism, 1945–1970* (University Park, Penn.: Pennsylvania State University Press, 2002), 196–97, 218–19; Dominic Sandbrook, *Eugene McCarthy: The Rise and Fall of Postwar American Liberalism* (New York: Alfred A. Knopf, 2004).

41. Roger Kimball, *Tenured Radicals: How Politics Has Corrupted Higher Education* (New York: Harper & Row, 1990).

42. David Brooks, *Bobos in Paradise: The New Upper Class and How They Got There* (New York: Simon & Schuster, 2000).

43. Christopher Lasch, The *Agony of the American Left* (New York: Vintage Books, 1969), 46, quoted in T. B. Bottomore, *Critics of Society: Radical Thought in North America* (New York: Pantheon Books, 1968), 80–81. The years 1920 to 1935, like most of the era since 1948, witnessed a stronger sense of alienation on the left, which issued forth in sharp esthetic and moral criticism of American life.

44. Todd Gitlin, *The Twilight of Common Dreams: Why America Is Wracked by Culture Wars* (New York: Metropolitan Books, 1995); Arthur M. Schlesinger, Jr., *The Disuniting of America* (Knoxville, Tenn.: Whittle Direct Books, 1991); Michael Tomasky, *Left for Dead: The Life, Death, and Possible Resurrection of Progressive Politics in America* (New York: The Free Press, 1996).

45. Martin L. Duberman, "Bring Back the Enlightenment," *Nation* 263, no. 1 (1 July 1996): 25–27; Robin D. G. Kelley, "Identity Politics & Class Struggle," *New Politics* 6, no. 2 (new series), whole no. 22 (winter 1997); Barbara Ehrenreich, "Why We're All a Bunch of Losers," *Progressive* 60, no. 7 (July 1996): 40–43.

46. Ehrenreich, "Why We're All a Bunch of Losers," 41.

47. Brooks, when reviewing Tomasky's book, cited Duberman's article, itself another review of *Left for Dead,* to ridicule "the multicultural left," and to argue that the American left showed little prospect of replacing "identity politics" with "class politics." David Brooks, "Class Politics versus Identity Politics," *The Public Interest,* no. 125 (Fall 1996): 118.

48. Robert Nisbet, *History of the Idea of Progress* (New York: Basic Books, 1980), ix.

49. According to a Harris opinion poll, in 2001 19 percent of Americans called themselves liberals (and 36 percent called themselves conservatives), while in 1968 17 percent had identified themselves as liberals (and 37 percent as conservatives). Humphrey Taylor, "Party Identification: Democrats Still Lead, but Their Lead (5 Points) Is as Low as It Has Ever Been," *The Harris Poll* #8, 13 February 2002, available at http://www.harrisinteractive.com/harris_poll/index.asp?PID=285. The American National Election Studies (ANES) Guide to Public Opinion and Electoral Behavior, based at the University of Michigan, shows a slightly higher proportion of liberals in the United States in 2004 than in 1972—23 percent versus 18 percent (with conservatives increasing from 26 percent in 1972 to 32 percent in 2004). The ANES numbers combine those identifying as "slightly liberal," "liberal," and "extremely liberal" (with corresponding categories for conservative identifiers). "Liberal-Conservative Self-Identification 1972–2004," ANES Guide to Public Opinion and Electoral Behavior, available at http://www.umich.edu/~nes/nesguide/toptable/tab3_1.htm.

50. Bruce Mohl, "O'Neill Calls Dukakis 'Progressive'; Former Speaker Rebuts Bush's 'Liberal' Charge," *Boston Globe,* 28 September 1988, 22. Dukakis was—as Republicans charged—somewhat more liberal across the board than he acknowledged, at least before the campaign's closing days, when he reversed course and took up the "liberal" standard, although without making exactly clear what he thought that meant.

51. Nader received 2.74 percent of the national vote for president in 2000. This data is available from the U.S. Federal Election Commission online at http://fecweb1.fec.gov/pubrec/2000presgeresults.htm. Wallace came in at 2.37 percent. Norman D. Markowitz, *The Rise and Fall of the People's Century: Henry A. Wallace and American Liberalism, 1941–1948* (New York: The Free Press, 1973),

295. The remark about Nader being "the real liberal" was made to me in 2000 by a Nader supporter, one knowledgeable about political history in recent years.

52. On the new style of class resentment, see Thomas Frank, *What's the Matter with Kansas?: How Conservatives Won the Heart of America* (New York: Metropolitan Books, 2004).

53. See David Harvey, *A Brief History of Neoliberalism* (New York: Oxford University Press, 2005).

54. See the documents collected at http://depts.washington.edu/wtohist as part of the WTO History Project at the University of Washington.

55. Christopher Lasch, *The Culture of Narcissism: American Life in an Age of Diminishing Expectations* (New York: W. W. Norton & Co., 1978), 3–7. As time passed, Lasch expressed increasingly baleful views on the idea of progress. See Christopher Lasch, *The True and Only Heaven: Progress and Its Critics* (New York: W. W. Norton & Co., 1991).

56. Intermittently, Internet blogs offer debate over the meaning of progressivism. Some of this discussion can be sampled at http://www.mydd.com/story/2006/12/6/175028/653 or http://www.dkosopedia.com/wiki/Progressive. Jerome Armstrong and Markos Moulitas Zúniga, *Crashing the Gate: Netroots, Grassroots, and the Rise of People-Powered Politics* (White River Junction, Vt.: Chelsea Green Publishing, 2006) is a leading account of this emerging political tendency by some of its best-known entrepreneurs.

57. A visit to the website of United for Peace and Justice, at http://www.unitedforpeace.org, quickly yields a sense of the political orientation and base of support of antiwar protest in this era.

58. The term is Timothy Brennan's. See Timothy Brennan, *Wars of Position: The Cultural Politics of Left and Right* (New York: Columbia University Press, 2006).

Index

Acknowledgments

I wish to thank the National Endowment for the Humanities for a Summer Research Stipend, which enabled me to move this project forward. Brian Balogh, Sara Evans, Louis Galambos, Jonathan Holloway, Daniel Horowitz, Michael Kazin, Nelson Lichtenstein, Robert Lockhart, Rebecca Lowen, John E. Miller, Dorothy Ross, and Julian Zelizer each provided helpful and encouraging comments on some or all of this book during its development, and I thank them all. Audiences at the University of Virginia's Miller Center of Public Affairs, at the University of Minnesota, at Wayne State University, at the University of Durham, and among my colleagues at Metropolitan State University helped me sharpen my ideas. In the history department at Metropolitan State, my colleague Kathleen Laughlin let me borrow lots of books and keep them as long as I wished. Rebecca Lowen found the cover art, an eye for such things being one of her many talents. Thanks, also, to Erika Gottfried and Michael Nash, of the Tamiment Library at New York University, for their help with that image. I wish to thank Erica Ginsburg and the editing staff at the University of Pennsylvania Press for their close attention to the manuscript. Bob Lockhart, Michael Kazin, and Rebecca Lowen have been especially generous with their time and attention. Bob has been a model editor: deeply engaged intellectually, ever willing to read new drafts, a creative thinker yet always a source of sound, practical advice. Michael, from our first conversations about this project, has understood exactly what I've been trying to do and has been unstinting in his praise and encouragement. Bob and Michael both have seen the forest and not just the trees. But only Rebecca knows the whole story.